When We Were Good

When We Were Good

The Folk Revival

ROBERT CANTWELL

Harvard University Press

Cambridge, Massachusetts
London, England

Library of Congress Cataloging-in-Publication Data

Cantwell, Robert, 1945–
    When we were good : the folk revival / Robert Cantwell.
        p. cm.
    Includes bibliographical references and index.
    ISBN 0-674-95132-8 (cloth)
    ISBN 0-674-95133-6 (pbk.)
    1. Folk music—United States—History and criticism. 2. Folk
songs, English—United States—History and criticism. I. Title.
ML3551.C36 1996
781.62′13′00904—dc20   95-20951

Title page drawing is an unidentified illustration from the album, *Folkways Anthology of American Folk Music.*

For my daughters,
Matilda and Madeline

Contents

Illustrations

A good song can only do good.
　　　　　　　—Pete Seeger

Anne Warner recording Frank Proffitt as neighbor children look on, in Beaver Dam section of Watauga County, N.C., 1941

Prologue: Tom Dooley

"**I** need a steamshovel, mama, to keep away the dead," Bob Dylan declared in 1965, having personally terminated the popular folksong revival, some thought, by picking up an electric guitar and sending his message around the world with it. "I need a dump truck, baby, to unload my head."

Having shared and brought to light so much of the experience of his generation, maybe Dylan was remembering an evening in the parlor back in Hibbing, Minnesota, in front of his parents' new television set, where in film supplied by the army department a man with a surgical mask, operating a bulldozer, was moving a naked trash heap of human corpses into an open pit. Or it may have been the sudden rising of a momentary sun over Bikini atoll, disemboweling the sky in membraneous sheets of dust and light and summoning out of the earth a pillar of smoke and steam in which the Pacific tried to leap out of itself. Or maybe he was remembering a dim Senate committee room where bespectacled men in front of microphones shouted at one another in anger and indignation or, like automatons, gravely intoned a refusal to answer on the strange grounds that their answer might tend to incriminate them. No wonder he saw history, on that same record album, as the work of a fancy promoter who, when asked whether he could produce the next world war, says "Yes, I think it can be very *easily* done!"—"just put some bleachers out in the sun" and have it out on the old Mississippi Delta highway, "Highway 61."

Between, roughly, 1958, when the collegiate Kingston Trio recorded an Appalachian murder ballad, "Tom Dooley," which sold nearly four million discs, and 1964, when the Beatles and other British groups began to colonize American popular music, folksongs, and original songs conceived and performed as such, enjoyed an unprecedented commercial popularity, inspiring thousands of young middle-class men and women to learn songs, to accompany themselves on folk instruments, particularly guitar and banjo, to search out and lionize authentic folk musicians, and finally to dress, groom, speak, comport themselves, and even attempt to think in ways they believed compatible with the rural, ethnic, proletarian, and other marginal cultures to whom folksong was supposed to belong.

In this process, many kinds of music that had already been commercially recorded—blues, oldtime, bluegrass, early jazz and swing, jugband and country western, even a few gems of early rock-and-roll, music in any case chiefly of southern rural origin—came to be regarded as "folk" music. This was the postwar folk revival. The commercial recording that set it in motion was a traditional ballad that commemorated the murder of Laura Foster, of Wilkes County, North Carolina, by a Civil War veteran, Tom Dula, and his lover Annie Melton, in 1866. Dula had a reputation as a desperado and a ladies' man. Reporters from as far away as New York covered his trial, and at least one of the ballads about him or attributed to him may have been composed by a journalist named Thomas Land.

Dula was hung for the murder in 1868. His song entered tradition in Tennessee and North Carolina, where in 1938 an ingenuous young mountaineer from Pick Britches Valley, North

Carolina, Frank Proffitt, sang it for a folksinger-collector named Frank Warner. Warner was visiting a dulcimer maker from nearby Beech Mountain, Nathan Hicks, Proffitt's father-in-law. "Then Frank Warner come to the mountains," Proffitt wrote, "and in him I saw an addgicated person who made me feel like somebody and I open my heart to him and gave him the old songs of my people. His eyes sparkled as I sang Tom Dooly to him and told him of my Grandmaw Profitt knowing Tom and Laura."[1]

Proffitt thought of Dula as a man who "didn't conform to rules." He had first heard "Tom Dooley" from his father, who taught it to him on a homemade banjo. "My earlyest recalection," he later wrote to Warner, "is of waking on a cold winter morning in a log cabin on old Beaver Dam and hearing the sad haunting tune of Tom Dooly picked by my father along with the frying of meat on the little stepstove and the noise of the coffeemill grinding the Arbuckle."[2]

Frank Warner, a dedicated singer of southern mountain ballads, had been using "Tom Dooley" in his own folksong concerts for twenty years and recorded it in 1952 for a fledgling folksong record company, Elektra, which operated out of a Greenwich Village shop called the Record Loft. Not a mountaineer himself, Warner grew up in Durham and studied under folklorists Frank C. Brown and Newman Ivey White at Duke University. With his wife Anne he became a pioneer in the use of portable recording equipment in the collection of folksongs; in 1940 the vice-president of Philco Radio had made them a battery-powered portable recording machine specifically for that purpose. In subsequent years Frank Warner distinguished himself as president of the New York Folklore Society, program director of the Pinewoods music camp, vice-president of the Country Dance and Song Society, and trustee of the National Folk Arts Council.

Warner had come to New York in 1931 as program director for the central YMCA, having already established several programs and directed a summer camp for that organization. It is probable that folksong proved useful in Warner's recreational work. By the early forties, living on West 19th Street, he was involved with folksong enthusiasts in Greenwich Village, among whom was the folklorist Alan Lomax. Lomax was preparing broadcasts of folksong for Armed Forces Radio, enlisting Warner among other performers such as Burl Ives, Sonny Terry, Woody Guthrie, and Huddie Ledbetter.

In 1947 Lomax printed "Tom Dooley" without the third stanza in his book *Folk Song U.S.A.*, attributing it to "that flavorsome North Carolina singer, Frank Warner."[3] Warner's version, as Lomax printed it, somewhat simplified the detailed narratives in the available traditional texts in favor of an evocative lyricism reminiscent of folksongs sung in school. But Ruth Seeger's sturdy musical arrangements in the book dispelled what to the school-trained ear are the melodic vagaries of the traditional Appalachian singing style.

Songs transmit themselves, for the most part, aurally. Singers and musicians are usually struck by what they hear, more than by what they may find in books, though they often have recourse to a printed collection in order to build a repertory or to reconstruct something they may have heard only once or twice. It is likely, then, that "Tom Dooley" entered oral circulation among folksong enthusiasts through the combined influences of Frank Warner's performances in New York, and after 1956 at Camp Woodlands, and through the Lomax collection. It was being sung in Washington Square in the late 1940s, for example, and by 1951 had been recorded on an esoteric Greenwich Village label, Stinson, by three local singers, Bob Carey, Eric Darling, and Roger Sprung, the Folksay Trio.[4]

By the mid-fifties the song was abroad on the west coast, where on a Wednesday night in 1957 three aspiring young men from Hawaii heard it sung by a graying folksinger who, like them, was auditioning for a job at a San Francisco nightclub, the Purple Onion. The melody haunted them, as it had Frank Proffitt—but for the words they went to Richard and Ruth Best's

New Song Fest, a paperbound campfire collection privately published in 1948 and again, commercially, in 1955, "in recognition of the present trend towards folksongs and ballads."[5]

Like the other songs in the collection, the Bests' "Tom Dooley," printed without attribution, seemed simply to be in the public domain—a song that belonged to everyone. With its major tonality and foreshortened melodic range, "Tom Dooley" is a kind of solemn duty, like planting a tree. Its simple tune, as declarative as a bugle call, climbs sadly in four nearly identical phrases from a fifth below the tonic to a second or third above it, where it pauses to rest, lingering in one of the two chords, tonic or dominant, that resignedly bear away the stanza. What is haunting about it is the strange, uneasy confederacy of its melody, which strikes an urbane note, with a harmony in which one can hear echoes, in a plaintive pentatonic mode, of some old fiddler's farewell—touching shame with a note of mockery and Tom's remorse with self-pity:

> This time tomorrow,
> Reckon where I'll be—
> In some lonesome valley
> Hangin' on a white oak tree.[6]

David Guard, banjo player in the Kingston Trio, had been inspired to undertake the instrument in 1957, when he was a student in Palo Alto. The occasion was a Weavers concert, with banjoist Pete Seeger, at Nourse Hall in San Francisco; a young Joan Baez was also in attendance, with her parents. Guard had learned banjo chords from Seeger's little mimeographed book, *How To Play the 5-String Banjo* (1948), and a three-finger picking technique, a "backwards" variant of the bluegrass or Scruggs style, from a Bay Area virtuoso, Billy Faier.[7]

Guard took to the banjo readily, having already learned to play guitar in the Hawaiian open-G tuning, traditional for the banjo as well. His own interest in folk music, however, had begun during World War II, when the director of the Melbourne Symphony, Fritz Hart, was detained in Hawaii and conducted choral singing of folksongs such as "Greensleeves" and "Shenandoah" for schoolchildren. "Everybody bought guitars," Guard recalls, when in 1950 the Weavers came out with their hit record "Goodnight, Irene."

By the time he entered college in California, Guard was a folksong performer as well as an enthusiast, and formed with Bob Shane and Nick Reynolds a band they called the Kingston Trio, in order to associate it with the calypso music recently catapulted to the top of the charts by Harry Belafonte. Belafonte himself had been introduced to the tradition by Irving Burgie, a composer who with West Indian singer Louise Bennet was performing calypso in New York as Lord Burgess and His Serenaders.[8] The popularity of calypso had grown with such swing tunes as Vaughn Monroe's "Rum and Coca-Cola" and Ella Fitzgerald's "All Day, All Night, Mary Ann"; the music had been migrating from the American naval base in Trinidad to the West Indian community on Long Island and thence to Greenwich Village nightspots.[9]

The Trio's lead singer, Bob Shane, went a step further by imitating Belafonte's husky, after-hours singing voice. A college-educated actor and ballad singer with Jamaican roots, Belafonte began his career as a folksinger in 1948 at Town Hall, where he played the role of the southern preacher in the cantata *The Lonesome Train,* a tribute to Abraham Lincoln composed by Earl Robinson and Millard Lampell in 1940.

From all this, the immediate background of the Kingston Trio's "Tom Dooley," one might surmise that the song did not spring full-blown out of the imagination of a Capitol Records promoter in 1958: it had a complex lineage of scholarly, entrepreneurial, musical, theatrical, and political activity of fairly long standing and thoroughly authentic origins. Neither the Kingston Trio, in fact, nor Frank Warner nor the Folksay Trio was the first to record "Tom Dooley." G. B. Grayson, a blind fiddler from Mountain City, Tennessee, and a descendant of the Grayson who had arrested the murderer, recorded the song for

Victor in the twenties, at a time when record companies were discovering regional markets for traditional music.[10]

We have only to scratch the surface of "Tom Dooley," then, as thousands of its young admirers did, to discover that the emergent commercial youth culture of the late fifties had suddenly been intersected by a rich and energetic tradition of folksong scholarship and performance extending back at least into the regional festivals, folkdance societies, and outing clubs of the 1920s, but which in the larger historical perspective belonged to a particular family of theatrical, literary, and musical representations of folk culture that had begun in America on the minstrel stage— in the 1830s, when T. D. Rice introduced a black stableman's torturous jig he called "Jump Jim Crow."

In 1912, for example, outdoorsman Teddy Roosevelt wrote a preface for John Lomax's *Cowboy Songs*, noting that in their "sympathy for the outlaw" the cowboy songs resembled British ballads, particularly those celebrating another outdoorsman, Robin Hood. Roosevelt had met Lomax at a Frontier Day celebration in Cheyenne and, since Frank James had supported his campaign in Missouri, especially approved the outlaw ballad "Jesse James."[11] It was the president's endorsement that hastened the book's popularity and launched Lomax's career as a folksong entrepreneur. In his year of graduate study at Harvard, Lomax had received the imprimatur of the ballad scholar, George Lyman Kittredge; with his son Alan he produced a series of influential folksong books and conducted a sweeping tour of the depression south that issued in the splendid collection of field recordings now in the Library of Congress. Among their discoveries was the great Hudson "Huddie" Ledbetter, nicknamed Leadbelly in prison, who in 1934 accompanied the Lomaxes to New York, where the tiny left-wing folksong community, which included a young Harvard dropout called Pete Seeger, enthusiastically, if uncomprehendingly, embraced him.

In 1950 Seeger's folksong quartet, the Weavers, made Leadbelly's "Goodnight, Irene" the most popular song of the year.

They also made a hit of Leadbelly's "Kisses Sweeter Than Wine" and of Woody Guthrie's dust-bowl anthem "So Long, It's Been Good To Know Ya," along with the South African "Wimoweh" and the Appalachian "On Top of Old Smokey." But in that same year *Red Channels: Communist Influence on Radio and Television* cited Pete Seeger thirteen times and terminated the Weavers' career. Show-business blacklisting drove folksinging underground for most of the decade.

It was precisely this momentary obscurity that opened the immense resources of folksong to the young and made it, by virtue of their recovery of it in the postwar period, their own. When folksong reemerged into the light of popular culture in 1958, with its ideological and cultural connections largely suppressed, abandoned, forgotten, or lost, it welled up with all the vitality of a cultural symbol eager for rediscovery.

The immediate foreground of "Tom Dooley" may also suggest what fertile cultural ground lay to be discovered in folk tradition. A learned long-playing reissue, released in 1952, of folksongs recorded commercially in the twenties, the *Folkways Anthology of American Folk Music,* reminded the folksong enthusiast and musician Ralph Rinzler of the Library of Congress field recordings he had heard in his youth,[12] and inspired him to journey to North Carolina in early 1961 to record the elderly banjoist and singer Clarence "Tom" Ashley. Ashley had been an early associate of G. B. Grayson on the medicine-show circuit; his "Coo Coo Bird," a mountain song with medieval English roots, became a revival standard after its reissue on the Anthology. Rinzler had met Ashley the previous year at the Union Grove Fiddlers' Convention, where Rinzler's group, the Greenbriar Boys, became the first northern bluegrass band, and certainly the first named after an exclusive mountain resort, to win the band competition. Ashley in turn introduced Rinzler to a blind rockabilly guitarist living nearby: Arthel "Doc" Watson, who, when he learned of Rinzler's interest in folksong, picked up a banjo and sang, at a lively mocking tempo, a version of

"Tom Dooley" that retained something of the ghastliness and moral squalor of an actual murder:

> You left her by the roadside
> Where you begged to be excused;
> Left her by the roadside
> Then you hid her clothes and shoes . . .
>
> You dug the grave four feet long
> And you dug it three feet deep;
> You rolled the cold clay over her
> And you tromped it with your feet.[13]

This "new" version, it happened, and the whole story of the murder, had been in Watson's family for generations. His great-grandmother, Betsy Tripplett Watson, was at the deathbed of Tom's accomplice, Annie Melton, to hear her confession. Yet Rinzler needn't have traveled far to find the version he knew from the Kingston Trio: Frank Proffitt lived only a few minutes down the road.

Tom Ashley, Frank Proffitt, balladeer Almeda Riddle, and other rediscovered mountain banjoists, many of them now quite elderly, returned with enterprising revivalists like Rinzler to play at university concert halls, coffeehouse circuits, and seasonal festivals at Newport, Philadelphia, Chicago, and Berkeley. Doc Watson, an expert instrumentalist and versatile singer intimately acquainted with traditional mountain music, became one of the titans of the folk revival, supplementing his already immense repertory from scholarly sources. Rinzler, after conducting fieldwork for the Newport Folk Foundation on Cape Breton and among the Cajuns in Louisiana, and managing both Doc Watson and Bill Monroe on the college circuit, went on to become, in 1967, the director of the Smithsonian Institution's Festival of American Folklife.

Rinzler's name, incidentally, had been suggested to James Morris, director of the Smithsonian's Division of Performing Arts, by Joe Hickerson, director of the Archive of Folk Song at the Library of Congress. The occasion was a memorial gathering in Washington for the man who nearly thirty years earlier had given away his father's song—Frank Proffitt, who died at the age of fifty-two in 1965. "The strange mysterious workings which has made Tom Dooly live is a lot to think about," he had written to Warner two years earlier. "Other like affairs have been forgotten."[14]

The Kingston Trio, 1958. From the top: Dave Guard, Nick
Reynolds, Bob Shane

1

We Are the Folk

Education would probably have been better served had I never attended highschool at all; I do remember, though, calculating in physics class, with a fresh pencil on an unspoiled page of my notebook, the difference in mass between an atom of U-235, an unstable isotope of uranium, and the sum of the masses of its constituent atoms, krypton and barium, when in the process of expelling an errant neutron the isotope splits in two. This tiny difference had been converted, according to Einstein's formula, into energy—roughly 200 million electron volts of it. A natural curiosity, this little difference, and startling, like the flame colored blossom of the wild jewel weed that pops open when you touch it.

Twenty-five years later, when I had learned to stop worrying about, if not exactly to love, the Bomb, I joined some friends around the television set to watch John F. Kennedy's former cabinet officers Robert MacNamara and Dean Rusk, knights of the aging Kennedy brain trust, recall the Cuban missile crisis. There was MacNamara, blank-eyed, efficient, and cold as Univac, epitome of the corporate manager, even in reminiscence looking genuinely frightened, and Rusk—ruminating, desultory, humorless, noncommittal—whose whole personality and even his physical presence seemed to have been sullied over by the gray cast of the famously unthinkable thought. I don't remember much of what they said, but the gist of it was simple: in October 1962 the Soviet Union and the United States of America had come within a hairsbreadth of destroying one another with nuclear weapons.

Though shocking, there was nothing really new here; in October 1962 we had believed, all of us who were seventeen or twenty-one years old, sitting around on the floor of a dormitory common room watching Kennedy deliver his dreadful ultimatum, that the ghastly mushroom-shaped thing lingering at the edge of our horizon since childhood would soon revisit us with the concentrated horror of a vast incomprehensible world war. I remember how we looked at one another—one of my dorm mates, wearing a Student Peace Union pin on his collar, broke into tears—as the years in which we were to have grown up into ourselves, our lives, disappeared, as if the sky or the stars were to disappear, and how our attention turned with an even more desperate intensity to the immediate world constituted, as it must be always for the young, out of youth itself: a generation destined to fall in love with itself, we would somehow seize history's canceled guarantees and, entirely on our own, make good on them.

As I drove home that night from my friends' house and the television program, the familiar streets of my leafy Ohio village suddenly turned alien and forlorn, I felt transformed, for a few hours stirred as if by a distant regimental anthem into remembering what twenty-five years earlier had been the spirit of the times—glorious, heroic, full of high purpose, of a revolution that would be fought without revolt, a patriotism without politics, an idealism mistrustful of ideas, a collective purpose lodged in a multitude of jealously independent hearts—aroused in me by a mercifully brief resurrection of the old spectre of nuclear annihilation.

This was an insight and, in the end, a theme, for the inward stirring was accompanied by the sounds and images of what we have come to call for convenience, but with an implicit sense of compromise or concession, the "folk revival," that popular cultural movement in which many of the young people of my generation were more or less swept up, and which, I understood that night, had been suffused with an apocalyptic dread so deep, prolonged, and pervasive that it had become unconscious—like all repressed nightmares stripped of the infinite fright that on the day of the Cuban missile crisis returned in a form as bloated and white as a corpse. Moved by the recollections of two aging men whom I had once despised, but for whom I now felt a kind of compassion for the terrible burden they had to bear, I remembered lovely Joan Baez, with her dark eyes and hair, her delicate shoulders, warbling to the plinking accompaniment of her guitar some British ballad in a voice somberly and exquisitely pure; images of Bob Dylan, the real inventor of punk, brazen, wasted, outrageous, excoriating racists and warmongers and capitalists in the drawling, swearing, muttering, doggerel-ridden songs we adored, and in the elliptic, visionary, lyrical ones that remade our world, but most of all felt again the defiant spirit in which we listened to them and the sense of strength and indomitability they gave us.

I was swept up in the folk revival—the ripening, I now realize, of seeds planted much earlier in life. For a time I supposed that "You Are My Sunshine," because my mother sang it to me, must have been some old Yiddish lullaby, translated into English. From my beginning years I had a radio and phonograph of my own; my uncle manufactured them. Among my records was "Red River Valley," illustrated by a drawing on the disc of a cowboy with his guitar, a running brook, and a maiden with a rose in her hair; Tom Glazer's "When You Lay the Rails, Boys," an Irish worksong complete with the puffing of a locomotive and the shouts of a section gang. I had a recording of "Sweet Georgia Brown" by the Billy Bones quintet, which though I couldn't have been more than eight years old always brought to mind the low gray skies, the somber parades of freight cars, the march of highways and high-tension lines across the prairie beyond my window; I had first heard it when my father took me to a Harlem Globetrotters game. And my older half-brother, something of a hipster, dead now, had given me—a private joke, it must have been, since I was very young—a recording of Dinah Washington's "Long John Blues," which when I rediscovered it more than forty years later gave up its sexual meaning without ambiguity.

With the little radio whose dial glowed late into the night beside my bed, I searched the broadcast spectrum, pulling in from distant parts of the middle west barndances, singing conventions, and gospel hours, until Elvis Presley, Carl Perkins, Chuck Berry, and the rest, swept Ernest Tubb, Hank Williams, Patsy Cline, the Chuck Wagon Gang, the black church services and boogie parties broadcast from the South Side, only a few miles away, out of my life. "Heartbreak Hotel" was my last 78.

But more than music lies around the deeper roots of the folk revival. I had played with capguns and dressed like a cowboy and caught all the western films that played for a quarter at the local theater every Saturday morning; I remained loyal to them when these same films came to television and inspired new weekly series like *The Lone Ranger, Wild Bill Hickock,* and *The Cisco Kid.* In 1958, sitting in my father's Oldsmobile parked at the curb with the radio on, I heard the Kingston Trio's "Tom Dooley." I was thirteen. Already I owned two or three of Harry Belafonte's albums; these I soon supplemented with albums by the Kingston Trio, the Weavers, the Limeliters, Bob Gibson, Joan Baez, and Pete Seeger. That this music might have, in its past, some political connection, I had no idea. By the time I reached fifteen my mother, who loved my rendition of "Lemon Tree" and liked to show it off to company, had bought me a little spruce-body nylon-stringed guitar with which I accompanied my few folksongs; but, having transferred to an urban highschool in a less-than-affluent northside neighborhood, I soon fell in with a group of aficionados who introduced me to the esoterica of the burgeoning folk revival—to blues and banjo fingerpicking styles from obscure scholarly field recordings, to Folkways albums recorded in North Carolina of an oldtime banjo player named Clarence Ashley and his neighbors, who included a blind guitarist named Doc Watson.

Struggling with our new guitar licks and banjo rolls, engrossed in record albums, photographs, and liner notes, tuning in on the long winter's Saturday nights to the *Midnight Special* on WFMT, at every opportunity singing to one another and to ourselves, our little band searched in the social ecology of the new Kennedy era for a niche in which to play out our rituals of adolescent self-making. By the time I entered college, I was practicing the banjo compulsively, my spirit daily venturing out on its bursting tones over the broken autumn cornfields that lay beyond my dorm window. In the summer of 1964 my friends and I made a pilgrimage to Newport, where for the first time I encountered the children of the northeastern cultural elite, children of real affluence, privilege, and power, whose strange beauty and confidence struck me with tremendous force. I knew I had reached the wellsprings of the folk revival. Guitars and banjos were everywhere. Young people thronged the streets, thousands of us, all studiously and precisely unconventional. Most were like me, imperfect copies. But a few were originals, and entirely convincing.

That, schematically, is one revivalist's story. When the Beatles brought their revolution I went along, until a few years later, in a bar, I met a hot country fiddler and joined a bluegrass band. In succeeding years I fell in with Ohio revivalists following the stringband renaissance flowing out of North Carolina, tried my hand with middling success at clawhammer banjo and oldtime fiddle, and flirted briefly with blues piano and slide guitar. At times it seemed as if all the reservoirs of a life passionately and exhaustively lived might open up to me if I could manage to overcome whatever it was that stood between me and the honest execution of some song or tune I loved; at other times it seemed as if my few gifts lay in another realm and that I had squandered them in the pursuit of a musical mirage.

History has a kind of conscious life in the institutions, ideologies, movements, and forces that seem to constitute the daylight workings of society; but it has a kind of nocturnal life as well—a dream world ruled by the various alchemies of metaphor and symbol, where the boundaries between one institution and another with which it is constantly at war, between an idea and its contrary, swim about in a kind of cultural ectoplasm where forms change places with one another, sending the spirit of one into the body of its sworn antagonist, bringing the dead back to life in new incarnations.

The postwar folk revival, in a straightforward way that may help us to understand the more complex social and cultural movements that followed it, was just such a series of transformations: when the carriers of a superannuated ideological minority found themselves celebrated as the leaders of a mass movement; when an esoteric and anticommercial enthusiasm turned into a commercial bonanza, when an alienated, jazz-driven, literary bohemia turned to the simple songs of an old rural America, when a Manichean cold-war mythology created a huge pacifist counterculture more fundamentally threatening to the political establishment than a handful of ideologues had ever been, when state capitalism generated a massive antiestablishment reaction in which it found, ultimately, one of its richest new market constituencies.

The atomic bomb did not cause the folk revival; Joan Baez was misquoted, but widely, when she said that she "sang to troubled intellectuals with the Bomb on their minds." And yet the revival as I knew it was permeated, if not by the bomb, then by the industrial, technical, economic, political, and social system of which the bomb was an emblem, a system that had achieved its highest level of organization, its most efficient coordination of various processes, powers, and interests, and its most stable institutional form during World War II.

Eisenhower's phrase, "the military-industrial complex," seemed for many years only a vague insinuation; but no one knew better than he the actual network of connections among congressional districts, Pentagon contracts, corporate managers, and local economies that has woven itself into the fabric of our democracy. It is perhaps too obvious to observe that American society, more thoroughly rationalized, regimented, and bureaucratized in the promulgation of the war at home than ever before in its history, had to show in its peacetime society and culture the many effects of that gargantuan collective effort. Of these effects, the folk revival was transient and transitional; but, precisely because it was transitional, because its prewar connections were for the most part with social and political elites, left-wing or progressive movements, and particular racial, ethnic, and regional cultures, the folk revival may have something to tell us about American society, then and now, that the more familiar features of the postwar social landscape—"postwar prosperity," automobilization, suburbanization, or television—cannot. When we consider the map of American culture as it organized itself around the folk revival, an unaccustomed picture emerges, one in which an intricate circulatory system of cultural ideas, often entangled with but essentially independent of the official and visible system, works through informal networks of people and communities to shape the collective experience in ways that are significantly more than a simple reiteration of social power. Above all, it is a picture of a *cultural* process, one in which the imagination proves more powerful than either the sword or the dollar, and in its moment capable of a permanent in-flight course correction.

Of that map, more in a moment. This book is not a history of the folk revival—it is an attempt to construct the context of a single image from the Newport Folk Festival of 1963 with which that event, and this book, closes. Such a moment has its own historical framework, and that framework in turn has a set of structural elements that also have histories, much of which is beyond the purview of this discussion. I have said little, for example, about the recording industry or, Chapter 6 excepted, about the canonical recordings that were the revival's primary aural and imaginative environment. The organizational, documentary, and archival initiatives of such organizations as the Newport Folk Foundation, which lent its material support to such significant enterprises as *Foxfire* magazine or North Carolina's Jugtown Pottery, and helped in generating state support of folk culture in Cajun Louisiana or the Georgia and South Carolina Sea Islands, have had lasting significance. But they too belong to another discussion, as does the entire background of folksong scholarship that has regularly intersected with folk revivalism.

My folk revival is not that of folklore scholars and activists, nor of highly influential pioneer figures such as Charles Seeger and Pete Seeger and Alan Lomax, nor of their children and protegés such as Mike Seeger or Ralph Rinzler or Roger Abrahams, born roughly ten years earlier than I; nor is it that of my contemporaries such as Dylan and Baez who won fame as performers in the revival. It is simply that of a participant, neither marginal nor central, one born in the last year of the war whose formative years by happenstance coincided with the brief and spectacular visibility of the folk revival in American popular culture. Hence much of what I have to say concerns the public life of the revival, which is why I have sometimes chosen over scholarly sources the commentary of a perceptive journalist such as Susan Montgomery, who after thirty years seems to have more to say about the revival than the oddly dated disputes of the revivalists themselves. Her frame of reference has endured; theirs have not.

What wants explanation for me, and I trust to many of my readers, is the seven-year period between the release of the Kingston Trio's "Tom Dooley" and Bob Dylan's appearance at the Newport Folk Festival in 1965 with an electric guitar and a blues band. These are artificial but not arbitrary points; by general agreement they mark the boundaries between which a longstanding folksong movement, with elaborate political and social affiliations, emerged out of relative obscurity to become an immensely popular commercial fad, only to be swallowed up by a rock-and-roll revolution whose origins, ironically, it shared.

What is to me most intriguing about the dissolution in the early fifties of the "folksong movement," the phrase I use to refer to the politically motivated singing of folksongs between, roughly, the emergence of the Popular Front in 1935 and the Wallace presidential campaign of 1948, is that it was induced by cold-war anticommunism, which drove not only folksingers but many others in the arts, education, and entertainment out of the public arena; it was just this suppression that "deideologized," or depoliticized, the folksong movement, preparing the way for the folk revival by sending the ideologically derived signs and symbols of the earlier movement into the postwar world apparently fresh, innocent, and untouched, ready to carry both the aspirations and the discontents of a new generation. Perpetually eluding conceptual closure, these signs and symbols seemed to demand absorption in ways closely akin to acting and the theater—hence my emphasis on issues of representation. The links between the stage and the revival, from the Carolina Playmakers through actors Ives, Geer, and Belafonte, to Broadway and the *Ballad for Americans,* to original Newport performers such as Theodore Bikel, Will Holt, and the Clancy Brothers is too consistent to be ignored. This was an essentially festive process that would ultimately overflow the stage into the wider public arena, partaking fully of the spirit of postwar consumer society.

Some readers may wonder why I have not paid more attention to the communist movement and to left-wing politics generally, given their importance in the genesis of the folk revival. Admirable work has already been done in this area, by scholars far better equipped than I to address it. Of the early centrality of the left in the revival there can be no doubt: one reads Richard Reuss or Serge Denisoff feeling that all the mysterious locked doors of the folk revival have their hermeneutic keys in the Popular Front, the American Music League and its revolutionary choruses, the Composers' Collective, the labor colleges, and so on; but for those of us whose revival began around 1958, these associations were absent and would have been, in our naive and compliant youth, a barrier to any enthusiasm for folksong. What is most interesting about the revival is not its political affiliations, but the absence of them. For we were good, and wanted to be. The left, in any case, was itself subject to the more pervasive cultural influences with which this book is concerned, and inseparable from them.

Hence new explanations and new interpretations are in order. It was, as I suggest, the suppression of the earlier political affiliations that enabled the folk revival to flourish as it did, outside any sectarian context. Nothing was more tiresome, once the revival was in full swing, than to endure the contributions of some antediluvian communist songster with a bag of "banker and bosses" union songs, stirring as they must have been in their time, who imagined that the labor movement of the thirties had come back to life. "The emphasis is no longer on social reform or on world-wide reform," John Cohen wrote in 1959. "The effort is focused more on a search for real and human values."[1] What had been their movement became our revival—and we insisted on assigning our own meanings to it. In retrospect, however, it is clear that the thirteen-odd years between, say, the release of "Heartbreak Hotel" and the election of Richard Nixon in 1968 were but temporary thaws in the sheet ice of reaction that is the recurrent theme of American political life.

In his monumental study of American folkways, *Albion's Seed,* David Hackett Fischer writes that Virginia's seventeenth-century ruling elite, recalling its own place in England's royalist hierarchy, "required an underclass that would remain firmly fixed in its condition of subordination." Prompted by a cultural nostalgia in which slavery figured both as an economic force and as a cultural opportunity, the Virginia gentry, Fischer writes, made its African slaves play the roles of English serfs: "to dress like English farm workers, to play English folk games, to speak an English country dialect, and to observe the ordinary rituals of English life in a charade that Virginia planters organized with great care."[2]

This was a kind of folk revival certainly, though one, perhaps, from which it would be idle to attempt any fixed conclusions, beyond the fact that the conspicuous role of coercion in it, even more of "charade," remains suggestive for us. The historical connection between the Virginia cavalier and the folk revival may seem remote at best; but as Roger Abrahams, exploring the same ground at closer range, points out in *Singing the Master*, one of these revived ceremonies, the English cornshucking or "harvest home," through its popular representations,

> formed part of the body of scenes and sketches of plantation life that became an important feature of the literary and dramatic life of the new nation. Not only in diaries and travelers' reports, but in novels and on the stage, Americans found the plantation South a compelling *mise en scene*. This popular interest had already produced, by the end of the first quarter of the nineteenth century, the beginnings of blackface minstrel entertainment.[3]

Blackface minstrelsy was the most popular entertainment of the nineteenth century. Indeed it was ubiquitous, embodied in a virtually infinite range of expressions from local plantation entertainments as indigenously African-American as could be possible in the New World to backwoods and frontier fun-fests that made use of whatever musical and comedic material was available, typically of rural black and backcountry origin, to famous theatricalizations of these entertainments such as Dan Emmett's Virginia Minstrels or E. P. Christy's Minstrels, to colossal choral spectaculars and outdoor pageants such as

Haverly's Mastadon Minstrels, scarcely distinguishable from Barnum's circuses.

Minstrelsy, as Abrahams reminds us, never really went away. Medicine, Toby, tent, and vaudeville shows sustained its life in the rural south, where with a little detective work one can still find traces in scattered fraternal lodges, VFW posts, and volunteer fire departments. George Hay's Grand Ole Opry and other radio barndances adopted minstrel conventions to frame the beginnings of country music as a broadcast and concert form, while such early television shows as Ed Sullivan's and Jack Benny's revived its social spirit. Early animations, including the copious barnyard symphonies as well as Disney's Mickey Mouse and Goofy—read Zip Coon and Jim Crow—owe much to minstrelsy; and if, finally, there is any meaningful distinction between the old *Amos and Andy* show, or the more contemporary country-music program *Hee Haw,* and the original minstrel show, I don't know what it is. Transformations of minstrel motifs still surround us, in everything from Disney's theme parks to Michael Jackson's videos.

In the minstrel show, American popular culture created its national clown, at once harlequin and tramp, a protean loose-limbed rag doll whose traces we can detect not only in Steppin Fetchit and Bojangles Robinson but in Charlie Chaplin, Emmett Kelly, and even Mick Jagger. Onto this figure, working- and middle-class audiences in an industrializing and urbanizing America projected the many challenges posed to cultural identity by the decay of religious, regional, ethnic, and occupational cultures, and resolved in a symbolic way the ambiguities endemic to a multicultural society.

But what is important for the folk revival is that the minstrel stage, well before the emergence of the romance of the west, was one of the earliest and certainly the broadest imaginative field in which America created its proto-discourse, not only of race and racial stereotype, but of rustic and pastoral life: its folklife. The cabins, cottonbales, wagons, steamboats, and rail-fences, the chickens, pigs, roosters, and mules, the "hogs and hominy, punkins and red gravy," the banjos, fiddles, guitars, and tambourines, the dandy, the rube, Sambo, Mammy, and Old Uncle, the "shuffle and breakdown"—all the trappings of the minstrel stage, as well as the piquant genre images of corn and cottonfields, the welcoming old plantation home, the harvest moons, the barefooted children, the magnolia, honeysuckle, and wisteria vine, all the wistful longing songs addressed to them, and the very "South" itself, magically invoked by mere names, Kentucky or Carolina or Alabama—are the visual and linguistic coinage of the minstrelsy that has been circulating in America for a century and a half in thousands of forms beyond the stage itself: in sheet music, songbook and magazine covers, panoramas, popular lithographs, postcards, bookjackets, scrapbooks, albums, catalogues, advertisements, product packaging, toys, as well as films, radio, television, folk festivals, and now even music videos. It is quite impossible even to think about "folklife" without recourse to the many motifs and images that descend from minstrelsy, which may be said to have formed the core vocabulary of an American vernacular romanticism, one inextricably bound up with questions of race and racial identity.

When the folk revival, taking up a cultural quest that began after World War I, rediscovered oldtime music, both in the form of reissued commercial recordings from the twenties and of the rediscovered mountain musicians themselves, it found one of the richest deposits of the minstrel show in banjo and fiddle tunes, play-party and nonsense songs, buck dancing and clogging; mountain people, like the world's other poor upland peoples, had proved highly retentive as well as provident culturally, recycling all it had inherited from the past, not only minstrel pieces but the celebrated ancient stock of British border ballads and songs as well as the revised or misremembered sentimental songs of Tin Pan Alley. It is nothing short of uncanny that one of the abiding symbols of the minstrel show, an artifact of its place in the abolition debate, the image of an aged Uncle singing of the old southern home to which he longs to return, should have become, in traditional mountain music and eventually in bluegrass, the expressive resource of rural people driven by agricultural depression into the burgeoning industrial cities of Baltimore, Cincinnati, Detroit, and Chicago.

Nineteenth-century representations in literature of the southern black owed a good deal to the minstrel show and to the many commercial uses of it, in advertising, pan- and dioramas, toys and dolls, and so on. Harriet Beecher Stowe's characters are a virtual encyclopedia of minstrel-show types, both drawing on and helping to reinforce their use on the minstrel stage as exhibits on every side of the slavery question. Others in Stowe's abolitionist circle, however, if not intimately acquainted with southern life, at least made contact with it through the bureaus, schools, and commissions of the Reconstruction South. The earliest collection of slave songs, that of William Francis Allen, Charles Pickard Ware, and Lucy McKim Garrison, as the last surname suggests (she married the great editor's third son in 1865),[4] had its origins after the Civil War in the second generation of New England reformers.

This is the tradition, that of enlightened social reform and genteel philanthropy, whose successive initiatives in the cultural sphere shaped the folksong movement and tied it historically to the waves of progressive social thought emanating from industrialized England in the writings of Robert Owen, John Stuart Mill, John Ruskin, and William Morris. The abolitionist, suffrage, settlement-house, and temperance movements are of course highly complex matters in themselves. One must look to the missionary societies of the Congregational Church, to the Unitarian creed of social service, to the millennial movements of the 1830s, and especially to Quakerism, whose antislavery, pacifist, and pluralist stances have consistently inspired reform in America and whose emissary to the folk revival was no less a figure than Joan Baez. One must also look to the literary inheritance of the New England elite: to John Milton, John Bunyan, and Ralph Waldo Emerson, epic, allegorical, transcendental, and above all Protestant poets who presided over the nineteenth-century synthesis of a redemptive cosmic drama with an ideology of self-reliance.

Though of course not exclusively or entirely, these movements appealed to a class of educated, affluent, northeastern women who, after the Civil War, found among the many varieties of socialism emanating from England an opportunity for personal fulfillment outside the home and a definite object toward which to direct their cultivated but diffuse energies, breaking what Jane Addams called "the snare of preparation." Genteel socialism was a complex synthesis of utopian thought and romantic feeling occasioned by the radical bifurcation of the social order into antagonistic classes by industrialization; in general it sought to relieve the material deprivation, as well as the spiritual alienation and cultural degradation, of the industrial worker, as well as to raise aesthetic standards through various configurations of model communities and enlightened leadership. William Morris, for example, took the medieval craft guild as his model and, with Ruskin and others, shared the object of redefining, morally, the process of work itself as an agent of both communal interdependency and artistic self-expression.

These were the ideas, however well or poorly developed, however inflected, whose general coloring can be detected in the craftsmen's clubs, arts and crafts leagues, architectural societies, and other establishments of this century whose influence in design extended to folk-art collections, museums, and craft guilds such as the Museum of American Folk Art and the Southern Highland Handicraft Guild. As for a standard of artistic perfection, the reformers' appeal was mainly to their own tastes—which, fortunately for their poetry, painting, architecture, decorative arts, and design, and for the folk revival as well, where taste has played a critical but largely unacknowledged role, was uncommonly fine. But it was taste nevertheless, stripping the surfaces of an imagined colonial and preindustrial

America to make the blazonry of a ruling-class crusade against mass culture.

The socialist romance that developed around the "folk" drove the feminist reform movement from the liberal northeast into Appalachia to create missionary and settlement schools, folk schools on the Scandinavian model, handicraft guilds and craft cooperatives.[5] Olive Dame Campbell, wife of the director of the Southern Highland Division of the philanthropic Russell Sage Foundation, in 1914 persuaded the English folksong scholar Cecil Sharp to set out in search of British songs in the southern Appalachians. Sharp's work, informed as much earlier European folklore scholarship had been by "romantic nationalism," ties together two traditions important for the folksong movement: that of the ballad revival, a literary enthusiasm whose sources are in romanticism generally and in Percy's *Reliques* and the works of Robert Burns and Walter Scott in particular, and of Fabian socialism, a gradualist creed that placed the impetus for social rectification in the hands of cultural lieutenants whose work, particularly in the arts, would achieve its aims by a kind of aesthetic consciousness raising.

Hicksite Quakerism, with its insistence on "mental integrity above all else," grounded Jane Addams' extraordinary call to service and secured for her, as for others in the settlement-house movement, what contemporary reformers do not enjoy: unflinching confidence in her own aesthetic, social, cultural, and moral standards. "Culture," she wrote in 1910, "is an understanding of the long-established occupations and thoughts of men, of the arts with which they have solaced their toil."[6] Hull House offered instruction in native languages, classic literature, and the fine arts, as well as various games, exercises, and amusements, including ethnic "folk festivals" of music and dance, and child-care, medical, and other social and personal services; but at bottom it was an oasis, in the midst of unprecedented urban congestion and disorder, of middle-class domestic taste, comfort, and refinement whose influence might in the end reconcile the violently dislocated people of Halstead Street to the realities of industrial capitalism.

To Addams, who had felt herself "smothered and sickened with advantages," and to many young men and women like her, life by the end of the nineteenth century had become something unreal, amorphous, and, as Jackson Lears puts it, borrowing Nietzsche's term, "weightless."[7] "She looked back upon her mother's girlhood with positive envy," Addams writes of a contemporary, "because it was so full of happy industry and extenuating obstacles."[8] A feminization of culture, as Ann Douglas terms it, seems to have driven culture out of the public sphere and confined it, much as it had confined women themselves, to the parlor and the parish house, isolated from the male-dominated spheres of effective social and political action.

Hence a masculine and "muscular" reaction, symbolized by the robust Teddy Roosevelt, which emphasized male independence, strength, autonomy, and virility, stressing the self-sufficient outdoor life of the soldier, the hunter, the scout, the cowboy, or the wilderness guide, arose to complete the bifurcation of antimodernism along gender lines. This so-called muscular Christianity, without its distinctly religious coloring, lingered on in American society until well after World War II in summer camps, scout troops, YMCAs, outing clubs, and the like, many of which became repositories of revived folk crafts and songs and, with the elite Anglo-American Country Dance Society, contributed to the postwar folk revival.

It became an appealing instrument of assimilation for German Jews as well, whose achieved status in American society seemed threatened by the masses of new Jewish immigrants from Russia and eastern Europe. The ethos of the strenuous life could be reduplicated in what Roger Abrahams calls the "sternly homoerotic environment" of German-Jewish summer camps, where communal living, campfire songs and stories, handicrafts and woodlore, athletic competition and ceremonial awards, in a setting of clear northern lakes and pine forests, ambivalently prepared the youngster for life in the capitalist marketplace. Various ideological strains, including Ernest Thompson Seton's "Friendly Indian" clubs, scouting's esprit de corps, and a nonsectarian love of the wilderness marked the summer camp both with class and nationalist meaning. At the heart of this project—a symbolic assertion of nativity, collective worth, and a kind of ecumenical transcendentalism charged with both Jewish Reform and Protestant elements—were ersatz Indian rituals, inspired perhaps by Seton but rationalized by Henry Lewis Morgan's studies of the "primitive democracy" of aboriginal America, often sounded in varying degrees alongside various progressive or socialist creeds.

By the 1920s a brisk trade in the representation of folk culture was securely in place. Pioneering record-company advance men such as Ralph Peer and Art Satherly, beginning in 1923, had begun to tap the immense resources in nineteenth-century social and display music, folk and commercial, still flourishing in southern folklife: familiar figures such as the Carter Family, the Stoneman Family, and Jimmie Rodgers won fame as performers and recording artists, playing and singing traditional songs as well as original pop tunes to regional audiences.

On the vaudeville circuit, where singers such as Ma Rainey and Bessie Smith supplied the African-American marketplaces with a newly intense blues and jazz music, a way was opening for many black rural singers and guitarists, such as Big Bill Broonzy and Leroy Carr, to find a wider audience; Charlie Patton and Robert Johnson, unheralded in their own time, left behind them on race records documents of prodigious musical and poetic power. Commercial broadcasting, too, with the Grand Ole Opry and other barndances, brought traditional fiddling, minstrelsy, and the Saturday night play-party, in performers such as Uncle Jimmy Thompson, Uncle Dave Macon, and Dr. Humphrey Bate and the Possum Hunters, to parlors throughout the south and midwest, recalling, with nostalgic caricature, the old times before the Great War.

Not all the activity in folk music was commercial. The intense concentration of European immigrants in urban ghettos, the squalor and desperation dramatized by such works as Jacob Riis's *How the Other Half Lives* (1890), stimulated an anxious nativist movement among people who, aroused by the lurid ethnic stereotypes promulgated by newspaper cartoonists, pulp novelists, and the vaudeville stage, feared that Anglo-American culture was being threatened with extinction; this outlook was often conjoined with the related idea that the offending agent was the spread of commercial entertainment, including the radio barndances but especially jazz, which to the nativist imagination was a poisonous brew of primitive racial elements both Negro and Jewish—what Robert Winslow Gordon, founder of the Archive of Folk Song, called "Hebrew Broadway jazz."[9] Modernity generally, or more precisely its threat to the cultural hegemony of the Anglo-American middle class, was the enemy, and folk culture, understood as a survival from a more respectable past, might be a bulwark against it.

Class anxiety and ethnocentricism, then, occasioned by swift social and technological change, provided an atmosphere in which, in 1926, the regional office of the Ford Motor Company in Louisville sponsored a fiddlers' convention, bringing together the winners from local contests held at Ford dealerships in the middle south. Industrialist Henry Ford, an outspoken antisemite and isolationist, sought like John D. Rockefeller to museumize the preindustrial artisan economy that his own enterprise had done so much to abolish, even to the extent of installing it among his own workers with instruction in square dancing and vegetable gardening; while the Rockefellers were collecting folk art and underwriting its exhibit in New York and Colonial Williamsburg, Ford was constructing his historical museum at Dearborn, Greenfield Village, constituted like Williamsburg from the relics of a renovated and rewritten preindustrial past. "Folk art" in this context—weathervanes, carousel ponies, funeral paintings, cigarstore Indians, and other commercial iconography—was really the folk objet d'art, with the craftspeople themselves quite eclipsed by it: precisely the condition of its "folk" as well as its antique and sumptuary status.

A new regional folk festival, music teacher Annabel Morris Buchanan's at White Top, Virginia, drew national attention when Eleanor Roosevelt visited in 1933; but another visitor, Charles Seeger, who came in 1936, was troubled by the parochial attitudes of a coterie of managers who seemed motivated as much by their contempt for what Buchanan called "crude modern folk productions with cheap tunes based on ancient Broadway hits," and a hatred of urban culture generally, as by a love for "the highest type of native material"; they saw no contradiction in excluding from the festival local people unable to pay the forty-cent admission fee. "Elizabethan frankness may be tolerated," Buchanan wrote of her festival, but "vulgarity is barred. The folk festival is not concerned with products of the streets, nor of the penitentiaries, nor of the gutter . . . high standards cannot walk hand in hand with simon-pure democracy."[10]

Seeger detected in the affair a veneration for Anglo-Saxon culture which, with its apparent indifference to actual mountain music and mountain people, was at bottom not musical at all, but social, an idol of the tribe, a self-styled cultural aristocracy. "Not for the mountain people alone," Buchanan intoned, "not for one region alone; not for one class alone: the White Top activities, if they are to endure, must be wrought slowly, carefully, measure by measure, for a *race* . . . for after all, the White Top festival belongs to *the folk*. And we are *the folk*."[11]

Other festivals arose with tourism in mind, as rubber tires and hard-surfaced roads opened rural areas into which railroads had not yet penetrated. In 1928 the Asheville Chamber of Commerce enlisted a local lawyer, collector, balladeer, banjo picker, and square dancer, Bascom Lamar Lunsford, to add a program of folk music and dance to its annual Rhododendron Festival. Asheville's development boom, founded in a feverish speculation in real estate, was on the wane—and waning with it was the hope that Asheville might become the resort center of the east coast.[12]

Conservative in politics and manners, and a former school-teacher himself, Lunsford saw in the domestic music and social dance of his region a reservoir of the old-fashioned rural gentility that a generation earlier had flowed from the country school-house, the law office, the Baptist pulpit, and the parlor. Lunsford would not brook a hellraiser or a rogue, types not unknown either in folk music or in mountain society, and certainly not a convict or a tramp; normally he did not extend his hospitality to occasional visitors from the urban folksong movement whom he saw largely as frauds.

The first folk festival to address conscientiously, with clear social and political aims, the cultural diversity of America was Sarah Gertrude Knott's National Folk Festival, inspired by Luns-ford's and introduced at St. Louis in 1934.[13] Knott had worked under Fred Koch in the Carolina Playmakers and, in 1929, became director of the Dramatic League in St. Louis. Like Anna-bel Morris Buchanan, she was concerned about the leveling effects of commercial records and radio, and, like most folklore scholars in that period, regarded folk culture as an endangered species; but, far from a commitment to a particular vision or strain of culture, with all the social and political allegiances such commitments imply, her outlook was generously democratic. Whether in preserving traditional cultures or in promoting international understanding or, after World War II, in improving the new leisure time or finally anticipating what would become a complex theoretical discussion, in attempting to distinguish between what she called "survivals" and "revivals" in folk tradition, Knott was able to ground her work in the ideological moment. "Our national culture is being woven from the warp and woof of the variegated and colorful strains of many nations," she wrote. "No one would want to dull the richness of that pattern. How bleak indeed would be the cultural outlook for the future if we overlooked the distinctive, individual cultures in a universalized, standardized, regimented culture."[14]

The folklorist David Evans divides the folk revival of this century into four stages,[15] beginning with the effort of classical singers such as Richard Dyer-Bennett, John Jacob Niles, Marian Anderson, and Paul Robeson to bring folksong into the concert hall, in effect defining a work of apparently humble origin, though many folksongs have been traced to court poets and academic composers as well as to cheap broadsides and chapbooks, as fine art. Niles, for example, was a foothill Kentuckian but Julliard-trained, and many of his folksongs, including the familiar and lovely "Black Is the Color," were of his own composition; occasionally he presented a Child ballad as one he had collected himself.[16] In the late nineteenth century, the Fisk Jubilee Singers and a short time later the Tuskeegee and Hampton Institute Singers offered a kind of genteel minstrel show of African-American spirituals, formal textual renderings of what were originally aural improvisatory choral songs, to support these nascent institutions—a highly successful effort that amounted to the appropriation of this music by polite society and the further confinement of black people, in some ways more invidiously than in minstrelsy itself, into the stereotype of Christian patience, humility, and other-worldliness that Victorian sentimentality had projected.

In the second stage, Evans says, during the heyday of the Popular Front, folk music came to replace the revolutionary chorus as a device for raising class consciousness in America, allying itself to the labor and antifascist movements. "All-purpose revival singers and groups like the Weavers appeared," he writes, who in a loosely Anglo-American singing and instrumental style "could perform 'songs of many lands,' mixed with a dose of leftist ideology." Liberal internationalism, after the League of Nations, as something quite apart from the ideology of class struggle, had been installed in every progressive agenda, and by

World War II had become national policy; "songs of many lands," absent the implied Marxist analysis, could be heard in the schoolroom and on the radio as well as the nightclub and concert hall. But McCarthyism drove the left, and the folksong movement with it, off the field, leaving it to such "nonideological" figures as the Kingston Trio and Harry Belafonte.

Reissues on long-playing albums constitute Evans' third stage, exposing revivalists to "real folk music" and inspiring the rediscovery of folk singers and musicians who enjoyed new careers as festival, coffeehouse, and concert performers. The *Folkways Anthology of American Folk Music* appeared in 1952; for most urban folk revivalists it was the first encounter with the commercial country music and blues of the interwar period.

Most of the intense reissue activity on a variety of small record labels followed the pattern of the Folkways Anthology, and there are few revivalists who do not remember their first experience of it. There are few, too, who do not remember their introduction to a new kind of record album, also on Folkways, called *Old Time Music at Clarence Ashley's*, recorded in the field by Ralph Rinzler, an album that aimed to reproduce in living musicians the sound of the old Library of Congress discs and prewar commercial records. Many other recordings followed, including Rinzler's own reissues of Uncle Dave Macon, the Carter Family, and Bill Monroe, the musician whose stringband, still touring the rural south in the shadow of rock-and-roll, had lent its name to the "bluegrass" music that would soon have, with Rinzler's conscientious intervention, a dedicated revival among urban folksingers. Another voice from the Anthology, Mississippi John Hurt's, would, on the strength of a one-word clue picked up by discographer Dick Spottswood on an early disc rediscovered by blues collector Tom Hoskins in Avalon, Mississippi, become a headliner with Dylan and Baez at the Newport Folk Festival. Many such reissues, discoveries, and rediscoveries followed, resulting in time in an extensive canon of what Art Menius calls "archaic commercial music."

The long-playing microgroove record, originally developed for symphonic music, had become an instrument for accumulating and storing music formerly dispersed in isolated private collections and company archives. "High fidelity," moreover, acted upon the music as an audial magnifying glass, bringing to the ephemeral discs of the 1920s, most of them languishing in flea markets and junk stores, an intense and vivid presence. A highbrow technology, then, which had reduced the symphony to a kind of elaborate miniature, had thrust the amateur music of the south's poorest and most despised peoples into the foreground of the high-cultural avant-garde.

From this activity, Evans writes, there emerged a fourth stage of the revival, as revivalists, like jazzmen before them, exhibited "an increasing competence and authenticity in the re-creation of folk style and a strong tendency towards conscious specialization and regionalism or ethnicity." Revivalists, Evans notes (in 1979), "are now mixing daily with 'the folk' on a level of social equality, and the musics of the two groups are becoming increasingly blended."[17] What began in Cambridge, Massachusetts, with the Kweskin Jug Band in the mid-1960s continued in the decades that followed in a proliferation of distinctive musical kinds, including New England contradance music, Cajun music, oldtime, blues, Klezmer, Irish caeli, until a profusion of eclectic folk styles from Latin America, urban Africa, Soweto, Indonesia, eastern Europe, and the Middle East absorbed the folk revival in the nineties into an ongoing process of musical incorporation and globalization.

Evans' account rings true, I suspect, for most revivalists; it is the received account, a revolutionary myth that celebrates the emancipation of the arts of ordinary people from the oppressive formality of high culture into a utopian condition in which the revivalist—urban or suburban, middle- or upper-middle-class, expensively educated, endowed from birth with wide access to the products of popular and elite culture, very likely established in a professional or managerial job—"mixes daily with 'the folk' on a level of social equality." It is a story of considerable force: derived on the one hand from its denial of the legitimacy of social power and, on the other, from its denial of the authenticity of social powerlessness, a story that validates the revival by claiming, like Annabel Morris Buchanan, "folk" status for itself.

Folk revivalists of the late sixties and seventies were hardly the first to "mix daily with 'the folk' on a level of social equality." Blackface minstrels regularly made the same claim; John Lomax, Carl Sandburg, John Jacob Niles, and especially Bascom Lamar Lunsford, later Jean Ritchie, Hedy West, and others, quite in spite of their educations, politics, and social affiliations, rarely permitted their audiences to forget that they were themselves grounded in the regional cultures of which they came to be agents, brokers, and retailers. Folksongs continue of course to supply the classical repertory. Evans' "stages," in other words, actually record successive intersections of new means of reproduction and dissemination with a unitary high-cultural process arising from the idea of the folk itself. It is not so much that the revival liberated folk music from the concert hall, revealing it at last in an authentic "re-creation" that dissolved any meaningful difference between the revivalist and the folk, but that the concert hall—that is, the high-cultural ideas, initiatives, resources, opportunities, occasions, and influences it represents—in time defined in its own terms who were the folk and in what authentic folk style consisted, so that the "increasing competence and authenticity in the re-creation of folk style and a strong tendency towards conscious specialization and regionalism or ethnicity," and the power of a revival so constituted to influence, by institutional and commercial means, the actual practice of music on the folk level, became, in effect, the legitimate high-cultural means of presenting folksong—as much as if it had been presented in white tie and tails.

The idea of the folk is a noble invention. To say so, of course, is always to risk grave misinterpretation, as if the folk were some sort of effete, narcissistic self-deception, like Marie Antoinette's milkmaid or Queen Caroline's thresher-poet. Not at all. That the "folk" are rarely such to themselves only suggests that the idea is the confluence of an objective social process, on the one hand, and a particular way of framing it on the other; in this respect it is a social, political, and aesthetic fiction which, like other useful fictions from the past, identifies a specific dimension of cultural life that, if it has not actually disappeared, and theoretically cannot really disappear, has nevertheless become awkward to construct in the same terms. From one point of view, the folk are simply what humanity appears to be from the prospect of social preeminence, as it gazes down on its dependents. Nobility in principle implies that dependency, to which nobility responds, in principle, with obligation; hence "folk" implies mutuality between high and low, and carries with it a predemocratic tradition grounded in feudalism—or, more accurately, in a memory of it—and inherently inimical to ideas derived from trade, from the town, science, money, mechanization, and mass production. If nobility loves independence, it is because independence is the definitive condition of nobility.

The idea of the folk is noble, finally, as the type of that which is eminently worthy and indubitably excellent, that which scorns whatever is base, mean, unworthy, or cheap. The principle of nobility thereby achieves a kind of consummation in the idea of the folk, for here it strips itself of the outward conditions of birth or fortune, discovering what is surpassingly fine among the lowly and least favored, thereby validating itself at the deepest levels. Like Fielding's Tom Jones, it is a foundling whose nobility runs in the blood and cannot but manifest its breeding in noble actions.

Like other noble ideas, the idea of the folk must be an invention, a substance sublimated by an aspiration, a poetry that like Wordsworth's half perceives and half creates, a frame of reference that locates the real even as it renders it ideal. Hence we encounter it, for the most part, as a representation. This is particularly true in folk revivalism. The performance of a folk-song is as much a representation as the pastoral painting or the proletarian novel, the movement of a sign from one order of signification to another, claiming and attributing but never confirming. That we may encounter pastoral scenes on the historical landscape suggests the referentiality of the pastoral image; but the pastoral image has always already shaped our recognition of the pastoral scene, which in turn provides further opportunity for the landscape painter—a reflexivity grounded neither in the scene nor in the painting but in historically contingent conceptions of space, ideas of property, instruments of exchange, techniques of husbandry, and conditions of consciousness embodied in both scene and painting.

And so with "folk," grounded in ideas of society, of self, and of time normally called romantic. What is confusing is that folksong or folklore, unlike arts conventionally understood to be images or fictions, may involve materially the representation of actual people placed or displaced from, discovered or imagined in, actual situations; though framed as folk, these situations and people, strictly speaking, belong to the order that framed them and are the consequence of the same agents, the achievement of the same forms, and the pursuit of the same ends as the painting or novel, more conventionally illusory or fictional. In that confusion lies the irresistible epistemological riddle of the folk.

A noble idea, then, but one immensely complicated by history. Those complications I will take up later; suffice it to say here that the traditional condition of nobility is in modern political theory occupied, but in social practice only aspired to, by the bourgeois self—that is, by a great many of us—and its frame of reference has become our customary way of encountering the other. To complicate matters still more, the postmodern self has become diffuse, its frame of reference shifting and uncertain, its substance traded away as a commodity and spectralized as pure sign. In these circumstances, a folk revival resembles a recovery of self—but at the same time is a revolution against the very forces that constitute the self.

I know of no better way to illustrate my point than through one of the great originals, and originators, of the folk revival, Mike Seeger. Along with his half-brother Pete and his sister Peggy, he was a child of the period's foremost ethnomusicologist, Charles Seeger, whose own father, Mike recalls, "was one of those oldtime gentlemen-businessmen who played the piano, drew well, and believed he was pretty high-class."[18] Mike himself was born after his grandfather's retirement from the import business to Charles and Ruth Crawford Seeger, impecunious avant-garde composers and music teachers who built their careers on the exotic and unusual sounds in American vernacular music. Ruth herself had grown up with Methodist hymns and knew something of mountain music—her father was born in the Cabin Creek area of West Virginia and he became a preacher. With his sister, Mike grew up in a household filled with folk music; while other children listened to merry nursery songs and didactic jingles, Mike and Peggy were exposed very early to Library of Congress field recordings and commercial discs of early rural stringbands, penitentiary worksongs, and blues that their mother transcribed for the Lomax books and sang to schoolchildren in her classes. As she notes in her own book, the Seeger children became "test tubes" for folksongs that she would include in her pioneering collections.

Like many another wellborn child, Mike, with his large intelligent head, sharp nose and eyes, his postbox grin, remains close to type, a face and figure on a light, elfin-like physical frame essentially out of the past, the very image of the storied frontiersman whose music he has been all his life reinventing, a smaller edition, it might be said, of Abraham Lincoln. The range of his musical versatility is remarkable: he is a master of guitar, fiddle, banjo, mandolin, harmonica, panpipes, jew's-harp, autoharp, dulcimer, mandolin, and banjo-uke; his repertory ranges over

Mike Seeger, 1995

the whole field of southern vernacular music, from bizarre nonsense songs and harrowing ballads to down-home blues, raun-
chy minstrel-show tunes, and weird frontier laments. His
musicianship is unfailingly spruce and craftsmanlike, sufficiently
expert to excel but never to exceed—it is better and more noble,

like Cyrano, to be "in all things admirable" than to place oneself ahead of others.

As a member with Tom Paley, John Cohen, and later Tracy Schwarz of the New Lost City Ramblers, Mike Seeger introduced oldtime and bluegrass music to young urban audiences, recorded a series of watershed field collections, and brought to the concert stage such notable musicians as the coalminer-banjoist Dock Boggs, autoharpist Kilby Snow, fiddlers Eck Robertson and Tommy Jarrell, as well as songster Elizabeth Cotten and country-music personality Cousin Emmy. His role, like other revivalist impresario-performers, has been that of mediator or broker—but in retrospect it is clear that whatever Mike Seeger played, recorded, or put on the concert stage has borne a certain indefinable mark, an elusive but consistent quality tending in some definite direction.

In recent years the originality of Seeger's work, as he passes his sixtieth year, has become even more apparent. With his fiddle tucked into his shoulder and his cross-key harmonica on a rack, he creates a strange, swimming, otherworldly sound that might, to a willing listener, suggest the image of a sun-blinded western wagoner of the 1850s at the limit of his endurance, his understanding clouded, his heart hardened and hopeless, his spirit harrowed by some sublime delusion. I say perhaps. Certainly no such musical sound was ever heard on the frontier or anywhere else; at the same time, it is impossible to say that it was not heard.

Surely, though, no Delta bluesman ever sang "Rolling and Tumbling" to the accompaniment of a guttering, gulping, fretless gourd banjo—Seeger's was built by a craftsman from a nineteenth-century artist's rendering of an antebellum plantation instrument—and yet in speculatively back-reading the Delta blues to a much earlier southern rural practice, Seeger wrests a musical truth out of a historical rupture. "Somehow," he writes in the notes to a compact disc, "I trust the years of oldtime and bluegrass experience enough to follow my imagination."[19]

Most telling, however, is Seeger's painstaking and deferential performance style. The white tie and tails are long gone, in favor of a pair of shabby cords, scuffed oxfords, and a set of black suspenders. There is no bel-canto delivery, but a style that by calculated artifice at once imitates and reinvents the traditionally strained, nasal, wood-grained mountain vocality, marking it with authenticity while at the same time claiming it as something both original and exotic. Seeger's allegiance to a standard higher than himself could not be more evident. What complicates the picture is that while he rescues in folk music the values dear to his class, values that typically include contempt for modern commonplaces such as mass production and mass culture, Seeger is also, through that music, in lifelong revolt against his class—and hence permanently exiled to that strange zone where the very phenomenon of social differentiation seems to have exhausted itself.

No ethnomusicologist will ever confirm or deny the relationships Seeger is claiming reside at the heart of his music. His claim is more interrogatory than declarative, more mythical than descriptive. In this he follows the work of the great folklorists from the Grimms to the Lomaxes, who understand that theirs is a work of cultural cathexis, dreaming the felt but untheorized political urgencies of the present into historical memory where they may reanimate the problem of the present with impulses that transcend the inertia and banality of fact. Such is the prerogative of nobility.

Like the returned Ulysses or the exiled Edgar in *Lear*, like the blackface minstrel, Mike Seeger can come most fully into possession of himself only in disguise. This is the classic Byronic gesture, that of the nobleman recovering through a reckless and brilliant condescension, choosing virtue over power, the essence of his nobility. To have it and to repudiate it, and thus to have it back again in its authentic form: of all the tales that nobles tell about themselves, this essentially allegorical and religious story has been, from Luke and John to the Wife of Bath, John Milton,

C. S. Lewis, and Hermann Hesse, the one most loved by the people of the town.

As an artist Mike Seeger is loyal to the noble tradition that shaped him, profoundly romantic, and in this sense he can be, like other romantics and, indeed, like much of the folk revival itself, handily dismissed—the very term has become dismissive—by the liberal, empirical, quantitative, positivist, utilitarian intellectual tradition for whom authenticity in folk music is a sociological, not an aesthetic, feature. But "romantic," the term and the concept, is only a late development of modernity designed to isolate precisely those human drives and forces, and the modes of understanding, knowing, and signifying, that stand obdurately in the way of its project.

At the heart of the folk revival, finally, lies what this writer at least does not attempt, a handful of passages excepted, to capture in words—a strange omission—the imaginative message of the music itself. What was once commonly said of folksong, that it has stood the test of time, seems valid still. Whatever these statements may mean ideologically I leave to others; for now I put politics aside to declare that folksong, whether high or low, old or new, traditional or original, survived or revived, reflects the deepest and most persistent of human dreams, and marks the human face and human habitat with their power. Often it is poetically subtle and precise, melodically and harmonically striking and fresh, elegant formally and structurally sturdy and ingenious, in performance a source of lasting inspiration and intense joy. Within its basic simplicity there is, in execution especially, a complexity that will always defy analysis.

Whatever we suppose it to be, whether it is a commercial disc recorded by a hillbilly pickup band of a barber, a car mechanic, and a local doctor on an afternoon in Bristol, Tennessee, in 1925, or a half-remembered British ballad descending on the maternal side of an old Blue Ridge family in western North Carolina, or a blues sung on the streets of Durham in the thirties by a laid-off tobacco worker, or a recital of "Negro spirituals" at

Constitution Hall by an African-American diva, or creditable imitations and recreations of any of these, folk music barters its episodes of the human story with a concreteness, immediacy, and economy commensurate with the best achievements of any art, at any social level.

Folk music has enriched my life immeasurably, as it has the lives of many others, and convincing performances of it are still to me a vital sign of an important human distinction. As someone who has over the years known a few marvellously gifted musicians, I can appreciate, as only an amateur with a small talent can, the distance between the merely adequate perform-ance and the consummate one, which carries musician and listener together out of their present life into the life of the music, grafting it with transfiguring force permanently to the body of their experience. In that distance is the measure of something so deeply and desirably human that many otherwise ill-advised, irrational, and often futile sacrifices have been made to traverse it. Whatever else it may be my book is intended as a tribute to those who went the distance.

And, in fact, thinking over my experience of the revival, I cannot at last separate folk music from folk revivalists. The story of the revival is, like other good stories, not finally about ballads or banjos but about real men and women and the moments in which they found their distinctive voices. With other revivalists I've had my musical heroes—Pete Seeger, Bob Dylan, Joan Baez, Earl Scruggs, Doc Watson, Bill Monroe, Robert Johnson, among others. I remember the initial shock of Dylan's raw and petulant voice, the almost unbearable limpidity of a lovesong in Baez's throat, the wildness and sublimity of bluegrass at its outer limit, the prodigious energy, at once poetic and erotic, of Robert Johnson at the eternal crossroads, sinking into the earth like one condemned.

The tunes I still attempt to play, the recordings that moved me, this or that unforgettable performance, have assumed over time nearly the status of persons—like brothers or sisters, perhaps, in whom one inevitably catches the old family resemblance, with whom one can always become reacquainted, in whom time collapses in upon itself, and yet who must finally remain independent, other, unconquerable. We cannot, finally, abandon them—for as surely as we must relinquish our youth, so must we honor and sustain the life force that is the gift of youth. As in any youth movement, what drove the folk revival was sheer erotic magnetism and beauty, idealism and aspiration, personal, social, and political striving, forces that, perhaps more than any other art, music is capable of communicating.

Consequently I don't forget the delicate young man, a student no doubt, with a few days' growth of beard, whom I encountered thirty years ago in the small hours of the morning on the backside of Beacon Hill, sitting in a doorway, working over on his guitar Dave Van Ronk's "Come Back, Baby" with application as intense as a lapidary's, playing with transparency and sensitivity, talking enthusiastically about his music and about bluesmen whose names I didn't recognize, since I was even more green and unschooled myself. Or the half-crazy, moon-faced, laughing sandy-haired fellow with yellowed teeth, a cheap guitar, and one chord, who drifted through our cornfield-bound midwestern campus one day singing Blind Lemon Jefferson's "See That My Grave Is Kept Clean" over and over again, with uncanny fidelity to his source, as if his voice and guitar had been beamed up from Waco, Texas, in 1919. Or the gruff, remote, obsessive banjoist in a business suit, his tie untied, whom I encountered at a party. He was standing in a bathtub, having filled the tiny room with admirers, ripping through "Dixie Breakdown" with a torrent of roiling notes that oddly seemed to reverse the flow of the music, as if Niagara were to fall *up*. Later I cornered him, and he showed me his secret. It was in the roll, you see: he played it backward.

Or a bluegrass festival I once attended, where one evening as I strolled back to my campsite, catching the sound of a fiddle coming out of the sun-streaked woods, I wandered off the path to find it. There was a solitary man, a poor man by all indications, about forty I'd guess, in a pair of old twill pants and a washed-out polo shirt, ruggedly handsome, with hollow pock-marked cheeks, a missing front tooth, and a mass of limp curly hair, his stout arms and huge workingman's hands fiddling some lonesome Kentucky farewell tune.

He seemed delighted to see me and began talking immediately, grinning through his broken teeth, something I guess about a certain difficulty in the bowing of the tune he was playing, and then began singing, with his fiddle, in the husky, high-pitched Clinch Mountain vocality associated with some old Stanley Brothers song—"Stone Walls and Steel Bars" or maybe "The Memory of Your Smile." He wore a wedding ring, but it occurred to me that in his world and past there might have been a few entanglements with women or with the law. Other people drifted in, crunching through the underbrush, to listen.

His musicianship, by any measure, was primitive, and his singing rough and uneven at best. But whatever folk music or mountain music or bluegrass music is, he had laid hold of it.

Arthur Godfrey, late 1950s

2

The New Minstrelsy

With his houndstooth jacket and open collar, his trade-mark Hawaiian shirt, lei, and ukulele, like a man on vacation, the round-faced, benign Arthur Godfrey, radio and television personality of the 1950s, can be said to strike the first note of that brief interlude in postwar American music we call the folk revival. Godfrey's program, with his idle, easygoing mono-logues, his leisurely conversations with ordinary people, his nascent suburban values, emerging like a new polymeric fiber from the collapse of prewar provinciality, and especially his hospitality to amateur performers, was as cozy as a coffee klatch, finding its audience mainly among women who had taken refuge in their suburban kitchens from the anxious managerial culture driving their ambitious husbands, war veterans with the buff and shine of military life still clinging to them.

Godfrey was hardly revolutionary. There was something tranquilizing in his avuncular good cheer, and in his suburbanism something congenially daft—particularly the almost doting delight he took in a postwar world where consumer products and laborsaving devices promised to inaugurate America's permanent vacation from political consciousness. With his ukulele, an emblematically amateur holiday instrument, an icon, along with the lei and a white Navy uniform, of the Pacific theater, Godfrey was almost camp, unconsciously recalling, even as he addressed the lower-middle-class migrant Californian with Iowa grandparents, the homosexual sailor on a weekend pass.

It is amazing how many revivalist guitar and banjo pickers claim to have begun on the ukulele, at summer camp or college, accompanying themselves on "Heart and Soul" or "Ain't She Sweet," two songs more fully established in American tradition, probably, than any British ballad or Woody Guthrie composition. Even Pete Seeger played one at boarding school and wrote a children's story-song, "Abiyoyo," about it. A miniature instrument played with a soft felt pick, two- or three-finger chords on nylon strings, with a light, shallow strumming sound, and decorated sometimes with tiny devices such as palm trees, hula girls, lariats, or sixguns, the uke lent itself to amateur entertainments in groups of adolescent and preadolescent children whose unawakened sexuality the uke with its devices seemed at once to concentrate and to dispel. Though not festive exactly, the mood of Arthur Godfrey and his ukulele is relaxed, sunny, recreational, the spirit of the package tour, like Hawaii itself the icon of an airline paradise strangely metamorphosed from World War II's initiating catastrophe, as the Bikini atoll was metamorphosed by its concluding one: the beginning and the end of history, paradise and apocalypse, staged at the same site.

It is curious, then, that the folk revival—the brief but spectacular commercial popularity of professional folksingers in the early 1960s—began quite literally in vacationland. Two highschool boys from Honolulu, Dave Guard and Bob Shane, had been playing parodies of folksongs for tourists at a Chinese restaurant, and later on the beach were joined by children of servicemen already familiar with Burl Ives, the Weavers, and Richard Dyer-Bennett. At that point, certainly, the folk revival was not the anomaly of culture most of us usually take it to be, the earnest handmaiden of radical politics and youthful bohemianism, a stream running underground in leftist intellectual circles, progressive urban schools, and summer camps, in scholarly song collections and esoteric recorded anthologies, but the self-conscious and self-directed irony of a collegiate generation emerging from the squarest decade on record, a decade of busy careerism, political somnolence, and inane fun designed as if to divert the attention of sensitive children away from the brutal face of the historical reality of the twentieth century. At this stage, the folk revival was simply another diversion in America's postwar festival of consumption and convenience, its temporary release from class anxiety and race hatred, its holiday in a new television culture that superficially effaced the old divisive ethnic distinctions in favor of a kind of classless, pan-ethnic, white suburban society grounded in consumerism, home ownership, and childrearing,[1] but in which Old World ethnic antipathies, by tacit agreement, silently prevailed.

Godfrey probably hated the folkies, if aware of them at all, but he embodies the cultural milieu in which the commercial folk revival grew up, when a radio-based mass culture of sport, drama, music, and advertising, the legacy of prewar urban America, was adapting itself to the new medium of television, essentially a commercial device disseminating a gospel of consumerism marked, not as in the past by the charm of convenience and comfort, not by any emancipation from labor or even by the glamor of luxury and status, but by the imputation of exclusion—the new television was a window that with stark florescent indistinctness placed everyone on the outside of American life, looking in.

Because it involves the movement of cultural materials across usually impassable social frontiers, from enclaved, marginal, usually poverty-stricken peoples toward the centers of cultural power, folk revivalism is inherently political and often, though not always, explicitly so. The blackface minstrelsy of the nineteenth century, among other things a theater for the formation of a working-class masculine identity played through a black mask that channeled a multitude of ethnic and racial images, absorbed the discourse of abolition and bandied the question of slavery about in many sentimental melodramas and irreverent farces; it left behind a body of racial and cultural ideas that still dominate our thinking about race and, at the same time, exposed to the popular imagination the emerging synthesis of European and African-American music which was our first "national" music as well as the pattern for most of the musical innovations after it.

"The reason my father and I got the backing to establish the Archive of American Folksong," Alan Lomax reflected, "was that we were supposed to find the tunes for a national opera that some American Wagner was going to come along and write—the American 'Ring of the Nibelung.'"[2] For Lomax, folk revivalism was a poetic project closely allied to the nineteenth-century literary quest for an American epic that would identify, glorify, and enlarge the primitive or natural man, the racial or working-class other, thereby yoking the history of European civilization to the continent's unfallen innocent state—either at the point of their meeting, as in Longfellow, or, as in Walt Whitman, in the figure of the Poet himself, at once a natural, common, and universal man, who in singing the multitudes represents, embraces, and absorbs them. And yet these separate strains, the one aristocratic and romantic—embedded in myth, turned toward the past, inscribed with rituals of Christian piety—the other visionary, democratic, secular, populist, progressive, converge in the central paradox of the American political experiment, designed to secure for the commonality the condition of nobility: independent, virtuous, honorable, but at the same time plain, modest, humble, serf as knight and knight as serf. At the heart of this paradox, and sustained by its own revolutionary energy, lies the idea of the folk.

The folksong revival of this century, with its various regionalist, nativist, radical, recreational, and countercultural strains, belongs to a complex response, with roots in the late nineteenth century, to the ongoing adjustment of newcomer groups, whether racial, ethnic, or generational, to the conditions of life under an industrial and post-industrial social and economic system—a process that has turned Irish airs into "Ethiopian Melodies," Yiddish lullabies into patriotic songs, and German hymns into cakewalks.

In an industrial economy that since the Civil War sequestered childhood and the family in a sacralized domestic sphere of affection, sentiment, memory, and ritual observance, the adjustment to the routines of industrial capitalism are in a sense structurally installed in the life cycle, demanded of every middle-class young person venturing out of home and school into the workplace. The folk revival, like other youth movements, took form in the personal and temporal zone between industrial society's period of prolonged cultivation of the child and the very different world offered to the young adult, who must face the sharply narrowed, dependent, and isolated version of himself it demands, having at the same time equipped him to take its fantastic injustices in an immediately personal sense.

Hence in successive periods a number of "progressive," alternative, or oppositional styles and ideologies, beginning in the generation of Jane Addams, variously inflected with class and ethnic meaning, gathering force at midcentury on the left, popularly consolidated in "the sixties" and continuing today in green, new age, punk, deadhead, grunge, and slacker movements, have ridden the waves of generations of youth recoiling from the real world as it confronts them after domestic and scholastic protections have receded, often adopting the more genuinely angry styles and postures of excluded ethnic, working-class, or minority youth.

At least one cultural theorist sees youth movements as displacements of generational tensions within the family into a social setting where the young "may express and resolve, albeit 'magically,' the contradictions which remain hidden or unresolved in the parent culture," achieving a kind of symbolic autonomy that at the same time preserves some continuity with the parent culture.[3] Others argue that industrial society's protracted adolescence has issued in a parallel postadolescent phase, devoted to the development of knowledge, skill, and initiative, that authorizes the young to postpone the assumption of adult roles.[4]

But adulthood, it would seem, cannot be delayed indefinitely; while a youth movement might postpone, especially in educational settings, the assumption of adult roles, it would seem also to imply resistance to that postponement, completing the cycle of adolescence by converting symbolic identities, roles, and occupations into the active resources of a reconstituted parent culture. Nor is it clear, in the folk revival, that generational conflict within the family was displaced into a youth subculture; on the contrary, the family of the early 1960s seems both practically and ideologically to have carried the brunt of conflicts whose underlying sources are outside the family, grounded in perennial debates over fundamental values familiar since at least the end of the nineteenth century. Christopher Lasch might have been talking as much about his own generation as that of Jane Addams when he wrote that "middle class parents found themselves unable any longer to explain to their children why their way of life was important or desirable. The children on their part found themselves equally unable to communicate a sense of why they could not pursue the goals their parents held up before them, unable to explain why they felt themselves 'simply smothered and sickened with advantages.'"[5]

The invention of a folk serves several purposes. It provides immediate relief from the sense of oppressive change emanating from vast, remote, and often inconceivable historical forces, and from an accompanying sense of personal disorientation, diminution, or fragmentation; the imagination may be set free into a completed familiar world that can be materially associated with residual social formations we incorporate into the historical and cultural narratives already available to rationalize such change, in whatever dimension it occurs. Like blackface minstrelsy, folk revivalism is a form of social theater in which we develop the protocols for negotiating relations among groups and classes, as well as our own transition from one state, condition, or membership to another, discovering ourselves contrastively as we invent the "folk," experiencing ourselves reflexively as we emulate them.

In this respect, folk revivalism tends to become associated with pastoralism, antiquarianism, the picturesque, and other nostalgic traditions; like other romanticisms, though, folk revivalism has both an epistemological and a political force undergirding its superstructure of fantasy, dream, and wish. In its very inventedness it embodies a structure of knowledge and an incipient system of affirmative values in which a critical historical perspective, an alternative or oppositional cultural politics, and even a prescriptive social-political program all become possible.

In 1845 J. K. Kinnard wrote a piece called "Who Are Our National Poets?" for *Knickerbocker Magazine.*

> In what class of our population must we look for our truly original and American poets? What class is most secluded from foreign influences, receives the narrowest education, travels the shortest distance from home, has the least amount of spare cash, and mixes the least with any class above itself? Our negro slaves, to be sure! *That* is the class in which we must expect to find our original poets, and there we *do* find them. From that class come the Jim Crows, the Zip Coons, and the Dandy Jims, who have electrified the world.

It is particularly significant that America's deepest social division, the one between black and white, should be the site of folk revivalism's most visible early efflorescence and its most persistent theme. Here the invention of a folk is historically allied to the larger collective project of inventing the black Other and of assigning the cultural indicators within which the black social being remains circumscribed and controlled. It is instructive that the leitmotif of blackface minstrelsy, the abolition debate, reemerged in the folk revival of this century as the civil rights movement, and that the folk-music heroes from both periods have often been those men and women who successfully negotiated the difficult passage between black and white culture, or who, while vigorously championing black political causes and expressive modes, remained cautiously on their own side of a cultural and racial boundary they had themselves drawn. Minstrelsy and blackface, and related forms of racial ventriloquism and imitation, were decisive means of accomplishing this.

What ties a man like T. D. Rice, who brought a black stableman's dance to the stage as "Jim Crow," or J. W. McAndrews, who brought the clothes, cart, mule, and cry of a black street vendor to the stage as "The Watermelon Man," to twentieth-century musicians like Bix Beiderbecke or Benny Goodman, studying the records of King Oliver and Louis Armstrong, or Jimmie Rodgers, "the father of country music," composing his "Blue Yodels" from the patois of black muleskinners, or Elvis Presley, tuning in to black country bluesman Arthur Crudup on Memphis radio, is the power of racial mimesis to deliver up for signification and enactment the cultural, social, personal, and sexual meanings otherwise secreted away in the all-devouring idea of race. Indeed, Woody Guthrie perfected his vocal delivery by listening hundreds of times to his handful of records of bluesmen Blind Lemon Jefferson and T-Bone Slim, and he performed during the war as the only white man in a quartet with Sonny Terry, Brownie McGhee, and Huddie Ledbetter.[6] Jack Kerouac called Guthrie, erroneously, "the first White Negro."[7]

When we remember "Old Corn Meal," the New Orleans street vendor who appeared on stage in New Orleans *as himself* in 1837,[8] we must remember too the great black singers of the folk revival, who performed and defined their own blackness within the constructions of white revivalists. Thus the racial and ethnic boundary crossings that characterize both minstrelsy and folk revivalism fortify these boundaries even as they facilitate a strictly regulated passage of cultural information over them. The result is a kind of infinite regression of identity into the insoluble—because misbegotten—but infinitely compelling question of racial distinction.

Antebellum minstrelsy, as Eric Lott explains, arose from the apprentice or artisan's sense of threat posed by a new wage-earning industrial working class—an anxiety exacerbated, at the bottom of the social ladder, where Irish Catholic immigrants (famine Irish) or half-castes competed socially and economically with free blacks, and by stirrings of antislavery feeling at the top. "Antiabolitionist and anti-black temperance riots in the 1830s and 1840s," he reports, "have been seen as angry correctives on the part of Irish and other workingmen to their own sense of political powerlessness and economic disenfranchisement—their resemblance, in both class and ethnic terms, to 'blackness.'"9 "Whiteness," David Roediger argues, "was a way in which white workers responded to a fear of dependency on wage labor and to the necessities of capitalist work discipline," so that the white working class began to construct an image of the black as Other—"as embodying the preindustrial, erotic, careless style of life the white worker hated and longed for."10

As many observers have remarked, minstrelsy exhibits in the realms of culture, class, gender, and sexuality the dynamics of a kind of sibling rivalry, in which one group projects its own oppression onto the group socially below it, oppressed like itself, both to deny its own oppression and to defer the guilt for its acquiescence, complicity, or even its initiative in it: that is, it subjects the Other to ridicule and parody, while at the same time it draws sharp distinctions, and in effect frees itself, from the Other.

But in this process there is a deep ambivalence: a recognition of kinship and perhaps, in their shared oppression, a charge of fellow feeling, but also an intimation that both groups are competing for the same resources, advantages, awards, and powers—and in this intimation, therefore, an attraction to what in the Other seems most capable of winning the oppressor's favor—a desire for what the Other has. This confused relation gives rise to a kind of hysterical enactment, with many reverberating layers of imitation and differentiation, claims of authenticity and brazen counterfeit, essentially a struggle between antipathy and identification, a sibling-like competition for resources with which each group, affirming its worthiness, soliciting or resisting the oppressor, engages its condition.

Thus far rivalry; but actual or symbolic identification with a marginalized group can also make one equally contemptible, in danger not only of the same subjection but of contamination by the Other. Hence, with one's own worthiness and power called into question, the minstrel or revivalist, actually or imaginatively squeezed into the same space as the Other, his own body inhabited by the Other's, recovers his power by first appropriating, and then mastering, the expressive forms and performances of the despised group: dancing the jig better than Master Juba himself, picking the blues guitar better than the Reverend Gary Davis or the banjo better than Earl Scruggs, or, as Jack Elliot and then Bob Dylan did, out-Woodying Woody himself—and in effect doing away with the Other out of love.

When the racial mask draws the black voice and the black body into the white, the mask becomes in effect transparent, exposing what for the minstrel-ventriloquist constitutes the Other while at the same time placing the minstrel in his "whiteness" on display. For however distorted or counterfeit, what is always at issue in minstrelsy, race itself having been formally neutralized, is the revealed cultural or other difference, a represented entanglement signifying a real one: not "white" imitating or parodying "black," but a racial imitation flushing out for examination the deracinated signifiers of difference, as a transvestite display will expose for contemplation the natural and social signifiers of sexuality, challenging the performer either to drive them further apart through parody or to unite them through impersonation, that is, to equal or exceed, to conquer the Other, to distance her or to become indistinguishable from her: a process in which new solutions to the equation of difference invariably proliferate.

The result, in either case, is the audience's heightened self-consciousness about its own standing: a fact that only intensifies the racial or sexual romance with all of its contesting desires.

And that is precisely the point. The mood of the minstrel theater, with the minstrel semicircle enclosing the audience, symbolically, is festive and comic; but within this closed circle the
minstrel performance itself is by turns sentimental or passionate,
humor flirting with pathos, ridicule with grotesquery, elegy
with banality, cupidity with cruelty, the racial burlesque like
sexual burlesque lurching unsteadily between the erotic and the
pornographic, desire and violence, always settling into the ambivalence that is the hallmark of romance.

In such troubled social-psychological zones, dialectically
elaborated types or "vernaculars" emerge both to claim what
Lott calls "indigeneity" for themselves and to become the constituent elements of the nascent imagined national community.
An economically and socially pressured group, as Roger Abrahams so astutely points out, with esoteric rituals of male bond-
ing on the one hand and the "open secret" of public disguise on
the other, challenges the authority of a reigning order and
claims a rooted social identity for itself. The mercantile captain
becomes country squire by getting up a harvest feast for the local
tenants and dancing the Sir Roger DeCoverly himself; a band of
yeoman farmers, in feathers and face paint, mobs the house of
the colonial landlord to demand its property rights; at the lodge
meeting or guild hall, the small merchant and the first selectman
rub elbows and, dressed like dervishes, display their camaraderie
in a civic pageant; in the minstrel show, a band of corked-up
Irish printers' boys travesties the only group more despised than
their own; an assimilated German Jew, honoring his young
campers for woodcraft and athletic prowess by bestowing "Indian" names on them, proclaims them peers of the gentile boy
scout and clubman—all rituals of making a community in which
demonstrated merit and natural hierarchy seem to argue against
traditional authority and arbitrary power.[11]

Constance Rourke years ago observed that in the first half of
the nineteenth century American life had a festive, comic-theat-
rical quality, the streets of its port cities crowded with various

characters who, like Jim Crow or Old Corn Meal, might pass back and forth across the proscenium with impunity, and without much modification. The Ring-Tail Roarer, the Yankee Peddler, the Long-Tail Blue, the Irish Cop, and the Jewish Tailor were in any case familiar figures on the social landscape before they became the stock characters of melodrama, minstrelsy, and vaudeville, and they owe their amplitude and clarity to the circulation of their images from stage to street and back again in a dynamic republic in which racial, ethnic, regional, and class distinctions were being redrawn, a process that gave us the Yankee, the Frontiersman, and the Black as archetypes of American identity.

In mass-circulation newspapers and pulp magazines of the early nineteenth century, embodiments of the American character, always located where some form of socioeconomic competition or domination had begun to inspire new self-representations, variously incarnated as Mike Fink, the barrel-chested Ohio River boatman, or as Davy Crockett, the braggart Tennessee frontiersman who ran for Congress in 1829, won the hearts of popular audiences with their humble origins, aggressively egalitarian postures, and copious speech; indeed, such emergent frontier primitives as the Ring-Tail Roarer and Mike Fink in blackface were already being called on to fill what for northern working-class audiences was the capacious, because "black" (that is, dark), category of race[12]—"the domain of a newly fascinating 'negro' or 'African' culture," Lott writes, in which guise "blackface minstrelsy threatened to lay claim to the title of native American genius."[13]

These figures in any case stand in contrast to the elegantly Rousseauean frontiersman Natty Bumppo who, like Daniel Boone, was essentially a gentleman. By midcentury they were joined on the New York stage by James Hackett's Brother Jonathan, the droll Yankee rustic, and Mose the B'howery B'hoy,[14] the brazenly chivalric volunteer fireman who rescued babies from burning buildings and protected helpless girls from seducers and innocent rubes from treacherous city slickers—all of whom were the American incarnations of age-old theatrical types, legible in Shakespeare and Ben Jonson, whose general office is to burst the pretensions of social power.

Whatever else may be said of these types, it is clear that they occur where class, ethnicity, location, occupation, all the surfaces of identity, intersect to form a three-dimensional social figure fashioning itself in revolutionary opposition to, in this case, urbanity, sophistication, gentility, and privilege. The search for an American national identity has been a genteel European project as well as a popular one—Tocqueville, Mrs. Trollope, Thackeray, and Dickens all tried their hand at it—and the "Americanness" of characteristic figures, entertainments, literary modes, and pictorial images is a function of the colonial or cosmopolitan outlook that produced them. Thus what is characteristically American is typically either of local or of provincial growth.

But with America's transformation from parochial to public, regional to national, entrepreneurial to corporate, the contest for an authentically American identity began to take on the form of a struggle either against appropriation by the commercial marketplace or for overweening success in it. In a context of European and internal immigration to America's urban centers, a circumstance that tends to enforce and to stereotype the old national or provincial identity, the elaboration of an American identity completes the social-psychological passage from the Old World or the farm and theoretically provides access to political and economic advantage. This may involve a superficial transformation, from Jewish peasant to Gibson Girl, or a more total one, like Jay Gatsby's. Paradoxically, though, it may also involve a symbolic embrace, often insistently political, of the old cultural identity—for this indicates precisely one's emancipation from it: one need not after all embrace, symbolically or otherwise, a cultural identity not already alienated, repudiated, or repressed.

Most of our theatrical stock characters, like those of earlier pulp fiction and theater, developed in the cities of the eastern seaboard, and mainly in New York, in a social setting of European immigration and its resulting urban population explosion, becoming over time the core vocabulary of our social stereotypes. "The one thing you shall vainly ask for in the chief city of America," wrote the journalist Jacob Riis, himself a Dane, in 1890, "is a distinctively American community."[15] During this same period, New York was becoming the principal producer of commercial culture for a national market and, through its many channels of information, the principal marketplace for the exchange of America's ideas of itself, ideas that over the course of a century took on what William Taylor calls the "social promiscuity" of New York's own cultural environment.

By 1870 publishing and communications had already become the city's largest industries—juvenile literature and comic ephemera, the yellow and penny presses, and Tin Pan Alley and vaudeville had established their production centers there. After 1920 national network radio, the theater chains, the newspaper wire services, the motion-picture distributing houses, and finally of course the television networks were identified with New York.[16] Geographically contained, like Venice or Amsterdam, its mercantile and business communities more influential, as Taylor notes, than either government authority or traditional cultural institutions, New York—and, until World War II, its cultural satellite, Hollywood—has been a fountainhead of cultural signification, its depictions and discoveries of America projected into its imaginative life and reincarnated in books, magazines, plays, movies, and television shows produced in the city.

Across the flowing proscenium of the Hudson, the New Yorker can behold, as Walt Whitman did, "successions of men, Americanos, a hundred millions." The very atmosphere of New York lies under a dramaturgical spell, as the mere passage of America's provincial life across the Hudson into New York lends it the unreal aura of the deracinated sign, displaced from its web of cultural and practical relations and isolated against the backdrop of New York's own strangely parochial cosmopolitanism.

This was the first principle of minstrelsy: the circus acrobat and banjo player or fiddler, marginal, errant, disreputable even in the frontier town of their origin, had merely to cross into the City, or the dancer and actor to bring the black stableman and street vendor by impersonation into it, to glow numinously with the untranslatable but powerful significance of their own cultural being, as well as to see it reflected back to them. It is the spell that transfigured Sweeny, Christy, and Dan Emmett, as well as Leadbelly, Woody Guthrie, and Bob Dylan after them, all of whom in a sense reinvented themselves by their passage into New York, converting their difference into an ideological, cultural, social, psychological, and commercial resource.

The midcentury folksong movement, a tissue of impersonation, enactment, spectacle, music, and narrative within a coterie, arose from the interplay of the ethnomimetic culture of New York, through its intellectuals, artists, and entrepreneurs, with the popular and provincial cultures that lay beyond it to the south and west. Its real beginnings are in New York radio and theater: for example, in Alan Lomax's radio program *Back Where I Come From* or Burl Ives's *Wayfaring Stranger*, in Broadway musicals such as *Oklahoma* and *Sing Out, Sweet Land*, or in high-modernist experiments of popular representation such as Agnes DeMille's and Aaron Copland's *Rodeo*. The commercial folksong revival it engendered was the return on the immense investment that the New York cultural establishment, in the forties and fifties, had made in entertainment, publishing, and education, particularly as these touched the imagination of the growing postwar generation at home, in school, on television and radio, and at the movies. Like all things theatrical, its characters inspired imitation and, through mobile and momentary performances of folksong, established a fluid dramatis personae and a portable mise en scene on the social stage, coaxing susceptible young people out of their inherited identities and touching the social background with hues of the past.

Many threads tie the representation of folklife, folksong, and folksingers in New York to minstrelsy and vaudeville. After the Civil War, emancipated slaves entered the minstrel profession in appreciable numbers, driving blackface minstrelsy's efforts at authentic depictions of plantation life off the stage and into elaborate glee-like entertainments with little connection either to southern folklife or to the northern working class. At the same time, black minstrel troupes, and the development of a black theater circuit with predominantly black audiences, created the arena in which postwar black music and culture developed, bringing ragtime, blues, jazz, and black performers such as comedians Bert Williams and Dewey "Pigmeat" Markham, blues composer W. C. Handy, and the queens of the blues, Ma Rainey and Bessie Smith, to national prominence in the 1920s.

Jazz had of course caught the popular imagination and was regarded by prescient intellectuals, who traced its lineage to primitive field hollers as well as to spirituals and blues, as the quintessentially American, that is, autochthonic, form. But urban blackface performance by the early twentieth century was mainly a *Jewish* phenomenon, what Irving Howe calls a "mask for Jewish expressiveness, with one woe speaking through the voice of another."[17] The popular music of the Jazz Age, Michael Rogin reminds us, was not the polyrhythmic, technically innovative and improvisatory performance later revered by jazz buffs and bohemians but, as in Irving Berlin's "Alexander's Ragtime Band," a cosmopolitan popular music derived primarily from the contemplation by Jewish songwriters of such black sources as ragtime. So it was both a sanction for the expressive freedom associated with the primitive and, in its early association with blackface, a site at which minstrelsy's idyllic South merged with the lost Yiddish past, converting the longing for innocence into a device of Americanization. "Al Jolson," Rogin writes, "plays a person of color instead of being confused with one. By painting himself black, he washes himself white."[18]

Fascination with jazz in the 1920s sent Benny Goodman, Mezz Mezzrow, and many young men of Old World backgrounds into the music, with its associated lifestyle and personal deportment, a tactic of assimilation to American life which recapitulated that of the young Irishmen in the middle of the nineteenth century who found in minstrelsy a gap in the wall of discrimination erected by polite society. As Lott cautions, however, the "class aura" of both jazz and minstrelsy was, at the outset at least, "scarcely elevating," and relations between self and other were contradictory at best;[19] minstrelsy and jazz created alternative communities, burnt-cork brotherhoods and hip congeries structured by musical and theatrical protocols and raised by their own popularity to a pitch of high cultural visibility.

The minstrels and jazzmen had colonized an illusionary cultural space informed by a kinesic style the whole world came to identify as distinctively American, what Walt Whitman called a "picturesque looseness of carriage" and Fanny Kemble a "languishing elegance," a style apparently deposited deep in the psychic strata of African-American culture that could be quarried out of it by painstaking, even laborious imitation, or by catching its spontaneous spirit when the combustion of black music released it into the moral atmosphere.

How did a "distinctively American" cultural trait fall into the hands of America's most injured and oppressed group? White and black southern folk culture, within many regional variations, shared a wide range of kinesic styles, musical forms, linguistic elements, culinary practices, religious observances, and the like, which contrasted markedly with the old Yankee mercantile culture of the north. But black culture was "frankly on display" in the north itself, routinely retailed on the streets well before the blackface minstrel began to appropriate the same performances.[20]

A "picturesque looseness of carriage," in any case, is no more distinctively American than it is distinctively Algerian or Australian. While Whitman himself may have exhibited it, while Lincoln certainly did, it is certain that such other "distinctively American" Americans as John Jacob Astor and John D. Rockefeller, or even the old soldier Andy Jackson, did not. The point is that such a trait, whether characteristic of frontier or plantation or both, whether it is West African or Scots-Irish, or some syncretic cultural trait, symbolizes and embodies the informality, unrestraint, freedom from rule, absence of servility, and confident natural dignity that a popular democracy is supposed to bestow, and it is always set in contradistinction to stiff interlocutor figures who represent polite culture, hierarchy, and privilege—a class distinction that was underwritten by an ethnic difference in the actors themselves, the one a Scots or border Irishman, the other a famine Irishman.[21]

Where ordinary social practice lies out of range of official standards and protocols, as on the frontier, or where institutional structures, such as the apprenticeship system of the urban north on the eve of industrialization, are deteriorating, or where social power rules with force but not with authority, as on the plantation or in the factory, a looseness of carriage or languishing elegance may be precisely the response of the devalued artisan or the driven slave to his condition, a show of defiance; Whitman's butcher boy, with his happy "shuffle and breakdown," joins his minstrel-stage counterpart in borrowing from the northern urban black a style of individual performance that declares his liberty, independence, and power from within his subordination. Hence while the putative stage black absorbed these meanings, so did the idea of black itself invade and saturate the blackface performer, the "negro minstrel" in whom racial distinction was effaced in the very act of being drawn.

From minstrelsy through ragtime and jazz, black music, and the people whose lives it evoked, amplified by published accounts and popular graphic illustrations, became the imaginary reservoir into which an old democratic tendency diverted from its course by mechanization, commercial capitalism, and the factory system increasingly flowed. In representations of black life, audiences sought the wellhead of a native culture; and so, moreover, did a increasingly stylized representation of black culture come to provide the codes for wider representations of American folk culture, through various deracialized or displaced forms of minstrelsy in the Toby show, the circus, literary works such as *Uncle Tom's Cabin* and *Huckleberry Finn,* and finally the radio barndance.[22]

In *Porgy and Bess,* presented as a "folk opera" in 1935, and thus identifying folk with black, George Gershwin combined the modalities of popular jazz with classical orchestration and the rich, multi-ethnic tradition of Broadway melodies. Gershwin's acquaintance with black folk culture extended far beyond Harlem's jazzmen; he visited black Charleston, South Carolina, and on Folly Island participated in Gullah ringshouts.[23] Set in Charleston's Catfish Row, the opera's central characters are strongly reminiscent of minstrel types, the pimp and pusher Sportin' Life and Porgy dividing between them the legacy of the dandy Zip Coon and the plantation clown Jim Crow. With its contrast of urban corruption to a paradisical "Summertime" of female warmth, fecundity, and ease, the opera continues the pattern established in earlier blackface minstrelsy in which racial and sexual desire could be covertly explored by satires of conventional bourgeois life disguised as a black travesty. But in the blacked-up pastoral allegory there were overtones of 1930s class conflict: Sportin' Life's meretricious polish—"I'll buy you the swellest mansion on upper Fifth Avenue"—smacked of the Filthy Rich, while the crippled Porgy, who must roll himself around on a goat cart, echoed a familiar depression-era streetcorner figure, also with "plenty of nothin'," on a wheeled platform, holding out a tin cup.

If Gershwin attempted to summon up black folklife by a kind of back-formation from jazz, the jazz impresario John Hammond sought it in a Hudson Terraplane, equipped with a car radio for scoping out blues singers like Big Bill Broonzy and Robert Johnson performing on Little Rock and Helena radio stations. A son of New York wealth—his mother was a Vanderbilt—Hammond became an early champion of black music and black rights, frequenting with other Jazz Age youth the clubs of Harlem. In 1931 he dropped out of Yale to work in jazz radio, and made his first excursion into the south as a reporter covering the Scottsboro trial for *The Nation.* Hammond is remembered as the Columbia Records advance man who discovered Billie Holiday, introduced Teddy Wilson to Benny Goodman, sponsored the first integrated jazz combo, and near the end of his career brought Aretha Franklin, Bob Dylan, and Bruce Springsteen into the Columbia studios.[24]

"For many years it had been an ambition of mine," Hammond recalled, "to present a concert that would feature talented Negro artists from all over the country who had been denied entry into the white world of popular music." His memorable "Spirituals to Swing" concerts of jazz and boogiewoogie musicians at Carnegie Hall in 1938 and 1939, to its first integrated audiences, were presented, under the sponsorship of *New Masses,* as a history of black music, opening with a recording of African tribal music and a lecture by Sterling Brown, a Howard University professor, on the folk roots of jazz, represented in the show by Sonny Terry, with his blues harmonica, the gospel-singing Golden Gate Quartet, and the blues guitarist Big Bill Broonzy, who had been "prevailed upon to leave his Arkansas farm and mule and make his very first trek to the big city to appear before a predominantly white audience," his "store-bought shoes pinching his feet."[25]

It was a "curious tableau," described by Charles Edward Smith in the album notes. "Jazz musicians blinking inwardly, or from lack of sleep, paunchy boogie woogie pianists wearing a bulbous self-assurance born of club and concert appearances, the regal bearing of a woman who sang the blues, the intimacy of a gospel group and the gawky awkwardness of a singer of country blues." Smith thought the program a cultural watershed, as much as the Armory show of 1913, though he couldn't resist asking, "What is the kitchen maid doing in the parlor?"

The search for the roots of jazz in the thirties, then, inspired in part by a deeper inquiry, along its deepest fault line, into the nature of American democracy itself, took the form it had taken in early minstrelsy: a quest for the grail of black cultural origins. It was a complex drive, grounded, certainly, in compassion, rivalry, sympathy, and desire, but complicated by a collective moral uneasiness that neither the championing of black causes nor an ultimately futile embrace of negritude could ever redeem. Black and blackface might be infinitely absorbent, culturally; but the conscientious invention of a black Other on the stage and elsewhere cannot vaporize African-Americaness itself. Neither slavery nor minstrelsy could reach into and subdue the forces of memory, imagination, and sheer human association in African family and community life; it has been argued, on the contrary, that the slave system supplied a structure for the syncretic nurturing of West African cultural norms. By a weird historical irony, what came springing out of slavery was the most manifestly unencumbered personality on the social landscape, endowed with performance forms that melted the rigid deportments of Euro-American hierarchies in the warmth of an interactive, somatic, aural-oral culture. The current running in what Mailer called the "existential synapses" of black America seemed to emanate from an original human gift that precisely by capturing and confining white America had let slip out of its grasp—and in this respect the contemplation of the black cultural Other both epitomized and essentialized the contemplation of "the folk."

"All the singing was done by Negroes," wrote John and Alan Lomax in 1934, after a collecting excursion into the cotton plantations, lumber camps, and prisons of Texas, Louisiana, and Mississippi. "Our purpose," they said, unconsciously echoing Kinnard's statement of 1845, "was to find the Negro who had had the least contact with jazz, the radio, and with the white man."

Both on the farms and in the lumber camps the proportion of whites to Negroes was approximately one hundred to one. In the prison farm camps, however, the conditions were practically ideal.

Here the Negro prisoners were segregated, often guarded by Negro trusties, with no social or other contacts with whites, except for occasional official relations. The convicts heard only the idiom of their own race. Many—often of greatest influence—were "lifers" who had been confined in the penitentiary, a few as long as fifty years. They still sang the songs they had brought into confinement, and these songs had been entirely in the keeping of the black man.[26]

John Avery Lomax (1867–1948) was the seventh child born of poor farmers who moved in 1869 from the Black River country of Mississippi to Bosque County, Texas, near the old Chisholm Trail. The first of his family to attend university, later a college administrator and banker, he had been impressed by the "idea of Texas" from easterner N. Howard "Jack" Thorpe's *Songs of the Cowboys* (1908).[27] Encouraged as a student in his folksong work by literature professors and ballad enthusiasts at Harvard, Barrett Wendell and George Lyman Kittredge, Lomax won a following in 1910 for a collection of cowboy songs endorsed, as noted, by Teddy Roosevelt.

"These boys in their twenties," John wrote of the cowboys he remembered, "who could ride and rope and shoot and sing, came mainly from the Southern states. They brought the gallantry, the grace, and the song heritage of their English ancestors . . . we know that the aftermath of the Civil War sent to Texas many a young Virginia aristocrat; many sons of Alabama, Mississippi, and Georgia planters; many a coon hunter from Kentucky; roving and restless young blades from all over the South."[28]

John Lomax's world of folksong was working-class and masculine, framed by his adopted Anglo-American ruling-class outlook and set in vivid contradistinction to the world of white-collar occupations and comforts and to middle-class standards generally, and in this sense echoed the scrapbooks, dime novels, picture magazines, calendars, postcards, and other ephemera in which the cowboy had his represented life. "Never has any singer of cowboy songs," said the historian Lloyd Lewis to Lomax, "made me feel the dust, the great grass ocean, the harried, bellowing steers as you did in that yodel."[29]

The "seven types" of the American ballad that Lomax distinguished in a 1915 scholarly article came from the miner ("of the days of '49"), lumberman, sailor, soldier, railroader, negro, and cowboy; another type included "the songs of the down-and-out . . . the outcast girl, the dope fiend, the convict, the jail-bird, and the tramp." *Cowboy Songs* accompanied its texts and scores with the lore of saddlemaking and roping, and explained such terms as "dogie" and "salty dog," to initiate the male reader, as a kind of grownup boy scout, into the survival skills of cowboy life.

In the world of folksong, the office and parlor-bound urban male might invest the better part of his secret longings—this was evident from the way in which Lomax couched his typology. "The life of every calling was spent in the open," he wrote, and "the occupation of each calling demanded supreme physical endeavor. The songs were made by men in most cases away from home and far removed from the restraining influences of polite society. They were created by men of vigorous action for an audience of men around the camp-fire, in the forecastle, in the cotton-fields, about the bivouacs of the soldier, during a storm at night when the cattle were restless and milling." The folksongs were "human documents that reveal the mode of thinking, the character of life, and the point of view, of the vigorous, red-blooded, restless American."

If folksong was, like the Grand Canyon or the Spanish-American War, an arena for the demonstration of a muscular male Christianity, it also retained the nineteenth-century emphasis on the innocence and purity of its polite, if not actually effete, Christian affiliations, even as it dramatized a longing to be free of them. "Dauntless, reckless, without the unearthly purity of Sir Galahad," Lomax continued in his article, "though as gentle to a pure woman as King Arthur, he is truly a knight of the twentieth century. A vagrant puff of wind shakes a corner of the crimson handkerchief knotted loosely at his throat; the thud of his pony's feet mingling with the jingle of his spurs is borne back; and, as the careless, gracious loveable figure disappears over the divide, the breeze brings to the ears, faint and far, yet cheery still, the refrain of the cowboy song."[30]

Yet Lomax collected his most famous song, "Home on the Range," not from a golden-haired prairie Galahad but from a black cook, who once worked a chuck wagon on a Texas cattle trail, in a "low drinking dive" of San Antonio. The Lomaxes' penetration into the enclaves of the southern black urban sub-culture, and more deeply into even more segregated lumber-camps and prisons, had uncovered what were actually the deposits of the late nineteenth-century Irish-American working-class culture, so richly represented in Huddie Ledbetter's reper-tory, in which the cowboy songs had originated. They crossed the racial line that consistently obscured black collaboration, not a "contribution" or a "corruption" but a full participation in the vernacular culture that black and white working classes in the south and midwest had created and shared throughout the nineteenth century. By a kind of cultural archeology, they reg-istered the stratified tempos of complex biracial cultural ex-change in terms of an exotic "black culture."

Embodied in black, in effect blacked up, the old ephemeral songs and dances from John Lomax's boyhood still to be discov-ered in southern saloons, on sharecroppers' farms, and in pris-ons took on a deeper mystery, touched with the fascination of the primitive, itself sexually inflected, whose power was now obscurely associated with a lost westward republic identified in turn with the male freedom, irresponsibility, and independence of Huck Finn's "territories." Delivering the cowboy songs retro-actively into the hands of an imaginary cowboy Galahad, even as it anglicized a racially and ethnically hybridized subculture, socially elevating and purifying it, also liberated the Anglo-American, now outfitted as cowboy, from the office and the parlor. In the cowboy song as in the minstrel show, the Anglo-American claimed the sexual and political potency of a black-inflected expressive tradition as his own remanded racial trait, the very command of which assured continued Anglo-American hegemony, thus conjoining its inherent racism to its vaunted self-control. "Why does the Anglo-Saxon race rule the globe," asks Henry Fuller's George Ogden in 1893, "except because the individual Anglo-Saxon can rule himself?"[31]

Shortly after the death of his first wife and having lost his job to a bank failure, with his seventeen-year-old son Alan behind the wheel of what to John was a not altogether trustworthy automobile, with a book contract, and with Library of Congress support, the incorrigibly restless John Lomax set out in 1933 with a 350-pound wire recording machine built into the back of the car across the black south, to record what is still the single most important collection of African-American field recordings in existence.[32] It was "a body of words and music," wrote Librarian of Congress Archibald MacLeish, "which tells more about the American people than all the miles of their quadruple-lane expressways and all the acres of their billboard-plastered cities."[33]

With his cocked fedora hat, three-piece suit, gold watch and chain, intrusive girth, and fat cigar, John Lomax styled himself a businessman; and we must think of him not in the company of the scrupulous ballad scholars who chafed at his reckless disregard of philological decorum, but with J. H. Haverly and Al G. Field, minstrel-show and circus entrepreneurs who understood that the commodification of indigenous song and dance involves their transportation, with fanfare, across cultural frontiers. It may make us uneasy now to recall that, after securing clemency for Leadbelly from the governor of Louisiana and his release from the Angola State Penitentiary, Lomax put the great black songster immediately on stage at the Modern Language Association's meeting of 1934 in New York and hired him as a chauffeur, dressed in convict or sharecropper's clothes for concerts, for a magazine photographer, and for a movie newsreel, "for exhibition purposes."[34]

John Lomax belonged to a tradition of cultural brokerage, that of the medicine-show mountebank of the rural south with his blackface banjo player and miracle cure. The language of the adventure magazine or romance novel, in the face of the genuinely savage and desperate America into which they ventured, cannot but arouse a kind of moral dismay:

> Was it the forbidding iron bars, the stripes, the clank of occasional shackles, the cruel-looking black bullwhip four feet long, which in some places hung in plain sight inside the door of the main hall—was it such surroundings that made the songs seem sad? . . . Eager, black, excited faces, swaying bodies, the ring of metal to mark the beat of the song, tones such as can come only from untrained voices—free, wild, resonant—joined in singing some semibarbaric tune in words rough and crude, sometimes direct and forceful, the total effect often thrillingly beautiful. While all around sat other men, alert and watchful, with guns in their hands![35]

This world, in which armed men gravely stand watch over the inner sanctum of a moral and spiritual emancipation won out of an economy of pain, is certainly the world that the ex-convict Leadbelly, his nickname turning him into his own gunshot victim, represented when at concerts he descended into the aisles to solicit small change or disappeared into the black districts to "sing himself hoarse."[36] Leadbelly gave the world "Rock Island Line," "Goodnight, Irene," "The Midnight Special," "Cottonfields Back Home," "Black Girl," and many other songs; his career had carried him through the cottonfields, lumbercamps, cattle ranches, pool halls, saloons, whorehouses, and prison farms of east Texas and Louisiana, a black southern subculture that few white people could imagine or understand. He was by all accounts an archaic, gentle, intelligent, isolated, powerful, and uncompromising man who, as Frederic Ramsey observes, could find no real place for himself in New York's musical, political, or social worlds. Severing his ties to John Lomax, he lived for a time on welfare and spent a year in jail for assault; after occasional radio and club appearances, he played for labor rallies and union meetings, at par-

ties, for children in public squares, and finally "at home, tire-
lessly, joyously, indestructibly, for all who would come and listen
. . . those who heard him then can never forget it." He died a pau-
per in 1949 at the age of sixty-four, of a sclerosis with "a pitiless
affinity for men of iron muscles."[37]

Leadbelly was a living representative of an inaccessible past in
which blackness could be contemplated as a universal condition,
signifying a temporal as well as a social boundary, at once a mask,
a mark, a surface, and a stain, not of a personal but of a collective
curse and a collective guilt as well as a potential power, one that
John Lomax could exhibit but not confront in its total meaning
because, unlike Alan, in whom Marx had awakened class consciousness and Freud the sexual subtext, his personal project, like
that of the other muscular Christians of his epoch, demanded a
strict policing of class, racial, and gender boundaries.

As a man of his time John Lomax could only enact the role of
Mr. Interlocutor in the minstrel show; his message was superiority, mastery, command. Unlike the blackface Tambos and
Bones who claimed to have done, he could represent but not
contemplate, and certainly not assimilate, the black Other; nor
like the racial-cultural androgynes such as Joel Walker Sweeny
or Dan Emmett, "nigger all over except in color,"[38] who mixed
with blacks "on a level of social equality" at the bottom of
society, could he embody and objectify America's bedrock racial
confusion.

This required a deeper identification, a poetic sublimation if
not a frank acknowledgment, of the racial fascination that had
driven John Lomax, and that Alan Lomax would consummate
by unmasking in American folk music the African spirit in
which, for Alan, all its musical, sexual, and political power lay.
If John Lomax can be plausibly compared to Haverly or Field, so
can Alan, a young southern white of humble origins earning,
after his father, his social stripes in the east, be placed alongside
"mean whites" like Christy and Emmett in a sibling relation,
with all its passion, ambivalence, and confusion, to the black

gandy dancers, chaingangs, convicts, sharecroppers, bluesmen, and spiritual singers whose songs the Lomaxes recorded. In them, perhaps, Alan saw vividly revealed the forces shaping his own situation—the legitimacy of his unique social and intellectual claim troubled by class contaminants in the social atmosphere, a sense of his considerable personal power compromised by an encroaching self-consciousness, at once unjust and inevitable—his own feelings complicated by their projection onto the Other and at the same time weirdly triangulated in the rather formal and fragile relation he bore to his father.

"I should like to look at the folk-songs of the country with you," the seventeen-year-old wrote his father in the spring of his first year at Harvard, fortified by infusions of the new social science of Professors Boas and Herskovits, trying the wings of youthful radicalism, "and do some research in that field from the point of view of sociology and anthropology. You and I are particularly well fitted for a partnership in this task . . . you have the practical experience in their field and an instinct for what is genuine and what is not. That experience I believe I can soon begin to supplement by making connections between the ideas in the songs and their social implications."

By Christmas of that year the solicitous son, now playing Father to his demoralized and vulnerable father, found an opportunity for expressing filial love in the paternal form he was seeking for himself: "For your own good and happiness I believe that your ballad-collecting and distributing for the lecture platform is the best way to earn money . . . you know more about that part of folk lore than anyone else. Mr. Dobie has created a popular demand for it. Why don't you supply it?"[39]

By "making connections between the ideas in the songs and their social implications," Alan Lomax would discover—which is to say, imagine—as in this passage about "John Henry," the primal scene of folksong, where sexual potency, physical beauty, strength, endurance, and grace, the search for authenticity, the recovery of democracy, and the industrial age itself make clandestine meeting in an actual and symbolic underworld where America's images of itself are forged:

> Far in the bowels of the mountains, lamps burn dimly in the foul air. Rock falls are frequent and ventilation is primitive. In the oppressive heat the workers strip down to the merest rags. Two men work in each steel-driving team. The shaker sits on the tunnel floor, the six-foot drill between his straddled thighs, twisting it by hand a quarter turn every time the driver strikes it. The driver, standing five to six feet away from the drill, swings his ten-pound sheep-nose hammer through a nineteen-foot arc, and comes down on the head of the drill like a man-made thunderbolt.[40]

These are the thunderbolts that, like the spears of Homer's warriors, lodge in human viscera, disclosing the interior of life at the same moment that life is spent, in both an organic and, in Lomax, an orgasmic sense. The drill the driver hammers into the rock is both the rivet that anchors America's vast industrial machine and the kingpin of the classic folksong that sets a man against it. The power that drives the drill is human power, "iron muscles" metonymically linked to sexual potency; but that power is secreted away, buried, like a minstrel in blackface, in its own blackness, as the workers themselves are condemned to the bowels of the mountain, symbol of a social unconscious into which repression has driven labor, the black race, sexuality itself, and the human engines of modernity, all conjoined in John Henry's self-sacrificial rite.

The fetid air and smoky lamps evoke the atmosphere of Hell—but of the coalmine and iron furnace too; burnt cork and blackface here merge with the soot of industrial combustion that blacked the entire nineteenth century. But it is also the atmosphere of the minstrel theater—where, as Constance Rourke wrote in 1931, "the persistent stress was primitive; it was often sorrowful; the effect was exotic and strange, with the swaying figures and the black faces of the minstrels lighted by guttering gas flames or candlelight."[41] "A stout unpretty woman," Sterling Brown said of blueswoman Ma Rainey, on the tent-show circuit

"John Henry, Steel-Driving Man," drawing by Eben Given, 1930

"with a necklace of twenty-dollar gold pieces glittering in the glare of the Coleman lanterns."[42]

Alan Lomax carried his father's chivalric romance to its transfiguration in a Pilgrim's Progress for the industrial age, where the way out of Arthur Godfrey's suburban False Paradise into the True Paradise of a realized democracy lay along the route that Woody Guthrie and all the revivalists after him would follow, through an underworld where the damned had labored to build America's gargantuan structure of exploitation, consumption, and excess. What had haunted, and ever eluded, the minstrel show, what played across its face with the flickering light, was the irremediable Wrong at its core that no complexities of play could dispel. The minstrel show was at once a propitiary and a penitential rite, conducted at the heart and on behalf of a society on the threshold of cataclysmic change, as the abolition debate grew into civil war, and chattel slavery into wage slavery, from one form of self-betrayal into another. The men who conducted it understood that their faces may have already been blacked by racial discrimination and economic oppression. By exteriorizing and symbolically controlling that process on the stage, and by summoning out of it the immense resources of the repressed African-American folk culture, they threw America's hypocrisy back on itself and opened a space of pure scandal where the implications of freedom might be played at, played with, and played out.

To understand the lesson in minstrelsy for the folk revival, we must look below the surface, under the skin: then we might fathom how America's most economically privileged and best educated generation of youth could feel itself socially bereft, culturally impoverished, and, above all, collectively and personally oppressed; and how, like the blackface minstrel, that generation turned from the flatly contradictory messages of ideology and lived experience toward the effaced "folk" cultures of the past, access to which lay mysteriously in the traces of doctrines that precisely because they were dark and forbidden had left behind only their romance, their innocence, and their hope.

Original album cover, 1940

3

Ballad for Americans

"**L**eadbelly and I were brothers," recalled Moses Asch, founder of Folkways Records, home of the principal recordings of Leadbelly, Woody Guthrie, and Pete Seeger: twenty-nine Seeger albums by 1955, with sales of a million records by 1962. Asch had met Leadbelly through Sy Rady, a producer whose *Pins and Needles*, backed by the ILGWU and played by worker-actors, was the first New York musical with a social message. John Lomax, Asch recalled, had just produced a *March of Time* newsreel about Leadbelly—"dressed him up as a convict, and he would drag him around to show what a great guy John Lomax was because he was his guardian."[1]

Asch had come to the United States with his father, the Yiddish writer Sholem Asch, in 1914, at the age of nine, having been raised by one of the first of Maria Montessori's pupils—an aunt who was an adviser to Lenin on early childhood education. Moe's Americanization began at once, with the western novels his father sent him from his travels as a correspondent for the *Jewish Daily Forward*: "Jesse James and Bill Hickock were early acquaintances of mine."[2]

After living for a time next door to Leon Trotsky, the family moved to Brooklyn, where Moe took an interest in his neighbors, ham-radio operators. "I saw the possibility," he remembers, "coming from Europe where there were only boundaries, that this was a medium that overcame boundaries, overcame customs."[3] Returning to Europe to study electronics, Asch met students from Brazil, Holland, Austria, and Russia, whose song fests, which required him to offer songs from America, taught him that folksong "expresses a *home* feeling of belonging and association." During a school holiday in Paris, he came across a copy of Lomax's *Cowboy Songs,* whose preface by Teddy Roosevelt inspired him "with the meaning of the cowboy and the west,"[4] and when he returned he could "show the kids at school that there was a uniqueness in our culture. It was not just a melting pot. Lomax showed clearly that there was a folklore in America."

Inspired by his father, whose aim in his writing had been to reconcile the Jewish and Christian traditions, but who forbade his children to become writers, and modeling himself after the collectors and preservers of rare Yiddish books and manuscripts his father had known, Asch wanted to create a record company, as he described it to the family friend Albert Einstein, that would "describe the human race, the sound it makes, what it creates." The first record he produced was his father's *In the Beginning,* Bible stories for children, accompanied by extensive notes and documentation, which set the pattern for his succeeding efforts in American and international folk music. "I always believed in the 'one mike' theory—I hate the stereo recordings, and mixing can never give you the accurate sense of the original sound," Asch remarked. "A hundred years from now it is as natural as the day I recorded it."[5]

The short life of Asch's partnership labels in the 1940s indicates both the narrow economic niche occupied by alternative music and the difficulties of the business itself. His first issue on the Asch label in 1939, after RCA and Columbia discontinued their ethnic series, was an album of Jewish folksongs by the Bagelman (later the Barry) Sisters; his efforts on the Disc label, after 1944, included classical, jazz, ballroom dances, children's songs, calypso, creole, gospel, music for "the ex-GI" and for "folk music lovers."[6]

"This was a way I could create a book without writing it," Asch observed of the recording projects that finally issued, in 1948, in his Folkways record company, named after William Graham Sumner's 1907 book of that title. Asch's fully annotated record albums reflected the wider documentary efforts of the New Deal period—Asch's brother Nathan worked for the Federal Writers' Project, was an associate of the artist/photographer Ben Shahn, and became an investigative journalist[7]— as well as the social science of ethnomusicologists Harold Courlander and Willard Rhodes.

Crossing boundaries, reconciling cultural differences, zealously embracing an idealized but alien cultural identity, preserving the documents of culture with scholarly exactitude—Asch's career reflects a cultural tradition, Yiddish, talmudic, diasporal, which in the 1930s did much to advance both the vision and the politics of the folksong movement. In Leadbelly, Asch found another embodiment of his own community—"a nonterritorial and oppressed national minority," as Jonathan Frankel writes, whose history had been "torn between integration and separatism, territorialism and cultural autonomism, organized immigration and violent opposition to the state."[8]

Massive immigration from the Pale in the first decade of the twentieth century had given to the cultural life of New York a distinctive Yiddish and socialist coloring. Russian Jews particularly were moving directly from a medieval to a post-Enlightenment condition, fiercely clinging to the past or fiercely abandoning it. Nearly a million and a half Jews had settled in New York by 1914, a third of them on the Lower East Side, and many brought with them ideas and sentiments from the Russian labor and revolutionary movements, a tradition that sought its constituency among the poor, the intelligentsia, and the young. Its lingua franca was Yiddish, its economic base the clothing industry, its political venues the Yiddish press, the public meeting, the trade union, and the political party. It placed its faith in planning, organization, and collective action, displayed "strong ascetic strand, pride in self-sacrifice, reckless defiance of objective difficulties, and a determination to translate thought into action, dream into reality," and glorified the outsider and the youthful rebel, repudiating existing conditions in the hope of a social utopia.

In the years after the Bolshevik revolution, this tradition had located the New Jerusalem in the Soviet state; but for American Jews this faith was a displacement, as the state of Israel would itself become, of millennial expectations grounded in Jewish eschatology but now associated with the immigration to America. Unlike the bourgeois German Jews already established in New York as bankers, merchants, manufacturers, and landlords, Russian Jews were still a strongly traditional folk community that, guided by the socialist intelligentsia, nevertheless hoped to achieve through their children a complete break with the European past and, through education especially, a thorough Americanization. By 1885 the established German Jews had rejected Jewish dietary laws and other tokens of the ancient culture in favor of the "modern era of universal culture"; but this group was at the same time the class of landlords and manufacturers whom workers in the ready-to-wear clothing industry blamed for tenement overcrowding and sweatshop conditions—a group that the new arrivals identified, in spite of the religious and cultural affinities between them, with the ruling class of Rockefellers, Carnegies, and Astors.

When the ongoing flight from Russian pogroms inspired anti-immigration sentiment in America, the German-Jewish elite, whose philanthropy was already responsible for hospitals and various social-welfare institutions, responded with organizations such as the American Jewish Committee to protect Rus-

sian-Jewish interests;[9] but not before a feeling of class antago-
nism, and an ideology of class warfare, had estranged them and
set the gaze of the younger generation toward a form of Americanization more compatible with their own community,
namely, toward American folk culture. A Martha
Graham dancer, Sophie Maslow—to cite, prematurely, but one
instance—admired Woody Guthrie's *Dust Bowl Ballads* of 1940,
because they reminded her of the Yiddish songs she loved as a
child. She choreographed a dance to two of Guthrie's songs and
used him as one of the guitar-picking storytellers for her dance
piece *Folksay*, based on Carl Sandburg's poem "The People,
Yes!"[10]

The early Jewish political and social clubs became virtually
mass organizations with the great immigrations after 1905. This
subculture, communist, socialist, and progressive, was marked
by activism and self-reliance on a grand scale. The Communist
Party—in 1927 only one-seventh of its members spoke English—eventually established schools, summer camps, a housing
project in the Bronx, and made significant inroads into the labor
movement; a closely allied, predominantly Jewish fraternal order, the International Workers' Order, provided medical care,
health insurance, and a social center. Though party membership
was relatively small, its influence was pervasive.

Intellectually, no single fact is as important in the contribution
of the left to the folksong movement as the social conditions in
Russia, "written in black and white" in Addams' words, which,
as remembered, were for many American Jews a conceptual
prism for viewing the American situation. At one end of the
spectrum was Count Leo Tolstoy, toiling beside his serfs, taking
up a scythe in deference to the pen, in order to meld theory and
practice in his own life. Tolstoy, wrote Addams, "had made the
one supreme personal effort, one might almost say the frantic
personal effort, to put himself into right relations with the
humblest people, with the men who tilled his soil, blacked his
boots, and cleaned his stables."[11] At the other end of the spec-

trum were the rural, often unlettered immigrants, who when they looked to the upper reaches of American society saw a confusing image of a capitalist who was either an American version of the old overlord or an image of that to which their sons and daughters might aspire.

These social conditions are of course those of an essentially feudal and agricultural society. At the end of the nineteenth century, Russia was still divided between a landed aristocracy and a largely preliterate peasantry, whose industrial revolution, more than a century after the dramatic social, demographic, and technical transformations in England, occurred in a very different social, cultural, and intellectual milieu. The tiny class of intellectuals and civil servants that engineered the Russian revolution, Russia's political romantics, turned neither to republican Rome nor to the contracts of Dutch trading companies for models of civil government, as the European mercantile bourgeoisie had done, but to their own national experience. Leon Trotsky, a landowner's son, conceived of the people as "a primitive illiterate mass of farm laborers, such as he could remember from his father's farm."[12] Lenin shared this bifurcated outlook. "We must always have before our eyes the workers and the peasants," he wrote in *On Culture and Cultural Revolution,* converting the Enlightenment's century-old poetic project into a political paradigm for revolution. "It is for their sake that we must learn to manage, to reckon."

The binary structure rooted historically in Russian feudalism, then, expressed itself in the familiar Marxist-Leninist model: a society of industrial and agricultural workers governed by a disciplined party of revolutionaries, mediated not by a middle zone of social mobility or a meaningful electoral process but by a party of bureaucrats and intellectuals that would construct an authentic workers' culture, including a musical culture.

Although this communist ideology was clearly incompatible with America's own Jeffersonian agrarian and artisanal ideas of democracy, which had centered on the figure of the independent English yeoman and not a revolutionary proletariat, it was nevertheless grounded in the soil and essentially aristocratic in temperament. For American socialists, communists, and fellow travelers—genteel reformers, urban artists and intellectuals, ethnic families from socialist and communist traditions, various other young idealists—some form of collective seizure of the means of production precisely answered the betrayal of America's political democracy by the grossly undemocratic conditions of industrial capitalism and the contamination of every quarter of cultural life by corporate consumerism.

In 1896 the German political economist Karl Bücher offered an idea familiar from early accounts of African-American worksongs and regularly repeated in the abolition debate in America: that song in primitive culture grew out of the rhythms of work. "The Negro laborer," the Lomaxes observed in 1934, "swinging his pick, fits the first phrases that occur to him into the rhythm of the pick-points . . . since the mind of the unselfconscious singer turns most readily to those things in his experience which are most important to him . . . these sentences are often terse and epic summaries of his important life relations."[13] Also in 1934 Maxim Gorky expressed a similar notion, like the Lomaxes' verging on a concept of oral-formulaic composition, that the Russian oral epic, which communists were attempting to dislodge from the aristocrats who cherished it, had been rooted in an effort to lighten the burden and increase the productivity of work—an idea already commonplace in American discussions of African-American song. "The beginning of the art of words," Gorky said, speaking as a writer to a congress of writers, "is in folklore. Collect your folklore, make a study of it, work it over."[14]

By the time of Gorky's statement, folklore in the Soviet Union had already been widely discussed, stimulating renewed folklore scholarship and study, enthusiasts' clubs in factories and collective farms, amateur collections by teachers, workers, and farmers, and official recognition, even stipends, for traditional singers and storytellers. Stalin had in the mid-1920s granted limited autonomy to the Soviet Union's various national minority groups in whom the raw materials of an authentic workers' culture might lay—not along the lines of a Herderesque "romantic nationalism" but as an official state spectacle that annexed folksongs and lore to revolutionary priorities. Under the new socialist realism, which Gorky and Andrei Zhdanov proclaimed in 1934, sweeping away European modernism, the vernacular forms of folksong, dance, and story would now solace travail, embody revolutionary aspirations, and lend a sense of hope and communal spirit—reflecting, as Richard Reuss writes, "hard times and real life."

The official proclamation of the Popular Front policy at the Third International in 1935, and in America by Earl Browder, shifting the ideological focus from a vanguard proletariat to an indigenous peoples' culture, reflected the hope of a worldwide closing of ranks against the fascist threat. But it also betrayed the inadequacy of early Soviet doctrine to address the realities of a multiethnic, multilingual, and otherwise economically and socially variegated Soviet culture, as well as of culture itself, which, after all, has an imaginative and practical life quite independent of official constructions.

For most Americans on the left, the distant Soviet experiment was, again, a millennial dream—deeply inscribed with Jewish eschatology, particularly compelling for secular Jews who understood that in American society a ceiling of discrimination hung over their heads—a dream in which the larger hope of the modern was to be played out in the Soviet political, social, and technical spheres as an example to the world. Hence communist ideology, and even state policy as it emanated from Moscow, continued throughout the period to shape the thinking and frame the discourse of the folksong movement, just as it shaped the general discourse on the left. But the folksong movement operated well out of range and beneath the notice of party regulars and bureaucrats, even when the party in 1936 declared for Roosevelt.

Though my interest is primarily in the protegés of Alan Lomax, who carried the folksong movement over the McCarthy period into the folk revival, it is important to note that during the 1930s interest in folk tradition was also penetrating the more orthodox sectors of communism. The immense hope that surrounded Roosevelt's social, economic, and cultural recovery efforts was, in an epoch of massive unemployment, necessarily focused on the improvement of labor conditions and the expansion of workers' rights, an enterprise in which communism had a principal part; and, like Kennedy's Peace Corps a generation later, it drew heavily on the idealism of the young. In their coal-camp and textile-industry work, young communist organizers were coming into direct contact with Appalachian and to a lesser extent African-American song traditions, bringing such labor anthems as "We Shall Not Be Moved" back to Brookwood Labor School near Beacon, New York, in 1931 from miners in West Virginia; in the labor colleges themselves, which taught ideology and grassroots organization, the movement was being increasingly charged with Baptist and Methodist religiosity by southern workers and activists generally aloof to official dogma and party bureaucracy.

The audience sing-alongs that Pete Seeger included in his concert performances, and indeed the spirit of inclusion, participation, and purpose associated in this period with folk music, emerges first on the left in the workers' choruses of the twenties, the best known of which was the Freedom Singers' Society, formed entirely of first-generation east European Jews, factory and sweatshop workers. The choruses took mass singing out of the picket line, the street rally, and the protest march into the recital hall where, even if he "could not fight in Spain or march on the picket line in front of 'Little Steel,'" Reuss writes, the young leftist "could still sit comfortably at a Garden rally or stand in a crowded room at a 'cause' party, sing songs implicitly or explicitly linking himself to his 'side' of the issues of the day, and thereby feel a part of the anti-fascist or 'people's struggle.'"[15] But to do so the doctrinnaire musical and political traditions in which they worked, alien even to the first American-born generation of the twenties, needed first to be domesticated. "Our comrades," a writer to the *Daily Worker* had complained in 1927, "can't sing."

Socialist Songs with Music had been first published by the International Workers of the World (the Wobblies) in Chicago in 1901.[16] But in the martyred IWW organizer Joe Hill, immortalized in Earl Robinson's and Alfred Hayes's song—"I dreamed I saw Joe Hill last night, alive as you or me"—the left discovered a figure in whom labor song and folksong could be credibly linked. "From California up to Maine, in every mine and mill . . . where working men defend their rights, it's there you'll find Joe Hill."

As early as 1915 Elizabeth Gurley Flynn, an IWW member who abandoned anarchosyndicalism for Marxist-Leninism, was celebrating Joe Hill for songs he sang "that kindle the fires of revolt in the most crushed spirit and quicken the desire for a fuller life in the most humble slave." Hill "has crystallized the organization's spirit into imperishable forms," she wrote, "songs of the people—folksongs."[17] The novelist Michael Gold, who with Flynn would be a regular visitor to Almanac House, made a similar association in 1933, after hearing at an Irish Workers' Club meeting "an old ballad in Gaelic, haunting and soulful with its ancient sorrow of a persecuted race," and, with a phrase that could easily have initiated the search for a Woody Guthrie, called in the *Daily Worker* for a "Communist Joe Hill."[18]

These developments help to explain why the folksong movement, in style and spirit, even perhaps in conscious imitation, owed the dominant strain in its descent, if not its every ideological inflection, to the singingest of the singing labor movements, the IWW. Unlike the communist movement generally, the Wobblies favored action over speculation; still the movement produced, Reuss writes, "its own band of intellectuals, men rough in manners who toiled with their hands as much with their pens, but who also read widely and argued violently about literature, philosophy, and art."[19] Reuss's portrait, echoing the literary portraiture of an earlier time,[20] summons up the unique proletarian figure to whom Pete Seeger and others in the folk-song movement were paying tribute, whose culture, without complicated ideological equipment, continued to circulate in the American left through the Roosevelt era, impressing young idealists even as the movement of working men that had borne it, never very cohesive and long subject to government repression, was fading into memory.

The Wobbly, like Jefferson's literate, disputatious yeoman farmer, was an independent agent, master of his own fate, in whom labor had brought not servility, ignorance, and brutishness but independence, understanding, and dignity as well as physical strength; he made a compelling masculine model for young men not born to labor but who saw in labor the real proofs of manhood—scions of privilege as well as sons of immigrant tailors and shopkeepers. For the main strength of the IWW was among western lumberjacks, miners, wheatfield workers, and stevedores, as well as migrant workers or hoboes—all figures on whom the romance of the west, and the image of the strenuous life, had long since settled. When the culture of the Wobbly met the ideological left in the thirties, it discovered a kind of resurrection of itself in the intellectual vigilance and austere personal discipline of Leninism, as well as in the heroic projects and worker legions of the New Deal. Under this cultural dispensation, to sing brazen and clever protest songs, to play the banjo or guitar, to speak eloquently in a union hall, to hold forth brilliantly among compatriots, could be just as manly, and as American, as driving piles or felling timber.

Thus the left's discovery of American vernacular culture, and of folk music in particular, arose generally from the failure of Soviet communism in the 1920s, with its sense of imminent worldwide economic collapse and its politicalization of all aesthetic expression, to create a workable native proletarian art.

The ideological proletarianism of the New York left in the early period had been quixotically out of touch with the actualities of the American working life and, until the concessions of the Popular Front, could not have assimilated its idea of the worker to American culture without making actual contact with it in coal camps, mill towns, and in the west. As Ben Shahn observed, actual human beings were not "uniformly eager" for revolution; instead he found "people of all kinds of belief and temperament, which they maintained with a transcendent indifference to their lot in life."[21]

To many American intellectuals and writers of the twenties, the American provinces had since the turn of the century become sordid, ignorant, and mean-spirited—in a word, provincial, but in an especially crass commercial sense as embodied in, say, Sinclair Lewis' George Babbitt or in the evangelical advertising pioneer Elbert Hubbard, who inspired Lewis' character.[22] The fount of high culture was to be found instead in European modernism, as represented by Picasso, Stravinsky, and Schoenberg, which with socialist realism was seen as an assault on academic tradition.

This was, initially, the posture of the Composers' Collective, a cell of the communist Pierre DeGeyter Club, founded in 1931 for the purpose of discovering ways of composing revolutionary music. The Collective included Charles Seeger, Elie Siegmeister, Earl Robinson, and peripherally Aaron Copland, all classically trained musicians with degrees from prestigious institutions who "shuttled from orchestral rehearsals in full formal dress to an unheated loft in Greenwich Village where they'd don their pseudonyms and proletarian-styled leather jackets."[23]

Classical composers had of course exploited folksong for political ends in the past. Grieg's use of Norwegian folksongs, Bartok's of Hungarian melodies, and Dvorak's of American spirituals are well known; but the Collective somewhat disingenuously regarded the classical tradition as an expression of the ruling class and folksong as "a badge of servitude"—as the

German revolutionary composer Hans Eisler put it, "defeatist, melancholy, morbid, hysterical and trivial."[24] Their ideal instead was the music of the Socialist Motherland, such as Rimsky-Korsakov's *Russian Easter Overture* or Mussorgsky's *Boris Godunov*—or a "'workers' chorus' singing clangorous, oddly formal compositions like 'The Scottboro Boys Must Not Die' or 'The Comintern.'"[25] A student of Arnold Schoenberg's, Eisler had seen fit to use the twelve-tone row in his revolutionary compositions, which, surprisingly to Americans, enjoyed some popularity in European cabarets and even in an occasional street demonstration.

But Charles Seeger, who called himself Carl Sands—and we should always recall, as we consider the elder Seeger, the life and career of his son Pete—felt that Eisler's street songs spoke a "basic musical vernacular," distinct both from the "melancholy folk-songs, dreary hymn-tunes, silly patriotic propaganda and sentimental aesthetics from Broadway," as well as from the Collective's modernist music, which as Mike Gold put it was "full of geometric bitterness and the angles and glass splinters of pure technic." But the occasional folksong had begun to appear in radical publications: the *Red Song Book* of 1932 included six tunes of Appalachian or popular origin, and a later edition added two of Lawrence Gellert's collected African-American worksongs. Folk music, Seeger conceded, is acceptable if "it shows clearly a spirit of resentment toward oppression or vigorous resistance."[26]

Gellert, the son of a Hungarian immigrant, a young Village communist and sometime editor of *New Masses*, had for health reasons moved to Tryon, North Carolina, in the mid-twenties to edit a small newspaper. He collected chaingang, work, and other African-American songs, many of them unnervingly candid in their expression of racial antipathy, regularly forwarded them for serialization in the magazine, and later published them under Mike Gold's title as *Negro Songs of Protest*. In 1934 Composer Collective member Lan Adomian proposed an expansion of the workers' chorus repertories to include Gellert's "Negro songs of protest," railroad songs, cowboy and hillbilly songs, virtually duplicating the categories developing in the Lomax collections, in order to "root our work in the traditions of American music."[27]

To this end a new American Music League, to which the Collective was an adjunct, of various choruses, bands, and orchestras on the left, mostly of east European and Jewish extraction, emerged in 1936 out of the Workers' Music League in order to "collect, study, and popularize," among other efforts aimed at reaching outside the party, American folk music. This is the context in which Robinson's American People's Chorus and Steigmeister's American Ballad Singers emerged later in the decade.

"Peter continued right on," Seeger told David Dunaway in 1980: "he did what we ought to have done . . . The Collective should have gotten together and made songs and sung to people. And if the people liked one song more than another, then they'd make more songs in that style. Well, that's what Peter did. You see, he went out with a theory based on all that had failed . . . He could see that we in the Collective were still looking at things from above down . . . Peter began to look at things from below up."[28]

Charles Seeger was a man of cool aristocratic bearing, Prussian temperament, and German ancestry who in 1914 was radicalized by the sight of a migrant labor camp in the San Joaquin Valley—deeply shocking to a young professor of music who had grown up on a Staten Island estate to the strains of Wagner and conducted the Cologne opera at the age of twenty-three. He was introduced to primitive music by the anthropologist Alfred Kroeber and made some field recordings himself of the Hoopa of northern California. Seeger's interest in the twelve-tone row and in Bartok's folk compositions was more than academic: he had been awakened to an enigmatic connection between music and society, which formed the basis of the ethnomusicological approach Seeger originated, and though he was constitutionally incapable of descending to the level of the common people, he thoroughly understood the alignment of musical style and social class.[29]

Thus, though John Lomax's *Cowboy Songs* had not touched him, it is not entirely improbable that mountain music, when Seeger first heard it, alerted him to the political power of the authentic *sound* itself. The occasion was the dedication in 1931 of Thomas Hart Benton's classroom murals at the New School for Social Research, where both men were teaching.[30] Benton was an amateur harmonica player, a member of a small oldtime stringband, and a collector of hillbilly discs, among which was a recording of Dock Boggs, the coalminer-banjoist who himself had taken much of his repertory from race records: that is, from contemporary commercial recordings of black singers. To Seeger and his son, also in attendance, Benton's performance of "John Henry" was interesting enough to warrant the loan of a few discs—and it should be emphasized, I think, that the Seegers' first encounter with mountain music occurred in conjunction with Benton's swimming, slithering images of the mid-American countryside and country people; and throughout the prewar period, folk music in New York was in like fashion consistently presented in the context of dramatic, pictorial, or aural representations of American folklife which not only fixed its imaginative associations but also linked it to the fine arts and through them to modernism itself.

For the text-oriented Composer's Collective, though, folk music had come first in book form. George Pullen Jackson's pioneering *White Spirituals in the Southern Uplands* had pointed to the antiquity of mountain shape-note hymns and explored the mysteries of folk tonality; Lawrence Gellert's series in *New Masses* on black protest songs were politicized spirituals and folksongs "unpolished, sentimental, and uncomplicated by political dogma," which at the same time "occasionally caught the essence of folk poetry."[31]

Not surprisingly, then, it was a poet, Carl Sandburg, who had been collecting and singing folksongs on college campuses throughout the previous decade, whose *American Songbag* of 1927 most inspired the Collective by releasing it from the ideological spell under which it performed its work. "Whenever I hear the 'Boll Weevil' song—about the little bug just a-lookin' for a home—I think of Carl Sandburg and how he sang it at the University of Michigan forty years ago," recalled one listener, Oakley Johnson. "Sandburg twanged his guitar and sang and smiled with pleasure at our pleasure. His longish reddish hair hanging over his forehead seemed a natural setting for the sad, salty, satirical ditties that came from his throat."[32]

Even more than Lomax, dreaming on his youth, Sandburg understood, and accepted with a midwesterner's equanimity, the egalitarian social ecology of folksong—that it moved up and down in the earth, was as likely to surface in a faculty club as in a cattle camp, and indeed that its social mobility was just what recommended its capture as an artifact of polite culture. Each folksong stored the energy of a restless democratic society that, though it might be differentiated by class and kind, was not as strictly segregated as class-based ideologies might assume; each song seemed to reveal, at the moment of its transmission, the otherwise hidden system of communications through which America's cultural life, observing no social boundaries, genuinely flowed.

"There is a human stir throughout the book," Sandburg wrote: "a wide human procession marches through these pages. The rich and the poor; robbers, murderers, hangmen; fathers and wild boys; mothers with soft words for their babies; workmen on railroads, steamboats, ships; wanderers and leavers of homes, tell what life has done to them." "This is precisely the sort of material," he affirmed, "out of which there may come the great native American grand opera."[33] As the poet Kenneth Rexroth later wrote, it was through Sandburg's songs that "the old free America in which he grew up was to transmit, as through the narrow channels of hundreds of capillaries, its value system, its life blood," to the countercultural generation of the 1960s.[34]

"A delicate imprint on a field of silence" was how Sandburg described his version of "Charcoal Man." "An old man selling charcoal used to proclaim himself to the residents of Springfield, Missouri, with this morning cry . . . I notated it, hazardously, from the singing of a faculty member of the State Teachers' College at Greeley, Colorado. She came from Missouri." Of "C. C. Rider" he wrote: "John Lomax and I heard this song in Austin, Texas, in an old saloon, *The Silver King*, operated as a soft drink parlor by a Mexican Negro, Martinez. After two negroes with guitars had sung 'The Original Blues,' 'Franky and Johnny,' 'Boll Weevil,' and other pieces, Martinez himself favored us with C. C. Rider."[35]

Many of Sandburg's songs reflected the intellectual and artistic circles in which he moved, and their various intersections with the vast reaches of a surrounding landscape both real and imaginary, the "old free America" receding into the past: "When the Rutledge and Rodgers mammoth and mastodonic minstrels travelled the mid-west many years ago," he wrote of "Good-by Liza Jane," they had this minstrel song on their program. "We give it here from the recollection of C. W. Loutzenhiser, of Chicago, who was a boy at the time." "Blow the Man Down" came from Robert Frost, who in his boyhood had heard sailors singing it on the San Francisco waterfront. "Somebody" was a "fugitive little lyric heard by Edwin Ford Piper from the singing of his pioneer mother in the 1880s on a farm near Auburn, Nebraska." Other songs, such as "Alice B," followed a more circuitous route:

> This is arranged from the ballad as sung by Arthur Sutherland and the buccaneers of the Eclectic Club of Wesleyan University. Sutherland, who is the son of a lawyer in Rochester, N.Y., first heard of "Alice B" when he was with the American Relief Expedition in Armenia, riding on top of a boxcar to Constantinople with a friend who came from New Orleans, Louisiana, and who in that gulf port

one day paid $1.50 to a hobo to sing "Alice B" as he, the hobo, had just heard it a few days previously in Memphis from a negro just arriving from Galveston, Texas.[36]

Folksongs for Sandburg, like Joel Chandler Harris' Uncle Remus stories, were poetic found objects, migrating into literature from the social spheres in which letters and literature have little part. The romantic tradition that sought folksong among workers, farmers, prisoners, or the poor was not inevitably compatible with democratic feeling—"but it was fun," remarked John Jacob Niles, "this thing of writing down the songs sung by your parents and your neighbors and your father's workmen and your mother's household help."[37]

But Sandburg seemed to be reaching out rather than down—and though he may have played the folk part in his performances, he was not perhaps as guilty of the disingenuous self-fashioning that from Niles to Jean Ritchie has marked the folksinger's professional presentation. When Elie Siegmeister finally asserted, in 1938, that the task of the composer was to break down the division between art music and folk music,[38] Earl Robinson, who had been deeply impressed by Sandburg's work, responded with two musical documents profoundly important in the folk revival, *Ballad for Americans* and *The Lonesome Train*.

The composers of the Collective, like intellectuals everywhere in America, had caught the patriotic spirit of the Popular Front. "Communism," said Earl Browder in a bold phrase, "is twentieth-century Americanism." Some in the Collective such as Herbert Haufrecht undertook folksong fieldwork. Charles Seeger joined the Resettlement Administration in 1935, directing the music programs for federally subsidized rural communities. "Go into the Resettlement camps as somebody from Washington," Seeger instructed his fieldworkers, "but for God's sake, there let it stop . . . The first thing for you to do is to find out what music the people can make. Then put that to the uses for which you're sent to the community—to make the people in that community get along with one another."[39] Even the aims of social democracy, it seems, can be advanced in a Prussian style.

Seeger's efforts on behalf of the Roosevelt administration provided another occasion for his seventeen-year-old son Peter's conversion when, in 1936, Charles took him along to Bascom Lamar Lunsford's Mountain Dance and Folk Festival in Asheville—"a very worthwhile affair," the elder Seeger called it, "in which promoter, performers, and audience shared a community of spirit and an agreed upon aesthetic." About other folk festivals he was not so sanguine. "A kind of vaudeville show," he wrote of the Pennsylvania Folk Festival at Lewisburg, "in which the traditional element was squeezed to the wall when it could not be made grotesque, sensational, or ludicrous." And as for Annabel Morris Buchanan's festival at White Top, it was "reactionary to the core."[40]

If in 1934 the search for the wellsprings of American culture seemed especially urgent, carrying the folklorist to the most remote corners of the society, it was because the collapse of the American economic system, as William Leach recalls, had drawn back the glittering veil of consumer capitalism that for more than a generation had been absorbing the forms of the traditional institutions of American culture into itself; the solution to social and economic recovery seemed to lie in the older provincial and republican society. "To the writers and artists of my generation," the critic Edmund Wilson wrote, "who had grown up in the Big Business era and had always resented its barbarism, its crowding out of everything they cared about, these years were not depressing but stimulating. One couldn't help being exhilarated at the sudden unexpected collapse of that stupid gigantic fraud."[41]

Between present and past stood the great gulf of a commercialized, technologized, and centralized society that seemed to have swallowed every last trace of the material order into which memory had read the continuity of the human community. "It seemed an aeon since the days of the nineteenth century," in William Leuchtenberg's words.

The task of industrialization had been essentially completed. Machines had replaced the old artisans; there were few coopers, blacksmiths, or cobblers left. The livery stable had been torn down to make way for the filling station. Technology had revolutionized the farm . . . The metropolis had shattered the supremacy of the small town, and life seemed infinitely more impersonal. It was proverbial that the apartment house dweller did not know his neighbor . . . The depression destroyed the Chautauqua, but it could scarcely have survived the competition of he radio and the movies in any event. "Now the players do not come to the towns," wrote Sherwood Anderson in 1932. "They are in Los Angeles. We see but the shadows of players. We listen to the shadows of voices. Even the politicians do not come to us now. They stay in the cities and talk to us on radio."[42]

"In retrospect," Leuchtenberg observes, "the years before World War I seemed like a lost Arcadia." To restore the old artisanship and the close community of the small town, and the sense of direct connection to a traditional collective culture, was a form of nostalgia at least as old as the work of Washington Irving and the Fireside Poets, but one to which the Great Depression added a powerful new economic intensity and a sharp political edge: a dream of social justice that would repair the dreadful racial, economic, and cultural rifts tearing the social fabric apart.

"Everybody in Washington was interested in folk music," Alan Lomax recalled. The Roosevelts

were the first prominent Americans even to take a position about it in public consistently, and the first Washingtonians ever to spend any money on it. The reason that the Roosevelts, the Tugwells, and the Hopkinses were interested in folk music was, first of all, that they were Democrats . . . and they wanted to be identified with it as a democratic art . . . they saw that the country lacked a feeling of unity; they saw that there were conflicts between various kinds of racial, regional, and class groups in this country. They hoped that the feeling of cultural unity that lies somehow in our big and crazy patchwork of folksong, would give Americans the feeling that they all belonged to the same kind of culture.[43]

All western societies in the 1930s, including the United States, were incipiently collectivist, held in the spell of powerful centralized governments that, if they were not outright fascist, had mobilized technical and communication resources on an unprecedented scale. The scale of human social organization envisioned in the thirties, particularly as it was rendered in futurism, modernism, and other movements glorifying industry, engineering, and technology, had not yet acquired the forbidding overtones of totalitarianism; on the contrary, the mechanically efficient world promised by engineering was something close to a rational, scientific utopia—a world of which the postrevolutionary Soviet Union, seen from afar, seemed the first earthly realization.

The Soviets, again, never had an industrial revolution; they were attempting the task of industrialization through rational planning which, by eliminating private property and the profit motive, would theoretically promote the common good, elevate the class-conscious intellectual to a position of leadership, and make of peasants and workers a conquering army that would bring about a millennium of prosperity and peace. In the west, writes Stephen Whitfield, Stalinism "appealed to feelings of human solidarity, to the brotherhood of the dispossessed and the excluded, especially when the Great Depression had dramatized the twin failures of free enterprise and the ethos of individualism. Before the incredible scale of Stalin's purges had become credible, Communism could present itself as the activated legacy of the Enlightenment."[44] From the perspective of the thirties, the communist system, for those who believed in its vision of social justice, was radically enlightened, democratic, and modern, the historical consummation toward which capitalism naturally tended and which seemed exhilaratingly imminent as capitalism seemed to be collapsing—it was, in short, a metaphor for the American situation.

"The Revolution," Trotsky had written, "is public, epic, and catastrophic." The millennial mood of the communist and progressive movements of the thirties was intensified by the emergence of European fascism and took on, even more than it had in the depths of the depression, the character of a moral world war with a global army of ideological footsoldiers who did not yet see that fascism and communism were twin children of the twentieth century's evil marriage of militarism and bureaucracy.

The Lincoln Battalion, formed in America as a response to the civil war in Spain, gave to crusading young spirits an appallingly literal cause in which to pursue the millennial dream: but the language of the period, with its "people's choruses," its "army of the unemployed," and the like, reveals the pressure of martial metaphor and machine-age imagery on political rhetoric. Even the pacifist slogan on Pete Seeger's banjo, "This machine surrounds hate and forces it to surrender," only sublimates the more straightforward sticker produced for war workers, typically seen on lathes and drill presses, that Woody Guthrie posted on his guitar: "This machine kills fascists."[45]

The historical convergence of worldwide economic depression and European fascism, then, forged in America a new cultural alloy out of discrete ideological and imaginative elements. From the nineteenth-century evolutionary metaphor of struggle, which had dominated all realms of discourse, came the concept of a proletarian army of workers and peasants; this was enforced in the Soviets' romantic and apocalyptic poster-art movement, whose consistent theme was "workers marching off to glory." With the rise of fascism, and the effort of communists in this country to Americanize their movement, the discourse of class war opened to admit the capacious republican idea of a "People," bearers of a grassroots American tradition that could survive the shocks of depression, and upon which the office of consummating history on American soil now fell. In this setting socialist realism, with its glorification of collective struggle and triumph, assisted by technology and the power of the machine, proved highly congenial to the historical moment as perceived in America.

Such a melding of ideas is extraordinary in itself; but, further, the expression of these ideas in America's cultural capital, New York, was shaped in significant ways by the work of Russian Jews and others of Old World descent whose own traditions already inclined them to the idealism, the initiative, and the talent for cultural synthesis the moment demanded—an urban, European-American people who by virtue of their isolation from American provincial society, an isolation that only repeated the Jewish situation of the European centuries, were uniquely equipped to imagine and depict it. We should remember that both "God Bless America" and "White Christmas" are the work of a Russian Jew, Irving Berlin; that after 1910 popular music was the nearly exclusive preserve of European Jews on the Lower East Side, a community of "piano-laden tenements, saloons with singing waiters, and promising young singers in the local synagogues," all supported on Tin Pan Alley by a network of boomers and pluggers.[46] An entire tradition of representation, then, enjoyed at last the broad sanction and the practical support of a liberal government, led by an aristocratic president from a philanthropic and humanitarian tradition.

There was of course nothing novel about representations of American folk, the People. But in popular culture at least, in theater, in regionalist fiction and journalism, the American folk figure had typically been a carrier of satire or melodrama. American realism at the end of the nineteenth century had produced no glorified folk figure, but at best a compromised and self-deceiving one, often morally benighted or confused. But in 1935, with a civil war in Spain, a world war on the horizon, and a metaphor of war penetrating the discourse of culture and politics, the depiction of the American folk sought embodiment in an art that might serve national unity and purpose.

In the 1930s the great historical engines of the state, the radio and the airplane, of technical progress, were visibly circulating in public consciousness, and we have all seen them at work, in murals still in post offices and banks, in the ranks of muscled, uniformed, universalized figures, in the forbidding machines, gigantic factories, bridges, dams and power plants, the very conceiving and building of which was heroic in power and scope—in which lives were sacrificed and Nature itself tamed. "The stolid mothers and brawny workers of New Deal art came to dominate public space," as Barbara Melosh writes: "visual icons of heroic common people, mutuality, and purposeful labor,"[47] which subordinated the previous decade's feminist and other liberationist stances to the depression's harder providence.

The hundreds of Farm Security Administration photographs, too, which have come down to us from Dorothea Lange, Walker Evans, Ben Shahn, and others, by bringing the highest standards of technical and aesthetic excellence to bear on the most humble and unprepossessing subjects, succeeded in transforming the brute facts of poverty, often carefully manipulated for the purpose, into images of dignity and beauty,[48] and with the work of regionalist painters conferred upon the American rural landscape the immaculate precision of portraiture.

All this was art *about* the people, celebrating the people both in the abstract and the particular. But the art *of* the people was, possibly, folksong—an art, Alan Lomax wrote, "which lives upon the lips of the multitude and is transmitted by the grapevine, surviving sometimes for centuries because it reflects so well the deepest emotional convictions of the common man. This is a truly democratic art, painting a portrait of the people."[49] Folksongs, along with Spanish Civil War songs, were being sung everywhere, as Oscar Brand recalls, by "unionists, left-wing political workers, communists, socialists and other groups at meetings, picnics, rallies and picket lines," under the sponsorship of the Spanish Refugee Appeal, the CIO, the socialists, and the American Youth for Democracy; and urban youngsters were learning to play guitars, banjos, and mandolins to accompany them.[50] "When the people of this country, under the impact of the war against fascism, looked about them for songs which reflected their egalitarian and democratic political principles,"

Lomax said in 1947, "there came a sudden rise in the popularity of folk music."[51]

Nor did composers of art music remain unaffected. Aaron Copland borrowed songs from Lomax's *Cowboy Songs* for his *Billy the Kid* and the Shaker hymn "Simple Gifts" for *Appalachian Spring*. Gershwin took elements from the minstrel show. So did modernist dancer Martha Graham, whose *American Document* of 1938 was literally a minstrel show—though not I suppose a very funny one—with an interlocutor who recited passages from the Declaration of Independence and the Emancipation Proclamation, striving to summon up an American hero out of sheer multiplication: "We are three women; we are three million women," he said as three dancers slithered across the stage, followed confidently by a solitary man representing "one million men." The show concluded with Lincoln's Gettysburg peroration "of the people, by the people, and for the people."[52]

Lincoln of course was the real hero of this piece; Sandburg had been developing Lincoln's mythology in a series of volumes since 1926, and in 1940 won a Pulitzer Prize. A common man, a raw-boned Kentucky frontiersman, Lincoln embodied the American character; and he had presided over a great war, in the midst of which he liberated a people who in the thirties had become, especially on the left, the symbol of the oppressed everywhere, keeping the flame of the American spirit. Earl Robinson adopted Lincoln as his hero for *The Lonesome Train*, for among composers it was Robinson who best understood that "three million women" or "one million men," the masses, could not communicate the real force of the people; that the People demanded incarnation in a Person.

Robinson was a classically trained musician who left the University of Washington looking for a "chance to write music that says something." He had composed songs for the San Francisco waterfront strike and about the Wobbly martyr Joe Hill, and set Sandburg's "The People, Yes!" to music. Later he composed "The

House I Live In," popularized in a short film by Frank Sinatra, for the war effort.[53]

In 1938, for the Federal Theater Project, Robinson composed, with lyricist John Latouche, what he called his "Whitman cantata," *Ballad for Americans,* as the finale of a musical history of America called *Sing for Your Supper.* Norman Corwin, a Popular Front radio producer, broadcast the piece on the CBS program *Pursuit of Happiness* on a Sunday afternoon in November 1939, with the black concert singer, All-American football player, Columbia Law School graduate, communist, and son of a runaway slave, Paul Robeson, in the lead vocal part. Soon school and community choruses, amateur theatrical groups, and church choirs throughout the country were performing it; the *Ford Hour* presented it with opera star Lawrence Tibbett, and a U.S. army chorus sang it for the Queen of England.

But the *Ballad* is best remembered as Robeson sang it. He followed his radio broadcast with performances in Lewisohn Stadium, the Hollywood Bowl, and the Republican national convention of 1940, with the American People's Chorus, which Robinson had formed from amateurs in the New York boroughs in 1937 to do protest songs and songs "of many nations."[54]

No musical document better captures the intellectual and social milieu of the folksong movement in New York than Robeson's *Ballad.* In calling on the tradition of the revolutionary chorus through the youthful American People's Chorus, the *Ballad* summons up local Jewish political culture and youth culture in a stroke, audibly dramatizing their interconnection and at the same time enunciating them in forcefully patriotic terms, quoting the preamble to the Constitution and, to the strains of "Let My People Go," the concluding phrases of the Gettysburg address. "That shore does sound mighty fine," a female voice declares from the chorus.

But in its leader-and-chorus, question-and-answer structure and its grand orchestral swells, all strongly reminiscent of *Porgy and Bess,* it sounds unmistakably like Broadway musical theater, annexing all the glamor and prestige of precisely that form through which representations of life beyond the Hudson had flowed most spectacularly into the city. The *Ballad*'s essential statement is an affirmation of political and social entitlement against the backdrop of a sense of powerlessness, invisibility, and marginality compensated, as it was in the union movement, by dignity, strength, and inclusion in numbers. It sketches in a series of verses a revolutionary theme as it is embodied in the patriarchs of the revolutionary war and in Lincoln as the Great Emancipator. "Nobody who was anybody believed it," Robeson the narrator sings of these historical crises—setting the revolutionary dream against the class-based language of status and celebrity on the one hand and, on the other, of urban anonymity, cultural invisibility, and immigrant powerlessness.

"Who are you, mister?" several voices from the chorus, as if out of a crowd on the street, demand indignantly of the anonymous narrator with his huge, all-encompassing vocal presence—a question the narrator repeatedly sets aside in favor of epic catalogues of America's working-class occupations, ethnic groups, and religious faiths. "You know who I am," he sings. "You see, I represent the whole of . . ." and "I am the etceteras and the and-so-forths that do the work," until in a triumphal finale he finally reveals himself as nothing less than America itself. He is a kind of Superman—a brown-suited, bespectacled man on the street, an everyman, and above all the champion of a faceless people: but one, perhaps, who can be catastrophically weakened by contact with his alien origins.

In his concerts Robeson typically combined Negro songs and spirituals with what Robinson later called "a musical tour of the world," with its "common denominator of human brotherhood." Robeson's cavernous voice, and certainly the man himself, embodied what had long been—from minstrelsy through Robeson's own roles in Eugene O'Neill's *Emperor Jones,* an *Othello* that toured the country, and the immensely popular musical *Showboat*—the type of the black giant-in-chains, "tired of livin' and scared of dyin'"; but it spoke too for the People, "the Nobody who's everybody, the Everybody who's nobody"—perhaps distantly echoing, for some who heard it, the little song called "Nobody" that Bert Williams used to drag sorrowfully around the vaudcville stage with the sad frown that every circus clown after him inherited.

Like the work of Moses Asch, Lawrence Gellert, Sophie Maslow, and many others, Robinson's *Ballad*, with Robeson in the lead, reflected the long-standing Jewish identification with the black minority to which the left had lent an ideological thrust. Michael Rogin notes that a nativist convergence of racial and ethnic stereotypes enshrined in the immigration-restriction bill of 1924 had tended to unify urban minorities against "the racial hierarchy of Protestant, genteel culture." The Yiddish press regularly compared lynching, rioting, and other racial violence to European pogroms; while the American Federation of Labor excluded blacks, the Jewish garment-workers' unions organized among them; Jewish philanthropic and legal agencies supported their African-American counterparts.[55] Hence the Popular Front's invocation of the People invariably cast, as it were, a black shadow, just as the figure of the Great Emancipator had both personified the People and represented them.

Though never as popular, Robinson's and Lampell's *Lonesome Train*, which followed closely on the *Ballad*, formed a bridge between the ideological folksong movement of the thirties and the commercial revival after the war. In a story told through the interplay of a chorus, a handful of narrator-singers, and the dramatic voices of Abraham Lincoln, various ordinary men and women, and a wounded Civil War soldier, *The Lonesome Train* conjures up an American landscape across which Lincoln's somber funeral train passes from city to city, greeted at each stop by crowds of mourners. "You couldn't quite tell where the people left off," goes the refrain, "and where Abe Lincoln began." The people are sketched typologically in a lively jiglike stanza briefly broken by a slow halftime couplet:

> A Kansas farmer, a Brooklyn sailor,
> An Irish policeman, a Jewish tailor.
> An old storekeeper shakin' his head—
> Standing over a loaf of bread—
> A Buffalo hunter tellin' a story,
> Out in the Oregon Territory.

But Lincoln himself leaves the funeral train: we see him at a square dance, "swinging his lady round and round" to the sound of a hoedown fiddler and a caller; we see him on a wooden bench "away in the back" of a black southern church, where a preacher delivers a stirring sermon, half sung and half spoken, about emancipation—"ain't got no deputies to chain us, no high sheriff to bring us back." Finally Lincoln himself addresses a wounded soldier, troubled "about killin' sir, it's wrong to kill," with angry words that echo the *Communist Manifesto:* "as long as there are whips, and chains, and men to use them, there will be no peace."

Such language was already abroad in the movement. Robinson's and Hays's song "Abe Lincoln" had drawn directly on Lincoln's first inaugural address. The Almanac Singers' wartime "Deliver the Goods," probably Lampell's composition, included this stanza:

> It's gonna take everybody to win this war,
> The butcher, the baker, and the clerk in the store,
> The men who sail the ships and the men who run the trains,
> And the farmer raising wheat upon the Kansas plains.[56]

But far more important than the play's syncretic social philosophy was Robinson's score, which caught African-American rhythms and tonality, the ballad singer's high-pitched, straining tone, and the drive of the five-string banjo, palette colors of a kind of auditory mural of American folklife supernaturally visited in each of its primal scenes by Lincoln's ghost.

Robinson first staged *The Lonesome Train* as a musical revue in 1942, and it found its way in 1944 to the Hollywood Bowl. But it entered the postwar folk revival principally through a Decca recording of 1945 under the direction of Norman Corwin, featuring Burl Ives, Pete Seeger on banjo, and Robinson himself narrating,[57] and then through a production at Town Hall in 1948, where Oscar Brand staged it with Harry Belafonte in the role of the southern preacher.

Yet just as Millard Lampell was composing the libretto for *The Lonesome Train,* trying to fashion the image of an American folk hero out of Sandburg's Lincoln biography, a real-life American folk hero was sitting opposite him at the kitchen table in Almanac House, making fun of him. Woody Guthrie had come to New York with Will Geer, a young radical actor who had met Guthrie in Los Angeles. In March 1940 Geer organized a benefit for the John Steinbeck Committee for Agricultural Workers; John Ford's film of Steinbeck's *Grapes of Wrath* had just been released. Geer made his reputation in leftist circles by his role five years earlier as a "ballad-singing Grandpap" in Albert Bein's *Let Freedom Ring,*[58] a proletarian drama about southern textile workers, but even more by his successful rallying, through song, of striking weavers in Paterson, New Jersey. He had a reputation as a composer-performer of western sketches and folklike topical ballads, and no doubt saw in Guthrie a reflection of his own stage persona. Guthrie himself certainly understood the type he was expected to play; he had been a professional country-western musician and, in the six months before coming to New York, contributed a regular column to the California communist publication *People's World,* self-consciously wrought in Will Rogers' crackerbarrel style.

The benefit was held at the Forrest Theater, where an adaptation of Erskine Caldwell's *Tobacco Road* was underway and in which Geer was appearing. In addition to Guthrie, described by the *Daily Worker* as a "real dustbowl refugee," the program included Alan and Bess Lomax, Aunt Molly Jackson, Huddie Ledbetter, Burl Ives, Geer himself, the Golden Gate Quartet, and Margot Mayo's American Square Dancers. Woody would shortly write a half-hour ballad called "Tom Joad," which told the story of Steinbeck's novel; at the Forrest, Joe Klein writes, "he stood alone, fixed by a spotlight slanting down from the balcony, and seemed to fit in perfectly with Jeeter Lester's tarpaper shack on the *Tobacco Road* set behind him. He scratched his head with a guitar pick and said 'Howdy,' squinting up at the cheap seats . . . as if he'd wandered in by accident, but didn't mind hanging around and singing a few songs as long as he was there."[59]

In radical circles, as we have seen, contact between Anglo- and African-American tradition bearers and ethnic American, particularly Jewish, progressives was far from unprecedented. Ray Auville, an urbanized mountain guitar player and fiddler, settled with his sister in Cleveland and was discovered by the local John Reed Club; he "fiddles with gusto and native style," Mike Gold wrote, "as rousingly as any old moustached veteran of the Great Smokies."[60] But most enduring for the revival, alongside Woody Guthrie, was the image of the singing unionist and midwife of Harlan County, Aunt Molly Jackson, who with her stepbrother, organizer Jim Garland, returned to New York with Theodore Dreiser's investigative committee to testify to the deprivation and terror wrought by the coal operators—and, blacklisted at home, settled in the city.

Corwin invited Guthrie to sing on *The Pursuit of Happiness,* where he had earlier introduced *Ballad for Americans,* and soon Woody was heard across the commercial radio dial on Sanka's *We, the People,* DuPont's *Cavalcade of America,* where he sang an original ballad about Wild Bill Hickock, and the Model Tobacco Company's *Pipe Smoking Time,* where his dust-bowl ballad, which would rise to the top of the hit parade after the war, "So Long, It's Been Good To Know Ya," was the theme.

Moses Asch remembers Guthrie as a man who "didn't like people, especially middle-class bourgeois people . . . He felt that he represented a group of poor people that needed to be spoken for."[61] But Clifton Fadiman wrote in the *New Yorker* that "Woody Guthrie and the ten thousand songs that leap and tumble off the strings of his music box are a national possession, like Yellowstone or Yosemite, and part of the best stuff this country has to show the world."[62] Even Steinbeck himself, in a sense conceding the limits of his own epic novel, agreed that Guthrie "sings the songs of a people and I suspect that he is, in a way, that people."[63]

But Guthrie's most consistent champion by far was Alan Lomax, who regarded him as the "great American frontier ballad writer." Lomax by this time was established in Washington as assistant director, with his father, of the Archive of Folk Song. In the previous year Lomax had secured a weekly morning spot on CBS's *Columbia School of the Air*, sending the romance of folksong into the nation's schoolrooms, and the following August would begin his CBS network program *Back Where I Come From*.

Back Where I Come From was organized around themes such as the weather, marriage, railroads, animals, and other subjects congenial to folksong, presented in the context of sound effects and dramatic readings from such authors as Melville and Whitman. This was the theatrical setting in which the voice of Woody Guthrie, and other folksingers of the period, was consistently presented. We may catch the flavor of Lomax's radio style on a Library of Congress recording. Against the backdrop of Guthrie's "Lost Train Blues," which like most of his harmonica pieces muddled the racial identity of the musician, Lomax introduces the dust-bowl balladeer:

> The song is "Lost Train Blues" played on harmonica and guitar by Woody Guthrie from Okemah, Oklahoma. Woody knows what that lost train means because he's ridden the "red ball" freights from one end of the country to another . . . Woody Guthrie is, I guess, about thirty years old from the looks of him, but he's seen more in those thirty years than most men see before they're seventy. He hasn't sat in a warm house or a warm office . . . He's gone into the world and he's looked at the faces of hungry men and women. He's been in hobo jungles. He's performed on picket lines. He's sung his way through every bar and saloon between Oklahoma and California . . . And listen to that "red ball" roll.[64]

One of the most interesting and poignant effects of these words, quite apart from their content, with Guthrie's blues harmonica whining in the distance, is Lomax's own voice, high-pitched, light, and whiskered like a blade of prairie grass, but with a certain fastidiousness too, the voice of a cultivated man given to eloquence that betrays the awkward and bewildering social gap between the two men, actually an ethnic and regional kinship fissured less by class than by advantage; Guthrie's apparent indifference to it only throws Lomax's isolation into higher relief.

Lomax's discovery of Woody Guthrie can be understood, then, as an aspect of his own self-discovery and only partly achieved self-invention. At once reared in and educated out of the condition into which both men were born, Lomax saw in Guthrie a cultural destiny at once escaped and lost, from which he was both compulsively alienated and painfully estranged. Lomax was offering to people who sat "in a warm house or a warm office," or who languished in the stifling old flats of Williamsburg, Flatbush, or Rockaway, the fresh republic of mountain, sky, and plain, railroad and highway, democracy and equality that he himself was rhapsodically celebrating, resolving his own ambivalence in a process of negotiation between the imaginary and the actual, in the ideological field of a racial and racialized "folk" that Lomax had staked out.

As a radio personality working in the realm of music and the spoken word, Alan Lomax was dedicated to creating conditions for the long-sought "great American novel" or an American *Ring of the Nibelung* that would not be constrained within the pages of a book but would incorporate an entire tradition of singers and songs ultimately beyond literature. In his programs, performances, broadcasts, concerts, and collections, as well as through his protegés, Lomax pointed to the epic or operatic plane upon which the "people's art" met the heroic, arousing by means of a grand weaving of song and story an exhilaration akin to patriotic fervor and religious enthusiasm, freed from the bankrupt institutional alliances by which these feelings had been structured in America since the 1890s.

That is why the insult was so profound and ineradicable when, in the 1950s, powerful men accused urban folksingers, so deeply patriotic, of treason and subversion. The public slander of the folksong movement, while driving it into an underground of private schools, summer camps, and college campuses, stripped it of the ideological discourse by which its whole semiology had been mapped and interpreted. But this prepared the way for a cultural recovery whose new discourse became articles of confederation for the last romantic counterculture of our century.

Woody Guthrie, 1943

4

Ramblin' Round Your City

Each generation, working from the mystery of its own origins, rewrites the history of the last. Among the many illegible legacies handed down to the generation of the 1950s is the complicated sectarianism of left-wing politics in America, whose links to the various leftist and popular movements of the thirties had been broken by the eruption of postwar anticommunism. The world war, like its predecessor, violently disrupted ordinary social and cultural continuities, laying the groundwork of a radically new postwar history in which the generation of the folk revival grew up, shaped in ways it did not comprehend by earlier ideas not embodied in texts or discourses or in any obviously political manifestation, but in the icons, symbols, and signs, all of them politically eloquent but ideologically mute, which the prewar epoch was able to insulate against postwar reactionary paranoia.

In the early 1960s, as the commercial folk revival gathered force, the ideological connections of the movement might have been readily uncovered by anyone curious enough to inquire of the many entrepreneurs, impresarios, folklorists, collectors, and folksingers who came into the field from the earlier period; but few did inquire—and, for their part, the chill thrown into the political climate by McCarthy's and others' investigations still lay over the speech and the memories of those who had been associated with the left, inducing a queer, cryptic, indirect mode of discourse, a kind of uneasy sidelong glance, and, at the same time, an unexplained energy and enthusiasm for the revival of folk music at once aggressively commercial and ideologically hermetic, as if, in a world in which an Inquisition had prevailed, some aging neoplatonists had found their philosophy rising again.

Calling himself "Pete Bowers" to protect his father's government job, Pete Seeger in the spring of 1941 lived in New York, first in Chelsea and later in a loft on 12th Street with a group of young people who shared his passion for folk music, his political commitments, and his sense of social and historical mission. Notables from the left were regular visitors, especially on weekends, when they had long folksinging parties. In February Seeger had brought two of his friends, Lee Hays and Millard Lampell, with him to a booking at the convention of the American Youth Congress in Washington, where they brought the house down with reckless songs that insulted the President.[1]

They called themselves the Almanac Singers. While the whole world descended into its long winter of barbarism, around the Almanac Singers a moral and political springtime was budding out of sheer youthful defiance of the munitions makers, corporate bosses, and politicians associated in their minds with the catastrophe: in the embattled communist movement of the Nazi-Soviet Pact period, the Almanac Singers found their opportunity. They sang in the May Day parade and in an antiwar revue, *Sign of the Times;* with a burgeoning new repertory of original union songs such as "Get Behind Me, Satan," "Talking Union," and Guthrie's "Union Maid," they performed for 20,000 striking transport workers at Madison Square Garden: "There once was a union maid, who never was afraid . . . Oh you can't scare me, I'm sticking to the union, sticking to the union till the day I die." After a concert at the Congress of the League of American Writers that included Burl Ives, Earl Robinson, Leadbelly, Josh White, Tony Kraeber, and the American Ballad Singers, the veteran communist Theodore Dreiser said of the Almanacs: "If we had six more like these boys, we could save America."[2]

Unlike Pete Bowers and his friends on West 10th Street in 1941, at what came to be called Almanac House, the revivalists of the early sixties, the "folkies," were not moved primarily by an ideologically inspired resistance, but by a generally shared belief in a world better furnished with the means of postwar society's tacit promise of personal fulfillment, dramatized by their common dedication to a social and cultural ideal mysteriously embodied in certain singers and musicians whom entrepreneurs and impresarios were bringing to light from the occult past before the war, from race and oldtime records and the forgotten folk festivals and fiddlers' conventions of the thirties. The music of these rediscoveries, saturating the atmosphere from ever more plentiful LPs, increasingly *was* their world, persistently and fully enough present to the imagination almost to eclipse the actual world of cities, suburbs, college campuses, and professional careers, and to substitute for it a tissue of illusion, of mountain cabins and southern canebrakes, desperados, tramps, maidens, farmers, banjo pickers, and wandering blues guitarists, a world of uncertain locale and shifting temporality which the revivalist was half-consciously struggling to reach on slow-moving freight trains or by hitchhiking, guitar or banjo slung over the shoulder.

As Jack Whalen and Richard Flacks describe it, the unifying theme of the sixties counterculture "was the romantic belief that the young could make themselves into new persons, that they need not follow their parents' footsteps, that they could build lives in which they could exercise a degree of self-mastery not given by the established structures of role, relationship, and routine."[3] In those summertime communal experiments in some northeastern or coastal city, the folkies may be said to

have been paying unconscious tribute to the founders of their
movement and to the circumstances in which certain stubborn
divisions, musical, social, and cultural, might temporarily disappear. Ideas, finally, did not give rise to the revival, but a deliberate refusal of ideas; it was not a particular kind of song, a
Spanish Civil War song or a labor song or a peace song that gave
rise to it, or even a particular way of singing songs, though this
became, alongside a certain mystification concerning folksong
"style," an ever more precise and exacting requirement, but
rather, the demand implicitly made on the music that it would
be personally transforming; that between the public persona
projected in the performance of music and the psychological
subject making the projection, a "folk" performance would
somehow bridge the gulf, melding one into the other, reinventing social and personal identity toward closely connected ends:
the effacement of received social identity, on the one hand, and
the construction of a new cultural ecology, on the other, in
which an imaginary self might find, or actually project out of
itself, the social and historical niche that authenticates it—a
project in which Pete Seeger, almost alone among folk revivalists until Bob Dylan, had actually succeeded.

Seeger was an idealistic and embarrassed young aristocrat urgently reinventing himself out of the epoch's peculiar coales-
cence of music and politics. Another Almanac was Peter Hawes, a
scion of the Houghton family of Boston, son of a writer of sea
stories for boys. Bess Lomax, daughter of John and sister of Alan,
though neither a blueblood nor heir to a publishing fortune,
enjoyed the advantages of her Texas origins, of distinguished
establishment connections, rigorous training as a child in classical
piano under an ambitious and conscientious mother, her family's
pioneering work in folk music, and a Bryn Mawr education—she
had begun her association with New York's left-wing community
on weekend excursions from school in Philadelphia.[4]

Millard Lampell, by contrast, was the son of a Jewish garment
worker in Paterson, but his assimilationist drive, as in many

working-class Jewish boys, was strong. The biographers of the revival persistently call attention to his good looks, his fondness for women, his way with words, and his football scholarship at West Virginia University. Lampell, whose heroes were Carl Sandburg, Stephen Vincent Benet, and Archibald MacLeish, was the aspiring writer that every communal house depends on, with a quick irreverent wit that his association with Woody Guthrie only sharpened. Lampell would eventually find his way, after the clouds of blacklisting had dissipated, to Hollywood.

Now Almanac House was hardly a community of farmers, mountaineers, sharecroppers, lumberjacks, fishermen, old nurses, and other putative singers of folksongs. On the contrary it was, at its core, a band of young radicals from whose ranks any pure representative of the vast American middle class was conspicuously absent. At Almanac House New York's left-wing bohemians gathered: poets, musicians, and intellectuals such as Nicholas Ray, producer of Lomax's *Back Where I Come From*, along with writers such as Dashiell Hammett and Walter Lowenfels, the artist Rockwell Kent, and other notables who orbited around *New Masses* and the Communist Party. That Pete and his friends were from privileged families, that he and Bess were the son and daughter of America's most distinguished scholars, collectors, and disseminators of folksong merely recapitulates the sociology of bohemia, from Oscar Wilde to Mabel Dodge to the Cambridge folk scene of the sixties, rooted at Harvard and the exclusive private schools that wait upon it.

With the invincibility peculiar to their class, and the drive peculiar to young men like Lampell, the Almanacs were dedicated to defying in word, in song, and in the manner of their life the entire capitalist system. Their outspoken antiwar songs of early 1941—"No, it wouldn't be a thrill to die for Dupont in Brazil"—had what Joe Klein calls a "puerile, insolent tone," the more so because couched in familiar melodies like "Billy Boy" or "Liza Jane"; these songs first shocked, and then thrilled, audiences such as the American Youth Congress because they not only attacked American foreign policy but brazenly ridiculed the President, figuring the European war as a capitalist dogfight and Roosevelt as a lurking imperialist.

This increasingly untenable position, neutrality, was as everyone knew that of the Communist Party. The Almanacs invested their labor songs as well with a communist outlook, hastily dividing the world into heroic armies of stiff-jawed workers and porcine bourgeois bosses, musical caricatures increasingly irrelevant to the special American form of capitalism that had long since drawn workers out of the social isolation characteristic of Europe's industrial operatives and into the marketplace, making consumers of them and identifying the original promise of democracy with the commercial buying power that could integrate the wage earner with the comfortable white-collar proletariat.

While the Almanac Singers and their auxiliaries in a career of less than two years enjoyed considerable exposure before the CIO, UAW locals, and even Harry Bridges's longshoremen's union, their principal audience was among radical youth, at "cause" parties, war-relief and private gatherings where they were accepted on their own terms—and not, as at a butchers' local in Queens, ridiculed because they weren't *real* working-class people.[5] In the querulous conversation on the American left in the late thirties, as war in Europe with each passing month shifted the terms of the debate, the Almanac Singers were more like weathervanes than almanacs; but as Alan Lomax reminded them, their "chief point of contact with America" was the soil and the folksong. "Don't become the 'Headline Singers,'" he cautioned, when it appeared that communist ties might spoil their chances for success as singing cheerleaders for the war effort, "even though you may be singing the 'Headlines.'"[6]

What for the Soviet Union had been a national security policy, cooperation with western democracies against the Nazis, a temporary working alliance with socialists, trade unionists, and liberals, the Popular Front in America had become an exhilarating national campaign for the extension of social democracy.

The "proletarian renaissance" was expanding on the left in all expressive spheres: literature, theater, photography, painting and design, as well as music and song, inspired by the Roosevelt administration's own documentary and recovery projects and by the labor movement itself, whose dramatic struggles in the coalfields and textile towns were lending epic grandeur to newspaper headlines. Even the apolitical middle class was involved as consumers of clothing, furniture, dishware, and other domestic goods in styles reproduced from traditional designs and, in some cases, actually manufactured in mountain cooperatives under radical leadership.

By the end of the decade, the communists' *Daily Worker* was fully engaged in the promulgation of folklore, the new "workers' culture"—a phrase whose semantic expansion in this period can hardly escape our notice now—publishing reports on cowboy songs, calypso, outlaw heroes, children's rhymes, square dances, tales and proverbs, Paul Bunyan, the WPA folklore project, W. C. Handy's lectures on the blues, Martha Graham's use of folk motifs, Paul Robeson, various reviews of collections, folk concerts, and regional folk festivals.

Nothing, however, could have more starkly exposed the fundamental incompatibility between the ideals of Marxist-Leninism and what had become a form of popular American nationalism, nor the near-mythical status the Soviet Union had assumed for American communists, than the Hitler-Stalin nonaggression pact of August 1939. At least one communist argued in defense of the pact[7] that, since Soviet overtures to France and England for mutual-defense treaties were ignored or rebuffed, the pact simply pursued, by a different means, what had been the essential aim of the Popular Front, the protection of the Soviet Union against an imperialist Germany. The war, in this view, was merely a competition among imperialist powers for control of markets in which the Soviet Union was not an ally but an adversary; many communists believed that the west was banking on a Nazi invasion of Russia. Indeed the war could, by this construction, hasten the inevitable collapse of the capitalist system and advance, under Soviet tutelage, the cause of communism throughout the west: a perspective that the history of postwar Europe, the rationale for the Marshall Plan, and the cold war itself would seem to bear out.

But as would become plain within two weeks in the partition of Poland, the Man of Steel had simply demonstrated his knack for realpolitik. To liberals and progressives swept up in the Popular Front, the pact challenged any ideological identification with Soviet communism, so beholden as it apparently was to Soviet national interest, and at a deeper level betrayed Stalin's fundamental hostility to western liberal democracy, both the child and the bride, after all, of capitalism. And at last, given the massive investment of Jewish idealism in socialist thought, the pact shockingly intimated that behind it, and under the foundation of both fascism's and communism's hatred of modernism and cosmopolitanism, lay horrid deposits of German and Russian antisemitism.

Think now of "the left" in broader terms: in association with urban ethnicity, particularly east European and Jewish, the drive toward assimilation and self-worth, and even more important, in terms of the young, who as the sons and daughters of European immigrants, as Jews, as citizens, and as Americans found in the broader movement a language at once revolutionary and prescriptive for describing the society in which, as adults, they wished to live. Robert Warshow, a child of the thirties who could look in one direction toward his immigrant parents and in the other to his son, born in 1943 and as a ten-year-old an avid reader of *Mad* magazine, lends us the perspective we need to make sense of the left, particularly the youthful left of the thirties, in more immediate terms.

The Jewish immigrant, Warshow writes, "was able to carry with him a sense of his own dignity and importance . . . In Europe, with the club over his head, he had nevertheless lived in a community which was in important ways self-sufficient, and which permitted him to think of himself as a man of value: he was a scholar, a revolutionist . . . To be a Jew was a continual burden, even a misfortune, but it could not have seemed to him a joke or a disgrace." Once in America, obsessed with the pursuit of the "infinitesimal advantages" upon which his survival depended, but buoyed up by the semi-European atmosphere of the synagogue, the cafe, the radical group, "he could contrive for his sad life the appearance of a meaning that went beyond the everlasting pettiness of which it actually consisted. He had a past."

Not so his children. For them, Warshow continues, "helping after school with the family's piecework or going themselves to work in the shops, and often suffering in addition under a severe moral discipline with no apparent relevance to the real world, the pretentions of the father could be nothing but nonsense." Beyond a "generalized ideal of moral and intellectual superiority without content," there was no personal origin for them in the parent generation. The melancholy consequence of this fact of immigrant life was that the father was inevitably "disappointed in his children, and his sense of disappointment was often the only thing he could clearly communicate to them. He succeeded at last in becoming a reproach to them, and the bitterness of the personal conflict which ensued was aggravated by the fact that they could never quite see from what he derived his superiority or what it was he held against them."[8]

To this social and psychological predicament, the left had offered a solution, one for which the second generation, in the broad tide of the Popular Front, had not paid so dear a price in parochialism and isolation. Never had "the left" been so fully included in America's public life as in the mid-thirties; the contract it was negotiating with American society was attempting nothing less than to reconcile, under the presiding spirit of America's depression-era fascination with itself and its people, the deep ethnic, cultural, and political divisions that had arisen in the massive systemic social changes of the previous generation.

By 1937 a new world seemed to be on the horizon, but Roosevelt's mandate had already begun to erode. The right was building its power in Congress; then came the pact; and by the following year the world had lapsed into nightmare. By the summer of 1940 France had fallen to the Nazis, and Britain lay under the blitz; and, though both political parties in the campaign of 1940 continued to resist American entry into the war, Roosevelt had begun a massive military buildup that in October brought America's first peacetime draft.

If on the left the prospect of war even against Hitler did not seem an unmitigated blessing, it may be because in the communist movement, the ethnic communities, and the labor unions there were many men and women who had been refugees from pogroms, conscription, and war, people for whom the conflict of nations was a quarrel among greedy and petulant gods that could only mean suffering for human beings. And a draft, of course, directly threatens young men: in October 1940, eight months before Hitler's invasion of Russia, another six before Pearl Harbor, World War II had not yet become the good war, the war that had to be fought and won.

In 1940, the year he would have graduated from Harvard, Pete Seeger was twenty-one. He staked his claim, in what would be in 1941 a gesture of commitment, almost certainly inspired by Hitler's invasion, every bit as dramatic and decisive as burning one's draft card would be in 1966, to the Communist Party and its affiliated community. To have abandoned the movement would have meant, practically speaking, an end to his nascent career and to the identity, the role, and the politics connected with it. Accepting membership in the party in 1941, on the other hand, had to be an act of faith, a political full immersion that like any great act of faith seems to measure its authenticity and meaning commensurately with its open defiance of both interest and reason. Loyalty to any authoritarian system necessarily demands more than acquiescence in what would otherwise amount only to an aggregate of private and independent agreements; indeed inconsistency and paradox only raise the stakes, by commanding allegiance to the shared reality mediated by a living community.

As the Popular Front deteriorated, dedicated communists withdrew into a sectarian isolation powerfully reminiscent of the Soviet Union in the twenties, even to the extent of adopting internal security measures and setting up an underground apparatus.[9] For now they were subject to a red scare, exacerbated by an antiwar position so militant as to verge on treasonous criticism of President Roosevelt for what in reality was a pragmatic defensive position.

This reflexive withdrawal, proportional in intensity to the broad acceptance the left had enjoyed in the days of the Popular Front, should I think be understood both by analogy to and as a recapitulation of what traditionally has been the response of second-generation immigrant Jews to the memory of Europe's recurrent cycles of antisemitism. To enjoy fuller participation in American life has been for most American Jews a desirable and worthy aim; but as every Jew understands instinctively, such acceptance can never be secure; in time of economic or political stress, anti-Jewish feeling, along with hatred and intolerance of every kind, will rear its ugly head, typically in conjunction with fascist or militarist styles and ideologies. In this crisis there arises the dilemma that German Jews faced as Hitler came to power: whether to mask one's Jewish identity wholly or to retreat into the rooted parochial community—to weigh on either hand the insult to conscience or to reason, the isolation of spirit against the extinction of hope.

This is the crisis that the left, as an ethnic, cultural, and political community, confronted in the peculiar period between August 1939 and Hitler's invasion of the Soviet Union in June 1941, the pact period, when "radical youth seesawed between pacifism and anti-fascism, first taking the anti-war Oxford Oath, then pledging to fight for Collective Security."[10] An interval of disillusionment and paralysis pervaded by a looming sense of grave international threat, it invites comparisons to the cold war as young people later experienced it: the sense of danger, at once global and personal; impatience and skepticism with cold-war propaganda and doubt as to the authenticity of the communist "menace"; a mounting conviction of the complicity of our own government and business establishment in promoting international tension; and, most important, dismay at the deterioration of a political and cultural consensus in which all the promise and possibility of the future lay.

For young people in the pact period, as at the end of the Eisenhower era, that critical moment of transition from child to adult, in which ideals, dreams, hopes, and expectations are invariably in peril, could only amplify the message of a threat to the body politic, to the broader cultural enterprise, to national security, as well as, many felt and believed, to individual life itself. The emergence of the Almanac Singers during this interval suggests that where formerly on the left the idea of an extensive vernacular American people had demanded embodiment in a people's hero, it now demanded a symbolic resurrection of itself in all its communality, demanded an expansion of the human compass toward the limits now set between itself and the larger polity. Like the folk revival after it, and indeed like any community that feels itself rebuffed, circumscribed, isolated, the folksong movement found itself politically ghettoized, driven back upon its own resources and, as Thomas Keneally writes of the Jews of the old Kazimierz ghetto, "consecrated to their own specialness."[11]

With Hitler's invasion of Russia, the antiwar repertory of the Almanacs had suddenly to be abandoned. Just before Pearl Harbor, with radical organizers achieving great successes within the CIO, the Almanacs' union songs had won cautious acceptance among the rank and file; after Pearl Harbor, these songs, marked by a divisive class-consciousness, had to be abandoned too, in the interest of general solidarity: labor, after all, had joined with government and management in a no-strike pledge to develop the wartime industrial economy. "Perhaps we were fools," Seeger said, recalling how the group had been impressed by Churchill's support of the Soviet Union, not to have seen that the historical situation would change. "When it did change," he added, "we weren't going to stand on any foolish consistency."[12] "I started out to sing a song," Guthrie wrote,

> To the entire population;
> But I ain't a-doing a thing tonight
> On account of this "new situation."

With a brief wartime resurgence of Popular Front feeling, then, the Almanacs' symbolic enactment of the voice of the people proved ideally suited to the sudden need for national solidarity. In this moment they achieved their greatest commercial exposure, introducing the first program of Norman Corwin's *This Is War* series on all four major networks with war songs such as "Reuben James" and "Dear Mr. Roosevelt," and rode a crest of popularity that took them to CBS's *We the People*, the Navy Department's *Treasury Hour*, and, thanks to Alan Lomax, even the U.S. Office of War Information broadcasts. While Guthrie as a performer and Lampell as a writer were both expanding their careers in radio, the William Morris Agency and Decca records expressed an interest in the group—the nature of which is implied by a near miss for a booking at Rockefeller Center's posh Rainbow Room, where at their audition the center's talent agents, though generally approving of their show, wanted what was already commonplace at the Grand Ole Opry and the National Barndance—hillbilly costumes to round off the act, gunnysacks, straw hats, overalls. "At the Rainbow Room the soup's on to boil," went their on-the-spot improvisation. "They're stirring the salad with Standard Oil."

As Lomax had predicted, their anti-Roosevelt songs recorded on the album *Songs for John Doe* were already coming back to haunt them. The New York newspapers, the *Post* and *World-Telegram*, in a way that foreshadowed the fate of the folksong movement in the McCarthy period, stopped the Almanacs in their tracks by announcing that the celebrated young patriots had also "warbled for the Communists." The "peace choir," as the *Post* put it, had "changed their tune."[13]

The much-discussed and apparently opportunistic ideological shifts of which the Almanacs were guilty are, in the end, beside the point. It is certain that the challenges posed to leftist orthodoxy during the immediate prewar period aroused debate at Almanac House and muddied the consciences of activists like Pete Seeger and Lee Hays, who only later understood Lomax's point, that the group's real significance ultimately lay not in ideological consistency but in a more distant place—at the social and cultural frontier to which their own advantages had led them, from which they could sing against the draft and in the next moment for the war effort, shamelessly criticize the President and almost simultaneously solicit his good will, set one class against another and in the same breath celebrate universal brotherhood—from a position, in other words, that already lay outside the institutional structures within which social and political discourse had, to that point, been carried out: especially, for them, the Communist Party.

The Almanacs' shifting repertory tended to discredit the tendentious role outlined by the left for folksong in favor of the iconography of American common life as regionalist writers, social-realist and academic painters, popular playwrights, filmmakers, and classical composers had constructed it. While their topical songs remain only as relics of the immediate prewar period, the sea chanties and cowboy songs they recorded under Lomax's tutelage in 1941 for a jazz label, General Records, including "I Ride an Old Paint," "House of the Rising Sun," and "Hard, Ain't It Hard" endured in the revival repertory along with the group's stylistic debts to traditional stringband music and blues.

What really animated Pete Seeger and Bess Lomax was a sheer love of a dreamed-of folk America, or more precisely of American folks, whom few in the group had ever known up close, in an atmosphere sweetened by the extravagant fantasies of Jewish immigrants, artists, and musicians anxious to discover native subjects, and by the moral energy of an idealistic political movement. "Outside of politics," as Burl Ives later testified to the McCarran committee, "there has been a sort of group which has some sort of cohesiveness, you might say, of all the ballad singers, and there are quite a number of them. Just by the nature of what we do, there is some kind of a relationship, a sentimental thinking about the songs and everybody interested in singing folk songs."[14] For some, of course, there is no "outside of politics," and what to some looks like cohesiveness to others looks like conspiracy.

Their collective vision was finally beyond ideology, the very condition of its possibility being the social, cultural, and physical distance between the left-wing community in New York and the great prewar American south and west, English, Scots and Scots-Irish, German, French, and Scandinavian, more than Polish, Hungarian, Lithuanian, or Russian, and, in the south, distinctively African-American. The American hinterlands and backcountry had shaped consciousness by an altogether different historical experience—along Protestant, republican, and agrarian lines, more individualist than collectivist, more egalitarian than authoritarian, neither proletarian nor bourgeois, strictly speaking, neither provincial nor cosmopolitan. It was instead a small-town society, aggressively entrepreneurial economically, complacently feudal socially, increasingly commercial culturally, consolidating itself around the mammoth urban markets whose agricultural and industrial implements, machines, consumer goods, books, magazines, catalogues, radio broadcasts, and advertising were forging an identifiable American identity such as Walt Whitman never imagined and of which doctrinnaire communism could not conceive.

It is particularly significant that living in Almanac House were not only young men and women of education, ability, and privilege but, incongruously, such picturesque American hinterland characters as Lee Hays and Woody Guthrie, and that from time to time other singing emissaries from the folk south such as Leadbelly and Josh White, Sonny Terry and Brownie McGhee, would join in the Almanac hootenannies.

Seeger had learned of Lee Hays, who was working simultaneously on a collection of labor songs, from their mutual friend Hawes in 1940 while compiling, with Lomax and Guthrie, the manuscript of *Hard-Hitting Songs for Hard Hit People,* which would not see print until 1967. More mature than the others at twenty-seven, the son of a Methodist minister from rural Georgia, Hays had concluded stints as a preacher, librarian, schoolteacher, and labor activist with two years as a drama coach, 1936–38, at Commonwealth Labor College in Mena, Arkansas.

Commonwealth had sprung in 1923 from a utopian colony in Louisiana founded in the late nineteenth century on the principle of making "moral conviction operative upon actual life," as Jane Addams reports, and "to obey the teachings of Jesus in all matters of labor and the use of property."[15] Its students, northern and urban for the most part, studied history, economics, political theory, and the practical arts in a Marxist framework. In 1937 the school's doctrinnaire pro-Soviet posture shifted dramatically under the Presbyterian minister Claude Williams, called the Red Preacher, who brought his original New Light fundamentalism to bear upon the Marxist-humanist social gospel with spirited song leadership and a deep engagement with local people.

Hays took to Almanac House his familiarity with the African-American song tradition, as well as the influence of Williams, whose example Hays had tried to follow as a teacher and organizer, regularly adapting spirituals and hymns to labor themes but, more important, singing them in a style shaped by the black pulpit. Hays had adopted the form of resistance politics most favored by the young minds of his generation, having identified himself, in a 1933 letter to *New Masses,* with "rank-and-file workers for a Soviet America";[16] but within his own personal politics, one can still detect the teachings of his father's Methodist evangelism, whose essence was to bring the message of God's mercy to the lowliest of people, in defiance of the Calvinist proposition that only the elect—election having been conveniently identified with worldly prosperity—might receive it.

As for Woody Guthrie, of whom so much has been written, I should only add that he was neither an unlettered dust-bowl refugee nor a pure-blood neolithic Pict, as Lomax fancifully identified him. It was Almanac House that put the finial on his bohemianization, since by the standards of Okemah, Oklahoma, Guthrie was decent folks, the son of genteel literate parents and a father who had made a small career in local business and politics, and even played guitar and banjo in a cowboy band. "You never harvested a grape in your life," the Oklahoma communist Gordon Friesen used to remind him. "You're an intellectual, a poet."[17]

Guthrie's life was tragically shattered while he was still a boy by his father's business failures, by a catastrophic house fire that killed his sister Clara and broke his parents' spirit, and finally by the Huntington's disease that took his mother into dementia and to which he himself would succumb. Guthrie was reduced to poverty and, bereft of attachments, set out into the world as the hapless drifter about whom we have all heard; the poignance of his story lies in the orphanhood to which, as a child of aspiring, even ambitious parents and a voracious reader who had considered both law and medicine as careers, Guthrie could bring the expanded awareness not of one born into poverty and desperation but of one blown into it by a bitterly ill wind, and who responded to it with the songs we have all recognized and celebrated.

> My mother prayed that I would be
> a man of some renown;
> but I am just a refugee, boys,
> as I go ramblin' round.

After learning guitar from an uncle while the family lived in Pampa, Texas, Guthrie played in a series of hillbilly stringbands and on the radio, in the heyday of the music, as a hillbilly singer, with a conscience pricked by the situation of the Okies in California. Had Will Geer never met him, had he never come to New York to be embraced by the left-wing community, it is possible that he would have been remembered as a gifted songwriter, and very likely not as a musician or singer, in the popular hillbilly tradition of the thirties, when Gene Autry and the Sons of the Pioneers were lending hillbilly music its country-and-western flavor and annexing the glamor of the Hollywood cowboy.

In his young manhood Guthrie was an errant husband, an indifferent father, with appetite for tobacco and whiskey—but more than anything else he was a brilliant, compulsive, undisciplined, indeed a natural writer and man of words, an eager consumer of books and a perpetual learner, in short a man who, absent the twin tragedies of his youth and his age, would have become, and within the limits of his personal destiny *did* become, one of America's great writers and poets, whom Bob Dylan in his touching "Song to Woody" placed among the folk heroes who had "come with the dust and are gone with the wind."

Hence there was a peculiar leavening in the social mix at Almanac House; it brought something to the Almanacs that party ideology, banjo playing, political songs, access to the greatest song collections in the country, or even Lampell's literary talent alone could not. Hays, in fact, was not long in the group, dropping out with complaints about his health; Guthrie's participation was intermittent. But both Hays and Guthrie had tapped into the southern—read "black"—way of handling a song, partly by birthright, having both been touched by the African-American strain in southern culture, and partly by experience; if Lee Hays learned his singing style in the black church, Guthrie perfected his by assiduous study of the eight or so blues recordings of Blind Lemon Jefferson and others that he played over and over in his upstairs room.

To be precisely what Guthrie was demanded the precise pattern of his tragic exile, which equipped him to mediate imaginatively, in his person and his works, between the world of the poor and the dispossessed and those who had never touched that world except as readers, tourists, journalists, artists, or photographers. If he did not actually live it, Guthrie tasted it; beyond that, his was an imagination able to grasp the implications of his own experience. If Guthrie helped to define the period, he was also defined by it; the imagery of his writings and his songs, indeed his personal image, riven into the very bones of his face, into his Chaplinesque carriage and his deadpan vocal delivery, was already widely distributed in a society consolidating itself at a new level of cultural homogeneity in commercial art and advertising, government propaganda, magazine illustration, public art, and a thousand other settings. As I have said, the heroic themes he articulated in his songs echoed the official rhetoric of a state dedicated to economic revival through heroic projects in planning and engineering, the deployment of youthful armies of conservation workers, bridge, road, and park builders, cadres of artists, writers, and intellectuals to document the vastness, color, and variety of the American continent.

Whereas Seeger, Bess Lomax, and the other Almanacs may have enjoyed special access to the various reservoirs of folksong, in scholarly collections and the regional festivals, whereas they could appeal to communist ideology and to political situations as a context for new compositions, Guthrie was breathing in the cultural atmosphere in his music, first as a hillbilly and then as an Almanac, and continued to breathe it in until he reached the physically negotiable limits of his disease, when as a skinny, tousled, unshaven bohemian in Washington Square, he became for a new generation the image that Jewish cowboys like Jack Elliot and Bob Dylan brought to perfection.

Like Charles Seeger, Guthrie had come into intimate contact
with the brutal discrimination against rural migrants, but unlike
Seeger was not socially and culturally insulated from it; his lived
consciousness of the gulf between rich and poor, shaped in the
peach orchards of California could, without grave distortions,
easily adapt itself to a Marxist analysis of capitalist society; or, at
least, could be put to service in the various projects to which the
party dedicated itself in the thirties. But as his own songs—"This
Land Is Your Land," "Pastures of Plenty," "Ramblin' Round,"
"Hard Travelin'" and many others—suggest, Guthrie's vision
was closer to Whitman than to Alfred Hayes, "an intoxication,"
wrote Robert Shelton, "with the richness and the breadth, the
variety and the promise of the American soil and character."[18]

Like Whitman, a literary man who liked to represent himself
as a carpenter, Guthrie glorified work and the working man; but
his own persona, that of the hard traveler who has ridden the
rails, worked the hard-rock mines, the wheat harvest, and the
steel mills, and spent ninety days in jail for vagrancy, is at one
with what he experiences and yet entirely aloof, "amused, com-
placent, compassionating, idle, unitary"; his vision is of a shining
open road, of a green and welcoming transcontinental paradise,
of a solitary wanderer with a knapsack moving on, as Whitman
wrote—

> Failing to fetch me at first keep encouraged,
> Missing me one place search another,
> I stop somewhere waiting for you.

—a singular man who, as his mythmakers understood, made up
his early bereavement and exile (in Whitman's case very likely
the issue of his sexual orientation) by the kind of universal love
that belongs to those who most long to be embraced by the life
denied to them.

Whereas the leftist program was essentially secular and historical, grounded in economic theory and tending toward more
or less radical reform, Guthrie's vision—or, rather, the vision

around which he and the other cultural seekers and idealists converged—was essentially pastoral and mythical, echoing Christian eschatology and rooted in the Gospel according to Matthew. Guthrie's extended "Ballad of Tom Joad" suggests the broad outlines of that vision: the pathway of redemption through suffering, secured by the ever receding, but ever visible, horizon of a glorified land, green pastures, fertile valleys, and fields of waving grain, which it is the destiny of the meek to inherit. In "Ramblin' Round," Guthrie's verses capture the ambiguity:

> The peach trees they are loaded
> The branches are bending down;
> I pick 'em all day for a dollar, boys,
> As I go ramblin' round . . .
>
> Sometimes the fruit gets rotten
> Falls down on the ground;
> There's a hungry mouth for every peach
> As I go ramblin' round.

This is at once a fecund and beautiful earth, heavy with its own fruit, and a world of hunger and want marked, like a Farm Relief Administration photograph, by the sorrowful faces of children. But no image of greedy grower-capitalist or bloated boss appears to arouse revolutionary anger; instead the solitary wanderer or refugee passes by to remark a condition that, even as it points to a specific injustice among the migrant workers of California, also suggests its place on the continuum of a universal human condition—a tradition more driven by compassion for the hungry and poor than by anger at the rich, which always carries traces of class resentment.

This strain of popular idealism, which Guthrie and Hays at a deeper level than their own adoptive politics embody, though its imagery is familiar in mid-nineteenth-century Protestant hymnody and though we often associate it with folksong, is in fact rare in folksong. It is far more an aspect of thirties popular culture, where the "ribbon of highway" and "endless skyway" owe much to Firestone Tires, Pan American Airways, and *Life* magazine, during a period when America's celebration of itself could include, without contradiction, its technological and commercial monuments, especially considered as the accumulated labor of its worker-armies, and a revolutionary thrust against the class that administered these projects, as if the massive organizational, managerial, and technical problems posed by highways, railroads, bridges, and dams did not demand corporate and financial coteries to plan and carry them out.

It is perhaps absurd to ascribe deeply religious motives to two incorrigible backsliders like Guthrie and Hays, drinking, smoking, womanizing, footloose young men promulgating a godless doctrine—certainly they themselves would have rejected the notion—but we are looking here at people who stand at a particular intersection of region, religion, and social class. That leftist politics may lend itself to certain aspects of the Christian Gospel, a "Christian socialism," need hardly be noted again. Ethnically, temperamentally, and artistically, Guthrie embodied the pragmatically egalitarian intermountain west, where such social distinctions as obtained along the east coast never really took hold, where the social spectrum in spite of vivid extremes of wealth and poverty remained comparatively narrow, where an old frontier Protestantism with evangelical roots, simple, plainspoken, generally unprepossessing, governed the moral imagination of even the most rapacious ranchers, oilmen, and land speculators.

As Guthrie remarked, the Almanac Singers were "the only group that rehearsed on stage." Beyond the protean topicality of their repertory, the class and ethnic traditions embodied in its members, the real meaning of the Almanacs lay in the social and musical space they opened for themselves in American popular music, the very space that the postwar revival would appropriate and enlarge. The Almanacs were incomparable. They were not pop singers, not ethnic singers, not quite hillbilly singers, though they would perhaps have been pleased to persuade some in their audience that they were. They did not perform in costume, either of the concert stage or of the radio barndance; and yet their street clothes, in which they ordinarily appeared, ranged from pieces of business suits in various permutations and combinations to dungarees, workshirts, and construction boots.

What the customary emphasis on the Almanacs' topicality neglects is that more than any urban folksingers before them, and more than many popular groups after them, they were able in their idiom, diction, vocality, phrasing, harmony, instrumentation, and especially their rhythm to capture authentic elements of the southern folk sound. The Almanacs were good. Through them young urban audiences were for the first time being exposed to the music with which the singers were familiar and which they could bring to the group—blues, hillbilly, mountain music, southern Methodist hymns. Guthrie's later participation only heightened this effect, while the accompaniment of Josh White's blues guitar on their Keynote recordings, alongside Seeger's eclectic banjo style that, with a combination of strumming and picking, evoked both jazz and frontier idioms, produced an ensemble sound not substantially different from, say, that of the Memphis Jug Band. One wonders what his audiences thought he was doing when in "C for Conscription," taking off on Jimmie Rodgers' "T for Texas," Seeger yodeled as forlornly as the Singing Brakeman himself.[19]

The very identity of the Almanacs was elusive. Pete Seeger, Lee Hays, Peter Hawes, and Millard Lampell formed a core, along with Bess Lomax and Woody Guthrie; after them came Baldwin "Butch" Hawes, Pete's younger brother, art teacher Arthur Stern, and, following Hays from Commonwealth, western labor activists Gordon Friesen and Sis Cunningham. Various houseguests occasionally sang along, with an errant unidentified voice from time to time finding its way onto a recording. Other singers participated who would later be celebrated in their own right, including Brownie McGhee and Sonny Terry, Leadbelly, and Geer's friend, the former actor

Cisco Houston. Discographers would seek in vain to disentangle the identities of these singers and composers, in the face of their stated policy, common in left-wing arts groups, to avoid individual attribution.[20]

This informal mixing actually resulted in several Almanac groups, sometimes answering different bookings simultaneously on a given night. By June 1942 a more rigorously rehearsed and disciplined band of Almanacs—Bess Lomax, Arthur Stern, Butch Hawes, and Charlie Polacheck—were enjoying a success that rivaled that of the original group, having moved to Detroit after a performance at the UAW's war rally in Cadillac Square. Union strength in the midwest was at a peak, so that among UAW locals, International Workers' Order affiliates, war-relief and other functions, including the UAW national convention in Chicago, these new Almanac Singers played over a hundred bookings within five months. The New York Almanacs were in the meantime disbanding. Seeger was drafted in July; Lampell withdrew to radio work before signing up himself; Houston, Hawes, and Guthrie all joined the merchant marine.

The mingling of these voices, in New York, San Francisco, or Detroit, produced a social image unknown before, at least in popular entertainment—though one might perhaps have found something like it among amateurs, in outing clubs, folksong and dance societies, and so on. None was a trained singer. Accents, phrasing, vocal timbre, and range, all mixed, both among the singers and within each individually, with a disarmingly unprofessional heterogeneity that drew on a number of flatly incompatible traditions. Seeger's voice alone was a network of contradictions: a lower Hudson Valley accent delivered in the tones of a schoolmaster affecting the idiom of a ranch hand with overtones of the Broadway stage. Lee Hays's stentorian enunciation smacked of the Methodist pulpit, through a kind of asthmatic fog, in the accent of the Mississippi Valley socially at the lower edge of respectability, but with vowels rounded by the reading of very grave and profound books. Millard Lampell, though projecting bravely, could not entirely put aside the galvanized consonants and elastic vowels of working-class New Jersey, nor could Cisco Houston fail to resonate like some smooth radio crooner singing the praises of a brand of cigarette or chewing gum.

Bess Lomax's bright, youthful, unmodulated voice would have been at home with piano accompaniment in a Bryn Mawr music room—but it was textured with the Texas wheatchaff that still sounded in her sibilants, as well as the little whimpering line ends inherited from genuine mountain ballad singing. The group's only real country singer could from time to time raise his reedy, drawling, but not particularly powerful voice above the cacophony, though his contribution was no more marked than the others'. Seeger's banjo stood out consistently as a kind of marker, at a technical level that rose and fell unpredictably, while Woody's guitar, with no more resonance in it than a steamer trunk, stiffly executed simple bass runs against a set of congested, shrubby chords. A mandolin tinkled, and even a fiddle squeaked occasionally. Plentiful but, it seemed, entirely spontaneous and uncoordinated harmonies and vocal decorations mingled, crossed, and wove around one another with an almost jazz-like improvisatory ease.

The Almanacs brought to their performances what Michael Rogin calls the "alternative, polyglot world" of New York's entertainment culture, "in which the children of Jewish immigrants found new cosmopolitan identities among Jews, other immigrants, children of old-stock Americans . . . and African-Americans as well."[21] This was the sound of their way of life: fanatically democratic, virtually unregulated, youthful, collective, and, like their stage of life itself, temporary. As a *People's World* reporter described it, each member in the process of composition would contribute lines and suggestions as Lampell pounded them out on a typewriter, occasionally joining together to sing a completed verse or two. Musical phrases from guitar or banjo would shape the evolving melody—until Woody, perhaps, would suddenly leap to his feet with a fully formed verse. After about an hour's work, they would all sing the completed song. Vivid social distinctions remained alive in the variety of vocalities even as they became meaningless in the common effort. An FBI agent who saw the Almanacs at a longshoremen's meeting in San Francisco called them "extremely untidy, ragged, and dirty in appearance," and claimed that the union's enthusiastic participation in a sing-along had been involuntary, the effect of some sinister "mass psychology."[22]

Mass psychology, indeed: the Almanacs were altering the conventional relation between performer and audience in a nascent social sphere. The group's informality and conscientious nonprofessionalism opened to the audience a new sense of access, as Guthrie noted, as if normally offstage operations had been opened to view, the entire performance space being redefined to bring audience and musicians together into active participation. It was a music of symbolic social leveling but not, as the federal agent supposed, one of social control. Quite the contrary: the audience had in effect been invited to one of the Almanacs singing hootenannies or rent parties, where people often widely divergent socially—upper class and working class, Jewish and gentile, black and white, easterner, southerner, and westerner—put these distinctions aside in a spirit of festive mutuality in a space apart from the quotidian world of social mistrust, suspicion, resentment, and conflict. This was a manifestly *popular* or people's music, at least in the collective enactment of it, one apparently free from the manipulations belonging to music in the commercial marketplace.

The group's urban audiences must have imagined—for what but imagination could resolve the band's confusing auditory and visual message?—that the Almanacs were somehow folk or hillbilly singers; "lanky" Pete Bowers and wiry Woody Guthrie would have helped to confirm the impression, even as Hays, Lampell, and the others might have disconfirmed it. At the same time, their music was emphatically not what was heard in the late thirties under that rubric, a mix of western swing and mountain stringbands, singing cowboys and country crooners, and the characteristic nasality of hillbilly singers. Indeed, though they would perhaps have wished it otherwise, the Almanacs would have been utterly out of place in the typical venues of hillbilly music—the morning radio shows, the barndances, the schoolhouses, athletic parks, country fairs, and jamborees on the rural circuit.

This gulf, between regional, rural, largely Anglo-American and Afro-American traditions and the urban ethnic working class, all idealism notwithstanding, was until the early sixties largely impassable; to that point only the Lomaxes had attempted to bridge it, with carefully managed emblematic figures whose legitimacy had already been established among artists, writers, and folksong enthusiasts for whom the distinction between the song and the singer might be abolished—indeed it was to these groups, not to the urban working class, that the Lomaxes addressed their programs.

It is interesting, then, to consider just what "folksong" had become in the Almanacs. Others were performing folksongs in public in 1940 and 1941: Elie Siegmeister's American Ballad Singers, John and Lucy Allison, Bill Bender, Burl Ives, Frank Luther, John Jacob Niles, Carl Sandburg, Tom Scott, Andrew Rowan Summers—a list showing that folksong, its retrieval, publication, and performance, had been almost exclusively the preserve of an academic, literary, and political elite. Indeed, the very concept of the folk belonged to an urban bourgeois culture whose roots were in nineteenth-century antiquarianism, romanticism, and nationalism. Folksong was a thing found mostly in books, whether it was a scholarly collection, a school text used for singing, or a campfire songbook. But the Lomax field collections had begun to thaw this freeze, and in 1941 both John and Alan Lomax released important new collections of field materials: Alan's edited from the Lomax collections in the Library of Congress and John's *Smokey Mountain Ballads* from

RCA's library of 1930s commercial hillbilly music. Still, few people actually knew folksongs in any meaningful sociological sense—at least not the repertory represented as folksong in the scholarly and popular texts.

The very textualization of folksong in the familiar forms demanded secure and inviolable social distances that the pioneers of the period had begun to explore. The most important instrument in this effort was the automobile—the Almanacs traveled in a '31 Buick—and after it the portable recording machine. The Lomaxes' collecting trips would have been unthinkable without them; the automobile figures again and again in the extraordinary contacts achieved in this period between urban impresarios and their isolated informants—only think, again, of John Hammond in his Hudson Terraplane listening to Robert Johnson on the car radio from a nearby station, or of Charles Seeger's trips to Asheville and White Top, indeed of Guthrie's and Pete Seeger's own cross-country ramblings, similarly accompanied.

With the radio and the photomagazine dominating popular culture, the music and the face of rural life had become a permanent element in the urban imagination, which in turn worked its own political and aesthetic transformations in order to bring them into conformity with prevailing modernist attitudes. It might be pertinent to ask why the vigorous entrepreneurial activity of the sixties revival, which brought many traditional singers out of their obscurity and isolation to university and commercial concert stages, had not begun earlier. Actually it *had* begun, with the Dreiser committee and the Lomaxes—or perhaps I should say, it continued, as venerable rural traditions, such as the minstrel and medicine shows, reached in new forms into the urban intellectual communities under the influence of the Popular Front. But for a variety of reasons, most of them quite practical, the traffic during this period flowed in the other direction. While avenues of transportation had opened up to the handful who thought to take advantage of it, very little in the way of an urban market for living traditional performers had emerged. It would not be until the early sixties that the Harry Smith collection, and other pre-depression commercial recordings, would emerge both to form the repertories of revivalists and to identify the traditional bearers of them still living in the south or in northern industrial cities.

Finally, the integrity of the performers themselves deserved respect; surely among thoughtful people, and perhaps among the Almanacs themselves, there had been some uneasiness about the sheer fact of Leadbelly's or Aunt Molly Jackson's or even Woody Guthrie's presence in New York, and about their appropriation by the left-wing community; surely there were some who saw exploitation in it, of the same old kind, along class and racial lines.

But there was another way to bring the living performer—"the people"—to the urban audience, and that was through impersonation. As Joe Klein reports, the Almanac Singers invented proletarian backgrounds for themselves, adopted a kind of method actor's version of a southern accent, one made of linguistic markers such as "you-alls" and "I reckons," rejected makeup, and dressed in what amounted to a theatrical designer's picture of farmers and workers. "There I was," Seeger recalled, "trying my best to shed my Harvard upbringing, scorning to waste money on clothes other than blue jeans. But Leadbelly always had a clean white shirt and starched collar, well-pressed suit and shined shoes. He didn't need to affect that he was a workingman."[23] Seeger's Harvard years slipped into obscurity, and Lampell claimed to come from Kentucky.

As the imaginative gulf between urban and rural, rich and poor, educated and uneducated, began to close—or, to put this more accurately, as *representations* of the exotic, the remote, the provincial, and the poor became more regularly accessible and even familiar—the enabling foundation of the song-as-text began to erode. As Alan Lomax in his wanderings had begun to discern, the folksong could not really be understood as text; it was a *style*, the issue of an entire way of life within a cultural community, and it vividly reflected both the person of the singer, in all her shocking social presence, and the emotional and moral imprint of her tradition on musical values. Nor, certainly, had this lesson been lost on Pete and Bess. Hence the Almanac Singers' deeper project was a personal and transformative one, one that reached into the machinery of personal and social identity—precisely the psychosocial site at which the leftist folksong movement begins to lay the groundwork for the postwar folk revival.

It is by turns endearing and aggravating to observe the urban intellectual left, in or out of the folksong movement, attempting to align itself with what it imagined as the working class or the "Negro." Working people had themselves been radicalized and inherited a radical tradition; and during the New Deal, highly committed political intellectuals had in fact succeeded somewhat in associating themselves, through party and union work, the Civilian Conservation Corps, and other avenues, with the working class. In the main, however, the idealists in the movement had little equipment or occasion for genuinely understanding either working-class or black culture in America, so inadequate were European-derived analytic models for grasping the complex forces that had contributed to the formation of working-class or black consciousness in a consumer economy or in a subculture shaped by the legacies of slavery. The folksingers had instead a grandly idealized picture of southern rural blacks and workers upon which to model themselves; and while recordings of traditional singers were newly available in the scholarly collections, the sources of folksong were still, for the urban revivalist, primarily literary.

Thus the Almanacs were attempting a new synthesis, one that preserved the ideality of the scholarly or recreational folksong as symbol of a shared American civilization and history, but which at the same time was a force for realizing personal identity in terms of that ideality in performance. In the ideological context especially, they were more real than real: as Richard Reuss

observes, Aunt Molly Jackson and Leadbelly, though unquestionably authentic, were ideologically unpredictable, while in
the Almanacs the left had, through impersonation, both embodied folksingers and trustworthy ideological exemplars. Nor was
this effort at realization merely theatrical, as an actor realizes a
character; drawing on the historical sources of America's traditional culture, the folksingers believed, accomplished a kind of
emancipation from received social categories and opened the
possibility of true communication with deeper social reservoirs
of the American character.

In taking folksong out of the library, away from the campfire,
and even in a sense out of the concert hall, and in making it a
way of life, the Almanacs and the movement they embodied had
marked folksong—or, more accurately, the performance of folk
music—as the performance of an actual or putative nonconformity with an implied countercultural program. At Almanac
House, and later in Washington Square and Newport, there was
no shortage of collegiate folksingers, dressed more or less for the
part, concerned to make the desired impression. But the really
admired figures, those in whom singing or playing seemed to be
a spring flowing out of the deepest sources of their moral being,
were those whose lives, by chance or by choice, had strayed off
the beaten track.

The dropout or drifter with the dusty cuffs and the odd name,
vague about his origins, in need of a haircut, appearing and
disappearing like an apparition in the dormitory corridor, never
for more than a week at a time, ostensibly to visit a girlfriend;
the conscientious objector, not following the fashion but driven
to it by his family's Mennonite tradition, doing alternative service in a drug rehabilitation ward; the barefoot girl without
makeup who played guitar, toured Europe on a motorcycle, and
lived with an older man; the brilliant doctoral candidate in
biochemistry, throwing it all over for a rat-infested carpentry
shop in Cambridge's Central Square; the army discharge teaching on a Navajo reservation in Arizona; or, as appeared in the

revival from time to time, the genuine social misfit, whose one chord, cheap guitar, and three songs were somehow more fraught with meaning than a whole volume of ballads—these figures, mostly young men with opportunities for independence that only the most daring young women could enjoy, were not the clichés of counterculturalism they ultimately became, but enigmatic, compelling, and profoundly disquieting figures, the practical or ethical foundations of whose actions remained mostly occult, especially when they lay in the advantages of a trust fund or some other accident of birth. When such characters condensed the moral atmosphere by singing with a guitar or banjo "Corinna, Corinna" or "Wreck of the Old 97," with more than the mere imputation of difference, they implied a new and original realm of existence that the young revivalist might enter.

As the Almanac Singers made clear for the first time, the folk revival was occurring in the interpersonal medium that communicates to perception the connections written into the organization of society—at the point where society's actual construction of its own reality occurs. Beyond their explicit political goals, the Almanacs were drawing on those resources of meaning which modern mass culture had forgotten or repressed. Many motives converged to account for this impulse. Chief among them, I think, was the embarrassment of privilege, the dual effort both of commonizing oneself and of elevating the common people—but of course in one's own terms, which generally did not include bringing them where they most wanted to be, into the consumer middle class. "One would be utterly blind," wrote Moses Soyer, "in these days of race hatred, depression, and the Blue Eagle not to align himself with the class to which he feels he belongs." Artist Rockwell Kent by his own account developed a social inferiority complex that he could redeem "only by becoming a workman myself."[24]

Class aspiration played a role as well, since the actual traffic in folk music was still very much an elite affair, carried out in a socially and ideologically rarefied atmosphere that included private schools, summer camps, youth congresses, and that most interior of inner circles, the party itself. As a way of life, however, it was a liminal realm in which young people, destined ultimately to carry out the responsibilities of privilege, could declare what Erik Erikson long ago called a "psychosocial moratorium" that freed them temporarily from the social imperatives working on them to find new forms in which to assimilate and master those imperatives.

Finally, we must not forget the political, social, and cultural idealism from which the folksong movement drew its energy. Whatever the ideological context, it is clear that to young minds freed by education and parental influence from official sanctimonies, alibis, and allegiances, the world of the depression and world war was not the best of all possible worlds. Something needed to be done and folksong, it seemed, as a symbolic as well as a practical instrument, capable of stirring hearts, of embodying ideals, and of discharging personal and collective motives that might be otherwise frustrated or crushed, was one way of doing it.

The sound of the Almanac Singers, and of the more stylized Weavers after them, would resonate in the waystation democracy of college life, where the young heiress, the plumber's boy, the banker's daughter, the tailor's son, the westerner and easterner and southerner, could enjoy both their own picturesque variety and the fleeting opportunity to experience themselves apart from the social forces that would inevitably, in the adult world, differentiate and estrange them. Operating in a cultural field that could still objectify the American identity and make it available for contemplation, as Moses Asch had contemplated it in John Lomax's *Cowboy Songs,* the Almanacs in a sense stablized and institutionalized folksinging as an instrument for prolonging just that condition, as a symbolic model of the American community visibly and audibly purified of all the bureaucratic, authoritarian, corporate, and commercial elements in American life, and yet somehow linked to the historical mythology that these institutions continued to advance as our founding narrative.

In twenty years or so, the social paradoxes and personal ambivalences that shaped the Almanacs would become pandemic in America among the most richly provisioned young generation in our history, and the model provided by the Almanacs, even as it was being deliberately forgotten, would help to fire a youth revolution, driven not by politics but by America's most powerful cultural engine, commerce, at once its creator and its destroyer.

Session of the House Un-American Activities Committee, 1947, with Richard Nixon looking on from the dais

5

Wasn't That a Time

"The rise of the demagogue," observed the president of Ohio State University in 1935, "is the direct result of radio . . . No silver-haired orator holding forth every night for a year to capacity houses of 10,000 people can be heard by as many people as listen to one local broadcast in a city of 100,000 or more in one evening."[1] If metaphor seeks to literalize itself, it is perhaps possible to predict events on the basis of the tacit comparisons that hold together the discourse of any period about itself. That our ultimate participation in the war in Europe was on the horizon in 1941 was apparent from any newspaper; but the way was prepared for it by the incessant recourse in public language and representation to images of collective, official, standardized, centralized, impersonal, technological, and essentially implacable campaigns against any resistance to the achievement of a state utopia. The standardizing mania of the engineering age had seized the modern imagination, borne on the voices of national leaders emanating like oracles or gods from a fixed center, amplified by radio receivers and loudspeakers where a concomitant narrowing of the frequency spectrum preserved the imprecatory character of political speech while muddying its content. Fascist states in Europe and, after the war, the Soviet Union only reflected the universal historical dream, so that the struggle against them, in the imaginative realm at least, was a struggle against those very forces, invisible to us as the very air of our national existence, that were transforming our own society.

An apotheosis of the divinities of metaphor generated in the New Deal came with the declaration of war, the "machine that kills fascists," realizing itself in a society dedicated to the promulgation of war. But it was the defeat of the enemy without, and the withdrawal of the national projection, that raised the spectre of the enemy within—of an all-powerful administrative and ideational force insinuating itself into the minds of teachers, artists, scientists, intellectuals, and civil servants.

Indeed such a force *was* abroad in American society, not as an extension of the Soviet program of world domination, an expedient object on which to project again the ungovernable fear, but what Herbert Schiller calls "a privately administered world order outside the known international structures" that executed, typically outside ordinary governmental control, the crucial decisions on production, investment, industrial policy, finance, and information. As Schiller explains, American companies hugely enriched by the war established in the twenty years after the war a system of manufacturing, advertising, and public relations throughout the world, assisted by expanding foreign banking interests such as the World Bank and the International Monetary Fund, laying the groundwork of what we now clearly recognize as a "global infrastructure of American-owned production, marketing, distribution and finance."[2]

The daylit historical causes underlying America's postwar turn to the right are many and various. The struggle with the Soviet Union over political spheres of influence, which became, in Frederick Siegel's phrase, a struggle over "the perception of power," released the powerful antipathies to the New Deal that the war had held in check. The "civil religion" of conservative Republicanism was rooted in traditional religious, ethnic, and racial constituencies, installed in education and public ritual, and of course vigorously championed by free-market capitalists. To Catholics, obdurately anti-Soviet, to German-Americans divided in their national loyalties, to businessmen big and small beset by taxes, government, and labor unions, to southern planters and oilmen threatened by the postwar liberalization of racial attitudes and labor policy, the New Deal had been nothing less than a usurpation of government by elites bent on sovietizing the United States.

With the Democratic vote of 1946 weakened by Catholic defections and the remainder split between Progressives and moderates, strongly antisocialist Republicans took control of both houses of Congress for the first time since 1932. Immediately they proposed a program of tax cuts, antilabor laws, and an ideological cleansing of the federal bureaucracy. "The ordinary props and costumes of the national political stage were stripped away," Siegel writes, "to reveal the white-hot anger and unleashed frustrations of nearly twenty years of Republican exile. Acting as much to punish their enemies as to revive true Americanism, the Congress was turned into a living theatre, a psychodrama in which senators and representatives felt free to spin out their wildest fantasies of homosexuality, intrigue, and treason, all of which were said to lay behind the New Deal."[3] Herbert Hoover thought there were 100,000 communists in official positions, and "unseen millions" of American sympathizers.

The atmosphere of national anxiety lingering from the war, addled by fears of depression, unemployment, even, in certain isolationist quarters, fascist revolution, is strongly indicated by the panic that followed the Soviet-backed Czechoslovak coup of 1948; even as sober a commentator as Walter Lippmann seemed to believe that the Russians were poised to march across Europe to the English Channel, and called in effect for a mobilization for war, including a draft, a war powers act, and a declaration of national emergency. To George Kennan, Bolshevism was a "Jewish disease," and the Russians themselves little more than barbarians who, according to Ambassador Averell Harriman, were preparing for an invasion of eastern Europe.

In the postwar period, as every schoolchild knows, the global purposes of the USSR, as well as the nature of Soviet society itself, campaigning to throw off western influences and to resist its economic overtures, had become mysterious, even inscrutable, the foreign policy of both countries drifting into a vague world of suspicion and mistrust in which inference, often irrational, often either politically expedient or purely theoretical, replaced diplomacy, negotiation, and compact.

Indeed, the Soviets' attempts to secure their borders and extend their sphere of influence by police-state tactics resonated forbiddingly not only with legitimate fears but with a resuscitated American isolationism and xenophobia. In 1946 alone, the Russian secret police, espionage agents, or actual army troops arrested sixteen members of the Polish anti-Nazi resistance, murdered a number of nationalist opponents, intervened in Hungarian elections, and, in an effort to attach oil-rich northern Iran to the Soviet Union, allied themselves, in violation of a wartime agreement, to secessionist Kurds. Joseph Stalin pictured a Soviet Union surrounded by hostile monopoly capitalists eager for another war. As the House Un-American Activities Committee turned to "Communist front" organizations, the Canadians arrested twenty-two Soviet atomic spies. Within three years China would fall to Mao, the Russians would test an atomic bomb, and New Dealer Alger Hiss would go on trial for espionage.

In fact both the Czechoslovak coup of 1948 and the Berlin blockade were reactions to what Soviet Ambassador Molotov denounced as an attempt by American capitalists to capture new markets: the European Recovery Program (the Marshall Plan), which the Soviets feared would absorb eastern Europe into the western economy as well as rearm and reindustrialize West Germany. Republicans recognized that such a plan, which proposed a joint reorganization of European economies through a transnational program of American investment, would never have been tolerated at home. Some form of the Marshall Plan, though, was inevitable, since its infrastructure, generated by the political necessity of maintaining the fragile war consensus, was already in place, a system of agreements between Roosevelt and business that had built up the arms industries and produced special legislation favorable to farmers and manufacturers as well as to individual capitalists, replacing New Deal programs and the ideal of social reform generally with what would in time evolve into the engine of a national security state, "the military-industrial complex."

The war had produced in both governments a sense of national insecurity that betrayed them into interpreting, largely for domestic political ends, complex world events exclusively in terms of the other's power or influence. It *was* the case that colonial societies had come to see first Hitler and then Stalin as potential allies against western imperialism. During the bitter European winter of 1947–48, moreover, with crippled economies nearly at a standstill and war-ravaged populations suffering from malnutrition and disease, the Communist Party gained strength, while in Africa, Southeast Asia, Indonesia, and India revolutionary movements were stirring against weakened colonial rulers. Though Stalin had shown himself unwilling to confront the west on behalf of largely independent European communists, Truman saw a "pattern of Soviet imperialism," ultimately picturing in 1947 a Manichean world of darkness and light, of "individual liberty, freedom of speech and religion," on the one hand, and totalitarian systems based on "terror and oppression" on the other. Every nation, he said, "must choose between alternative ways of life."[4]

The Truman doctrine, Siegel notes, "threatened to put the United States in the impossible position of foolishly trying to

hold back the ceaseless waves of rebellion and revolution unleashed by the growth of the world capitalist economy, which
had everywhere shattered traditional societies and left little in
[their] place." Now the United States would have to police the
globe, Walter Lippmann predicted, "recruiting, subsidizing, and
supporting a heterogeneous array of satellites, clients, dependents, and puppets," defending unstable dictatorships in the
name of anticommunism.[5] To this problem, and to the global
involvement and government expansion it posited, the insubor-
dinate General Douglas MacArthur, called back from the 38th
parallel by an indignant President Truman, offered a proposal to
both save the world from communism and America from itself:
nuclear weapons delivered by air.

This is the political tidal wave that washed the left, and the
folksong movement with it, off the field, preparing the ground
for a folk revival in the next generation.

Communists had enjoyed a temporary rehabilitation during
the war, supporting the people's war against fascism by con-
demning overly militant campaigns for black rights or equal
employment, and by supporting the no-strike pledge and soft-
pedaling the rhetoric of class conflict. But the crisis of mid-twen-
tieth-century America was not the war itself but the end of war.
War had produced unity, prosperity, and opportunity; yet little
of this, either during or after the war, flowed significantly into
the labor force, nor had increased opportunity for women and
minorities in the military and defense industries done much to
improve their postwar status. The returning army created an
immediate instability in housing, wages, and race relations,
exacerbating wartime anxieties at a time when the long-awaited
social and economic security seemed on the horizon at last, the
wartime sacrifice having fallen most heavily on ordinary people
while elites in government, education, and science remained
protected. Even within the army there had been, after the
armistice, a left-inspired rebellion against the privileged officer
corps and, among returning soldiers, a debt of resentment

against those who had gained a head start by remaining at home. Sustaining the overheated patriotism of wartime proved expedient after the war both as an expression of class hostility and as a propaganda tool for a military-industrial complex eager to prevent the postcolonial world from breaking away from the world business system into socialist economies.[6]

"The postwar anti-communist consensus," argues Daniel Yergin, "existed first in the center, in the policy elite, before it spread out to the nation."[7] The House Committee on Un-American Activities acquired permanent status in 1945, contributing, along with Truman's loyalty oath for federal employees and the attorney general's list of subversive organizations, to an atmosphere of social and political paranoia. These seem to have been as much political tactics designed to win over the defense-minded Republican Congress on behalf of expensive assistance programs overseas as they were responses to fear of Soviet-directed internal subversion.[8] Truman's personal position is unclear; publicly he declared the threat of internal subversion a "red herring"—but confided to his diary that "Reds, phonies and the 'parlor pinks,'" among whom he included the actors and artists in "immoral" Greenwich Village, "seem to be banded together and are becoming a national danger."[9]

As Frank Kofsky has suggested, the Truman administration's reaction to the Czechoslovak coup, raising the spectre of war with the Russians in western Europe, however otherwise motivated, also promised to revive a flagging domestic aircraft industry. The threat, in any case, disarmed congressional and popular resistance to a renewed military buildup.[10] Churchill's "iron curtain" image of March 1946, finally, brilliantly distilling fifty years of wartime propaganda and converting, in a stroke, the utopianism of the thirties into the Orwellian nightmare of the fifties, came to dominate the popular imagination and to shape both popular and official thinking about geopolitical organization.

The purge touched every level of society. Robbie Lieberman writes:

> Local, state, and federal legislation and committees, as well as self-appointed vigilantes, harassed individuals, groups, and institutions. People were fired from their jobs; discriminated against in housing, social security, and unemployment benefits; and deported. Such actions were justified on the basis of past membership in subversive organizations, guilt by association, reliance on the Fifth Amendment, and refusal to cooperate with congressional committees. Whatever genuine crisis existed was translated into a nationwide sense of crisis in the form of widespread anticommunism.[11]

"Anyone who'd ever joined a committee against racism," Joe Klein recalls, "anyone who'd supported the 'wrong' side in the Spanish Civil War, anyone who could be called a 'premature anti-fascist,' anyone who seemed suspiciously idealistic, one-worldly, permissive, well read, or immune to the lures of materialism, was suspect."[12] The fanatical anticommunist (and ex-communist) Whittaker Chambers unwittingly betrayed what lay at the heart of the crusade when he noted "the jagged fissure, which it did not so much open as reveal, between the plain men and women of the nation, and those who affected to act, think, and speak for them. It was, not invariably, but in general, the 'best people' who were for Alger Hiss." No matter that Senator McCarthy and other anticommunist crusaders were financed by Texas oil and other Big Money; they drew enormous support from working-class Catholics and Protestant midwesterners hostile to the eastern establishment. For "it was not the less fortunate . . . who have been selling this nation out," McCarthy warned, "but rather those who have had all the benefits."[13]

As incredible—the McCarran Act actually specified detention camps for leftists—as the period to which McCarthy has lent his name may seem in retrospect, it is perhaps now that its authentic structures become more visible to us. Racism, xenophobia, antisemitism, anti-intellectualism, and class resentment have a long history in America, as does their exploitation by powerful political and corporate interests. In the fifties these chronic parochialisms swept in, exacerbated by broader fears of what Elaine Tyler May calls the "new secularism, bureaucratic collectivism, and consumerism,"[14] to lend names and faces to the communist phantom and to excite a deeper hatred of it. World war had demanded acquiescence in its profound economic, social, and political dislocations and conformity to the ideology that justified them; the cold war and its mythology, which installed the wartime reorganization as a permanent structure, infused American society with a pervasive sense of collective and personal insecurity and helplessness, indeed of imminent danger, under a huge, vague, vacillating, and remote power. This pervasive insecurity necessarily produced a reaction, not against the mythology itself or its fabulists, since these had already been ideologically immunized against criticism, but against an imaginary communism that directly symbolized the strange insidious force, official, propagandistic, totalitarian, afoot in society at home.

But the anticommunism of the postwar period differed from its historical antecedents in several respects. Fear of anarchism and Bolshevism has of course rattled the ownership classes since the massive industrialization of the post-Civil War era. Populism, moreover, has always had two faces, represented during the depression by the Popular Front, on the one hand, and on the other by resurgent anticommunism, anti-Catholicism, and antisemitism, which are really strains of an entrenched popular fear and resentment of authoritarian systems, urban cultural elites, foreigners, and intellectuals.

Postwar anticommunism was institutionalized and, in Schiller's phrase, "legislated into daily life," as the fear of internal subversion became identified both with domestic communist agents and with the nation's shadowy mirror image, the Soviet Union. As May argues, the foreign-policy concept of containment was projected psychologically into domestic politics and even into family and personal life, tying the so-called national security, now more a "perception, a state of mind" than a formulated policy, to a new posture of permanent alert that read subversion into almost any form of deviance, but especially deviance from the emergent political, commercial, sexual, and family norms.[15] Those who dissented from anti-Soviet foreign policy and rose to the defense of labor and consumer groups, and ultimately anyone who did not conform to a widely promulgated picture of American middle-class life, all were suspect.

From the officially constructed Soviet threat, many interests benefited. American corporations on foreign soil were protected by a global network of military bases, which provided a huge protected market for American industry as well. Schiller writes:

> The vast military shopping list, underwritten by unstinting congressional appropriations, meant that aircraft, shipbuilding, electrical equipment, automotive, and, most consequently for the long-term, the new information industries had a ready buyer: the Pentagon. The new information technologies—computers, satellites, and a growing number of electronic marvels—owed their existence to military interest and support. This high-technology sector became the main hope of achieving ultimate military superiority over the Russians and providing an edge to the American economy, hopefully enabling it to maintain a global position of authority into the twenty-first century.[16]

Anticommunism eventually appropriated the labor movement along with many other forms of social and cultural dissent, and at the same time provided an object for genuine anxieties arising not only from Soviet political interventions, the missile buildup, or the spread of anticolonial revolution in the Third World, but from the material alterations in the structure of American daily life evolving precisely from the industrial expansion that Schiller describes. What the consequences were for the immediate postwar generation I will take up later; suffice it to say here that the national dread of subversion by alien ideas and forces, the vague sense of conspiracy in high places, and the general erosion of a sense of public and personal security were all abundantly justified by developments within American society at home, not the least of which was the cold-war mythology itself. The official and unofficial stifling of dissent, the sharp narrowing of the permissible range of political difference, the utter starvation of political and cultural discourse, and the conviction of a growing nuclear threat were its immediate effects.

But these were simply a political expression of the displacement of our massive wartime mobilization onto the interests that had conducted the war—manufacturing and information industries whose collective enterprise for the first time became a social and cultural standard to which all Americans were obliged, largely because of the social pressures lingering from the war, to conform. Moses Asch understood the development in terms of the impact of mass culture on personal identity:

> Just at the time the United States became conscious of being a homogeneous people . . . "Americans"—and we discovered our musical heritage, our folksong and music, technical changes, such as mass communication through the radio, television, movies and the phono-record, made all of us behave according to the pattern set by these media. An American became an "average man." He dressed, acted, wanted and behaved in the image of what the advertiser and manufacturer and song plugger said was "normal."[17]

In the 1950s, American neighborhood and community life became fields of industrial production, distribution, and consumption. No longer regional but national in scope, with new commodity, consumer, information, and entertainment markets opening in the suburbias, the wartime capitalist economy had become the peacetime public culture, like war itself strangely delocalizing, depersonalizing, propagandistic, and above all emanating from agents hidden out of sight in committee rooms, boardrooms, and executive offices. The war had raised the task of purchasing, especially as it belonged to the new suburban woman, to a patriotic level; consumerism had become the index of the international contest, of the superiority of the American way of life. "As a normal part of life," William H. White commented in 1956, "thrift is now un-American."[18] Participation in the market, whose promise had driven the expansion of the American economy until the crash in 1929, had a peculiar new imperative attached to it, as if the very survival of the social order were at stake. No longer was it an appeal, a seduction; it had become compulsory.

In 1946 Harry Truman asked for the resignation of the last New Dealer in his cabinet, Secretary of Commerce and former Vice-President Henry A. Wallace: in a speech at Madison Square Garden, while acknowledging the authoritarian character of the Soviet government, Wallace had argued for peaceful coexistence and cooperation with the Soviet Union. A true child of the thirties, Wallace flew in the face of Henry Luce's "American century" and called for the "century of the common man." But his claim to the Roosevelt legacy was partly countered by Truman's shift to the left on domestic issues—Truman's Fair Deal after all, which the new Congress tried to block, called for full employment, an end to racial discrimination, an increased minimum wage, extended social-security benefits, price and rent controls, public housing, and even universal health insurance. While Wallace's Progressive Party stood for racial integration and an end to the draft, and against the denial of civil liberties to party members and front organizations, the New Deal constituency had largely dissolved into the relative prosperity of the late forties. More significantly, the Progressive Party's position toward the Soviet Union, echoing the bewilderments of 1939, was undermined not only by Czechoslovakia and Berlin but by Stalin's 1946 prediction at the Soviet party congress of war against the capitalist west.

In spite of these inauspicious signs, the Progressive Party, one member recalled, "seemed like a historic fulfillment, an independent Farmer-Labor party, the authentic American form of the People's Front that would unite the majority against imperialism and war and serve as a transitional stage in the march toward socialism." Most important for us, though, is the fact that the Progressive Party created what Lieberman calls "the most dramatic alliance of folk music and electoral politics in American history."[19]

On the last day of 1945, Pete Seeger met in his Greenwich Village basement with some thirty folksingers, choral directors, and union education officials, including Lee Hays, Millard Lampell, and Woody Guthrie, to found People's Songs, an organization dedicated to the dissemination of folksongs that, as an early recruiting document put it, "talk about life as it really is." People's Songs was the first group in the folksong movement to appeal to a generation of young enthusiasts who had been raised on folk music in left-wing urban homes and were exposed to the discourse and imagery surrounding it in communist and left-wing summer camps.

People's Songs collected folksongs, published a monthly bulletin as well as songbooks, songsheets, filmstrips, and records, taught classes in political action, organized concert tours and hootenannies. Leonard Bernstein called its *Song Book* "a long awaited record of a kind of American folk music which should long ago have entered the consciousness of the American people."[20] The organization was conscientiously inclusive and egalitarian, welcoming jazz aficionados as well as members of workers' choruses, classically trained musicians, and even popular composers such as the lyricist for *The Wizard of Oz* and *Finian's Rainbow*, E. Y. "Yip" Harburg. In the immediate postwar period, and especially under the influence of the Progressive Party, the atmosphere recalled the days of the Popular Front, when unions, communists, socialists, and progressives hired folksingers for their meetings and social functions. In two years People's Songs had established a booking agency and opened branch offices in San Francisco, Los Angeles, Chicago, and Boston, spreading the hootenanny to colleges, labor unions, and private gatherings.[21]

Music in the Wallace drive for the presidency in 1948, under the direction of Alan Lomax, lent it the character of a religious revival, sending out folksingers on soundtrucks to rallies and placing the mass singing that would later become the hallmark of every Pete Seeger concert at the heart of the campaign. People's Songs booked singers for meetings, arranged campaign tours for musicians, and in Cleveland even became the party's organizing base. Paul Robeson and Pete Seeger led the singing at the Philadelphia convention and later the 30,000 attendees at the rally for the newly nominated candidate, with whom they later traveled, drawing impressive crowds. Young folksingers were inspired and exhilarated but, like their counterparts in the sixties, also confused to find that their beloved candidate and what he stood for did not enjoy universal approbation or that, in spite of the enthusiasm they aroused at campaign rallies, clever campaign songs composed to folk and popular melodies would not necessarily win voters to the Progressive cause. Birmingham Sheriff Bull Connor, later infamous for firehosing Martin Luther King's nonviolent army of students and children marching for desegregation and employment, arrested Wallace's vice-presidential running mate, Glenn Taylor, for addressing a group of black supporters, while Wallace himself was pelted with eggs and his campaign workers were jeered, beaten, and even knifed.

After the failure of the Wallace campaign, several notable folksingers, including Burl Ives, Josh White, and Oscar Brand, repudiated the left. People's Songs disbanded in 1949, but not without contributing to the folk revival a song by Lee Hays and Walter Lowenfels, "Wasn't That a Time"—"a time to try the soul of man . . . Wasn't that a terrible time?"—which captured the idealism of the campaign, linking it to Valley Forge and Gettysburg.

Its successor organization, the booking agency People's Artists, quickly encountered the menacing national mood in Peekskill, New York, where local vigilantes recruited from veterans' groups and the Klan broke up a Paul Robeson concert under People's Artists sponsorship in support of party leaders on trial at Foley Square; after the successful execution of a rescheduled show on Labor Day, a mob with the complicity of the police stoned the cars and buses of the departing audience.[22]

This foul mixture of race and class hatred and impotent rage heated by inflation, housing shortages, and unemployment marked a fault in the bedrock of American society, opening upon a deeper and more sinister gulf that in our own time has not only distorted the political process but seems to be dissolving the social fabric itself with toxic inundations of hate, resentment, and bigotry. Peekskill looks forward to the lines of newly deputized uniformed state troopers at Newport shouting racial and sexual epithets at scandalized young folkies who could scarcely fathom how they had offended, and drove them from the beaches with kicks and billyclubs; it anticipates the teargas and firehoses in Birmingham, the nightsticks in Chicago; Peekskill echoes today outside abortion clinics, on talk radio, on ghetto streets, and in Congress, like a moral acid eating away at the tacit social agreements once relied on to give a modicum of civility to political speech, to restrain legislative rivalries, and to sustain in public discourse a sense of civic, moral, and historical responsibility. The abiding divisions along the lines of class, race, religion, and gender continue to situate our antagonisms and define our conflicts; but the extensive strife on the social surface, and the angry, brutal, and dishonest language that accompanies it, is useful in distracting our attention away from the polarizing engine at the core of society that drives our political culture.

World War II was a watershed in American history, a great wall built across the continuities that sustain any multiplex society in the reconciliation of its varied purposes. But, as I have emphasized, the war machine, like the Pentagon building that never became the veterans' hospital it was designed to become, was not dismantled; the web of industrial production and Pentagon procurement, the extensive worldwide military installations, production facilities, labor supplies and markets, intelligence operations, and most important the interpenetration of corporate and government agencies in the forties all persist to this day in a kind of sustained national emergency whose overriding interest, everywhere embodied in public discourse, absent a cold war or some other politically expedient object, is nothing more or less than the continuing expansion, at whatever social, cultural, and environmental cost, of itself.

Business has always been effectively in the saddle in America; as many European commentators from Alexis de Tocqueville to Alan Trachtenberg have remarked, America from the beginning has seemed more like a commercial opportunity, organized along military lines, than a political experiment. "All of warfare and its breathless audacity," wrote one nineteenth-century French observer, Paul Bourget, lay behind "the enterprises of this country."[23] Yet even the most unapologetic free-market capitalist of the late nineteenth century, as James Gilbert has suggested, worked within a developed antebellum cultural and moral vision shaped by the Protestant utopianism of the Great Awakening;[24] the failure of that vision to humanize the industrial workplace gave life to the labor movement and to a range of progressive reforms. But the victory in 1945, and the sudden withdrawal of a unitary object from the vast machinery fashioned to win it, stripped the old business community of its traditional social, civic, and cultural roles, which had derived from its embeddedness in historical, regional, familial, and other culturally informing contexts, turning it collectively to the single aim of self-preservation. The way was now open for a rationalized profitmaking system, in which scientific management and Fordism, with an assist from the postwar shift to automobile and air transportation, microwave communications, and finally computerization, would give way to the organization man and then to what Robert Reich calls the "symbolic analyst," while the industrial proletariat gave way to an urban underclass.

Eisenhower himself exemplified the new managerial class of social engineers that controlled the great postwar bureaucracies; his cabinet of Protestant businessmen included midwesterners George Humphrey, president of National Steel, and Charles Wilson, president of General Motors, who made the remark that popularly became "What's good for General Motors is good for the country"—after all, Americans had spent by 1955 fully a fifth of the value of the gross national product on automobiles.

By that year fifty corporations accounted for fully one quarter of the gross national product, with 3 percent belonging to GM alone; Chrysler, General Electric, Goodyear, and Westinghouse devoted the bulk of their advertising budgets to sustaining production of military weapons under Pentagon contracts, linking the defense budget to technical superiority and domestic prosperity. During the Eisenhower years, the volume of military business exceeded the total profits of all private enterprise. In California, especially the Los Angeles area, cultural fountainhead of the postwar suburban way of life, military spending incredibly accounted for almost 60 percent of all gainful employment.[25]

The extent of corporate power, as well as the ideological linkage of commodity and military production, is amply illustrated by the Federal Highway Act of 1956, supported by auto, tire, glass, steel, and concrete manufacturers, oil refiners, and construction companies, which effectively eliminated public transportation, hastened the decay of the old industrial cities, and underwrote suburban expansion as, among other rationales, dispersal against atomic attack. The government, observed Paul Hoffman of Studebaker Motors, was simply the nation's largest business and should be run like any other giant corporation. Frederick Siegel observes:

> In a sense, then, the economy had been socialized into private hands. A fairly small group of businessmen now made private decisions that determined a good deal of the economic and public life of the country.

> Big businessmen, like their socialist critics, recognized that the distinctions between private choices and public policy, business and politics, no longer made any sense.[26]

In short, the war had won us—and we live with the result. Domestically the exponential expansion of American corporate power has increasingly atomized, privatized, depoliticized, and detraditionalized American society, bafflingly narrowing the scope of collective decisionmaking in all spheres. The framing of opinion and debate according to traditional alliances, constituencies, and memberships, expressed historically in religious affiliation, ethnic identity, regional economic interest, class or educational status, or some other discriminating factor, structures that were sufficient to explain American political history well into the 1930s, had by the end of the war largely broken down, confronting Americans with a featureless new social landscape ready to be reflected in schools, government, religion, and entertainment, along the lines of a cold-war mythology, in the process transforming the word and concept of "communism" from a category of political philosophy, and an ineffectual fringe party, into a demonology embracing literally everything that ordinary Americans could be told to fear and hate—social nonconformity, homosexuality, the black race, its music, Jews, immigrants, science, education, and even the group upon whom all the blessings of the American marketplace were to fall—their own children.

The centrality and singularity of communism as a controlling myth in the 1950s should suggest to us how that period, superficially so different, in fact laid the foundation of our own. With vested interests holding hostage the core agendas of both liberals and conservatives, legislators mired in private obligation and thrust into a pseudo-environment of professional lobbies, corporate-funded studies, and "grassroots" movements, their insulation from public scrutiny stripped away by new electronic modes of access and surveillance, the deliberative processes of government effectively grind to a halt.[27] Our collective debates, once embedded in specific historical discourses and communities, have crystallized around an incoherent set of specific social, economic, and moral flashpoints most negotiable in the political marketplace: matters of personal conduct and sexual orientation, family and sexual relations, the rearing, nurture, and education of children, broader community, workplace, and professional relations, and perhaps most egregiously the very dreams, ideals, and values that once anchored those spheres.

In the 1990s there is no longer one issue around which both the electorate and the consumerate can be influenced and manipulated, but many, their polarizing power arising from the deracinated character of the issues themselves. Much has been made of the role of communication technology in producing what James Davison Hunter has called the "culture wars"; in fact, however, the reduction of public discourse to campaign soundbites, of foreign-policy adventures to political advertisements, of corporate rapacity to a total environment of mind and eye, is not a cause but yet another effect of the transformation of America's public and private institutions into implements of business, to the exclusion of every other modulating claim. And, as the language of the New Deal predicted the mobilization for war, so does the language of our own period, with its pervasive cost accounting, market research, management science, public relations, advertising, and other corporate discourses, betray the penetration of the for-profit model into government, education, science, and health care, and the vitiating logics of Wall Street into areas of cultural production such as book and newspaper publishing, movies, radio and television, sports, and food, as innumerable small manufacturers and retailers, their products, services, and sites long installed in our material culture, fall to huge conglomerates.

Nothing, finally, more vividly reveals the sociopolitical imperialism of the postwar corporation than its regular appropriation of countercultural agendas, from self-actualization to communalism to "empowerment," "diversity," and "multiculturalism," to promote the aim of higher productivity. John Locke's social contract, it seems, is at last about to realize itself not as a metaphor for liberal government—only, apparently, an intermediate stage—but in the literal form of the trading companies that were the source of the idea.[28]

It is essential to place anticommunism in the context of the postmodern spectacle in order to understand the transformation of the folksong movement from a herald of millennial change into what Pete Seeger was to call guerrilla warfare against the domination of American life by the conjoined corporations, the military, and the government. From this vantage point the otherwise short-lived postwar folk revival looks quite different even than it did ten years ago. The repression that descended on the folksingers of People's Songs and on the left generally should perhaps be seen now at the cultural level, where the polarizing engine in American society, dividing the historical culture—"life as it really is"—from the spartanized, mobilized corporate society, began its work in the psychosocial zone that separated the wartime and the postwar generations. A new youth movement would arise that took it upon itself to sustain the historical culture that more mature men and women, the parent generation, had abandoned in depression and war.

"Generation gap" is of course only a journalistic formula, since the social and cultural boundary it designates was not inherently generational but instead historical, a conflict between demographic cohorts that had coalesced around the widely shared experiences, preoccupations, and issues of pre- and postwar America. But the metaphor effectively locates what had become by the early sixties a struggle, dramatically embodied in the youth movement of the period, for the imaginative legacy of an entire society, a struggle in which the folk revival, only a friendly overture at first, became the opening salvo.

By the mid-1960s that struggle had taken on a strikingly bipolar character, as the young had come to represent a massive human resource over which two huge interests, the corporate marketplace and the war machine, represented on the one hand by the Beatles and on the other by Lyndon Johnson, were in open competition. We think, conveniently, of the advent of the Beatles as the beginning of the end of the folk revival; quite so—because the Beatles, with their veneer of counterculturalism, drew the power of social and political resistance away from various folk-based alternative musics and from the subcultural economy in which early rock-and-roll and the revival were still grounded, into the corporate-commercial mainstream.

This titanic struggle ended in 1968 when the adversaries discovered their common purpose: when politics fell almost entirely into the domain of marketers, advertisers, and publicists, where an endless proliferation of momentary images distracted attention from the working policies of a plutocracy whose primary aim is to extend the commercial-political system championed by Ronald Reagan and ambivalently carried on by George Bush. Nixon was the first president to conduct politics purely on the corporate-managerial, public-relations model; Carter attempted to meet the competition from the marketplace by shifting the national discourse into a techno-utopian mode, the "energy crisis"; but his austere moral program was no match for the spectacle of a political commodity retailed, like margarine, as "morning in America."

Hence the practice of the folk revival of retrieving cultural material from the poor and isolated people who kept it alive in many ways reflected the symbolic practice of the postwar establishment in rallying various "traditional" prejudices, fears, and beliefs around the issues of communism, Americanism, liberty, patriotism, family, and the like. The folk revival and the establishment were together dipping into the historical resources of culture to fashion a new public life, a mythology and a countermythology each seeking to establish itself as the fountainhead of value in postwar society.

It is entirely consistent with these developments, then, that the folksong movement should have exfoliated in the 1940s with the emergence of new *commercial* incentives for folksinging. In January 1941 a consortium of radio broadcasters, incensed by an increase in ASCAP licensing fees, imposed a ban on ASCAP-controlled material, and through their newly established publishing arm, Broadcast Music, initiated a search by radio stations for previously unrecorded singers not yet bound by the prevailing ASCAP contract. Thus began the demise of Tin Pan Alley and the entry of increasing numbers of amateur musicians and songwriters into the music business. Technical advances in record production, with the appearance of the LP in 1948, while delayed by a musicians' strike and by wartime restrictions on the use of vinyl, contributed to the decline of sheet music as the principal carrier of commercial song.

Military service brought together many young people of widely diverse backgrounds, so that hillbilly music and western swing, alongside the popular big bands, came together on armed-forces radio as well as in the barracks and dancehalls. Norman Corwin, who had produced Paul Robeson's recording of *Ballad for Americans,* featured Woody Guthrie on his Sunday afternoon variety show and used the Almanac Singers on *This Is War,* a four-network national pep rally that introduced the armed services to Leadbelly, Ives, Seeger, and Josh White. Bess and Alan Lomax too, both employed by the Office of War Information, produced at least one hundred hours of similar programs.[29]

For financial and legal reasons, then, it was expedient to use unpublished, nonprofessional folksingers on radio broadcasts, a practice that had begun in the twenties not only on local stations in the rural Carolinas, Tennessee, and Virginias but on network radio with George Hay's Grand Ole Opry from WSM in Nashville and the National Barndance from Chicago's WLS. In the late thirties in New York, CBS's School of the Air, on a program called *Folk Music of America,* sent Lomax and his guest singers into city classrooms every Tuesday morning at 9:15, teaching folksongs to students who followed the music in manuals, complemented by some well-known classical theme derived from folksong—no doubt to provide the appropriate educational content of the program. Lomax's program was later joined on the air by one from the Brooklyn Public Library called *Folksongs of the Seven Million* on Tuesday evenings, which offered a series of urban folksongs, stories, traditions and customs hosted by Elaine Lambert Lewis, who had studied with folklorist Stith Thompson at Indiana. As the *Journal of American Folklore* later reported, *Folksongs of the Seven Million* "stimulated listeners to send in folksong material from as far away as Haiti." In 1945–46, guests included folksingers Tom Glazer, Leadbelly, Richard Dyer-Bennett, and Frank Warner, as well as folklorists and collectors Ben Botkin and George Korson.[30]

The well-known music historian Gilbert Chase had also been planning and writing for NBC a series preparatory to his landmark book, *Music of the New World,* to present folksong from an ethnomusicological perspective, anticipating the credo of People's Songs. The series, he said in 1944, would be "designed to show how music is related to ways of living, both in the past and in the present. It presents folk music not merely as something exotic or 'quaint,' but in organic relationship to the historical, geographical, and ethnological backgrounds which shaped the music. It views music primarily as human experience, and it is predicated on the assumption that this experience is most fully revealed in the music of the folk."

Clearly folksong had ventured out of the left-wing community into the larger commercial culture and was already informing the imaginative lives of children who would come of age in the next decade. Indeed, one of the prime markets for folksong on record was the children's market. Young People's Records and the Children's Record Guild both hired Tom Glazer, who sang on WNYC's *Folk Song Festival* on Sunday evenings as well as on *Folksongs of the Seven Million,* and who had sung with Alan

Lomax and Helen Schneyer in Washington with the Priority Ramblers, for records of "I've Been Working on the Railroad," "Clementine," and other familiar school songs.[31] Even Standard Oil, on their *Standard School Broadcast* in 1948–49, aired on the west coast over NBC, produced a series of programs for children based on folk characters such as Barbara Allen, Old Stormalong, Paul Bunyan, and Pecos Bill, setting their stories in a context of sea chanties, ballads, and worksongs.

But perhaps the most powerful indication of the expansion of the revival out of the left-wing community was its elevation to the theatrical stage in the 1940s. The Folksay group of the American Youth for Democracy, in addition to its petitions, blood drives, picket lines, and lobbies, held evening "dance arounds" of folksinging and square dancing, and produced folk plays such as Irwin Silber's *Circle Left,* a recitation of "The People, Yes!" accompanied by topical folksinging, reaching an audience of 100,000 young people in nearly sixty productions in the late forties.

In 1948, again, Oscar Brand staged Earl Robinson's *Lonesome Train* at Town Hall—but Broadway was already swept up in something of a craze. Robert Anderson and Elia Kazan recruited Brownie McGhee and Sonny Terry for *A Streetcar Named Desire* (1947); publicists had earlier characterized the groundbreaking *Oklahoma* of 1943, its hero Curley probably inspired by Woody Guthrie, as a folk opera; after it the Theatre Guild produced, in 1945, *Sing Out, Sweet Land,* a musical revue starring Burl Ives, Alfred Drake, and Celeste Holm, with an orchestra under the direction of former Composers' Collective member Elie Sieg-meister.[32]

Ives, like Sandburg, came from Illinois, son of tenant farmers, a college dropout, and a familiar figure at Almanac hootenannies, who studied acting and voice in New York. He got a singing role in *The Boys from Syracuse* and had his own radio program, *The Wayfaring Stranger. Sing Out, Sweet Land* staged a series of stereotyped scenes and characters of popular life as settings for folksongs: a country square dance, a Civil War encampment, an urban-industrial honkytonk, a Puritan town square, a New Orleans gambling den; characters included a watermelon vendor and even Burl Ives in an engineer's outfit as a version of Jimmie Rodgers, the Singing Brakeman. Many of the songs most associated with Ives found their way into the production, including "Wayfaring Stranger," "Blue Tail Fly," and especially "The Big Rock Candy Mountain." Lomax had printed "Big Rock Candy Mountain" without attribution in his *Folk Song U.S.A.* of 1947; it had been recorded in the twenties by Mac McClintock, who versified it from hoboes' folktales. "Haywire Mac" was to become, after an adventurous youth, one of America's most popular radio and film personalities, hosting a program of stories, cowboy songs, and ballads on San Francisco radio and in 1938 joining a network radio program, *Happy Go Lucky*, in Hollywood and landing bit parts in a number of Gene Autry films.

While the other songs in *Sing Out, Sweet Land* were delivered, as elsewhere on Broadway, in light operatic style, typically with a small chorus, Ives's songs came out in his piping, foggy midwestern voice and small-town accent. Elsewhere in the program the show's accompanying singers executed "Didn't My Lord Deliver Daniel," "Trouble, Trouble," and "Basement Blues" in a studied African-American call-and-response style, accompanied by acoustic guitar and barrelhouse piano.

It was in this cultural ferment that People's Songs came to life, and out of their hootenannies the chief figures of the later revival began to emerge—among them Irwin Silber, who had been a student at Brooklyn College and a Wo-Chi-Ca camp counsellor, cofounder of the aforementioned Folksay group of teenage singers and square dancers, and ultimately the editor of *Sing Out!*; Brooklyn-born Fred Hellerman, a member of the Young Communist League who had learned to play guitar in the Coast Guard during the war; Ronnie Gilbert, whom Hellerman had met at Wo-Chi-Ca, also a People's Songster, born to a

Ukrainian father and a Polish mother who worked in a garment factory, was a member of the ILGWU, sang in a Jewish Bund chorus, and introduced her young daughter to the Wobblies' songbook and May Day parades.[33]

Pete Seeger, Lee Hays, Fred Hellerman, and Ronnie Gilbert, the Weavers, began singing informally at Seeger's house on Wednesday afternoons in 1948 in the wake of the Wallace campaign, becoming the first of the folk revival to win a commercial following. Their earliest public appearances were at the Thanksgiving and Christmas hootenannies of the waning People's Songs and at various radical gatherings through early 1949, including a rally for the "New China" with songs from Mao's liberation army; with the novelist Howard Fast narrating, they recorded a polemical account of the Peekskill riots. As the Foley Square trial of communist leaders started, Hays and Seeger collaborated on what would become one of the most popular songs of the folk revival, "The Hammer Song": "If I had a hammer, I'd ring it in the morning . . ."

Before they chose their name, from a play by the German leftist Gerhart Hauptmann about rebellious weavers in medieval England, they sang on Oscar Brand's weekly folksong program on WNYC until Max Gordon, owner of the Village Vanguard and long an admirer of Seeger's, booked them for Christmas week, 1949. Alan Lomax, ever alert to the historical significance of the moment, brought Carl Sandburg to the club, who with impeccable cultural discernment said of the quartet, "When I hear America singing, the Weavers are there." They are, he averred, "out of the grass roots of America. I salute them for their great work in authentic renditions of ballads, folk songs, ditties, nice antiques of word and melody."[34]

Hoping "to do for folk music what Benny Goodman did for jazz,"[35] and with contract proposals from Decca and Columbia in the offing, Seeger contacted a friend from the Wallace campaign, Harold Leventhal, a song plugger for Goodman and Irving Berlin, and incidentally a communist, who agreed to manage the Weavers and guided them into an agreement with Decca and a relationship with that label's house arranger, Gordon Jenkins. Jenkins had loved the Weavers at the Vanguard—but he presented their music to the public on their first record, "Tzena, Tzena" and "Goodnight, Irene," floating on a mixed chorus and swimming in violins. As Seeger put it, the Weavers were willing to do almost anything to "make a dent in the wall that seemed to be between us and the American people . . . we'd now gotten into such a box that we were just singing to our old friends in New York."[36]

"Goodnight, Irene," adapted from a Leadbelly song, itself very likely an oral descendant of a Tin Pan Alley song of 1886 by Gussie Davis, became the most popular song of 1950, only months after Ledbetter's death. It inaugurated a string of hits: "On Top of Old Smokey"; "Wimoweh," a composition by South African Solomon Linda from a traditional Zulu chant; another Leadbelly derivative, "Kisses Sweeter Than Wine"; and Woody Guthrie's "So Long, It's Been Good To Know Ya." Both "Tzena, Tzena" and "Goodnight, Irene" attracted covers by established pop stars, including bandleader Mitch Miller, Vic Damone, and Jo Stafford, who recorded an entire album of folksongs (later acknowledged by Judy Collins as her introduction to folk music). Even Frank Sinatra, hoping to stage a comeback, attempted "Goodnight, Irene" in 1950. "Never in history," wrote Stanley Edgar Hyman, "has a craze so ruthlessly captured every phase of our lives, has a cult been so ingeniously exploited to make every nostalgic longing for the purple sagebrush in the distance, or the raven hair of an imaginary true lover, ring up its exact cash equivalent in the till."[37]

Perhaps the last expression of the progressive spirit behind the folksong movement occurred on 28 January 1950, at a Leadbelly memorial concert in Town Hall. After Hot Lips Page and Sidney Bechet sounded the leitmotif of the evening, the kinship of the jazz and folk traditions, Woody Guthrie and Pete Seeger sang duets and led the Good Neighbor Chorus in a medley of songs. Jean Ritchie and her dulcimer were prelude to Count Basie, balladeer Tom Glazer to West Indian calypso singer Lord Invader, and gospel singer and guitar wizard Reverend Gary Davis to a dixieland band. The formal tribute to Huddie Ledbetter belonged to his close friends Brownie McGhee and Sonny Terry, and to the Weavers' "Goodnight, Irene." But perhaps most significant for the revival to come was the appearance of "genial Frank Warner," who sang a few songs from his private collection, among which was the little-known murder ballad collected from a mountaineer in North Carolina, "Tom Dooley."

The seeds of postwar anticommunism were ready to sprout. Labor unrest—five million workers were on strike by the end of 1946, their gains undermined by inflation, automation, and the withdrawal of federal subsidies to industry—exacerbated by chronic shortages of jobs, schools, and housing, aroused earlier anxieties and summoned up the traditional spectres toward which to direct them. The onset of the Korean war in June 1950, and its immediate catastrophic casualties, turned international communism into the enemy that propaganda and policy had designed it to be. Shortly the hapless Julius and Ethel Rosenberg, later convicted on the basis of little more than the national mood, political facesaving, and a few elementary and meaningless drawings, were arrested; *Red Channels: Communist Influence on Radio and Television* was published by the FBI editors of *Counterattack;* and September brought the Internal Security Act.

Sales of over four million records, writeups in *Variety* and *Downbeat,* appearances in Chicago, Los Angeles, Reno, and Houston, even a spot on Milton Berle's television show *Texaco Star Theater,* could not in the end insulate the Weavers from their pasts. Duncan Emrich, director of the Archive of American Folk Song, had in the previous year turned over his copies of the *People's Songs Bulletin* to Hoover's agency, inaugurating a parade of People's Songs and People's Artists members into hearing rooms on Capitol Hill. In the summer of 1951, while "Kisses

Sweeter than Wine" and "So Long, It's Been Good To Know Ya" were on the Hit Parade, the House Un-American Activities Committee was defaming New Deal radicals, and a federal court sentencing the Rosenbergs to death. An FBI informant, Harvey Matusow, alias "Harvey Matt," conspicuous in the left-wing community as a distributor for the *Daily Worker* and briefly posing at People's Songs as a record salesman, stirred the suspicions of the bureau against the Weavers; in February 1952, tutored by Roy Cohn and the editors of *Counterattack,* he testified before HUAC that three of the group, excluding Lee Hays, were party members. Matusow was later convicted of perjury—but he had destroyed the Weavers.[38]

By the autumn of 1952, the folksong movement in New York seemed to be over. Leadbelly was dead. Woody Guthrie had begun to exhibit the disabling effects of what most assumed was alcoholism, until the final diagnosis of Huntington's chorea in September. Exhausted and embittered—even his own musicians' union local had questioned his loyalty—in 1949 Pete Seeger retired to the cabin he and Toshi had built in Beacon, New York. Alan Lomax, winning a Guggenheim Fellowship in 1947, accepted a contract from Columbia to undertake a collection of the world's folk music and left for England, where he remained for seven years. Earl Robinson went into music teaching, and Burl Ives, in an action that would alienate his former associates for forty years, supplied names to HUAC and went on to success as a recording artist and actor.

But political repression could not entirely crush a cultural movement that went deeper than politics. Moses Asch, like the rest, was in retreat from topical music, but in 1952 he released the pathbreaking *Folkways Anthology of American Folk Music.*

The entire trajectory of the urban folksong movement, as its rank-and-file participants shaped and were shaped by it, may be glimpsed in the career of the psychologist Helen Schneyer, a member, with Alan Lomax, of the aforementioned Priority Ramblers.

Born in 1921, Schneyer grew up in a Jewish family in the Bronx, learning Yiddish and Russian songs at home—but also attending church several times a week with the family's black housekeeper. Her parents sent her at the age of six to a progressive boarding school, Manumit, where folk music and household crafts including weaving, basketry, gardening, carpentry, soapmaking, and canning were taught. The family moved to Buffalo, and at sixteen Helen was copying songs she had learned from her black schoolmates into a looseleaf notebook.

Schneyer's professor of English literature at New York University was the folklorist Mary Elizabeth Barnacle, who one day in the late thirties brought to her class Huddie Ledbetter and Aunt Molly Jackson; soon Helen was singing with other young folksingers in Washington Square and attending the basement hootenannies at Almanac House. In 1947 she was invited to sing at the first interracial nursery school in the District of Columbia.

But she recalls, "Somebody picked me up there, noticed me, and began bothering me about wanting to talk with me."

> I couldn't figure out what he was selling me on—something about "artists having to take crumbs from the rich man's table," and actually it sounded to me like a pep talk for the Young Communist League . . . He was checking all my records, and I went to answer the phone at one point, turned around—and the guy was going through my mail on the coffee table!

Her suitor was an employee of the House Un-American Activities Committee.

Folk music had given Helen Schneyer the "sense of yesteryear" so perennially compelling to the sons and daughters of immigrant parents seeking to gain psychic possession of their adoptive culture. The ideological atmosphere in which she imbibed it alerted her to the sources of folksong in America's underprivileged peoples as well as its connection to varieties of preindustrial culture. But the incident convinced her to abandon folk music because, as she puts it, she "got scared out of it." A decade later the folk revival brought her back to the coffee-house circuit.[39]

Two developments, one demographic, the other technological, emerged in the early 1950s to determine the direction of American life until the end of the century: children and television. The United States at the end of World War II had been invaded by its own army, which like Roman legions encamped on the plains of Gaul brought along their suburbs, scarcely distinguishable from army bases, their military engineering, organizational, communications, information-gathering, and intelligence techniques, their burgeoning nuclear families and, certainly, their memories of America as it had been before the war. The birthrate had risen during the war and, in the years immediately after the war, increased by one million; after a peak in 1957, postwar births eventually accounted for 76 million people—roughly a third of the total U.S. population.[40] This was the baby boom, which over time saturated the marketplace with its buying power and popular culture with its image. It created a dynamic consumer group marching through society, each successive stage in its life cycle followed with eager solicitude by the retail establishment.

An increasing general preoccupation with children in the early fifties is evident from the popularity of juvenile entertainments in the period, especially in television. One million TV sets were sold in 1948, but by 1953 half of all American households had them.[41] Children's programming, in everything from *Howdy Doody* to *The Mickey Mouse Club*, has become the period's most durable cultural marker. But the music charts even earlier had begun to reflect the trend. Among the several music publicists and executives who caught the Weavers' act at the Village Vanguard was Howie Richmond, a music publisher who made a specialty of novelty songs such as "Mairsy Doats" and the Woody Woodpecker song, which had enjoyed exposure on the

Hit Parade. Richmond saw the Weavers too as a novelty act, whose Israeli folksong "Tzena, Tzena" was to him reminiscent of his recently successful number "Music, Music, Music."

He had discovered, moreover, what folklorists such as the Lomaxes already knew, that traditional songs, with only minor alterations, were subject to copyright and consequently represented, especially now that radio and records were the main carriers of popular songs, a new commercial resource. In 1950 the search by radio and record producers for such a resource had a new urgency, since these carriers were feeling the competition from that other novelty, television. Interestingly, it was in children's programming that television began to discover both its own nature as a medium and its social niche—the middle-class suburban household where the reduction of the family to nuclearity, the explosive growth in the enrollment and stratification of public schools, and the overnight appearance of new neighborhoods with no social, cultural, or demographic depth was producing a generation of unsupervised children enthralled by the screen of ruminating light that greeted them upon their return from school at 3:30 in the afternoon and on Saturday morning at 6:00, while parents slept.

As Lynn Spigel remarks, television was becoming the focus of a general obsession with the renewal of family life, the elaboration of new gender and generational roles, and the reconstruction of traditional domestic values.[42] Wartime disruptions had of course destabilized all of these forms; more significant, however, is that their rehabilitation had begun during the war as one dimension of the propaganda of national solidarity, and continued to be deployed by the postwar corporate establishment, which made the family its most powerful propaganda machine: witness *Ozzie and Harriet.*

Well into the fifties, television continued to appropriate the contents of earlier forms: film westerns such as Tom Mix's and science fiction serials like *Flash Gordon,* long the staple of the Saturday afternoon movies, variety and vaudeville shows such as Berle's and Ed Sullivan's, and radio dramas such as *The Goldbergs, Amos 'n' Andy,* and *The Lone Ranger.* But the miniature scale, narrow scope, shallow depth of field, and low visual resolution of the TV screen, with its "cool" or participatory character, as Marshall McLuhan and others have observed, as well as the domestic and private rather than the theatrical and public audience, lent itself far more readily to the intimate disclosures and laconic tempo of the hosted talk show, in which a genial central figure mediated between program content and the viewer in a closely confined dramatic space: hence the popularity of *The Arthur Godfrey Show,* the pioneering work of Dave Garroway's *Today* show, and, for children, *Howdy Doody* and *Kukla, Fran, and Ollie*—the latter in effect consultative talk shows in which the conversation is with marionettes or puppets.

The Weavers were of course more than a novelty; but as the society sought to reestablish itself according to the traditional patterns of prewar American life, which were more imagined than real, and as radio and television, with other institutions and interests, sought to control the process both materially and imaginatively, the Weavers spoke directly to the ambivalence inherent in that idealism. Their repertory, with its Slavic, Indonesian, Spanish, Israeli, and African folksongs, its spirituals and slave songs such as "Follow the Drinking Gourd," its reworkings of Ledbetter's and Guthrie's compositions, its British ballads and mountain hoedowns, its traditional gospel songs as well as Lee Hays's "Lonesome Traveller," its lullabies and retrievals from the Almanac repertory such as Guthrie's "Reuben James," embodied, without invidious ideological designs, the broader values of the progressive period—racial justice, ethnic tolerance, and global brotherhood; and it imparted to these ideals the colors of America's romance with its own regions and characters.

The movement from the left-wing community into the popular sphere, moreover, lent to the Weavers' presentation a quality of self-deprecating irony that made a quaint joke of folksong's long association with literary scholarship. "I gave thee this, I gave thee that," a well-rehearsed Seeger complains, at the 1955 reunion concert at Carnegie Hall, of the forty-eight verses of the English ballad "Greensleeves": "each verse is duller than the last—I've never had enough stomach to be able to sing 'em." Although folksong bore on its back twenty years of sectarian ideological struggle, the Weavers dispelled at once the combative tone of class conflict, the partisanship of electoral politics, and the elitism of the folksong movement itself, marrying Popular Front idealism, ideologically declawed, and the power of folksong to reimagine the lost America that lay in the historical hinterlands behind the great wall of World War II.

If the eclecticism of their repertory and the humor of their presentation did not accomplish this marriage, their unique vocal sound certainly would. Like the Almanacs, the Weavers' four voices gave the impression of social breadth, heterogeneity, and happy conviviality, sexually, generationally, socially, regionally, and even culturally mixed, as if there were twelve or fourteen rather than four of them. Under Seeger's plank-built tenor and Hays's avuncular baritone were two younger voices: a bookish but mellifluous one, Fred Hellerman's, and the protean and brilliant alto of Ronnie Gilbert, who had many voices, by turns gentle as a nursing mother's, innocent as a child's, lusty as the Wife of Bath's, and stern as a suffragette's.

Though far less casual than the Almanacs, submitting most of their songs to professional arrangers whose guidance was often overlooked, the Weavers remained more a confederation than a consort and, though not quite as communal as the Almanacs, strongly bonded in their differences—a kind of extended family on a reunion picnic. Looking elsewhere on the musical landscape of the forties and fifties for a comparable sound, I would settle on the Chuck Wagon Gang, the family quartet from Bledsoe, Texas—father "Dad" Carter, his son Jim, his daughters Rose and Anna—who in spite of forty years of wide popularity in gospel music never abandoned the southern harmony style of the old singing schools. This was the sound the Weavers took to

their Carnegie Hall reunion concerts, whose recordings on Vanguard went into the collections of every folk revivalist.

A new audience was taking shape. Beyond the residential
rings of the northern urban centers, on Long Island, on the
Illinois prairie, in the hills of Orange County, suburban tracts
that had lain undeveloped during the depression and war, un-
tenanted streets, vacant lots, and the occasional private park
began to receive under the roofs of mass-production bungalows
and cottages and ranch houses their legions of urban emigrés
with children. Out on the city's advancing frontier, the new
suburbanites found a remnant of the old prewar rural life—the
farmhouse, with its yard and outbuildings, and a piece of the
farm itself still under cultivation at the end of the street, a
roadside fruit and vegetable stand in the summer, perhaps even
an awkward but agreeable farmer in overalls or his wife and
daughter selling eggs and butter door to door.

In this meeting, over the isthmus of the war, lay a kind of
surmise, a dim recognition of the world that was and of the
world that would be, sounding in the voices of the Weavers.
Their voices, if not the Weavers themselves, survived the winter
of the McCarthy period to emerge among the first blooms of the
sixties folk revival, carrying the cultural signifiers, the "sense of
yesteryear," on which the new generation would draw to affirm
the existence of what all the voices of government, education,
and commerce had promised them.

Original album cover of the Folkways Anthology, 1952

6

Smith's Memory Theater

The political folksong movement of the early 1950s had scarcely broken into the marketplace with the Weavers' "Goodnight, Irene" when the reactionary right drove it out of nightclubs and off radio. But the movement succeeded nevertheless in bequeathing to the politically more innocent folk revival of the next decade a cultural text that would become its enabling document, its musical constitution: the three volumes, twelve sides, and eighty-four selections of the *Folkways Anthology of American Folk Music,* released in 1952.

Much of the recorded music circulating in the folksong movement, including Library of Congress field recordings, Woody Guthrie's *Dust Bowl Ballads,* and Huddie Ledbetter's *American Folk Songs as Sung by Leadbelly,* represented the energy and enterprise of folklorists John Lomax and his son Alan. The younger Lomax wanted to construct an idea of folk music consistent with an activist political program and an idealized populist outlook. Under Moses Asch's Folkways label, the Anthology could not have but won acceptance in left-wing culture, which would ultimately appropriate it; but it drew on a body of recorded music from a former generation of entrepreneurs who in the early days of electrical recording had cultivated the ethnic and regional record markets that urbanization, mass marketing, and federal regulation would soon undermine.

Microgroove technology had made possible the anthologization of traditional vocal and instrumental performances, insofar as these were represented on the commercial discs of the twenties, releasing them from their own contexts and reconstituting them in the milieu represented by long-playing records, whose affinities at that period—because an LP could contain a twenty-odd-minute orchestral movement without interruption—were mainly with classical performances, highbrow record clubs, and high-fidelity buffs. Hence the Folkways Anthology in effect legitimized its material, investing it with the cultural authority both of its advanced technology and its rarefied sociopolitical connections. What had been, to the people who originally recorded it, essentially the music of the poor, the isolated, and the uneducated, the Anthology reframed as a kind of avant-garde art.

The music reissued on the Anthology was already selectively, conscientiously, and conspicuously revivalist when it was originally recorded. This quality had recommended it, at the height of the Jazz Age, to its various parochial and provincial listeners; the Anthology recovered that music not in a spirit of resistance but ethnographically, with an almost mystical drive to comprehend the material in relation to itself and as a whole. The Folkways Anthology was a kind of curriculum in mystical ethnography, converting a commercial music fashioned in the twenties out of various cultural emplacements and historical displacements into the "folk" music of the revival.

Moses Asch was himself a kind of ethnographer, continuing his father's ambitious philosophy in the technical sphere by proposing a complete acoustic record of the human lifeworld. The Folkways catalogue came to include, in addition to the famous recordings by Guthrie, Leadbelly, and Seeger, Native American ritual songs, mountain ballads, black gospel singing, creole music, sea chanties, cowboy songs, Kenyan folksong,

Hindu religious ceremonies, folktales of Oceania and Caribbean dance, lullabies and children's games from the streets of New York, the speaking voices of Martin Luther King Jr., Sigmund Freud, W. E. B. Du Bois, Margaret Mead, and Carl Sandburg, documentary recordings associated with the suffragette and labor movements, the Spanish Civil War, the Holocaust, civil rights, and Solidarity, and, extending deeper into the human and natural environments, infant cries, technological sounds from office equipment and locomotives, bird calls, and the sound of the rain forest.[1]

But the *Folkways Anthology of American Folk Music* was assembled, edited, and annotated not by Asch but by a west-coast artist, filmmaker, discographer, collector, and literary editor named Harry Smith, from his own holdings in early race and hillbilly recordings. Smith's enormous collection, of which the Anthology represented only a small portion, would find its way into the New York Public Library, where it became, through the taped transcriptions of revivalists Mike Seeger and Ralph Rinzler, what Rinzler called the "motherlode" of the strange, idiosyncratic, often exotic, sometimes occult or bizarre oldtime repertory that Seeger's New Lost City Ramblers would disseminate throughout the urban folk scene in a style that by its studied imitation of original folk performances, frequently converted them into enigmatic rituals that other musicians could incorporate only by further and even more exacting repetition.

It was the Smith collection, moreover, which sent Rinzler, Seeger, and many other young revivalists into North Carolina, Virginia, Tennessee, Georgia, and Mississippi to seek long-lost musicians such as banjoist Dock Boggs and Clarence Ashley, or blues singer John Hurt, whose younger voices had been preserved there, and to coax them out of retirement; these excursions led into an endless proliferation of new recordings, not only of reissue anthologies modeled on the Folkways Anthology but of new recordings of rediscovered Anthology performers, as well as newly discovered younger musicians such as Doc Watson, who could be encouraged to take advantage of the growing commercial viability of traditional music by returning to the style and repertory of the previous generation—as well as to repertory supplied by the urban revivalists themselves from scholarly collections.

Literary anthologies of folksong were of course already familiar; John Lomax's *Cowboy Songs* and Sandburg's *American Songbag* had taken folksong out of academic departments and collections and introduced it into outing clubs, dance societies, recreational and fraternal organizations, scout troops, summer camps, school choirs, and other voluntary, educational, and amateur communities. But the Folkways Anthology brought forward what could only be preserved aurally, the sound of the folk performance itself; its exploitation as a cultural resource, which is the implicit purpose of any anthology, demanded a broad encounter with divers musical styles, all of them wildly at odds with polite musical convention. Revival musicians, in turn, became themselves living anthologies, purveyors not only of a repertory of songs but of instrumental and vocal styles, limited only by the broad categories such as "race" and "oldtime" introduced originally by the record companies to define their markets. By a long and arduous process perhaps a decade or longer in completing itself, the Folkways Anthology continued the Almanac Singers' project of detextualizing folk music—and in thus dismantling the entire conceptual structure in which folk music as such has its existence.

As it came to us in the early sixties, a decade after its original release, the absorption of the Folkways Anthology by the folksong establishment of the northeast, with its headquarters in Greenwich Village, its house organ *Sing Out!* now reaching a vastly expanded audience of college-age folk revivalists with its unreconstructed Marxist-Leninist editorial message incongruously mixed with newly intensified commercial advertising in recordings, instruments, professional concerts, and nightclub appearances, was overtly signaled, appropriately, by new packaging. On the cover of each of its three boxed sets, in green, brown, and blue, appears the image of a grinning, unshaven, poverty-stricken, self-conscious man, a tenant farmer apparently, who had been photographed by Ben Shahn years earlier for the WPA. Wearing overalls and an old hat, the blackness of a door framing his face with its famished mouth and lantern jaw, the man glances to his right with a kind of smirk; he isn't an old man—but his several days' growth of beard and the deep erosions on his face of hard work, weather, and sheer travail make it impossible to fix his age. He might be seventy, but he could be forty. He is a totem of the New Deal, whose brilliant photographers used their art to stylize rural penury and dependence, turning exhausted women, broken men, and naked, sorrow-eyed children into icons of the socialist romance.

The Anthology's participation in that romance, however, seems suspended the moment we remove its covers and open the boxes. For that romance is among other things an ideology of social distinctions—particularly of the distinctions of race and class and emphatically, in the New Deal period, of the distinction between the industrial and preindustrial ages with which that whole romance was historically bound up. These distinctions, which had lain over folksong collections like lines of latitude and longitude, have been effaced in favor of three simple musicological classes: ballads, or songs that tell a story; social music, secular and religious; and songs, including blues, which are lyric structures of traditional phrases and verses—all functional distinctions, with implications for poetic form.

We do not have, then, Labor Songs or Mountain Songs or Songs of the Cowboy or Songs of the Negro, picturesque conceptions that enforce in one realm distinctions proper to another by supposing that music observes racial, occupational, regional, and other social boundaries. Of course music *does* observe such boundaries—but with hopeless irregularity and inconsistency. In fact Smith recognizes the association between folksong and particular cultural communities. But by erasing the popular categories, and the stereotypes grown up around them, he opens the Anthology to the intense hermeneutic effort into which so many of its listeners have been drawn, which struggles to comprehend the dynamic and consistent way that folk music confuses the classifying impulse, striving to bear out of itself an auditory Third World that will not be located at any point on the globe or submit entirely to colonization by the First, but lives in its body undetected—while its migrating influences signify the thickening complications and finally the complete breakdown of the old cultural geography.

Once we open the boxes, then, and perhaps even before we place the first record on the turntable, we begin perusing the curious catalogue or "handbook," as it calls itself, that accompanies each of the three volumes. Photostatically reproduced, strongly reminiscent of the organs of transient or marginal political coalitions (it doesn't in any case look like a corporate annual report), the handbook is at once a catalogue, like the republished antique Sears-Roebuck catalogues, a discography, a manual, a scrapbook, a sort of stamp or coupon book, a sort of official document, like a passport, as well as a tabloid newspaper: a bricolage of printed ephemera that like junk sculpture incorporates many alien forms, each set off in its own character against all others and against the whole.

Quaint old printer's devices—the American eagle, a pointing index finger, the bearded figure of an eighteenth-century musicmaster, the liberty bell, a blacksmith, a horse, a pig, an Arcadian piper—festoon its covers: so many of them in fact that the catalogue seems at first to belong in a printshop, not a record collection. This festive abundance of emblems is reiterated inside the handbook by imperfect photographically reduced reproductions of the catalogues and dustjackets of old record companies, which include photos of the performers—the Carolina Tar Heels, Reverend Gates the holiness singer, the Carter Family, Stoneman's Mountaineers, and so on, all from the 1920s—along with old record labels and musical instruments such as the fiddle

Cover of the Folkways Anthology handbook

and banjo as well as the bass drum, clarinet, trumpet, harmonica, jew's-harp, kazoo, mandolin, autoharp, triangle, tamborine, and accordion, all from the mail-order catalogues that used to advertise these instruments for sale. With its playful elaboration of commercial graphic and typographical forms, the handbook calls up the socioeconomic milieu of the recordings and at the same time silently asserts, with a grin, its complete emancipation from such forms and their purposes.

Most interesting of its photolithographical charms are perhaps the original record jackets themselves. These borrow from old sheet music satirical and sentimental images of folklife: a barefoot lad in overalls, shirtless, with a guitar, intoning a love song outside a mountain cabin while a barefooted girl and a scowling man look on; a black stevedore with a banjo, howling through hornlike lips and strumming with clawlike hands, leaning against a cotton bale while behind him in the distance a riverboat plies the wide Mississippi; a saucer-eyed bluesman-dandy sitting upright on a cafe chair while a voluptuous creole woman, draped in a careless sarong, dances seductively nearby. These conventional tableaux, which represent the effort of early record companies to convert elusive human performances into elements of an immature social vocabulary they could reduplicate in the marketplace, may be seen now as the incunabula of a multimillion-dollar record industry operating in a culturally variegated market in which the music we listen to virtually pinpoints our locus on the cultural map: or, to put this more precisely, in which sustained attention to mobile and privatized sound generates a multitude of virtual cultural environments.

On the frontispiece of his handbook, speaking not in the authoritative, impersonal tones of print but from a hoarse, photo-reduced manual typewriter, Harry Smith provides us with an introduction to his work. Not surprisingly perhaps, his own interests seem to reflect Asch's fascination with the place of audio technology in cultural change. We learn that "many important recordings of folk songs had been cut on cylinders" by 1888 and that, with the perfection of the gramophone disc by Emile Berliner, about thirty folk performances were issued between 1895 and 1899. Smith tells the story, now well known and itself part of revivalist folklore, of Ralph Peer's trip to Atlanta, where he recorded the circus barker Fiddlin' John Carson, whose "Little Log Cabin in the Lane," which Peer believed

would only sell locally, in short order sold out its original pressing of 500 copies and compelled Peer to bring Carson to New
York to make further recordings;[2] he reminds us that recordings
reveal historic changes in music that written transcriptions
alone cannot, and notes that the records themselves helped to
stimulate those changes "by making easily available to each
other the rhythmically and verbally specialized musics of groups
living in mutual social and cultural isolation." The music was
recorded, he writes, during the five-year interval between the
advent of electrical recording and the onset of the Great Depression, when "American music still retained some of the regional
qualities evident in the days before the phonograph, radio and
talking picture had tended to integrate local types."[3]

Eavesdropping on an eavesdropping, auditioning an audition, imaging an image—caught up in its own reflexivity, the
Folkways Anthology attempts to recover a recovery even as
the nature of recording itself thrusts the performance away
and into the past, opening in its absence an imaginary field
in which all its sounds are immediately and urgently present.
That urgency is perhaps what the pages of the handbook, each
one patched up like a newspaper page proof, reflects: a mosaic
of boxes, one selection assigned to each, each entered in a
standard form diagrammed for us on the opening page. This
includes a kind of record label, white on black, that oddly
resembles the old duplicated official documents we used to
get from the county clerk in the days before xeroxing, as if
each selection were issued its own discographic birth
certificate; a headline-like condensation of the song lyrics; and
a paragraph of information and notes, followed by several lines
of scholarly citations that refer to the discography and bibli-
ography supplied at the end of the text. The strange electronic
quality of the page arises from the fact that it seems to have
been printed, before its duplication and reduction, by teletype:
as if all its titles and information had been freshly telegraphed
from that front where love, betrayal and murder, train wrecks,

robberies, assassinations, chaingangs, courtrooms, and gallows hangings, Saturday night dances and Sunday morning church services, as well as the intimate recollections, brave homilies, and lonesome complaints of mountain and blues singers, wage continual war against the tyranny of abundance, safety, order, convenience, and comfort.

In an oral tradition, of course, folksong *is* news. In the Anthology handbook, we learn who Frankie was, where and when she shot Albert, and who wrote the song about her: it was Mammy Lou, a singer at Babe Conner's cabaret in St. Louis. We learn that Stack-O-Lee, the gambler, belonged to a family that owned a line of Mississippi steamers—privilege, no doubt, having contributed to his dissolute life. The sinking of the *Titanic* comes to us as if the wire had just delivered news of it, as does a ritual murder of a child by a gypsy, subject of a Child ballad, which occurred in 1255. The headlines summarizing the content of the songs contribute to this newspaper-like immediacy, and at the same time seem to have been fashioned as aides-memoire. The old mountain song with Elizabethan roots, "Froggie Went a-Courting," could be on the front page of a supermarket tabloid: ZOOLOGIC MISCEGENY ACHIEVED IN MOUSE-FROG NUPTIALS, RELATIVES APPROVE, while CRACK ENGINEER JONES IN FATAL COLLISION might have been clipped from *Railroad Weekly*.

This conflation of the forms of the newspaper, with its immediacy, its communal character, its effect of assimilating the simultaneity of events to the two-dimensional mosaic of the newsprint page and to the Anthology's recorded material, is of course a metaphor: it captures the character of the music itself, which has been gathered in just such a combined field through which the linear history of the literary collector, with its several versions standing like mileposts in the evolution of a song, cannot find a path. Hence one of the most peculiar features of the handbook—the bold, black entry numbers standing at the head of each citation, by far the most conspicuous element on the printed page—is at once the most ironic and the most arbitrary. What principle can have determined this forceful enunciation of seriality in a body of music that has no inherent sequence, chronological or otherwise?

It is the aural imagination that shrinks the shell of time, brings the background forward, and it is the literary imagination that expands it, locates the anachronism on the scale of history. Whatever else may be said about the dream of America rising out of the Folkways Anthology, its form is one of ceaseless heterogeneous activity located not at a particular point in the past, but in a wider field of a disintegrated time revealed to us by the door that the retrieved collection opens onto it. This world has little to do with the study of folksong, and it has an altogether different shape; but it is an aural expression of the intimations and speculations that drive the tireless and futile search for an original and authentic text. It is a world, above all, we must first suppose to have existed, for sound implies presence; and a world, because of the ventriloquist trick of the recording, which makes present what is not, that must inspire a search for, or a reconstruction of, its source.

Marshall McLuhan observed that new technologies create new environments that transform the supplanted environment, otherwise imperceptible, into a counterform that provides us with a means of perceiving the environment itself. In the *Folkways Anthology of American Folk Music* we can view the birth of a counterculture at the very moment that a new medium, television, was making a spectacle of American life and drawing us all unwittingly into its audience. In 1952, the year of the Anthology's release, we saw the coronation of Queen Elizabeth and the nominating conventions of the two political parties on national television; soon the demise of the man whose name attached itself to the period, Joseph McCarthy, would take place with all of society in the committee room—not reading about it or hearing about it, but participating in it directly, intimately, and collectively.

Much has been made of the power of television to provide access to the world and to widen the horizon of events. But to grasp the transformation that occurred in our culture between, roughly, 1950 and 1960, one that created the noetic environment in which the Folkways Anthology and the whole folk revival has its meaning, we must look at television differently—not as an extension or expansion but as a violent contraction and confinement of the unbounded space in which the cultural imagination wants to move. Television was certainly impressive as a device of communication, a sort of radio with a window in it; but as a medium for the representation of life, it was desperately impoverished. With its almost nonexistent depth of field, its narrow frame, its dollhouse scale and grainy low-contrast image, technically limited by cumbersome equipment to contrived situations and cramped studio stages, television of the fifties, while seeming to raise a curtain on the world, also put a curse of unreality, banality, and triviality on it, reducing the most momentous human events to humbug and shaping, over the period, modes of entertainment compatible with humbug. At the same time, the luminosity of its corrupted picture drew the bewildered visual cortex into an involuntary trance, familiar to all parents who have tried to get their children away from the TV set, which assured the ascendancy of the medium and its hegemony in the realm of popular culture. As the idiom surrounding television has long indicated, the tube was nothing less than a form of nonsurgical lobotomy, a pervasively commercial medium whose content has been ever more crassly and straightforwardly determined by advertising, what Daniel Czitrom calls "the greatest marketing machinery in history."4

Print literacy had reconstituted structures of thought along alphabetic, textual, and typographic lines; radio had led a mass society demagogically into global catastrophe; but both of these modes, literate and aural, invited the imagination, for better or worse, to work—to complete the circle of perception by fleshing out the body of the word from memory and desire. In the 1950s a strange detergent culture, a kind of spectocracy, evolved under the expanding diffusion of the video image, arousing in the transitional generation, raised on books, radio, and records, a passion to escape into the fresh, colorful, fecund, and limitless imaginative landscape the word had promised, and a deep moral hunger after real experience that the word had compelled. It is significant, then, that though the folk revival found limited exposure on television, its real milieu was extra- or subtele- visual, one of records, concerts, and clubs.

Interesting, too, that the Folkways Anthology should have emerged from a social setting that in 1952 was deeply and abidingly countercultural. Of that counterculture the editor of the Anthology was a living exemplar.[5] Harry Smith, who died in 1992, was an engaging intellectual and artist who grew up in the thirties and forties in the Pacific northwest, and whose social and artistic inclinations carried him to the great bohemian centers of the coasts: to Oakland, Berkeley, and Greenwich Village, all well before these beatnik watering spots appeared on the map of pop culture. He won a reputation among his friends for his capacity to live without earning a living—a beat article of faith later. His interest in a wide variety of exotic art forms gave him a circuitous career of making and collecting: dejected at one point with his abstract films, which later elevated him into the ranks of respected avant-garde filmmakers, he left them behind in a theater; "by mischance," he says, he happened to destroy all of his paintings, though some of his work did find its way into the Museum of Modern Art. Recordings he had made of Kiowa Indian music in Oklahoma waited years for release because he hadn't completed the design for the cover.

As for his record collection, it had grown to a mass of several thousand discs when he attempted to sell it to Moses Asch. Asch suggested, on the analogy of a jazz anthology his company had just produced, the idea of a folk anthology, and Smith painstakingly made phonetic transcriptions of all the words in the songs—but lost the notebooks in which he had made them. John Cohen describes Smith's apartment:

> The closet is filled with women's dresses from the Florida Seminole Indians. One corner of the room, marked with a "Keep Off" sign, is filled with Ukranian Easter Eggs; on the bureau are stacks of mounted string-figures; behind them is a movie camera alongside portfolios of his paintings and graphic work. In another corner is a clay model of an imaginary landscape which is re-created from a dream. On the walls hang empty frames from which the pictures have been ripped out. Under the desk lamp is the only other living thing besides Harry—a solitary goldfish in an orange clay bowl. A 19th century Pennsylvania Jacquard woven spread covers the bed. At other times there have been piles of beautiful quilts and other weavings from that area as well as a collection of paper airplanes from the streets of New York. Small file cabinets of index cards are distributed between the stacks of research books. Each book becomes more exotic by its juxtaposition with other such books—Mayan codices beside Eskimo anthropology studies, under a collection of Peyote ceremonial paintings etcetra etcetra.

In a way that provides the type of many major figures in the folk revival, Smith grew up in a family marginalized by its own gentility. "My parents came from good families," he reports. "My great grandfather was the Governor of Illinois, my mother came from a long line of school teachers in Alaska." And yet "we were considered some kind of a 'low' family, despite my mother's feeling that she was the Czarina of Russia. We were living down by the railroad tracks, and I only realized a month ago that probably the rest of the people in town looked down on us."

Smith became acquainted with esoteric thought and exotic peoples at an early age: his theosophist grandfather's collection of alchemical books, such as a treatise by the Elizabethan neoplatonist Robert Fludd, and other arcane materials—he recalls a book on Bacon's authorship of Shakespeare—were shelved in the basement; the family lived in Anacortes, Washington, an island that had been settled by whites in the 1890s ("if you want to classify people by color"). Its original inhabitants were of course native Americans; and, after hearing a classmate's report on a local dance in which a human skull was swung around on a string, the boy took to visiting the reservation frequently—daily, in fact, by the time he reached highschool, taking photographs and making recordings, following the lead of "standard anthropology books about what was liable to be the culture elements in that area."

Smith's mother sang him Irish ditties, and his father, who had been a wrangler, cowboy songs. But Carl Sandburg's *American Songbag,* which his father brought home, introduced him to English ballads, and one of the first singers he heard was the elite revivalist John Jacob Niles. Thus began his search for folk music on record: seeking out Niles's records, he found versions of the same songs in the Sears catalogue, repressings of old recordings, "a curiosity because something that had survived orally for a long time suddenly turned into something that Sears Roebuck sold, and you could order it from Pakistan or wherever you might be."

Smith remembers the basement of a funeral home in Seattle—as fine a place, I suppose, as any for the folk revival to begin—which had been converted into a Salvation Army store, where he heard Grand Old Opry star Uncle Dave Macon for the first time. He notes that great masses of old records were being collected for conversion into war materiel. He had bought his first record, a blues, in 1940 and recruited his friends to help him in his search for more. "I was looking for exotic records," he recalls; Rumanian bagpipe discs joined his collections of Chinese records, Japanese records, some as early as 1895, hillbilly records and blues. By consulting scholarly discographies, among which was a Library of Congress document called *American Folksongs on Commercially Available Records,* issued in 1937, he learned the names of the artists: Memphis Minnie, Blind Lemon Jefferson, Blind Willie Johnson, the Carter Family. Finally, by one of those turns of fate that seem to characterize his whole career, Smith found himself living in Berkeley one floor below the ballad scholar Bernard Bronson, with whom he exchanged records of mountain ballads.

By background and training—he had studied anthropology at the University of Washington—the man who created the single most important oral anthology of the folk revival approached the world scientifically, habitually collecting and investigating, searching for patterns and the principles that linked them in aural and visual realms. "The type of thinking that I applied to records I still apply to other things like Seminole patchwork, or to Ukranian Easter Eggs. The whole purpose," Smith explains, "is to have some kind of series of things."

> Information as drawing and graphic designs can be located more quickly than it can be in books. The fact that I have all the Seminole designs permits anything that falls into the canon of that technological procedure to be found there. It's like flipping quickly through, it's a way of programming the mind . . . as it goes in through the vision, it is more immediately assimilated . . .

What is the origin of this curious way of thinking, and what has it to do with the *Folkways Anthology of American Folk Music*? For the answer to the first question, we may find a clue in Smith's original cover for the Anthology, a drawing he correctly attributes to Theodore DeBry from Fludd's four-volume *History of the Macrocosm and the Microcosm*, published in Germany between 1617 and 1619.[6] The drawing shows the hand of God tuning, on what appears to be a dulcimer, the Celestial Monochord, that is, creating the heavenly harmony to unite the base elements of earth, air, fire, and water, which the originally planned four album sets, in brown, blue, red, and green, were to reflect.

Smith seems to have called upon the hermetic epistemology that fascinated the learned minds of Elizabethan England in the decades before Bacon and Descartes refined it into the scientific method. Robert Fludd had developed out of the old art of memory pertinent to the study of eloquence a so-called memory theater—Frances Yates suggests that Shakespeare's Globe Theater was modeled after it—whose aim was to present the entire cosmos of knowledge in the form of alchemical, astrological, and cabalistic symbols arranged in particular sequences on the terraces of a small circular amphitheater; a scholar could enter the theater to study, discovering in drawers or cabinets beneath each emblem those manuscripts summarizing the information represented by the emblem.[7]

This was a kind of mnemonic library, an early thinking machine; its aim, to borrow Smith's prescient phrase—a computer metaphor was esoteric in 1968[8]—was to "program the mind." The architecture of the theater reflected Fludd's vision of the cosmos, "in which Jehovah, presented in the form of the Name of God in Hebrew in a glory, reigns over the schemes of concentric circles consisting of angels, stars, elements, with man at the centre."[9] Can it matter that Fludd's pictorial representations of his cosmos look for all the world like long playing records with their concentric circular bands?

The memory theater called upon a peculiar mental discipline, the *ars memoriae*, which orators in the universities used to retain the subject matter of their addresses. The essence of memory, sequence, was the psychological heart of this practice—hence Smith's big bold numerals—and odd, grotesque, or exotic imagery, the most memorable imagery, was its sensible surface. By diligent study in the memory theater, the scholar could retain knowledge and retrieve it by systematic recall. In this synthesis, of the *ars memoriae* with a cosmology embodied in a complex architecture of symbols, Fludd hoped to restore human consciousness to its Adamic state of pure unmediated apprehension of the laws and powers of Nature.

The Folkways Anthology did not exactly restore us to an Adamic state; but to the existence of a prelapsarian American harmony it does mysteriously allude, and by methods clearly those of the memory theater. It is a theater for the ear, arranged in a sequence of eighty-four memorable selections divided into six discs, each set of two representing one of three musical kinds, which taken together seemed to tell us, as John Cohen puts it, "where traditional music came from." It was the profound, even unshakable, memorableness of this set that made it the basis of the new aural tradition that developed among folk revivalists and "predicted everything that followed in popular music."

When we first enter it, the memory theater is strange, even sinister: a closet-like enclosure from which the world is shut out, spangled with occult symbols whose meaning we have not yet learned, fitted to an obscure design or purpose and harboring a vague threat, like the gypsy's tent or the funhouse, that by some unknown force will subject us to an ordeal over which we have no control and which will leave us permanently marked. But our deeper intrigue dissipates these fears, and we will become, in time, lost in the process of discovering, by assiduous study, the meaning of the signs; some will stand out boldly and others remain opaque, while the sequence through which we are meant to pass will fall apart into great awkward fragments with no apparent connection. Finally, in time, we will master the theater: the sequence restores itself, with each of its plateaus, sections, and themes reintegrated like a completed puzzle. At this point the theater replaces the world, having become, on one hand, a fixed structure that maps the plan of the cosmos and, on the other, a dynamic process that tells the story of its completion—a story that, because it is complete and all-embracing, is always a comedy.

If Lomax's folksong cycle is a kind of epic or opera with overtones of Protestant allegory, the Folkways Anthology, with its three volumes, six discs, twelve sides, and eighty-four bands, is a kind of *Commedia* in its very structure and, like Dante's poem, is suffused with strangeness. Entering the Anthology, we meet, first, a babble of voices—strange, even outlandish voices, everywhere unbeautiful, in some instances comical, caricatures of voices, in others bathetic, in still others forbidding or unnatural. In this atmosphere a dialectical energy develops between the vocalities that lie reassuringly within the boundaries of familiar traditions and those that transgress them; Lemon Jefferson's strong tenor or John Hurt's wise, conversational one, Sara Carter's diligent alto or Julius Daniel's mellow baritone, ground the Anthology and maintain a standard against which the more exotic vocalities can be measured. Like so many Virgils they accompany us, revealing in the Anthology's eerie environment of whines, cries, shouts, growls, and other weird sounds, the path our own traditions have taken, at the same time positioning our own voices in relation to sounds lost, abandoned, or forgotten.

The Folkways Anthology has taken a sounding of American culture at a time when its psychological forces had worked the human voice into timbres that are now mostly strange to us. We hear them, occasionally, on recordings of old radio broadcasts. One is tempted to apply the old epithets to them—to say that the voices on the anthology are untutored, rustic, primitive, and so on. Of course they are these things, from the viewpoint of our own art music and polite speech; but as the sheer fact of recording suggests, they are exotic in other ways as well. With certain important exceptions, most of the male voices, black and white—and we have to remember that the accompanying text does not assist us in such distinctions and even takes care to efface them—sound aged, even when the singers are young. But that is imprecise. More accurate to say that the male voices, with certain important exceptions, carry the imprint of a culture in which the warmth, relaxation, and sensuousness by which human sexuality finds expression in the voice is uniformly repressed: with the unlikely consequence that sexual differentiation is at once sharper and, because of what sounds like harsh constraints placed on the vocal mechanism, conscientiously reinforced.

Yet within their number certain distinctions can be heard. The Kentucky-bred concert singer and Baptist minister Buell Kazee, striving to lay the stately measures of a ballad over the racing rhythms of his banjo, which consequently sounds as if it were pushing him along in double time against his dignified demeanor, bellows like a rotarian; Clarence Ashley, the North Carolina medicine-show minstrel, sings with a kind of cozening, conspiratorial tone, like a stage usurer, a Shylock, through one side of his mouth—but with a balance and straightforwardness in his phrases that suggests he is a candidate for some local political office. Dock Boggs, the coalminer and banjo picker who learned much of his material from race records, sings with sour, nagging irascibility, as if singing for him were like paying taxes; while Frank Hutchison, the mountain blues guitarist, sings with gruff self-importance, like a policeman. The voices of these men are deadpan and humorless, all tied up in knots; their banjo and guitar rhythms hurry along anxiously, as if to outrun the recording machine.

Not all the white male voices are so fraught with tension. The good-natured voice of Bascom Lamar Lunsford has not only a suppressed laugh in it but an ingratiating tenderness; Lunsford was a country lawyer but a very indifferent one, preferring folksinging to the law and its rigors. Uncle Dave Macon sings with a swagger, like the teamster he was, laughing all the while, handling his banjo like a dancing partner—and, interestingly, these same two men accompany their singing with relaxed, experienced banjo rhythms, Lunsford's loping and lyrical, Macon's driving and gregarious.

On the other side of the racial line—but it is essential to remember, again, that the Anthology does not draw the racial line—we hear similar curiosities. Voice masking, by means of a deliberate rasp or a roar or a kind of growl, is the favored form of vocality among black singers on the Anthology. The Mississippi Delta blues patriarch Charlie Patton, identified on the original Paramount label only as "The Masked Marvel," delivers his song "Boweavil Blues" in the esoteric style identified with him, one designed, it seems, to garble the words to one audience while opening them to another—rolling them around in his mouth, swallowing them, ruminating upon them, and spilling them out again with a heavy vocal gravel mixed deep in his chest. Blind Willie Johnson stoutly roars out his paean to "John the Revelator" as if he were made of granite, while William Smith's litany to the *Titanic*—"Wasn't it sad when that great ship went down?"—filled with the smooth abrasive of his voice, refines the vocal substance to a kind of pumice: many writers have cited the origin of this vocal tone in African sacred music; many have heard it in Louis Armstrong's voice.

Significantly, both Johnson and Smith are accompanied by women: Johnson by a sweet, youthful female voice that answers his question, "Who's that writing?" with a happy "John the Revelator"; Smith by his wife, whose high-pitched wail carelessly follows the lead a few steps behind; in both recordings a yawning sexual gulf separates the singers. The voice of Ashley Thompson, who sings "Minglewood Blues" with Cannon's Jug Stompers, buzzes like the membrane in a kazoo, and at such a pitch that he sounds like a woman, while sanctified singer Reverend Sister Mary Nelson, in the trio "Judgment," sounds like a man—the vocal rasp in this instance not limited to male singers.

And what, indeed, of the female voice on the Folkways Anthology? There is, to be sure, no sultry Bessie Smith, no vulnerable Billie Holiday, and emphatically no pure Joan Baez, even in such songs and ballads that might most likely be found in the nursery or by the hearth, or in any case in the repertory of women. While the Anthology is overwhelmingly a collection of male voices, the occasional female voice—always in an accompanying role, as the second voice in a dialogue or in a mixed chorus—is similarly strained: piercingly high-pitched, warbling, sometimes wailing. In dialogues such as the Stoneman Family's "Mountaineer's Courtship" and "The Spanish Merchant's Daughter," the female voice, supposedly Mrs. Ernest Stoneman's, is so caricatured that it hardly seems female at all: surely the quacking, quavering voice in the "Mountaineer's Courtship" is the falsetto voice of a man. In the Williamson Brothers' version of "John Henry," a female voice, presumably that of "Curry" cited on the label, answers each line with a shrill cry. Versy Smith does the same in her husband's song about the *Titanic,* echoing one or another word as it passes by with a sorrowful wail.

Yet these same pinched, narrow women's voices, borne on the surges of lining and shape-note hymns, such as the Alabama Sacred Harp Singers' thrilling "Rocky Road" or F. W. McGee's "Fifty Miles of Elbow Room," lend them an emotionality that seems to belong only to the intimate occasions in which communities of men and women revisit the spiritual bond that holds them all in its embrace—occasions that, though we have access to them through recorded sound, seem not to have been created with us, or any audience, in mind.

There are, again, exceptions; there is the aforementioned voice of Sister Mary Nelson, with its rough, mannish texture: but is she, finally, an exception? The very absence of deliberate sexual designs, which we regularly find in our popular music, actually sharpens our consciousness of sexuality—not as a quality belonging to this man or that woman, a personal power, but as the impersonal force that distinguishes them; and voices that through texture or pitch confound such a distinction only heighten our awareness of it. It is perhaps not so extraordinary, then, that the exceptional voice of Sara Carter, with its buxom and officious shape—the voice of the young woman behind the desk at the public library who steadfastly refuses to acknowledge that she is beautiful—is replete with sexual power: we have seen her, in photographs of the period, a girl in late adolescence, still wearing the short dress, anklets, and cropped hair of a schoolchild, as awkward, unnatural, and unhappy in her costume as a convict in his stripes.

The anomalies of the Folkways Anthology—and Harry Smith concedes that the songs "were selected because they were odd"—are not merely perverse. Like all anomalies they speak

directly to the entire conceptual system by which we understand them as such. These selections place a strain on our
aesthetic standards, but do not altogether deny us performances
that will keep those standards alive. Merely to have answered
the old expectations—for English ballads in the concert style,
say, or for cowboy songs or Negro spirituals or the blues, still
inextricably linked in the minds of urban listeners to
jazz—would only have sustained the precious illusions, deeply
rooted in the established order, of which these forms could be
taken to affirm. But Smith's memory theater—one cannot but
think of a country mountebank and his gaudy show wagon—is,
with its presentation of folksong in its most raw and even most
tortured forms, subversive, disabling with its shocks our resistance to the very consummation that though we don't know it,
we are seeking.

And it is not, finally, all oddity, curiosity, and anomaly: the
strange landscape of the Anthology is marked with reassuring
cairns. In the opening ballads we hear, in Dick Justice's touching
rendition of "Henry Lee," a lady condemn the knight she has
stabbed and thrown into a well—to "lie there until the flesh
drops from your bones." In the "Fatal Flower Garden," two sad,
tired, desultory singers, one, as if he did not remember the
words, lagging behind the other, accompanied incongruously by
a Hawaiian guitar, relate a tale from the middle ages, in which
a gypsy lures a child into her flower garden and thence to her
bed, where she murders him.

Indeed there is scarcely a song in the Anthology that does not
reveal, like the magical objects in fairy tales, some memorable
event or image, such as the Carolina Tar Heels' song about
shoemakers' instruments displaced by machinery in 1804, "Peg
and Awl." Two young ladies, disappointed in love, die by their
own hand, another by her lover's; two presidents are assassinated and two murderers executed by hanging. A riverboat
dandy shoots his adversary over a poker game, and a betrayed
woman shoots her man, *in flagrante delicto,* through a solid oak

door. Two trains crash, the *Titanic* goes down, and several farms
fail; a cuckoo bird sings, patriotically, on the Fourth of July, and
a big old hunting dog shakes the earth as he dies and goes down
to his grave on the end of a golden chain. Other elements, of
style and instrumentation, linger in the memory: the jugs and
kazoo of the Memphis jugbands, the tamborine and hand-clapping rhythms of the sanctified songs, the fa-so-las of the sacred
harp songs, each syllable sung as if it were as full of meaning as
a new-coined word.

This sketch of some of the Anthology's many memorable
features indicates that the larger classes into which the collection has been divided, ballad, social music, and song, have been
further subdivided in ways that, like the racial division, are
implicit or, perhaps, deliberately hidden, and yet at the same
time describe a movement—a movement in time certainly, but
a movement too in the entire geology of the collection and in
the relationships of all its strata. The opening sequence of ballads, for instance, though largely Appalachian in style, are all
rooted in British tradition and, like the story of the murdered
knight or the house carpenter, who seduces a young mother
away from her baby, or a nagging wife carried off by the devil
or the frog who marries a mouse, belong to imaginary realms far
removed from the world of the hillside farm or coalmine.

That sequence is succeeded by a string of original American
ballads belonging, roughly, to the first decade of the nineteenth
century: the ballad of Omie Wise, who was murdered in 1808,
the aforementioned "Peg and Awl," and especially the haunting
"Willie Moore," which belongs to the sturdy stock of American
folk ballads that join Irish and border melodies, usually pipe and
fiddle dances and airs, to narratives of life in the new land.

In the set of songs that follows, however, an intriguing reorientation of singer, style, and song takes place. The subject of the
songs has become particular people and events of the late nineteenth century—from the early 1870s, when the historical John
Henry most likely lived, to the sinking of the *Titanic* in 1912.

Here are the tributes to the heroes and desperadoes of the post-Civil War period: to Cole Younger, who in the voice of Edward L. Crain, rues the day he haplessly murdered a brave bank cashier in Northfield, Minnesota, in 1876; Garfield's assassin, Charles Giteau, in the voice of Kelly Harrell, sadly remarks that as a child he never imagined he would end his life on the gallows. The Carter Family tells the story of the capture of John Hardy, who was hanged for murder in 1894, and Frank Hutchison of the murder of Billy Lyons by Stackolee, the gambling black sheep of a Memphis family that owned a line of Mississippi steamers; Charlie Poole and the North Carolina Ramblers deliver their peppy ragtime peroration to the dying President McKinley; and John Hurt, supported like summer roses on the intricate trellises of his guitar work, relates the story of Frankie and Albert in a wry and genial way, as if he knew them.

On the other side of the disc we hear commemorative songs of the great disasters of the period: the *Titanic* again, the wreck of engineer George Alley's "Fast Flying Vestible" near Hinton, West Virginia, in 1890, and, in Furry Lewis' sardonic version based on an early ballad about a pimp, one of the casualties of trying to make up lost time, Casey Jones. Agricultural disasters are the subject of the disc's three concluding numbers, "Down on Penny's Farm," Charlie Patton's "Mississippi Boweavil Blues," and the Carolina Tar Heels' "Got the Farm Land Blues"—all of which engage in a bit of merriment at the farmer's expense.

It is here that the recording medium begins to work its peculiar magic. The recordings, again, have been collected from a relatively brief period, 1927–1932, and are thus removed by one and two generations from the people and events they describe; but it was part of the purpose of these producers, and of performers such as A. P. Carter who collected material from the grandparent generation, to reach into the past and retrieve it, assimilating the historical gap to the temporal gap that lies between any musical performance and a recording of it, thereby securing the formal unity of subject matter and technical medium which is the essence of artistic illusion.

The style of the singers, both black and white, belongs to the epoch in which the songs and the events they commemorate came into being; however painstaking the scholarship for each song, however plain the simple fact that the performances are separated from the events by at least twenty years, the actual sound of the music evaporates these distinctions. It is as if Cole Younger and Charles Giteau themselves had spoken; as if somehow engine 143 had been summoned into existence by the Carter Family's song about its demise. No longer do we have singers and songs, as we might in concert or chamber performances; they have been absorbed into each other and together call up a universe in which they are aspects of a single reality. In the developing culture of the Anthology, a new kind of history has begun to form, a kind of aural hologram hovering where musical forces gather independently of time and text; like culture itself, with its residual and emergent forms, the Anthology becomes a reservoir of the various tributaries and currents of history, in which time flows against, around, and into itself, and takes on the qualities of a vast, active, living body in which many independent processes share a vital medium in itself unknowable but capable of manifesting itself in many different forms.

That is the wide delta into which the Anthology flows as we enter Social Music, the second set of discs. These selections, like those of the first set, can be variously located in folk tradition. Bunt Stephen's jolly "Sail Away Ladies," a fiddle tune, belongs to that cheerful and cheering tradition of dance tunes, the first to be forged in America out of native elements with British and African forebears, growing up behind the first frontier along the great water routes—the Ohio River and its tributaries, the old canal system, the lower Mississippi. J. W. Day's "Wild Waggoner" is of much later date—probably a stage tune of late minstrelsy or early vaudville; "Wake Up Jacob," by Prince Albert

Hunt's Texas Ramblers, is a border tune from Kentucky mixed with eastern European elements probably from Bohemian pioneers to the west; and the Cajun foxtrot "La Danseuse" sounds more like a German than a French song. But the dance tunes range still more widely—to a fiddle rag, the "Indian War Whoop" that is more a cowboy yodel, and a polka performed by a jazz orchestra.

The religious songs are just as varied. They include Rev. J. M. Gates's surge songs, or lined-out hymns, whose origins are in seventeenth-century psalm singing and whose long history carried them quite early to the American frontier, especially in the black churches where the essentially oral character of the psalm songs was not transformed by text-based hymns; fa-so-la hymns like "Rocky Road," on the other hand, record the heady conjunction of the passionate and spontaneous southern spiritual, product of the camp meeting, with a mechanical discipline imperfectly imposed by the shape-note text—a discipline that in the Middle Georgia Singing Convention's "This Song of Love" becomes almost robotic. Rev. Moses Mason chants a sermon, and Blind Willie Johnson a blues-like homily; Bascom Lamar Lunsford offers a mountain song, "Dry Bones," whose antiphonal structure and narrow melodic scheme suggest it has been cobbled together from overheard black songs, secular or religious, while the Carter Family's "Little Moses" seems to have been borrowed from a popular waltz.

Urban traditions are represented too. Ernest Phipps and his Holiness Singers' "Shine on Me" begins as soberly as a Nebraska "Rock of Ages" but quickens into a spirited, hand-clapping shout, while Rev. F. W. McGee's "Fifty Miles of Elbow Room" ushers his whole congregation into sheer pandemonium. These selections, along with the Memphis Sanctified Singers' "He's Got Better Things for You" and Rev. D. C. Rice's "I'm in the Battlefield for My Lord," which come out of urban churches in Memphis, Birmingham, Atlanta, and Chicago, show, like contemporary sanctified and holiness churches, the influence of popular music: in this instance, of commercial gospel harmonies and jazz.

Yet this entire perspective—the songs and their histories, the history and origin of the style in which they are performed, indeed the whole machinery of folksong scholarship—has become, by the time we are set free in the second box of discs, largely irrelevant. We enter, now, not a textual universe but an aural one, where every performance is a kind of eddy or maelstrom or ring in the surrounding medium of human vitality. Though we hear them in sequence, they are going on simultaneously and are disturbances in the medium of our own being. Somewhere obscurely to the south and west—in east Texas or the Mississippi Delta, in the north Georgia hills or along the Blue Ridge, on Beale Street or on 47th and Cottage Grove, in some Memphis or Chicago darktown—where the demography and geography of cultural identity spills outward into the landscape and history of the country, the genuine common life in all its variety is burgeoning. Moses Asch himself, writing on the last page of the handbook, records his astonishment: "Little do we realize that to the people who live in these localities, the tunes and songs heard on these records, although they listen to radio, watch movies and television . . . are still the intimate part of their lives."

Asch was mistaken, of course: by 1952, country western and rhythm and blues, carried by men such as Hank Williams and Muddy Waters, had largely displaced older rural forms. But these were continuous traditions nevertheless, of which the Anthology had taken an earlier sounding; and in any case Asch's mistake was, cognitively speaking, necessary. Like any recording, the Folkways Anthology eclipses the face and world of the author, which we must supply imaginatively. We knew little of the actual social and commercial context of these recordings, and still less of the people who recorded them, in the sixties; they came to live in the world evoked by their own voices and the stories they tell—that, again, is one of the principal movements of the Anthology, the absorption of singer into song—a movement that permits us to embrace Asch's promise largely unaware of the art at work. Initiated into the aurality of the Anthology, we come to see it on its own terms, as a collection not of songs, but of sounds: and, looking back to "Henry Lee" and forward to Songs, the third set of discs, it is a story of sounds, their progress, their integrity, and their moral center, that we are following.

First we heard British and Anglo-American ballads; then dance tunes and religious singing; now we hear singers singing, it seems, out of their own identities, in blues and in what Paul Oliver calls the "nodal ballad," a form whose "verses are sung as a succession of discrete, encapsulated comments on a situation rather than as a narrative."[10] The nodal ballad, because it does not have the autonomy of a linear narrative, cannot so readily disentangle itself from the singer as does the ballad, which even in folk tradition often has an independent existence in the form of a written text; its existence is in oral tradition, as a body of free-floating verses, couplets, and epithetic phrases, which in any given performance coalesce into a song and an implied narrative inseparable from that performance.

That is why, as the Anthology moves out of a textual into an aural universe, the blues and the nodal ballad come to the surface; and it is why, too, folk-revival singers, unlike their counterparts of an earlier period, who depended on text collections and transcriptions, favored these forms of song: because they sang it, however implausibly, however allegorically or symbolically, about themselves. Indeed we might look ahead for a moment and observe that folk revivalists divided on this issue along gender lines: young women, of whom Baez was the type, whose balladry linked them to the literary ballad and hence to the polite conventions of the Victorian parlor, and young men, of whom Dylan was the type, whose blues and songs thrust them into the world of the hobo, mountaineer, laborer, prisoner, and pariah. These were songs that seemed to demand, out of their own original energy, not that we modify them stylistically to conform to some polite standard, as concert performers of folksong had done, but that we change our very lives to bring song and singer into alignment. One could not, of course, change the style of the song: in an aural universe they *are* their style. True compatibility, then, between singer and song demanded that we reach down to the bedrock of song style and rebuild it out of new experience.

It is amusing, perhaps, to recall all the young revivalists who only appeared to do this—who were content with theatrical changes in themselves and in their sartorial and tonsorial styles to create the desired impression of authenticity. But what of the many young people, the lost generation of the 1970s, who couldn't content themselves with less than thoroughgoing economic, political, and personal reform?

We can hear, once established in the aural cosmos of the Folkways Anthology, the formation of its promise and its gathering momentum. Listening back into its city of shadows, we hear it reorganizing itself, like an animal that molts in the dark, making a new sequence not of songs but of voices and rhythms, a sequence, finally, of human presences that will permanently change us as only rogues, gamblers and clowns, tramps and vagabonds, drifters, forsaken men, innocent girls, wounded women, and an unregenerate cowboy can do. We can trace, now, threads running through the Anthology whose paths do not observe its announced categories—or, for that matter, any traditional categories; instead they run over and around these boundaries and through the very songs themselves, dissolving them into constituent elements that, finding their like among the other freed elements of the set, form new alliances, less like intellectual classes than like living communities.

Through the entire set, now, rolls the cool backbeat of Maybelle Carter's guitar, an instrumental ventriloquist carrying the rhythms of black banjo pickers hidden in the silence behind the earliest recordings; presiding over it is the holler of Deacon

Lemon Jefferson, his guitar muttering the oracles of some dead child in mystical riffs no musician has yet been able to translate. In this milieu, which extends on one side into the cottonfields of the south and on the other into the blues clubs and storefront churches of Chicago and New York, several of the Anthology's voices speak out with new authority. Returning to Dick Justice's "Henry Lee," we hear not a Child ballad but a Baptist whine, such as we might hear from the pastor of an Old Regular Baptist church both in the hymn he sings before his sermon and in the sermon itself. In Burnett and Rutherford's "Willie Moore" and G. B. Grayson's "Omie Wise," the singers tell their tales not as guilty men, but with the sobriety and awkwardness of witnesses before the judge's bench, acquaintances of the principals, echoed by a fiddle in rueful concurrence: but where do those sad, sliding tones come from, the sinking blue notes with which the fiddler worries the chilly hollows left in the old pentatonic melody?

These same notes will be heard in the testimony of jugbands and blues and religious singers, who speak not to the authorities but to their own people, in voices relaxed by the ambient human presence: this is the voice in which John Hurt speaks, intimately, as if he were surrounded by spellbound children, a domestic voice; it is also the voice of Bascom Lamar Lunsford, whose audience might be some visitors from the Asheville Chamber of Commerce who he knows have never learned to take seriously the musical traditions of the class just beneath them. It is the voice in which, in more public circumstances, Henry "Ragtime Texas" Thomas issues the bold declamatory shouts of "Old Country Stomp"—square-dance calls and lyrical cries erupting out of guitar rhythms: guitar rhythms, in fact, which sound like those of the country fiddle. The same calls and cries are heard on a Saturday night in the North Carolina hills, in some old piper's tune bent double by plantation counter-rhythms emanating from a banjo. That is what we hear in Clarence Ashley's banjo, though he plays it in an ancient modal tuning and recovers a fragment from the Middle Ages about a cuckoo bird; the notes he makes with his fingernails might as well have been made by a griot of Senegal, and with the same motion of the crooked arm over the track of the strings of his gourd instrument.

It begins to appear that the racial line has not been drawn across the Folkways Anthology because it can't be drawn—not without breaking its performances into pieces. "Before the Anthology," Harry Smith tells John Cohen,

> there had been a tendency in which records were lumped into blues catalogues or hillbilly catalogues, and everybody was having blindfold tests to prove they could tell which was which. That's why there's no such indications of that sort (color/racial) in the albums. I wanted to see how well certain jazz critics did on the blindfold test. They all did horribly. It took years before anybody discovered that Mississippi John Hurt wasn't a hillbilly.

The Anthology did with sound what the discourse of folklorists and ethnomusicologists, with the endemic distinction between Afro- and Anglo-American, could not do: drive home the essential integrity, in American folk music, of African and European traditions—for the very language of scholarship preserves the distinctions that scholars want to eliminate. But in the performances of songsters and musicians themselves, discrete cultural elements deposit themselves freely, especially in the blues and ballads whose verbal elements have been forged in a common life, where the mutual absorption of singer and song so confounds the division of style and subject that they become one—songs that have to be sung in a certain style, a style that in turn falls upon only certain kinds of songs.

Where a traditional social system regulates, as it has in the south, relations across boundaries of class and race, and secures social identity in those terms, boundaries may insulate even as they separate, becoming thresholds or frames that both define a difference and occasion a relation. The very stability of social categories provides for close social interaction; and the system predicated on the fear and denial of cultural influence disarms resistance and opens people on both sides to unconscious cultural mimesis.

This is in essence a theatrical world, where culture enacts itself on a social stage and with reference to an audience, cultivating differences with a self-conscious intensity that enlarges, exaggerates, and stylizes the cultural message. Such was the character of American popular culture in the middle of the nineteenth century: along the river routes of the early frontier; on plantations, as late as the turn of the century when in Mississippi the blues began to form; in coal and logging camps and railroad towns; in minstrelsy, especially where it penetrated on riverboats into remote areas and mountain towns; in the mountains, especially where fugitive and manumitted slaves sought refuge; on the seas, where British song and dance met African and Polynesian inflections; in the west, where black and white cowboys melded the songs and ballads that came from Kentucky, Tennessee, and Arkansas; and of course in the cities—New Orleans, Atlanta, Memphis, Kansas City, Chicago—where the races and classes met at every level of society.

The Folkways Anthology reproduces this condition in its own organization. By confounding the familiar racial, regional, and sexual categories, or by cutting them so finely that they are reduced to a heterogeneous new substance, or by juxtaposing them with such violence, or such subtlety, that they tend either to paralyze or to mimic one another, the Anthology robs us of the handy frames in which we transport our folksong and presents it nakedly—or, rather, greets us after we have been stripped naked, intellectually speaking, so that we can't really conceive it at all. Instead we must experience it directly, something utterly strange and yet, because it is made of things we know, hauntingly familiar, and because we can't readily form a conception of it—this must wait for years, if it is ever achieved at all—enact it, again and again, until we have relieved the neuralgia produced in our own soul when it resonates to its perceptions but cannot assemble the idea by which it integrates perception into the rest of its experience.

The seeds of this change are planted inconspicuously early in the Anthology: in the songs and tunes already cited—not only in John Hurt's "Frankie," Charlie Patton's "Boweavil Blues," Henry Thomas' "Old Country Stomp," but in Jim Jackson's "Old Dog Blue" and Lunsford's "I Wish I Was a Mole in the Ground." Other listeners might fix on other songs, but no matter. What is important is that these songs, by virtue of a peculiar mix of subject matter, structure, style, and performance, look deeply into southern folklife through several layers of its history, and communicate something of the richly transformative energy that arose from the constant exposure of white to black and black to white, each group playing out before the eyes of the other its reading of the human drama; each group filling out its imaginative life with comic narratives of the other, in which it embodied a shadow version of itself; each group annexing, too, the narratives of the other group into the repertory of its own, strangely hybridized as, for example, commercial "coon songs" entered black oral tradition with a few new words and a new irony;[11] each group—and here is the force that gave to southern folklife its authenticity and color—unconsciously shaping itself under the influence of the other, both under its direct influence and through the imaginative universe in which both groups lived.

Southern folklife between the end of the Civil War and the outset of World War II was a life perpetually reinvented, like the lives of lovers who create themselves in the heart of the other, a life that, like any genuine culture, was striving to represent itself—on the minstrel and vaudeville stages, the medicine-show wagon, the tent show, the dance hall, the folk church, ultimately on the radio and in the picture show—and to perpetuate itself in the mutual absorption of life and its representations which is the dialectic of culture.

On the Folkways Anthology the south's idea of itself, expressed in song and dance, shaped by the minstrel stage and by other commercial forces of distant origin, by radio and phonograph, swinging dialectically between its black and white folk communities, has *become* the south. This is a world in which imagination, not formally insulated in "art" or hoarded as "culture" by a ruling elite, penetrates life and speech, daily entertainments formal and informal, social and domestic, traditional and original—sharpening and emboldening one's experience, transfiguring it, galvanizing it against the corrosion of unreality that custom, habit, and sloth throw over it. It is a world of animal fable where animals are not in zoos but at the edge of the field, in the trees, in coops and pens and on the table; of comedy, melodrama, tragedy, and farce perpetually being played out on the other side of town or across the street, as well as in one's own family, across generational lines; a world where you don't think of what you should have said or done but where you actually say or do it, because instantly accessible in your own idiom or standards of conduct is some powerful resource that emblazons the moment with its own vigor: the cool phrase, the trenchant expression, the perfect gesture, and beyond these purely decorative devices, the vow, the oath, and the reckless or violent deed.

The singers are of course southern folksingers and bearers of folk tradition: but not in any pristine sense. Lunsford, as we have seen, from Madison County, North Carolina, was an educated man, a conscientious collector and festival promoter; Jim Jackson, a blues singer from Hernando, Mississippi, and a veteran of southern roadshows, recorded extensively in Memphis and assisted in scouting performers for the producers of race records.[12] But it is perhaps just these facts that account for the power and beauty of these apparently simple songs. They probably began as little narratives of the play-party or cornshucking, or perhaps as artifacts of the commercial musical theater and Tin Pan Alley; they entered folk tradition; two singers, both of whom, for their own reasons, took a special interest in traditional songs and became professional performers—not naive folksingers recorded in the field by some intrepid songseeker, but self-conscious exponents of discrete musical traditions.

And what delicate, aspiring, and tender souls are here revealed! Different as they are, the melodies of "Old Blue" and "Mole in the Ground" both belong to that dialect of pentatonic tunes that spread from Scots tradition all across the south and, by virtue of close tonal similarities, readily assimilated Afro-American tonalities. Both have the dreaming and, depending on its reach, poignant, melancholy, or glorious force of a scale that repeatedly evokes its own internal harmonies. Above all, these melodies are not intellectual; they do not, like many ingenious dance tunes that developed on the fiddle or the pipes, fascinate us with many swiftly passing adjacent notes. Instead the pentatonic scale is right-handed, simple, square, and ingenuous, a scale meant to inspire us when it dips into the grave matters that music touches below the tonic, or sometimes with a kind of collective purpose, like battle, when it ventures above the octave, where the voice goes to cry and to shout.

"I Wish I Was a Mole in the Ground" has such a melody—an adventurous one that opens and closes with honest declarations of itself tied together by two stirring affirmations, one on the sixth above the tonic and the other at the frontier of the melody, on the third above the octave. But the valiant soul framed on these notes, who in other circumstances might have led an army, only wishes—and that's how he puts it, like a child, "I weesh"—surrealistically, and with disarming specificity, to be a mole in the ground, the epithetic phrase, so characteristic of oral-formulaic song and speech, and the repetition of the line with the completion of its thought in the third line of the quatrain, maybe implying, to the alert musicologist, that though Lunsford may have learned the song from one Fred Moody, a college classmate from Haywood County, North Carolina, it has come from some place in African-American folk speech. Other verbal elements—the "forty-dollar bill," the "baby, where you been so long?" and the possible prison reference—all suggest this: it is a song that is both and neither a blues and a ballad.

And why does Bascom wish to be a mole in the ground? Perhaps because he is a man not at home where destiny has placed him. He has been in the "Bend," quite likely a prison, too long, "with the rough and rowdy men" of whom, I think it is fair to say, he is not one. And he has had a bad experience with railroad men, who "drink up your blood like wine." Even Tempe, his woman, doesn't love him in the way he deserves, wanting him only when he can supply the cash for the nine-dollar shawl she covets; that doesn't prevent him, though, from loving her: Tempe, he urges her, let your hair roll down, "let your bangs curl around." To hear her sing, he would wish himself not only a contemptible mole but a vile "lizard in the spring."

A lizard, a mole: Bascom is not the first man in love to feel his rodent-like unworthiness and reptilian cupidity, as well as a gross impatience with the world as it is: a mole, maybe, but one that "would root this mountain down." Nor is he the first to feel, under the influence of love, the roughness of his own sex, or whose heart has learned the arcane and curious language in which nature, in the form of mole and lizard, little miracles of creation and perhaps, in the metaphorical field of sexuality, covert genital symbols, both speaks to his condition and brings him into unconscious sympathy with his beloved.

Yet the singer's voice registers none of these discontents. For these are the discontents of youth, and his mood is a kind of gladness, the gladness of one who has been through it all, left it behind him, and is wise enough to know that it is, after all, an old story; his voice has the quaver and the sagacity of one who has narrowly escaped into middle age, the contraption of his banjo rattling like some old farm engine. Lunsford was forty-six when he recorded this version of the song; he recorded it on at least six other occasions. His voice swells nearly to a laugh as he sings, as if with a renewed conviction of the truth of the old song, and perhaps with a memory of the night twenty-seven years ago when he and his college classmates sat up in a railway station singing it, waiting for the train to take them back to Asheville.[13]

How is the imagination to resolve these contraries—the voice that tells the story, a figure of folklore, whose heart is fixed on the lizard and the mole, on Tempe's curls and her nine-dollar shawl, on rough convicts and the long days behind bars, the treacherous railroad men—what unseen incidents tie these images together we can only guess—and the figure of the voice that sings the song and plays the banjo, a figure of culture and history, touched with the spirit of a particular historical moment, a particular moment in a life to which the singing of the song gives meaning and form?

The answer is that it is not to resolve them. Listen to "I Wish I Was a Mole in the Ground" again and again, learn to play the banjo and sing it yourself over and over, study every printed version, squander your time in the bargain, and you still won't fathom it. The folksong has created a whole new man and a new world in which to live.

Into that world "Old Dog Blue" loses us even more thoroughly. Jackson's song probably has no more to do with the singer's actual experience than Lunsford's does with his; and yet he sings with the arresting honesty and immediacy of pure presence. You can actually hear Jackson composing the song on the spot, reaching out into the limbs of the oral tradition, coupling new-won lines to the song on the spur of a rhyme. Like "Mole in the Ground," "Old Blue" is a pentatonic tune, but it doesn't venture far from its home territory. In fact, like many songs in the Afro-American tradition, the melody tends to linger at its center, dropping with each line like a sentence finally to the sixth below the tonic, where the song acquires its somber, melancholy tone, then in a bridge climbing to the sixth above, where its sadness takes on the momentary sublimity of a cry—but, because the melody remains confined between the sixths below and above the tonic, can go no further. Jackson's guitar repeats a sober riff that sets out deep under the tonic, on the fifth, lingers on the sixth below, and ascends briefly to the second above, where it mingles with the song; his voice, which seems to flow directly out of his breast, is burdened, it seems, even in its tenor range, with a weight of grief that we cannot but attach to the memory of an old dog made almost visible to us.

Who would think a man could love a dog so much? Or, indeed, that we could love him, love his feet, "so big and round," love him because he is so loyal, companionable, and smart? Sending the craven marsupial into a tree is the least of his accomplishments; he can also corner a possum in a hollow log and maroon it on a tree stump, and even watch over the one in a sack "until I get back." Because he is so like a friend—"Blue looked at me and I looked at him"—when his time comes to go, "Blue laid down and died like a man."

There are probably hundreds of versions of "Old Blue." Folklorists have collected them in Mississippi, Texas, and the Carolinas, in which the dog, who can tree a possum anywhere, is in the company of other wonderful animals that figure in fables and tall tales. But Jackson's Blue, even when the singer pays his dog the Miltonic tribute of digging his grave with a silver spade and letting him down on a golden chain—"every link I called his name"—seems to have scratched on our own backdoor. Perhaps it is because, with the fugitive stanzas from some lost song interpolated with this one, the singer has become not only Blue's celebrant but a man in his own right, who in the opening lines of the song tells us that he's on his way back to where he came from, where "me and them pretty girls ganged around"—a place he recalls even in the midst of his tribute to Blue, by remembering the "pretty little girl with the red dress on." It is more than a conceit, then, when the singer imagines Blue treeing possums in the Promised Land or in Noah's Ark, because he still hears, as we hear the voices of our absent children in grocery stores and on the street, "Old Blue bark." It's a song about a dog, certainly; but it's a song too about love, loss, and the persistence of the past.

And yet, as on its twelfth side the Folkways Anthology ushers us out, we come to understand that there is, finally, no "real life" that has not been transfigured in imagination, that we seem not to experience ourselves at all until we have formulated our experience in language and thought, in declaration, recollection, and propostion, in memory and wish, in song, story, and image.

Whatever reading may have led us to side 12 of the Folkways Anthology, all listeners meet there for seven of the most memorable performances ever collected on a recorded disc. Except for Uncle Dave Macon's merry introductory pieces, which are fully formed melodies in a diatonic mode redolent of the roadshow and the coal camp, the songs on side 12 seem to share a broad southern tonality formed from the melding of the pentatonic scale to the blues mode, on the one hand, and to the mixolydian mode on the other, closely related tonal realms that account, melodically at least, for the fertile symbiosis of Scots-Irish and African-American musical traditions in the south; all of the songs are deeply embedded in southern language and experience. What that experience may be is darkly suggested by the subject as well as the style of the songs: the first three touch life on a prison workgang, while the two that follow, Smith's notes assure us, did originate as worksongs—all five, in fact, are "structurally adapted to responsive chanting by workers," with the "characteristic leader and chorus pattern."

Still, if the first five songs are in some sense about bondage, they are also about freedom, or the dream of it: for the concluding songs of the Folkways Anthology, Ken Maynard's goofy "The Lone Star Trail" and Henry Thomas' glorious "Fishin' Blues," sing to us from a world uncomplicated, bountiful, and limitless.

One can trace this movement. The clever diatonism of Uncle Dave Macon's songs supports his wit and topicality, with the ironic references to forced labor, drink, and sex. With his celluloid collar, suspenders, and button shoes, his ingenious banjo picking that defies authority, the grinning gold tooth that twinkles like a roguish eye, his wild clog dance that laughs at oppression, poverty, and age, the boisterous and ungovernable min-strel becomes a deposed monarch and muledriver who has made of his condition an artifact of transcendent gaiety.

In John Hurt's "Spike Driver Blues," though, Macon's cheery diatonic scale withdraws into the characteristic flatted third and seventh of the blues; as Smith notes, Hurt sings introspectively, recalling John Henry's story but reading it differently: as the story of a strong man who nevertheless "went down," not the hero who triumphed over a machine but a fool who let himself be worked to death. "That's why I'm gone," Hurt announces to himself, while still compelled to swing the hammer that killed John Henry but that "won't kill me." We seem to eavesdrop; the sinister geometry of his guitar picking, with its insurgent counter-rhythms, is the very subterfuge by which he will make his escape and travel the "long ways from east Colorado, honey, to my home"—intelligent and keen as his resolve, though, his voice betrays a gentle nature capable of bearing its suffering philosophically but likely doomed, nevertheless, to bear it.

In the Memphis Jug Band's "K. C. Moan," however, the in-ward ruminations of a man in the workgang, attaching his longings to the sound of a distant train whistle and thence to the thought of a woman, have been reconstituted in a fraternal quartet of fellows who, in the lonesome refrain of harmonica, kazoo, jug, guitar, and bass, seem to throw their arms over one another's shoulders, like they do down at the Domino on Friday nights, recollecting some old time past and gone. Their single voices loosely commingle, their casual harmonies shift as each finds his position in the chorus. The blue notes seem gradually to fade out of existence as the song draws to a close—and with them a world lapses behind us, a door closes, an old dispensation runs out; a new land opens up, an Oklahoma territory, vast, sunlit, and virginal, spread in the silence lying beyond the last notes of the Anthology but glimpsed in the merriment of its concluding pieces that, ranging in youthful and energetic open scales, have actually won the freedom of which men on the chaingang, Uncle Dave and John Hurt and the Memphis Jug Band, and all of humanity, can only dream.

The title of J. P. Nestor's "Train on the Island" most likely is descended from an Irish reel, "Lady on the Island," which, with its haunting shift a whole tone below the tonic, has flourished as a dance tune among southern fiddlers; but the tune with which "Lady on the Island" is traditionally coupled as a medley, "Callahan's Reel," has apparently provided, at some remote time and place, the rude melody of a worksong, almost certainly of African-American origin, whose half-intelligible fragments tumble out of Nestor's throat like the plaintive shouts of a railroad conductor, cobbled together of archaic and ingenuous phrases and isolated sounds and images: "go tell my true love" from English balladry and, as if from a Pentecostal hymn, "it's happy I do feel"; somewhere a locomotive charges ahead, its whistle screaming, "interpreted," as Smith notes laconically, on the banjo and fiddle, the one racing at an exhilarated tempo, the other urgently trailing with its fenders on the tracks. The singer hears it squeal and blow; "go tell my true love," he says enigmatically, that "I can't roll the wheel," while he and his fiddling companion traverse the strange, dark, rolling terrain—perhaps, somehow, the mountains around Galax, Virginia, crisscrossed by lumber and coal railroads, where Nestor and fiddler Norman Edmunds lived when they recorded the song—as if the mountains themselves could open their mouths to speak.

Ken Maynard was a rodeo rider and stuntman whose "Lone Star Trail," the penultimate song on the Anthology, comes from the sound track of *The Wagon Master,* a western movie of 1929.[14] In a squeezed nasal voice that briefly recalls the hillbilly singers of earlier cuts, Maynard blunders onto the stage of the Anthology with comic buffoonery, the classic bumpkin, utterly out of place, bringing a momentary pause to its varied forces, which hang in suspension while he brags to us, in the formal diction of the nineteenth century, of a carefree life on the Texas trail, of his skill and ease with the lasso, his love of the rolling prairie "that's far from travail and strife." He recalls the "dusty billows" that rise up fifty miles from water, where the "grass is scorching dry" and the gentle rains bring lakes "full of water," grass "waving fine," and a "pleasant smile" to the boss's face. Evening falls, and the fire of the setting sun plays on the horns of the cattle; we hear the horses shake their saddles and the startled longhorns rise to their feet in a mass. He can reflect happily on the "sweetest girl in the whole wide world" who has fallen in love with him, and swear that he'd marry her if he had a stake; but, as his wild and lonesome yodel reveals, there really is no other life for him but this one: "behind a bunch of longhorns I'll journey all my life."

It's a pastoral idyll, of course, but also a curious interlude in the movement of the Anthology. Its two-odd minutes of high-pitched upland nasality and stiff, nervous rhythms, placed within sight of the Anthology's closing selection, in a musical context now steeped in complex and driving beats, dark open calls, languid melismatic detours, and sliding blue tones, have a cloying impertinence. In a sense the song, in this place, is absurd. Side 12 of the Folkways Anthology dwells on pain, dislocation, forced labor, and imprisonment, even when it does so with comic irony; its promise, in Uncle Dave's grim satire on the ball and chain and his outspoken commentary on convict labor, in John Hurt's savvy, muttering, futile defiance of a vast and faceless oppression, in J. P. Nestor's ecstatic shout, where the drive toward liberation comes in the face of an unabridged and intimate confrontation with suffering, reaches beyond the innocence and glamor of the Hollywood western, and beyond the repressed, narrow vocality that is in flat contradiction to the claim of the lyric. Yet I think that "Lone Star Trail" has been ingeniously placed to arrest the gigantic techtonics of the Anthology and to stabilize our attention for its contemplation of the end—and at the same time to sketch what the shape of that ending might be.

On its last band the Folkways Anthology returns us to the hardy, generous, open voice of Henry Thomas. His "Fishin' Blues" is a cheerful, straightforward song, almost a march, free of blues tonalities but not of its vocality, regularly but lightly syncopated—a little rag, in other words—about catching a catfish and frying it up in a pan. It is surprising how few folksongs there are about fishing. But as Paul Oliver suggests, "Fishin' Blues" may have been a series of sexual innuendos until Thomas emended it for the recording machine: that is the context in which the idea of fishing normally occurs in the blues. It is the metaphor, moreover, employed in a nearly identical song collected by W. P. Webb in Gatesville, Texas, from a streetsinger named "Rags" who very likely was Ragtime Texas Thomas himself.[15]

The fish, like the hound dog, is sometimes in the blues a female symbol; but isolated from the contexts that would alert us to its specifically sexual significance, it acquires a more compellingly erotic and mysterious character, verging on the other realm in which the fish has its meaning, the spiritual, with its suggestions of descent to the unconscious and to the deep sources of life. On the face of it, "Fishin' Blues" is simply a song about a man *gone fishing,* with all that implies; but in the context of the Anthology as a whole, the fish is an almost palpable sign, as much as if its image had been painted on the record label.

The very concept of "song" as a fixed text, even one fixed in memory, somewhat misrepresents the mercurial mind of Henry Thomas, which was an echo chamber of tune fragments, lyric phrases, lines, song titles, and guitar riffs that could be combined and recombined with the ready resourcefulness of the streetsinger living by his wits, whose performances can be almost indefinitely extemporized from bits and pieces of folk and popular music: Thomas' recorded repertory reveals transient performances often nonsensical in themselves but echoing lines from other songs—"Molly and Tenbrooks," "Little Red Caboose," "John Henry," "Make Me a Pallet on Your Floor," "Honey, Won't You Allow Me One More Chance," among others—from minstrelsy, vaudeville, and Tin Pan Alley.[16]

Thomas' aim, like all minstrels, buskers, and other roving musicians, is to win a coin from the pedestrian by honoring requests—by serving the purpose that radios and tape players serve today, of speaking to the moment; with a fragment of the melody and the lyric, and of the title line, he can by filling in the gaps from his own ragbag produce a song that sounds tolerably like, but textually speaking cannot be, the coon song "Honey, Won't You Allow Me One More Chance" strangely joined to a fragment from Lemon Jefferson's gospel song "See That My Grave Is Kept Clean":

> One kind favor I ask of you
> Honey, won't you 'low me one more chance?

Or of "John Henry," oddly coupled to a fragment from mountain tradition itself descended from British balladry:

> Henry went on the mountain top
> Give his horn a blow.

Or of a Kentucky racehorse song of the 1870s, "Molly and Tenbrooks," hitched up nonsensically to a line from "Liza Jane" and to another from an unknown train song:

> Run Molly run, run Molly run,
> Run Molly run, goin' to have some fun.
> Oh Liza! Oh Liza Jane! Died on that train.

Indeed among Thomas' sources may have been other recordings from the same period. As Tony Russell observes, Thomas' "John Henry," "Arkansas," "The Fox and the Hounds," "Jonah in the Wilderness," "Shanty Blues," and "When the Train Comes Along" had all been recorded a few years earlier by Uncle Dave Macon, while Thomas' medleys such as "Bob McKinney" echo Macon's "Wasn't He Bad," "Make Me a Pallet on the Floor," and "Bully of the Town." Russell suspects that the Brunswick Company, "for whom Thomas made all and Macon the bulk of his titles, was attempting a sort of comparative issue programme—Macon for the whites, Thomas for the race . . . of course the songs concerned were so old that Thomas need not have learned from, nor even have heard, Macon's interpretations."[17] It is likely that Thomas reproduced Macon's records by ear, after a few listenings; Macon's own repertory, in any case, drew consistently from African-American music.

Who can tell what songs have left their traces in "Fishin' Blues"? Thomas chants a narrative that effaces the sexual reference, whatever it might have been, in favor of a kind of loafers' idyll, reminiscent of Walt Whitman at his ease on the grass: he cuts his pole on the hill at noon, buys his hook at the hardware store, and gets down to the river by one—wearing a watch, it seems—where a catfish waits to be caught; in the third verse he uses a fragment from "Shortnin' Bread," the one about the skillet and the lid, to help him imagine frying his catch.

Between these verses, which are nearly monotonic recitations, he sings a nine-line chorus whose lyric, melody, and harmony—including the tonic, subdominant, dominant, and second chords—are so fully developed as to suggest an origin in some popular composition: perhaps in a ragtime piece, the tradition to which its jaunty melody seems to belong. "Any fish bite, you got good bait" might be part of the song's hokum subtext, and so would be the line "You bet your life, your lovin' wife, I'll catch more fish than you"; but "here's a little something I would like to relate" is the idiom of the music hall. You can almost see Ragtime Texas bent forward in the buzzard lope, shuffling along the footlights, shaking his head at us, while his rhythmic, full-chorded guitar and his shouting voice seem to rise up over the unheard noise of an unknown thoroughfare to spread around us the light and shade of a cool spot by a river where the catfish linger near the bottom and sleep. Henry has turned out the light, locked the door, and hung up a sign, since that's what "gone fishing" means. But he knows what time it is.

And through it—breaking in its midst like a tattoo, a little countermelody, a barbaric, ethereal faerie sound, a human calliope, a kind of flute, but more open-voiced, as if some unknown deity of field or wood had suddenly by some espionage planted her voice in the Anthology from some undiscoverable place in unremembered time, a pastoral spirit that its hours of spell, chant, chorus, and incantation have at last awakened. It is the sound of something breaking free, something not of this world, Andean, forged in that limbic region where natural forms, animated by human forces, return to throng a human consciousness evacuated by its own projections.

It is the sound of panpipes: called "quills" in the south, cut from southern canebrake. It must be that Henry Thomas, who is after all a street performer, wears them around his neck on a rack, like a harmonica, and toots on them between choruses; it must be that he has cut them and tied their several lengths together himself.

In Ragtime Texas Thomas, his very identity, and the songs that constitute it, utterly in rags—and we should imagine him in rags, like the old minstrel and circus tramps, their silk hats opened up like tin cans—Smith has fashioned a moment in which American culture lies beyond reach of its historical origins and social structures and discovered the anthropological first principle, which continually dismantles the ever-proliferating rational forms that our civilization has erected around us. The quills write the story of American folk music into the greater inventory of human sounds, and blow it back to the savannahs of human desire to remind us of what, in the remotest and least accessible regions of memory, in spite of all appearances, we actually are. This is transient, but transcendent, knowledge, never thinkable except in the moment of the disintegration of the structures of thought, inseparable from the narrative that produces it and hence never knowable in itself except by an endless process of repetition and becoming.

Powerful prevailing winds converge on the Folkways Anthology, producing a cultural gyre that as it turns forms an ever more still and lucid eye in which the ariel sound of the panpipes seems to fly unmolested. Among those currents is the Anthology's narrative content, which carries the rage, jealousy, and passion of fully engaged and literal sexuality, such as we find in the ballads, toward the two realms in which sexuality elaborates itself—in the festive occasions, secular and religious, in which people reconstitute their solidarity, and in the broader field where social forms issue in structures of power and oppression, where recklessness, defiance, and outlawry gradually bring the individual personality up to the surface of the Anthology—where in its own voice it reports its increasing loneliness, isolation, bondage, and, as the set approaches its concluding side, begins its movement toward freedom and transcendence.

Thus far the Anthology's sheer verbal report. But, again, this narrative development is undergirded by deeper changes produced on the one hand by the shifting orientation of medium to material and, on the other, by a stylistic evolution in which African vocality, tonality, and rhythm gradually transform European musical structures and practices. The aural medium comes into more intimate contact with the song material; the recorded ballads, with their third-person narratives in which the singer has only a narrative role, give way to choral performances and finally to first-person songs in which traditional materials have been united with recorded performances by the temporal indeterminacy of the recording process itself.

Reflecting this reorientation of singer to song is the Anthology's stylistic movement. African musical practices are characterized, in general, by a relaxed or masked vocality, a plastic and nonmechanical tonality, and a rhythmic interaction that at once individuates and integrates, the entire process intimately associated with language and speech; its cultural meaning, at least in relation to stratified European harmonies, mechanically realized quantitative scales, and abstract musical scores, militates against rationalized, disciplinary power in favor of the aural, the improvisatory, the formulaic, the agonistic, and the participatory.

Thus flowing below the narrative trajectory of the Anthology, from engaged sexuality, sociality, and festive community, from community to resistance, resistance to isolation, and isolation to bondage, is a deep countermovement, one that dissipates, insofar as such forces and structures can be embodied in musical sound, the very forces and structures that issue in the repressive and disciplinary effects on sexuality and the personality against which the Anthology's heroes and outlaws have ranged themselves, which holds its prisoners in bondage, and which registers its presence in the voices of nearly all its singers. By dissolving the historicity that holds singers and songs in a temporal network, the singers in effect take control of the counterhistory that is evolving on the Anthology and populate it with a putative folk culture; that culture absorbs the African musical temperament—a process in southern folk culture of which the Anthology is, as Harry Smith knew, a powerful sociocultural index. The Anthology thus loosens the articulations of the European-American psychosocial framework and, like jazz, blues, and other African-American musical forms, transfigures them, adopting them simply as one element in an ironic interplay of textual fixity and spontaneous invention, the implication being that within disciplinary structures there is always a creative energy that can weaken the instruments of social control and at the same time preserve them as frameworks for the play of erotic forces. *This old hammer killed John Henry—but it can't kill me.*

The Anthology in a sense ratifies, but at the cultural and not the ideological level, the program of subversion with which it has been associated historically. It anticipates the popular music that followed it in a more than musical sense. Its own end point may perhaps be taken as the formal end of Folkways Records itself, whose total project, recording the sounds of the human lifeworld, animates the absent universe by stealing away its sounds that *as* sounds register life and presence: a revivified world in which not only infants, great men, and folksingers, but office machines, crickets, and monsoon winds, great and small, like gods, all speak. We should recognize that the *Folkways Anthology of American Folk Music* achieves its ends aurally—working as a kind of solvent on the fixed distinctions of continuous rational space, with its visual-tactile gradient, and transforming it into an altogether dynamic, discontinuous, and irrational space: a multifarious, simultaneous universe, all of its differentiations uncertain, its boundaries permeable and its forms protean, the ephemeral world whose perceptual surface we must continually penetrate to construct a palpable reality, one that always partakes of our own experience.

Vivified by intelligent presences, the aural universe is thick with angelic agents, alive and embodied. It is the cosmos that scholasticism elaborated through dialogue and debate, grounded in obedience to the voices of secular philosophy and divine revelation. The memory theater was a transitional device, as institutional knowledge collapsed and every confidence in traditional authority was called into question, used by magicians and mystics to learn the cosmos, by means of the ductile and mechanical symbolic methods that mathematics would soon displace. Smith's memory theater for the ear, and perhaps now the whole environment of electronically preserved and transmitted information in which we live, suggests another moment of transition, in which, as an unintelligible world massed itself on our horizon, we sought to master the forms of its creation.

Pete Seeger at the Newport Folk Festival, 1965

7

He Shall Overcome

In their romance with folksong, revivalists often thrust upon brilliantly gifted but sometimes sheltered and unworldly people, or on tough, ill-used, implacable people, the unaccustomed, occult, and capricious role of "folksinger." Some flourished in that role; some didn't. Better perhaps in the end, as Joseph Conrad put it, "in the romantic element to immerse one-self"—even if the signs are not entirely auspicious. This is what Pete Seeger did—and he did it voluntarily, penitentially, in a redemptive, self-effacing career born of a uniquely inventive reconciliation of gifts and opportunities, of a peculiar bravery that, while signifying profound and inarticulable injury, at the same time emboldened him to jettison the fears and prejudices that usually prevent us from negotiating an agreement between personality and society all our own.

From a welter of influences and occasions, Seeger fashioned a character and a career frugal but imaginative in its economy, rugged but genteel in its texture, simple and consistent in mo-tive, one that spun the fibers of diverse cultural traditions into a continuous thread to lead him out of, but has remained stead-fastly anchored in, his basic sadness. Though he allied himself with ideologues, his ideas were not complicated, and his convictions, deeper than ideas, deeply contradictory. Had Seeger turned out differently, had he become a casualty of idleness, depression, or failure, causes enough might have been unearthed from the record; but he outdistanced the record. Though Seeger's unique personal document has been anathema to some, many have been signatories to it, and it has become a permanent part of the literature of American identity.

Once I asked a friend, a cloistered monk, if I might meet the abbot of his monastery, said to be a holy man. "There wouldn't be much point in that," he answered. "There's nothing to meet." Seeger is notorious for his inaccessibility, his general withdrawal from personal or intimate relations. "Only Pete knows Pete," Moses Asch once told Gene Bluestein. "I don't think even Toshi"—Pete's wife—"knows Pete."[1] Alan Wald notes, "Seeger is an enigmatic figure, who closely guards his personal life; he is a man who appears anti-intellectual and warm-hearted in public life, but is said to be quite otherwise in private."[2] I doubt it. In Seeger the personal presence that emerges through engagement with others, in a series of negotiated social gestures, is sublimated, a larval stage lingering only in vestiges, its forces marshaled on behalf of an achieved self—originated, not negotiated—that appears not through engagement but in affiliation, commitment, and, most of all, performance.

His performances have changed lives: unlike the great mass of performers who have secured their personal privacy behind a facade of public masks, Seeger makes in performance, I believe innocently and unconsciously, a most intimate revelation. All of him is there: the elegantly disciplined and vigorous awkwardness; the moral imperiality humbled by a conviction of unworthiness; a fundamental embarrassment put temporarily at bay by energetic, liberal, and scrupulously amateur musicianship; the refinement politely disguised, the delicacy waived, the theme of social injustice persistently sounded with beseeching gestures from within a private sorrow. Revealing himself, he remakes us.

A doctor's son from Passaic, Ralph Rinzler, and a lawyer's son from Philadelphia, Roger Abrahams, heard Pete Seeger together at Swarthmore College in 1953. As a boy Abrahams wanted to become a popular singer; he had been stage struck, captivated by Burl Ives in *Sing Out, Sweet Land*. Both he and Rinzler were Gilbert and Sullivan fanatics.[3] But in the encounter with Seeger "we realized that this was what we wanted to do for the rest of our lives"—that's how Abrahams remembers it. Seeger was a man with "clarity of spirit and vision," who gave no evidence in his presentation of any particular ideological associations—with the Communist Party or the Popular Front—through whom life flowed purely, without subtle ideological convolutions. For Rinzler, "everything fit together" in Seeger; "he seemed absolutely coherent."[4] Immediately the two young men went out to buy banjos; in a few years both were well established as revivalist musicians; in the fullness of their careers Abrahams became one of the most creative folklore scholars and theorists, and Rinzler, who died in 1994, became a leading figure in the federal folklife establishment. Rinzler's friendships with Mike and Peggy Seeger, formed at the Swarthmore festival, issued in an association with the Seeger family that consistently shaped his activist outlook.

There is a peculiar kind of authenticity in what Rinzler calls "the coming together of ideology and musicianship." But whether creed or ideology, philosophy or faith, it offers to the literate young person in a multiplex society, who has not yet learned to tolerate much ambiguity, whose identity in the moment of its annealling demands a certain definiteness and rigidity, a way of achieving the apparent unity and singularity of mind, not hobbled by self-consciousness or crooked by guile or sickened with irony, which is the apparent blessing of folk culture. "In folk societies," John Cohen writes, "the limitations are often clear and strong."

> The influence of tradition is heavily respected and goes unquestioned. In the city, each individual is constantly in search of values . . . This search for values is becoming the tradition of the city. If

we from the city are attracted to folk music, it is because we appreciate the clarity of the limitations within which folk music developed. But ultimately we appreciate the *order* that comes of these limitations.[5]

In folksong, that order is the order of culture; in urban, secular, literate society, it is the order of ideas, the textualization of culture that is ideology, and the declaration of commitment that is what we call belief. Somewhere between these poles lay the folk revival and all the youth movements that followed it, with a commitment to an order of signs, not words.

It is not immaterial that both Rinzler and Abrahams were young men of German-Jewish background, both powerfully influenced in boyhood by admired but aloof elder men, an uncle and a father, respectively, with socialist leanings; Seeger touched them clearly on a level deeper than ideas, though in retrospect ideas provide a useful way of explaining the force of Seeger's presence. Still, as the boys' first impulse—to go out and buy a banjo—indicates, it was in his musicianship that his meaning seemed to be concentrated.

Any music or musical instrument has a social as well as an historical meaning; band or orchestral or jazz instruments, classical or cabaret or pop singing, could be taken as signs of participation in complex institutions and social structures, elite, popular, and commercial, extending outward into certain classes and communities, establishments, cultural fields, and standards of taste. The cellist or French horn player, saxophonist or pianist, could not have her meaning in and of herself, but in relation to the extensively ramified character of her participation in these systems.

The same could not be said of the strange lanky fellow ambling up Fourth Avenue with a banjo on his back. The social connections of the banjo had been obscured by its repeated disappearances from popular music; its marginality, its obdurate indissolubility in social meaning, gave it an eerily unlocatable quality, a "signifier in isolation"—comparable, perhaps, to a soldier's carbine protruding uncannily, unbelievably, from a book-depository window—no longer grounded in our understanding of how the material world articulates with the social system, producing a fissure in social reality itself. The banjo in a sense reversed the current of signification, becoming intensely fascinating *in itself*, as its devotees sought to absorb it into their phenomenal life by inscribing it with new orders of meaning that would pacify or subdue it.

As Alan Lomax and many others have observed, Pete Seeger looks like, and in a sense *is*, his banjo—the anomalies of anomalies in his anomalous personality. Seeger's own banjo was an oddly elongated variant of its nineteenth-century original, with a tuning peg fixed halfway up a neck to which three extra frets had been added—an innovation of Seeger's in 1944 that, while it permitted him to play in more keys, also exposed the conspiracy of elongation, legs, arms, and banjo neck, in which man and instrument were passionately involved.

Culturally, the banjo was an enigma, having been thrust out of a series of social niches through associations that had themselves become indefinable: abandoned by black culture, which reconstructed it from an African progenitor, forsaken by the Gilded Age parlor society in which it had a brief vogue, repudiated by jazz as jazz moved uptown—it was the instrument that history left behind. To take it up, as Seeger had, was a gesture at once disarmingly candid and hauntingly emblematic, a fundamentally comic piece of cultural scavengery that like a clown's broken umbrella solicits ordinary good will in conventional terms as it also legislates some independence of norms and conventions.

The banjo, as Karen Linn recounts in her illuminating *That Half-Barbaric Twang*, had done service in this way before. In 1883 Joel Chandler Harris asserted that the banjo "savors strongly of the plantations through which the back streets of New York City run."[6] As banjo music loiters on the edges of western musical categories, so it has tended to linger where sexual, social, and political boundaries are most ambiguous. In minstrelsy, sharp racial distinctions obscured the fact that blackface and the banjo were instruments for producing such distinctions where cultural forces had muddied the fine social discriminations so vital to an emergent class.

Inscribed with images of a languid and aristocratic Old South, the banjo of the Gilded Age had been particularly significant to leisured young women whose social and sexual status was called into question by the emergence of a class of semiprofessionals—stenographers, typists, telephone operators—exploiting new opportunities for economic independence. It was significant to another embattled class as well—that of industrial foremen, skilled tradesmen, new mechanical specialists and tinkerers, public servants such as police and firemen, record-keepers and clerks who expressed their sense of their rarefied and elusive social station—sandwiched between the working class and the petty bourgeoisie, neither one nor the other—by adapting the musical artifacts of bourgeois culture to a nonserious, even in some quarters a despised, instrument, but one made by machines and demanding a craftsman's dexterity to play. Now, in the emergent folk revival, Seeger's banjo and the folksongs it accompanied were emerging again, in a new form, to announce that a demographic group—"the young"—had emerged as an unconvinced, unassimilated class demanding some sort of contract with social power.

That independence was economic, like the independence represented by the jazzman's horn or "ax," but moral as well: with his banjo on his back like a soldier's carbine, the solitary Seeger seemed a footsoldier in a vast invisible banjo army, at once crusader and apostate. As minstrelsy's signature instrument, the banjo embodied not only the victimization and marginality of the plantation slave but the spartan and adventurous spirit of the itinerant theatrical player or circus roustabout, uncompromised by ties to family, community, or society; to play it was a homely occupation, a kind of trade, like carpentry—hence

Seeger's rolled shirtcuffs. In short, it was the perfect icon of Seeger's achieved self—and to the young imagination of the folksong revival, which looked across the landscape of postwar society and found not a single opportunity to its liking, the banjo was a door, and Seeger was knocking on it.

I first encountered Pete Seeger, though I didn't realize it, in the early 1950s at summer camp. It was his banjo that had fascinated me in our little pantomime of *The Lonesome Train*, in which my best friend Ricky, whose growth spurt had sent him into the air a foot above our heads, played the role of Lincoln. Seeger didn't visit us as he did so many other camps during the period, no doubt because we were in Wisconsin; but our camp director, a rabbi's son from New Orleans who spoke rhapsodically of the lakes and pines and filled our hearts with holy dread when he donned a great ceremonial headdress of eagle feathers and carried his giant frame like a brimming cup around our council ring to the beat of an Indian drum, liked to play Weavers' songs on the public address system—especially, at summer's end when we were all packing our trunks, Woody Guthrie's "So Long, It's Been Good To Know Ya." I loved that song, maybe because I associated it with going home; but even then I could hear something in that gang of voices—Hays, Hellerman, Gilbert, Seeger—a kind of neighborliness, which I never forgot.

Of folksong, then, I knew a little: my uncle gave me a little plastic record on which the folksinger Tom Glazer told the story, with some catchy Irish worksongs, of the completion of the transcontinental railroad. But I was innocent of politics. I knew nothing of socialism or the Spanish Civil War and still less of blacklisting, though I'd seen the Army-McCarthy hearings on our new Emerson television—without of course understanding anything about them. Of communists I knew only that they were sinister men with eyeglasses and neckties whom I was supposed to fear. My mother's father had emigrated from St. Petersburg in 1898, peddled fish, and lost a hard-won real estate fortune in the depression; she voted, with the rest of her family, for Adlai Stevenson. But my father voted for Eisenhower. He was a midwesterner, son of an oldtime Methodist preacher, and reminded everyone, me included, of Gene Autry.

Some years later a young man I admired, a bit ahead of me, already in his first year at the University of Michigan, the son of a Jewish patriarch who owned a furniture store and of an affectionate, bookish, chain-smoking, goggle-eyed woman, who had been one of my mother's childhood playmates, introduced me to two artifacts of his world: Peter Gunn, the hip television detective, and a Vanguard record album called *The Weavers at Carnegie Hall.* There were those voices; and on the cover was a tall man with a big nose, a tuxedo, and a banjo, whose name was Pete Seeger.

Soon all my friends had guitars or banjos and were singing everything from "Railroad Bill" to "Havah Nagiela." I had a beautiful long-necked banjo, the "Pete Seeger" model, with a smiling white face, white as table linen, a whiskery surface, and a set of shining steel strings that crossed it like the Golden Gate Bridge, and I played it constantly. I had a sweetheart too, who gave me a Pete Seeger album for my birthday, and we let one of his lonesome banjo tunes carry us out over the yellow hinter-lands beyond the bower of tender new caresses where we lay. At last Pete Seeger came to Chicago's Orchestra Hall, and spread wide his arms as we sang to him, and it changed me. It was thirty years ago, and I have not changed back.

Peter Seeger was born in 1919 and grew up on his grandpar-ents' fifty-acre estate near the Taconic Mountains in upstate New York; his unhappy young parents sent him away to board-ing school at the age of four and divorced when he was eight.[7] His grandfather, having made a fortune in sugar refining and rubber, expected his boys to follow him in business; but Charles, Pete's father, perhaps because of the elder Seeger's enthusiasm for Wagner, studied music at Harvard and aspired to become an avant-garde composer—a fitting aim within a moneyed family that traced its ancestry to German aristocracy. But by the time of Pete's birth he had lost a teaching position at Berkeley because of his opposition to America's entry into World War I.

Charles had his family's "probity, self-control, and strict table manners," one of Pete's brothers recalled, and expected perfection in everything. Pete's mother, Constance de Clyver Edson, raised in Tunisia and Paris, was a self-conscious young woman persistently anxious, apparently, about matters of money and respectability, devoted to her violin and inflexibly conservative in her musical tastes. She never convinced Pete to play the classical violin, for he had absorbed his father's contempt for "fine" music; but she infused in him a sense of what is classical in music perhaps even more exacting than her own.

Until he was seventeen, Pete saw his family only on school holidays, boarding in what was the only home he knew as a child, the barn at the family estate in New York; family life itself was strict, coolly formal, tightly controlled emotionally with, as family friend George Draper noted, "no tears allowed at family separations." Not perhaps the childhood we might want for our own children—but thoroughly compatible with the Seegers' Calvinist ancestry, with its watchful asceticism, its self-reproving moral rigor, and its all-pervading conviction of sin.

Here, it seems, must be the real fountainhead of Seeger's politics: a repressed and repressive personality, competent, dependable, and proud, given to detachment and reasonableness, often compulsively self-sacrificing but capable of intimacy only with difficulty, the habitual suppression of anxiety, anger, loneliness, and hurt, a tendency to place the needs of others before one's own, acquired of necessity from the emotional frustrations of childhood. "Toshi reminds me of something we've been through that's very unpleasant," Pete told his biographer, "but I haven't the faintest memory of the occasion. It's as if I have some protective device inside my brain; instead of causing grief by remembering it, I simply erase it."

Privilege does not guarantee that parents will bestow the unequivocal love from which spiritual freedom flows, or earn the trust on which worldly confidence is based. But it does confer a certain sense of immunity, warranted or not, from the spectres of disgrace and indigence, and hence a certain independence of social convention—and this may better equip a child to compensate early emotional deprivations. Certainly such a sense of immunity helped Charles Seeger to resist the enormous tide of anti-German political opinion in 1917. The true child of privilege need not think or do as others do; on the widened field where he will squander, repudiate, or sublimate his advantages, he enjoys a feeling of indomitability. Hence the phenomenon of the young gentleman-adventurer, like Pete's uncle Alan Seeger: Harvard man, friend of John Reed and Mike Gold, Greenwich Village bohemian, volunteer in the French Foreign Legion where he was shot to death leading a charge—and a poet who wrote the famous line, "I have a rendezvous with death."

The Calvinist personality was a formula designed to issue precisely in the efficiency, indefatigability, and moral ardor which brought it to prominence in the industrious mercantile society developing in the seventeenth century. But spiritual growth in every tradition entails the transcendence of personality, which in Calvinism, as in other religious traditions, discovers the long-sought infantine lost love in a divine love abroad impersonally in nature or in humanity. With a precision that robs all his actual and potential biographers of their thunder, Pete Seeger compared himself in his regular column in *Sing Out!* to John Chapman, the Swedenborgian mendicant from Massachusetts known as Johnny Appleseed, who in the early nineteenth century prepared the wilderness for the westward expansion by setting out apple nurseries throughout the Alleghenies into central Ohio. Chapman believed that the innermost human soul was divine and that, with resistance to temptation, and strict obedience to the word of God, human nature could be glorified by its indwelling influence. In folklore Chapman was remembered for his kindness to animals, his feats of strength, his ability to live in the wild, and for the stew-pot—how like a banjo!—he wore for a cap.

Seeger's longing for the "morally consistent life," then, was a venerable Yankee tradition—but it found its fulfillment in an original structure of influences from the experiences of his own family, class, culture, and times. Seeger was only one of many boys who read the works of Ernest Thompson Seton, founder of the Woodcraft League, who challenged his young readers to "survive in the woods with just yourself and an axe." Through woodcraft and Indian lore Seton promulgated a juvenile version of muscular Christianity, with its basic analogy of physical fitness and cleanliness to moral rigor and purity, bodily hardiness being a hedge against sexual temptation—particularly that bugaboo of the period, masturbation—and a corrective for the feminizing influences of bourgeois society.

New Russia's Primer, the Bolshevik children's book Seeger discovered as a boy in the Spring Hill school library at Litchfield, Connecticut, inculcated a similar message: to remain watchful for decadent tendencies in parents and teachers, and to help those nostalgic for prerevolutionary Russia to see the error of their ways. Seton's Little Savage and Lenin's Young Pioneer expressed the idealism and discipline that were Seeger's both by temperament and by tradition, and the young man's embrace of them may have started him off on the synthesis of politics and folksong that became his vocation and identity.

Though isolated and very shy, Seeger had already found his favorite social mode at Spring Hill, where he and a roommate, accompanied by Peter's ukulele and at the end by an entire auditorium of voices, led a program of sea chanties. At sixteen, just over five feet tall, and with his fresh complexion and long curls, Peter found himself in theatricals at Avon Old Farms, a prep school for "the elite of the well-ordered mind," in female roles. He was already subscribing to *New Masses*, memorializing his uncle Alan by reading John Reed and Mike Gold, and for spare change shining his classmates' shoes. At Avon, attracted by Gershwin songs, he put aside his uke, bought a disused tenor banjo from a faculty member, and joined the Hot Jazz Club.

But he couldn't reproduce on his four-string tenor banjo, a ragtime and jazz instrument, the sound he heard on the Library of Congress recordings his stepmother Ruth Crawford was in the summer of 1936 transcribing for John and Alan Lomax: the sound of the five-string southern mountain banjo, played by Bascom Lamar Lunsford, Pete Steele, Buell Kazee, Wade Ward, Lily May Ledford—names that became household words to folk revivalists of the sixties—and Uncle Dave Macon, whom Seeger considered the best banjo player in the world. That the folk banjo had five strings, not four, Pete didn't discover until, later that summer of 1936, his father took him to Lunsford's folk festival in Asheville. "I lost my heart to the old-fashioned five string-banjo," he said, "played mountain style."[8]

Discovering the five-string and playing it, however, were different matters. Seeger's career as a folksinger began inauspiciously in New York where, having dropped out of Harvard and taken up residence with his brothers on the Lower East Side, Seeger felt powerfully the synthesis of personal authenticity and politically meaningful activity that possessed the youthful imagination of the period; at seventeen he had worked at a socialist summer camp operated by family friends alongside men and women only slightly older than himself who, instead of returning to school the following fall, volunteered for duty in the Lincoln Brigade. But unable to find work in his chosen career as a newspaper reporter, Seeger was forced back on his banjo—and, in a sense, on the necessity of turning the banjo itself to these same ends. His sister-in-law had dared him to perform on the street: so he stood on Park Avenue and sang "Old Man River" and "Cindy" to his banjo accompaniment, earning 75 cents in three hours. His aunt Elsie Seeger, principal of the Dalton School, got him a job at a dance, where he earned

5 dollars and an invitation to repeat his performance at other private schools, among which was the progressive Little Red Schoolhouse, where Margot Mayo, founder of the American Square Dance Group, was on the faculty.

Mayo's group at that point anchored New York City's folksong movement; her cousin, the Kentucky mountain banjoist Rufus Crisp, showed Seeger the arcane clawhammer or "frailing" style of banjo playing, a technique of West African origin nearly impossible to understand by either listening or watching alone, in which lay the secret of the folk banjo's driving, rhythmic sound. Seeger's adaptation of this technique, what he called his "basic strum," became his musical signature and a versatile method for accompanying folksongs of all kinds. By nestling a resonant chord between two precise notes, a melody note and a chiming note on the fifth string, Seeger gentrified the more percussive frailing style, with its vigorous hammering of the forearm and its percussive rapping of the fingernail on the banjo head.

At precisely this moment, folk music was emerging into the culture of the left in New York City, whose major preoccupation, as we have seen, was the representation of a political idea, the idea of the People: not as a philosophical abstraction, but as a palpable reality, one that could be painted, photographed, interviewed and recorded, chronicled in novels, championed on the stage and screen, and celebrated in music and dance. Leadbelly was a people's hero incarnate, and so was a few years later Paul Robeson. The year 1938 had brought John Hammond's first Spirituals to Swing concert, Aaron Copland's *Billy the Kid*, and Martha Graham's *American Document*; in 1939 came Earl Robinson's and Robeson's *Ballad for Americans*; in 1940 Alan Lomax's radio program *Back Where I Come From* made its debut, and Woody Guthrie arrived in New York.

Literature had produced images of populist heroes, in Carl Sandburg's Lincoln and John Steinbeck's Tom Joad, both of whom the folksong movement made part of its iconography—Lincoln in Robinson's cantata *The Lonesome Train,* in which Seeger played a banjo part, and the Okie Tom Joad in Guthrie's ambitious ballad of seventeen-odd stanzas, which was introduced at the *Grapes of Wrath* benefit for migrant workers in 1940. "Woody Guthrie just ambled out," Pete Seeger recalls, "offhand and casual . . . a short fellow complete with western hat, boots, bluejeans, and needing a shave, spinning out stories and singing songs he'd made up . . . I just naturally wanted to know more about him."

Seeger himself appeared with Guthrie that evening—his first concert performance—although stage fright, he says, deprived him both of the words to his song and the ability to accompany himself on the banjo. But his involvement with the heroes of the folksong movement was already intimate. Alan Lomax had introduced the fledgling banjoist to Aunt Molly Jackson, whom Seeger knew from Library of Congress recordings, and to Leadbelly as well, from whom he took lessons on the twelve-string guitar. By the summer of 1939 his musical skills had improved so much that he could travel as a banjoist and singer with the Vagabond Puppeteers, two of whose members had trained in the rural education campaign of postrevolutionary Mexico; this radical band offered to perform for the dairy farmers' union in the midst of New York state's violent milk strike. Seeger hadn't banked on becoming a soloist, which was anathema to him; but his audience of farmers was enthusiastic about his banjo and asked to hear it—a crisis of self-consciousness that Seeger resolved by coaxing the audience to sing along with him. By degrees he was discovering his calling, whose moral tone was perhaps deepened when the union steward who had offered his hospitality to the group was struck by a scab driver and killed.

As a boy Pete Seeger watched volunteer squads from Communist Party unemployment councils replenish the shattered households of evicted tenants on the Lower East Side; in the cold lofts of Greenwich Village, where the Composers' Collective held its meetings, he heard Aaron Copland speak on the role of music in the class struggle. Still the impulse to remake himself by his own rite of passage was irresistible: with Woody he set out for Oklahoma in Guthrie's new Plymouth—bought on credit—literally singing not only for striking oil workers but for haircuts, gas, lodging, and food, while absorbing the music of Gene Autry and Bob Wills from the car radio. Then in 1940 Seeger set out on his own, hitchhiking and hoboing through Missouri, Wisconsin, South Dakota, and Montana, sleeping in a Salvation Army overcoat. He mangled his banjo in a leap from a moving freight train, hocked his camera for a cheap guitar, and for money played cowboy songs in a saloon: a creditable narrative for a rather delicate boy. A month after his return he set out for Alabama, looking for Joe Gelders, a radical labor organizer and former University of Alabama physics professor[9] in whom he seems finally to have located the social and cultural pole around which his career, and the entire folk revival, was to revolve. "You can have your Radio City Music Hall," he wrote, "your Hotel Savoy, your Hollywood Kleig lights, and your tuxedos, but as far as I'm concerned the best music I ever heard came out of that old shack in Townley, Alabama."

Seeger's late adolescence converged auspiciously with an extraordinary historical moment, subjecting him to the influence of men and women of great personal amplitude and power, even of genius. In the years of the folk revival, many young people then put on Seeger's identity in the hopes of making it their own. But Seeger's identity, while self-made, was not put on; it was sought and won, a segment of a social and psychological arc that at its apogee worked an irresistible influence on thousands of young people, altering their lives forever, and that, as Seeger approached fifty, returned, carrying the moral souvenirs of its remarkable transit to the point at which it had begun.

Seeger is the type and, for the young people who encountered him in the fifties and early sixties, the original of the fresh, untempered youth who, dizzy with a sense of his own insubstantiality, despising the class and education that made him but

Seeger at the Washington Labor Canteen, 1944, with Eleanor Roosevelt

filled with the romance that only class and education can im-
part, projects out of his heart the adventure by which he will
season himself, and in which he will discover the self that will
authenticate him—or, more accurately, court the self that, if he
is worthy, will accept him. All lives follow, like the energy that
runs along a powerline, a direction determined by the compass
points of class, education, and the like, and defined by the
particular terrain of personality and experience; all people carry
in the current of their being the resulting articulations of its flow
that constitute the message of identity. For most of us, the life
force flows in one or two directions; experience follows, for
most, a beaten track, and individuality falls readily into familiar
patterns and categories. But Seeger, though in himself a point
nearly refined out of existence, is the intersection of many such
lines, each of which has left a betraying sign in him, each sign

isolated from its own medium but nevertheless imparting its message, coexisting with other signs in a tension of contradictions that can only be read, like a poem and, for people accustomed to making painstaking interpretations, a compelling puzzle.

In the early 1960s, at the height of the commercial folk revival, the American Broadcasting Company declined to include Seeger on its short-lived TV program *Hootenanny*—a fact particularly ironic because Seeger introduced the word "hootenanny" into the national vocabulary, having learned it in Seattle on a singing tour with the Almanac Singers. Blacklisting was in part responsible of course, but as one producer noted, Seeger was "too slow and thoughtful" for the show. What he might have said was that Seeger, to be understood and appreciated, demands not the mercurial television audience accustomed to monolithic television "personalities," but a slow and thoughtful audience, one willing to read the signs of a complex identity to which the television screen is mostly insensitive.

That would be the college audience, among whom Seeger had most of his influence in the fifties and sixties. In spite of his own record as a dropout, Seeger has something of the university about him. At his school concerts, with his knitted ties, rolled shirtsleeves, and bright red socks, he might be a physicist of the forties, engaged in some obscure way in the war effort; in his more familiar dungarees, workshirt, and workboots, though ostensibly proletarian, he might be a geologist on a field trip. These clothes, in any case, even the tuxedo he wore at the Weavers' Carnegie Hall concerts, never quite fully assume their office; instead they hang on his tall frame like bunting, as much symbols of the realms of life to which they belong as artifacts. Seeger cannot dress at all, it seems, without making a statement.

Part of the reason is certainly that the awkwardness of his late growth—Seeger grew nearly a foot between the ages of seventeen and eighteen—has never really left him; always his ankles, wrists, and head seem to thrust out of his clothes as if he had suddenly, in the night, shot up like a sunflower. And with this growth came, it seems, a hormonal surge that coarsened his jaw, enlarged his nose as if he had a permanent cold, and put gristle in his long, graceful limbs: caricaturing, but not effacing, his fundamental beauty—the quality that recommended him for female roles at Avon Old Farms—which can be seen in its original freshness in an early portrait of his mother Constance, whom he resembles, with her wide mouth, almost oriental cheekbones, and her large, watchful eyes. As a young man Pete still had her rosy complexion and her fine, wavy hair, gleaming like chrome on the top of his head or hanging in a childlike ringlet over his temple. Craning his neck to sing, with his chin raised, his aerodynamic pompadour poised for highway travel, Seeger might have been a brazen college youth at the wheel of an open roadster, college pennant flying, speeding toward an ivy-league football game with a carful of girls singing the fight song; but he might have been too, with his raw, innocent, uncouth face, an Iowa farmboy, with German parents perhaps, reciting the pledge of allegiance.

When Seeger returned from a tour with the army in the Pacific in 1944, he was, Bess Lomax remembers, "a very different man. He had matured physically and become a stronger singer. Now he was physically vibrant. He'd always been tense, lean, and bony, but the years of physical activity had put some weight on him. He was as hard as nails." This was the figure who, with outstretched arms and cuffs rolled, a man manifestly at work, could set an entire auditorium singing with him in four-part harmony, summoning up what all the art and journalism of the thirties could not do, an immediate, existential image of the People, a people not idealized at a distance but present, at once flowing out of and into the self, a personal and a supernal force, and bring to that experience an almost religious sense of collective grace and purpose. "Shameless rhetorical devices become as magic in his hands," writes Jon Pankake. "Before an audience that has never seen him before he will offhandedly say, 'I think I've told you many times about . . .'" or, of a strange song, "'You all know this one . . .' and one is immediately enrolled in his corner, as friend and intimate."[10] His eclectic repertory leaped telephonically from an Appalachian ballad to an Indonesian lullaby to an African chant to a Guthrie song, translating them all through Seeger's simple musical arrangements, designed for spontaneous choral singing, through his vocality, speech, indeed through his very being, into a familiar and authoritative cultural idiom.

Other concert singers such as John Jacob Niles and Richard Dyer-Bennett had attempted to elevate the folksong socially through, in Niles's case, melodrama, and in Bennett's, bel-canto style—but this was merely an articulation of polite culture in the name of folksong. Seeger, by contrast, suppressed all the *overt* signs of his social affiliations and substituted, with his banjo, his proletarian costume, and so on, signs of a deliberate identification, in the iconography of thirties populism, with what were variously called workers, the people, or the folk. Those in his audience prepared to reject polite society were disarmed; while Seeger stood for the worker, the farmer, or the black, he embodied not mere polite society, with its bourgeois impulse to enunciate itself, but hereditary caste, by Seeger's own embarrassed testimony "all upper-class." For however rustic or exotic his song, Seeger delivered it not with the affected drawl of later folk revivalists, but in the honest accents of New England gentility, with its dignified, rotund vowels, every word articulate, and the raised voice of a scholar at the podium, lifted out of its element, projecting with the emphasis and drama of the elocutionist, as if out of a Latin primer; the folksong through his mediation became an artifact of the highest culture, normally itself hidden in corporate boardrooms or behind the hedges of private schools and great estates. Seeger's performances are covertly a disclosure and, in the archaic sense, an act of courtesy, in which he opens through song the ark of the social covenant to reveal what in a democratic society is the one treasure that individual initiative cannot win: privilege, *real* privilege.

Europeans are familiar with the figure of the aristocrat-radical or reformer who from time to time appears on the social horizon. Allied with Seeger's physical resilience and social standing was the political radicalism with which he was increasingly, and to his everlasting detriment, identified. Even at his acquittal for contempt of Congress in 1962, the presiding judge could not forbear referring to him as "one who may appear unworthy of sympathy." He had embraced radical causes at Harvard; in 1941 he joined the American Communist Party, sang at the opening of its headquarters in the Bronx and at lectures sponsored by the American Labor Party, taught classes on labor songs at the Marxist Jefferson School of Social Science, helped to raise money for the *National Guardian,* and, having led the People's Song movement in New York in the forties, traveled south in 1948 with Henry Wallace's Progressive Party campaign—these among many other Popular Front activities.[11]

And yet Pete Seeger was not, strictly speaking, ideological. His sympathies and antipathies were powerful and persistent: but not the result of the conscientious embrace of a system of ideas quarried from texts, refined through reflection and debate, reembodied in memory and championed as a description of reality. Seeger inherited his radicalism from his father and his father's associations, from the experiences that arose from them, as a streak in his temperament, just as the child of the Catholic, Presbyterian, or Jew inherits the codes of those traditions even though he may not practice, or may even consciously repudiate, the rites at the heart of them. Beyond the deposits of radicalism in his temperament were the lifelong associations, formed in New York's culture of the left in the thirties, with people like the writer Mike Gold, whose radicalism, like Seeger's, was grounded on simple antipathies—a hatred of waste and greed on the one hand, a love of ordinary people on the other—to whom Seeger paid tribute with Gold's favorite "Guantanamera," the Cuban revolutionary song, at his deathbed in 1967.

Seeger's politics, then, are more like a creed than an ideology, rooted morally in a fundamentally religious sensibility that despises waste, ostentation, and worldly power, all the more so because his own origins lie in wealth and its prerogatives. Politically, it is an unsophisticated though often systematic opposition to commercialism and monopoly, especially in entertainment; socially, it is a repression of the personal in favor of the collective and participatory; and personally it is a guarded asceticism sublimated by its identification with an idealized working class. As David Dunaway reports, Seeger carried his boyhood Setonism well into manhood. "A person shouldn't have more property," he used to say, "than he can squeeze between his banjo and the outside wall of his banjo case."

But such an embodied, unarticulated creed, present only by inference, is far more powerful than ideology, which apart from direct political action has only verbal argument in which to advance itself and is therefore always vulnerable to argument; and the disarticulated ideology, which is what Seeger's became after his blacklisting in 1950, is even more powerful—for it had the mystique conferred by the cynical political opportunism of anticommunism and the House Un-American Activities Committee. Arising only briefly and enigmatically in speech, never fully revealed in the unstable ambiguities of structures of words, but seeming mysteriously to inform every gesture and every note, bringing its moral energy into the music and elevating entire audiences with its communal spirit, Seeger's ideology is actually a silence that can absorb the meanings assigned by his audiences, each person individually—which accounts for the powerful allegiance, or revulsion, he inspired.

"I've never heard nobody yet get a whole room full of friends or enemies both to sing and to ring the plaster down singing out a novel," Seeger exclaims—and in this he summons up both his father, employee of the Resettlement Administration, and the young audiences of the sixties whose growing disaffection had begun to touch even the classrooms and books that had awakened them to their own situation. Seeger's radicalism was a matter of desire more than of words, and hence something far more authentic than words; and the system of thought with which it was associated had been violently disarticulated by the demonology of anticommunism.

He emerged, then, as a system of paradoxes: masculine and feminine, patrician and proletarian, cosmopolitan and provincial, cultivated and uncultivated, educated and anti-intellectual, conservative and radical, hermetically private and gregariously public, a solitary wanderer and at the same time an entire movement, a richly heterogeneous cultural symbol. And this was his power: the power to arouse the need to speak.

In the 1940s Pete Seeger sang for the labor movement and the Progressive Party; in the fifties, after his blacklisting, he took his music to schools and camps throughout the country and planted the seeds of the folk revival to come. He sang for the peace movement in the late fifties and sixties, for the civil-rights movement in the early sixties, and in February 1968 sang his "Waist Deep in the Big Muddy," the antiwar song that CBS had censored six months earlier on the prime-time *Smothers Brothers Comedy Hour*.

But the civil-rights and antiwar movements were now dominated by young leaders who openly advocated revolutionary violence. And the youth counterculture, begotten by a rapacious commercial establishment upon the baby boom, waged a moral and, in battlefields such as the 1968 Democratic National Convention at Chicago, a literal civil war against the political establishment, exposing the fault lines of class, race, gender, and family that the myth of generational conflict had obfuscated. In April Martin Luther King Jr. was assassinated, and in June presidential aspirant Robert Kennedy; night riots in Washington, Chicago, Detroit, and Los Angeles set the ghettos burning throughout the summer. Without his leadership, King's Poor

People's Campaign produced massive but ineffectual demonstrations in Washington and foundered in the squalor of Resurrection City, the encampment on the National Mall, mired in mud and uncollected trash, hung with the teargas deployed by police against the firebombing of passing motorists by young demonstrators, which was finally razed by bulldozers. Camped there with Toshi and his daughter Tinya, Seeger had helped other activists to lead the singing—but the blacks, native Americans, and others of the poor and dispossessed in the city could not feel, as Dunaway reminds us, that "This Land Is Your Land" applied to them.

Professional setbacks, however, cannot finally terminate a career whose basis is a moral project. Twenty years earlier Seeger had anticipated what would soon become the response to the wretched America of 1968 of thousands of young adults who, with their organic gardens, VW buses, and woodstoves, paid him unawares the tribute of their imitation. Seeger had built, with the financial assistance of family and the contributed labor of friends, a log cabin on the banks of the Hudson near Beacon, New York. With its small woodlot, its garden, workshop, and fireplace, with the narrow clearing through which the river gleamed in the sunlight, the Seegers' cabin was a haven into which one could with dignity retreat from the physical and intellectual violence that now ruled in the political sphere. But the political sphere is where you find it: it expands with the consciousness of the political burden laid on every aspect of existence, dilating into moral and spiritual realms where "political" is only a metaphor—but a metaphor with a keen edge, ever seeking to divide good from evil. Contending against evil was of course in the tradition of the "old clergyman," as Seeger once called himself, even in Beacon, where as recently as 1965 vigilant local conservatives mounted a campaign to prevent him from singing in the highschool auditorium.

The year 1968 sent Seeger, and half the counterculture with him, back to the land; and the land—actually the Hudson

River—became his new cause. Although the history of environmental conservation lay largely with the upper classes, environmentalism, alongside the energy efficiency prompted by the Arab oil embargo, became one of the political themes of the 1970s, dear to young activists now growing into their childrearing and householding years. So it was disconcerting to his radical friends when Pete donned a Greek fisherman's cap—the kind you can order from the back pages of the *New Yorker,* and see around the wharves of Vineyard Haven—and proposed to build a highly expensive replica of a nineteenth-century Hudson River sloop, to bring together "wealthy yachtsmen and kids from ghettos, church members and atheists," in the cause of cleaning up the river.

The Hudson River flowed with everything from raw sewage to carcinogenic chemicals destined to poison the waters for a thousand years, and Seeger was disturbed by it. Sailing, moreover, in a small fiberglass skiff, had provided a happy pastime in the years after the absorption of the folksong revival into the youth counterculture. With Toshi's administrative initiative, the Seegers raised sufficient funds from concert performances, local millionaires and historians, and, contrary to its stated objectives,[12] even from the Newport Folk Foundation, to build at last the half-million-dollar sloop *Clearwater,* which with its several less expensive progeny has become a symbol of one of the country's more successful environmental causes. Because his association with the sloop was a continuing source of controversy, Seeger eventually detached himself from the project; but to the children of the seventies who never knew him in his earlier incarnations, Seeger will be remembered as the graybeard with the nautical chin, the fisherman's cap, the sailboat, and the banjo who with his crew of folksingers and schoolkids brought back the birds and the fish.

"I am a product of my family and my childhood," Seeger told his biographer. "One thinks that one creates one's own life. So there I was at nineteen . . . going out to do what I thought needed to be done. To my surprise, thirty-five years later, I found that I was practically carrying out what my family had trained me to do." Seeger is eminently a man of his class, with conscience, energy, and originality culturally ordained to realize the responsibilities of his class in ways sensitive at once to the historical moment and to a standard of courtesy: a standard to which ideologues on the right and the left have been mostly blind. To the radicals of 1968 Seeger seemed to have lost touch with the Movement; but like the redbaiters of the early fifties, they had seen him only superficially, unable as ideologues always are to understand a complex human being, full of inconsistency and doubt, his ideas only approximately fitted to his experience, unable to know himself fully, as anything but a point on the map of their own thought. Personally remote, sometimes tiresome, childish perhaps, consumed with the perpetual inward struggle that is the psychological legacy of New England Calvinism, often remorseful, self-chastising, despairing, occasionally given to violent outbursts of anger, Pete Seeger is nothing more or less than an imperfect mortal whose personal performance is of concern to himself and to his intimates alone.

To his public, however, he belongs with the religious dissenters and abolitionists who were his ancestors, and in time will perhaps join John Chapman, who shared his legacy, in that realm of memory, imagination, and speech where folklore translates history into story, conferring identity and strength. "I have never in my life said, or supported, or sung anything in any way subversive of my country," Pete Seeger told a federal judge in 1961, recalling his dissenter and abolitionist progenitors. "I do no dishonor to them, or to those who may come after me."[13] The sound of Seeger's voice echoed long ago from the New England pulpit and the schoolhouse, and the sound of his banjo from the circus ring and the minstrel stage; the sound of his ax, bedded in the hills above a river both blighted by civilization and touched with sublimity by art, recalls the isolated clearings of the first frontier, emblem of a fallen nature's New Beginning.

Yet this man is no historical spectre. Destined to go one way, he went another; favored with modest natural advantages, he turned his many cultural advantages to a lifelong identification with people struggling to prove that we need not capitulate to oppression, whether it proceeds from God, nature, history, our parents, or ourselves.

Folksinging in Washington Square, 1959, with Dave Sears on banjo

8

Happy Campers

"I wish joyous successes to the noble musical-enlightening activities of the magazine," wrote Dmitri Shostakovich to the editors of the new *Sing Out!* in 1950. "It is a call for friendship and for the uniting of all peoples under the great canopy of song," added directors of the Bolshoi Theater. "It is a mighty call of millions of voices resounding around the earth."[1]

With offices on East 14th Street, *Sing Out!* started off in May 1950, lineal successor to *Peoples' Songs*. Joining editor Irwin Silber on the masthead were Paul Robeson, Earl Robinson, Waldemar Hille, Howard Fast, and Sidney Finklestein, who in the first issue asked, "Where else but in the Soviet Union would composers be inspired to study the greatness of people?"[2]

The Popular Front, with its cultural armies drawing together the masses under the banner of universal socialism, its cosmos divided between owners and workers, bourgeois and proletariat, apparently still prevailed on East 14th Street. To the Marxists of the thirties, Ella Mae Wiggins and Aunt Molly Jackson represented precisely the alignment of capitalism, ethnicity, and class conflict that obtained in the Soviet Union, where long-oppressed peasant groups, the true folk cultures of the Caucasus and the Balkans, were being drawn into a modern nation-state without the historically mediating stage of an industrial revolution, or even of an Enlightenment tradition to disentangle the idea of social contract from the deeper cultural contact it assumed.

But the great fissure that lay across American life was not primarily that between mine operators and mill owners and the folk groups who in isolated and economically underdeveloped regions supplied their principal laborforce. Indeed, by the end of the war, the old working class, originally constituted of exploited ethnic groups, coaxed away from European depression and famine by American industrial agents, was scarcely visible on the social landscape. Soon the industrial worker in the major urban areas might own his own house, car, and television set; he might be enrolled in company health and pension plans; his children might attend state university or even a private college.

No, the new fissure in American society was not primarily one of class or ethnicity, though these certainly figured into it, nor one of the generations, though it would soon manifest itself as a generational quarrel. Rather it was a cleavage of memory, a division between the historical cultures formed before, during, and after the war. What came to be known broadly as the Establishment had prosecuted the war and sustained its power in the elaboration of postwar society: legislators, policymakers, and a legion of federal bureaucrats, particularly military bureaucrats; captains of industry, banking, transportation, communications, and business; decommissioned officers entering government, corporate and financial management, education, and the professions; soldiers returning as heroes to small communities, local schools, governments, and police forces, voluntary civic and youth organizations, and businesses; workers to whom wartime productivity had brought a rise in social and economic standing.

The consolidation of this establishment arose partly from the advantages extended by the government to returning soldiers in the forms of housing and educational loans, medical and tax benefits, and preferential hiring in federal, state, and local governments; by 1947 the GI Bill accounted for fully half of college enrollment and half of the veteran population.[3] Such entitlements enabled employers to replace union workers and eroded labor's seniority arrangements as well as the gains made by women and minorities in the workforce.

There were many people of course who were not part of the postwar establishment upon whom wartime patriotism had nevertheless been deeply impressed, and who in their social exclusion could not but cling to those attitudes ever more jealously: displaced and dislocated workers and their families, especially urban minorities; socioeconomic and regional subgroups returning to their systemic marginality; and women, whose expanded wartime roles were swiftly reduced by the restoration of men to the workforce and the household.

Where, then, was the locus of antiestablishment feeling? Among a few artists, intellectuals, certainly, what remained of the political left, in the black urban subculture that developed around jazz, and in the white bohemian subculture that identified with it; even, perhaps, secreted away in the hearts of older people, the grandparent generation, too skeptical and self-reliant either to have been shaken by the depression or swept away by the promise of the New Deal. Indeed antiestablishment feeling, if it existed, could scarcely speak out as the cold-war mythology gradually came to dominate the collective imagination, public and private.

But if America had been invaded by its own army, it was on the threshold of a new invasion, that of the postwar generation, not, as we shall see, altogether identical to that statistical bubble called the baby boom, but a dynamic community whose collective memory could reach only dimly into the war years and, at the same time, stride with seven-league boots over the wider territory of the American cultural imagination and build its identity on the basis of it. In the end it was fortuitous, for the revival, that folksong had in the early days been joined to the left, and that the repression of the left had extended to singers of folksongs—for it drove them underground, not to party cells or clandestine meetings in the coal camps and mill towns but to the seedbed of elite American culture in schools, summer camps, and private homes, to prepare for the young a new vision of society.

Theirs was not yet the authentic vernacular music of the cottonfield, Atlanta streetcorner, Delta juke joint, country church, tobacco factory, coal camp, textile mill, or auto plant, such as later revivalists would retrieve and imitate, but the communal music of an urban political-intellectual youth culture, with an explicit message of brotherhood, peace, and justice, and its implicit message of cultural continuity and a new love of country, not so much the patriotism of a wartime society but a kind of matriotism, centered on a love of the mother culture and its nurturing memories.

It was to the children's underground that Seeger took his music. "For many years," he recalled in 1961, "I pursued a theory of cultural guerrilla tactics."

> I could not hold a steady job on a single radio or TV station. But I could appear as a guest on a thousand and one disc jockey shows, say a few words while they played a few records. I could not hold down a job at the average college or university, but I could appear to sing some songs, and then be on my way. I kept as home base this one sector of society which refused most courageously to knuckle under to the witch hunters: the college students. Now, I figure, most of my job is done. The young people who have learned songs from me are taking them to thousands of places where I myself could never expect to go.[4]

Seeger had inaugurated in 1954 a new feature for *Sing Out!* magazine, his Johnny Appleseed Jr. column, dedicated "to the thousands of boys and girls who today are using their guitars and their songs to plant the seeds of a better tomorrow in the homes across the land. They are lovers of folksongs, and they are creating a new folklore, a basis for a people's culture of tomorrow. For if the radio, the press, and all the large channels of mass communication are closed to their songs of freedom, friendship, and peace, they must go from house to house, from school and camp to church and clambake."[5]

John Lomax, Carl Sandburg, and John Jacob Niles had all given folk concerts in colleges in the twenties. The Detroit contingent of the Almanac Singers held their last concert at Wayne State University in 1943. By 1955 the folksong movement was resurfacing in colleges and universities. Irwin Silber traces the beginnings of the collegiate folk revival to a lunchroom at City College of New York in the late forties, where Tom Paley, Joe Jaffe, and Jerry Silverman, former Folksay activists, entertained their fellow undergraduates on guitars and banjos. But an annual folksinging weekend during the same period at Swarthmore, begun under the physical education department's square-dance program,[6] started earlier, in the late thirties, and counted Woody Guthrie among its visitors. By 1954 student Ralph Rinzler was involved in its production and with the Swarthmore radio station and its extensive folk-music collection. When Mike Seeger suggested that Rinzler introduce living stringband traditions such as bluegrass into the Swarthmore festival, Rinzler responded by joining the younger Seeger on his visits to the New River Ranch at Rising Sun, Maryland, a country-music park where Bill Monroe, Lester Flatt and Earl Scruggs, and the Stanley Brothers regularly performed, along with oldtime guitarists the McGhee Brothers and banjo player and singer Ola Belle Reed. From this activity two influential record albums on Folkways, *American Banjo, Scruggs Style* and *Mountain Music, Bluegrass Style,* which Seeger and Rinzler recorded in "kitchens, boarding house rooms, bedrooms, basements and recreation rooms," as well as the taverns of Baltimore, emerged to define bluegrass as a type of traditional music and to graft it onto the folk revival.[7]

The Swarthmore festival attracted students up and down the eastern seaboard, inspiring similar events in the midwest, at

Antioch and Oberlin, in the south at Arkansas and Chapel Hill, and in the west at Berkeley and Reed.[8] Susan Montgomery, a fashion writer and an astute observer of the folk scene in 1960, noted the interest in folk music at Yale's outing and ski clubs, and the galvanizing impact of vacation concerts by Pete Seeger and especially the Weavers' Christmas Eve concert at Carnegie Hall in 1955. "Ivy League girls from all over the East found themselves in New Haven on a Friday night," she writes, quoting John Cohen, "confronted by a roomful of guitars."[9] At the outset the campus folksingers constituted a small group of rebels and intellectuals, principally art and math students, since many students, not without reason, believed that any association with folk music would seriously impair their careers.

Pete Seeger performed at Swarthmore in 1953 and at Oberlin four years in succession, from 1954 to 1957, watching his audiences increase from two hundred to a thousand.[10] In response to his performances, Oberlin students Joe Hickerson, later to head the Archive of Folk Song at the Library of Congress, and Steve Taller, who had been a sales representative for Folkways, Stinson, and Electra Records on campus, formed the Folksmiths who, charged by their mentor to quit school and travel the roads of America spreading folksong, did the next best thing and took their summer vacation in camps throughout New England, teaching folksinging, dancing, games, and instrument making.[11] Also a member of this group was Dave Van Ronk, a New York jazz guitarist who entered the revival as a bluesman with a voice so textured and dramatic that early reviewers took him to be black.[12]

The apparently natural affinity of group singing and dancing with camping, well developed by the twenties in scout, YMCA, and ethical-culture camps was not lost on Jewish and left-wing camp directors. The borscht-belt booking agent Leonard Jacobson, whom the Almanac Singers took on to handle their concert engagements, used on their behalf his connections to the Catskill resort circuit and left-wing summer camps. "The camp was in an uproar," Earl Robinson recalled of his attempt to bring Huddie Ledbetter to Camp Unity in Wingdale, New York, where in 1936 Robinson was employed as a counselor, over "songs of bad women and gun toting Negro gamblers . . . with just an occasional jail song where the protest could barely be understood through his dialect."[13] Robinson had better luck with his own song, "Joe Hill," which he introduced to the campers on Joe Hill evening; poet Alfred Hayes, who wrote the lyric, was also on the staff.

Even Commonwealth Labor College, advertising in *New Masses*, offered "hiking, swimming, folksongs and dances, fishing and tennis" to prospective students—which should remind us that the web of relations that embraces the political idealism, the spirit of protest, the love of the outdoors, all bound up with vacationers' ethnic and ideological esprit de corps and the singing of folksongs, has as its background Old World immigration, urban ghettoization, and the barriers to full assimilation into American cultural life.

The Folksmiths' summer-camp tour suggests that if folksinging had been catching on in colleges, it was perhaps because the exposure of children to folk music had begun much earlier in their lives. Hickerson, in fact, had been a camp counselor himself, at Camp Woodlands in the Catskills, founded in the late thirties by Norman Studer, director of a liberal private school in Greenwich Village. Studer's aim was to achieve, in microcosm, an egalitarian interracial community and to bring the campers into close association with what Pete Seeger called the "old American stock" in the surrounding villages and countryside.[14] "The importance of this work," wrote Beatrice Freedman, "lies not only in the collecting of material, but the use of it as a living force, in interpreting the Catskill region to itself, and giving city people a deeper understanding of country people and their culture."[15]

As Seeger recalls, Studer turned his students into folklore fieldworkers. "A station-wagon full of twelve-year-olds," he writes, "would come unannounced to a cross-roads country store inquiring if there was anyone around who could tell them when the tanneries were running, fifty years ago . . . In one house they might see a battered fiddle on the wall, and its owner would be invited to a camp square dance." By the end of the summer the campers had organized a folk festival in which several dozen locals participated with the youngsters in balladry, dancing, guitar and banjo playing, storytelling, and basketmaking or woodcarving.

Camp Woodlanders would be well represented in the vanguard of the folk revival. In the mid-fifties Eric Weissberg, who with Roger Sprung was one of New York City's few three-finger-style banjoists, formed with Erik Darling, Alan Arkin, and Bob Carey the Tarriers, who reached the pop charts in 1956 with "Cindy" and the "Banana Boat Song." The following year Harry Belafonte turned this last into a million seller; Darling replaced Seeger in the Weavers in 1958; Weissberg later introduced bluegrass banjo to the world on the soundtrack of the film *Deliverance.* John Cohen became a founding member, with Mike Seeger and Tom Paley, of the New Lost City Ramblers. Paley himself, though not a Woodlander, had worked at the nearby resort, the Woodlands, along with Israel Young, who later opened the Folklore Center in Greenwich Village. Richard Bauman ultimately joined the faculty at the University of Texas at Austin and became the director of Indiana's Folklore Institute, while Bruce Langhorne distinguished himself as a guitarist and session man.[16]

Not all of the early folksinging and folkdancing summer camps were in the northeast. At Oglebay Park, West Virginia, in 1939, an autumn folk festival had begun as a conclave of folk-dancing 4-H clubs; by 1946 it had become a biannual three-to-six-day summer camp built around folkdances, songs, square dances, play-party games, and crafts, as well as ethnic meals served in costume and a festival presented by the hundred-odd campers, who included 4-H, scout, and church leaders, college students from Antioch and Harvard, as well as "unexpected guests" such as a black music teacher from Pittsburgh and a local oldtime fiddler, to audiences of over two thousand.

But if this was guerrilla warfare, it was of a different stamp from Seeger's. "Much of the atmosphere," reported recreation specialist Jane Farwell, "is created before camp begins—created by the gay peasant decorations, which are always different. This year . . . about 1,000 feet of wide paper 'eyelet embroidery' ruffles were made and used to festoon the log recreation hall. The center wagon wheel light fixture over the fireplace was adorned in a gay ruffled paper petticoat with pantaloons peeking below."[17]

Cultural warfare extended to schools as well. As early as 1910, Archie Green reports, a schoolteacher from Milwaukee named Frances Elliott Clark had begun to use recorded folksongs in her classroom; in the next eighteen years she directed the educational department of the Victor Talking Machine Company, supervising the recordings for use in schools of songs that included Stephen Foster and James Bland compositions and Scottish ballads.[18] The association in the minds of record producers as well as performers of folksong with children would in the end prove to be its most potent connection, since even as it juvenilized folksong, consigning it to a child's minor world, it also established it as one of the ontological touchstones in the child's developing imagination.

We have glimpsed the role that radio played in disseminating folksong to New York schoolchildren in the 1940s. One of the best-remembered performers of children's albums, Frank Luther, had been in the late twenties a prolific recorder of hillbilly songs, and in 1934 began with Decca records a series of Irish, Civil War, Stephen Foster, and cowboy songs, collaborating in 1941 with Thomas Hart Benton in an album of folksongs called *Saturday Night at Tom Benton's*. To Luther, folksongs belonged to a broader romance that like fairytales or old-fashioned popular music seemed to immunize the past against ideological struggle and at the same time promulgated, in the form of picturesque imagery, caricature, and idealized human exemplars, social and political ideas bound to work their influence on children at a level at once ideological and deeply subjective.

In 1939 the poet Archibald MacLeish, then Librarian of Congress, had successfully approached the Carnegie Corporation for funds to manufacture pressings of recordings from the Archive of American Folk Song for sale to schools, colleges, and the public.[19] Following MacLeish's lead in 1944, Ben Botkin, president of the American Folklore Society, greeted the annual meeting of the Music Teachers' National Association in Cincinnati with the announcement that his society was "striving to promote folksong activities" and conscientiously enlisting music teachers in the project. "Until folk music is accepted by music teachers as basic to a living and democratic musical culture, our interest in folksong must remain academic. Before we can reach the folksong audience and supply the growing demand for folk music, we must first reach you, who in a sense control the supply and help shape the audience."[20]

Ruth Crawford Seeger's influential *American Folksongs for Children in Home, School and Nursery School,* published in 1948, was among the first fruits of this effort. Presenting it as "a book for children, parents, and teachers," acknowledging the influence of her husband and her associations with the Bentons and the Lomaxes, Ruth Seeger introduces the book with what could be regarded as one of the master texts of the expanding folk revival. "This kind of traditional or folk music is thoroughly identified with the kind of people who made America as we know it," she writes. "Our children have a right to be brought up with it."

If it is one of the aims of education to induct the child into the realities of the culture in which he will live, may we not say that this traditional music and language and ideology, which has not only grown out of but has in turn influenced that culture—and is still influencing and being used by it—should occupy a familiar place in the child's daily life, even though it may not be current in the particular neighborhood in which he happens to be living. Many of us open a savings account at the bank when a child is born, and add layer after layer of small deposits which he can later draw on for a college education. Perhaps a fund of songs might be begun as early, and added to layer after layer—an ever-growing wealth of materials which he can draw on at will and can take along with him as links from himself to various aspects of the culture he will be going out to meet.[21]

Seeger argued the case for folksong as a "bearer of history and custom," as an embodiment of "democratic attitudes and values," and even that, conforming to the ethos of the postwar period, it glorified the family. Because it was participatory and improvisational, because it was rhythmically vigorous, because it could adapt itself to many situations, folksong, she argued, was particularly attractive to children and useful as an educational tool. And she predicted that "as the performer's age increases, so also does the range of his appreciation of such songs. And that is, after all, the prime test of a permanent cultural possession."

Ruth Seeger's book underwrote, as a resource, the further promulgation of folksong to the young—but it was also the record of a process already well established. Seeger had been singing folksongs to children not only, of course, at home but as early as 1941 in exclusive day schools throughout the Washington area—sites at which the research of the Seeger family would transmit itself to the children of the nation's political and cultural elite.

Ruth Seeger's painstaking transcriptions reflected her familiarity with the original oral performances as well as the exigencies of actual singing. As she recalls, the Lomax recordings were played perpetually in her household as she was transcribing them, while her children Barbara, Peggy, and Michael, then aged three, five, and seven, would be her "test tubes." The success of the songs with schoolchildren led to a series of meetings with parents who wished to learn the songs themselves. Often an untrained voice, Seeger explained, "will convey to the child a greater enjoyment of the song itself than will the voice which has been made to concentrate hour after hour on the manner of singing the song . . . and do not have contempt for your voice if it is reedy or splintery or nasal. Remember that some of the finest traditional singers have similar qualities of voice, and that the songs not only are at home with voices like these, they sound well with them."[22]

Ruth Seeger's role in disseminating folk music to the young, and the lasting impact of early education in the revival generally, is illustrated in the career of the folksinger Kathy Shirnberg. Ruth Seeger was Shirnberg's early piano teacher; by the time Shirnberg entered fifth grade she had heard the recordings Seeger was transcribing, participated in her Saturday sings, and learned to square-dance. In highschool, having moved from Boston to a rural community in Indiana, she took up guitar, discovering that unlike the classical music that her parents treated as a background to living, people "actually *listened* to folk music." Later in life Shirnberg and her husband, both urban professionals with university degrees—she entered Berkeley in 1960, after a period at Radcliffe—followed the back-to-the-land movement to rural upstate New York.[23]

Between 1950 and 1952 *Sing Out!* urged its readers to carry the folk gospel to schools, summer camps, and other small venues, and in 1956 altered its editorial policy and copyright, no longer identified as People's Artists, Inc. but as Sing Out!, Inc., symbolically dissociating itself from its ideological forebears. By 1959 *Sing Out!* called itself *The Folk Song Magazine,* and by 1962 its circulation more than doubled—a subscription list of 500 in 1951 grew to 25,000 in 1965[24]—and its advertising represented nearly every folk record label and instrument manufacturer. Its credo was that of a global youth movement without an articulated politics:

> We are, first of all, interested in folk and traditional music, as a living heritage—a link to the past—as an aesthetic experience, and as a vehicle for contemporary music, or, more specifically, folk music which is sung and traditional in the United States. We are also interested in the folk expression of other peoples and cultures as a means of broadening our understanding of the world we live in and as a key to learning more of the ways in which folk music

is created and preserved among all peoples . . . One of the functions of *Sing Out!*, we believe, is to make these songs more readily available to the thousands of young people who play guitars and banjos, and who are the lifeblood of what has been called "the folksong revival."[25]

In the critical years, then, between the blacklist and the appearance of the Kingston Trio's "Tom Dooley," the folksong movement was becoming in schools and camps a folk revival. Margot Mayo continued her emphasis on folksong and dance at the Woodward School in Brooklyn, finding over the late fifties and early sixties that her students consistently favored folk music over other music.[26] Sam Hinton recalls "a little green book of folksongs" distributed to California elementary schoolteachers by the state department of education in the early fifties.[27] The staff at the Lincoln Farm Work Camp, in Roscoe, New York, included a guitar-playing Unitarian minister and a banjo-picking rabbi among schoolteachers, singing and playing African, Israeli, and European folksongs alongside spirituals and bluegrass. A "folk chorus," an ensemble of banjos and guitars, performed on an impromptu basis at state parks, farm auctions, and country fairs in the region, and even made an appearance at the Boston Symphony's Tanglewood.[28] Camp Quinipet, a Methodist youth-training center on Staten Island, drew on the Folksmiths' repertory for its music program, while Camp Pinewoods in Buzzard's Bay, Massachusetts, sponsored a folk-music week, bringing in professional singers such as Frank Warner and Cynthia Gooding to perform.[29] Warner was at the same time working at Long Pond, the Country Dance Society's summer camp in western Massachusetts, with banjo player Lee Haring, an English professor at Brooklyn College.[30]

Guerrilla warfare had accomplished what the people's army could not, introducing into the cultural stream folk images and sounds, dehistoricized and yet replete with the past, deideologized but inherently political, in the gentle and sequestered headwaters where the cultural stream originates. By an uncommon kind of forgetting, which elected to reinvent history rather than to retrieve it, these tributaries would shortly emerge above ground and gather themselves into a kind of flood. It would not have been apparent, or relevant, to the audiences at the first Newport Folk Festival, in 1959, that featured performers such as the Kossoy Sisters or Barry Kornfeld had learned their music from "camp counselors playing the guitar and singing."[31] The counselors and schoolbooks would be forgotten in the urgent project of reframing the history of one's culture and one's self, and in opening and surveying the social space in which the new folksong-formed identity might realize itself.

We should not imagine, however, that young men and women nurtured on folksong as children could, as they moved out of the enclaves of exclusive schools and camps, find a society altogether hospitable to the attitudes, values, and personal styles associated with folksong. But the way had been prepared for them by the jazz-centered urban bohemian subculture that after the war had modeled itself loosely on the life of left-bank Paris, where the ghost of Lenin still haunted the theaters and cafes, discovering in the French resistance a metaphor for the conduct of an awakened mind in postwar consumer America. This was the world of the coffeehouse, existentialist philosophy, symbolist poetry, paperback science fiction, and the rest—the world, as one commentator put it, of "barren lofts, damp cellars, bearded men, candles in bottles, wine, free love, intellectuals, pseudo-intellectuals and total disagreement with the Dale Carnegie system."[32]

"When I was in college," one unsympathetic observer, Mike Collins, recalls,

> there was a hard-core underground of real folkmusic enthusiasts. Among their other enthusiasms were things . . . equally obscure: serious music composed prior to Bach or after Schoenberg; the psychoanalytic theories of Wilhelm Reich; the stories of Kafka and the paintings of Mondrian . . . their idea of real folkmusic was a

Library of Congress recording of a blues sung by a 95-year-old Negro woman in Louisiana, accompanying herself by beating her wash on the rocks of the Mississippi.[33]

By 1959 the association between folksong and the left had been largely replaced in popular consciousness by a new association already well furnished, as the columnist Harriet Van Horne suggests, with beatnik stereotypes. "It's the kind of folk-music," she writes, addressing Lomax's *Folksound U.S.A.* radio program, "I associate with far-out bohemian types":

> I mean the kind who wear leather thong sandals and entertain you after dinner (a casserole of garlic bulbs and goat hearts, stewed in bad wine) with their scratchy old recordings of blues songs by Leadbelly and Blind Willie Johnson. "Listen for the falsetto break!" they cry, spooning up another helping of goat. No, this kind of music is not for Miss Square Toes. I know it's part of our musical heritage. I know the poetry of the earth is never dead, I know every note has pathos and guts and minstrelsy and lots of old-time religion. But I keep remembering that stewed goat and the candles in wine bottles.[34]

Beat culture had been jazz-centered, assimilating the cool, misanthropic stance of the black bebop musician, the radically introspective spell of his music and his nocturnal, pot-pacified style of life. The association of French existentialism and jazz reached back at least to the Franco-Creole beguines imported from the French colonies of Martinique and Guadeloupe in the twenties; black American writers and jazzmen had been welcomed hospitably in Paris by artists and literati, living embodiments of Richard Wright's Outsider, the existential hero in whom the act of rebellion alone signified, if it did not secure, his freedom. The interest of philosophers had turned from society to psyche, from primitivism and transcendence to the undifferentiated anxiety of self thrust into a universe pervaded by the imminent, prolonged, faceless, unredeeming apocalypse of nuclear annihilation.

Jazz, in the meantime, had "wandered into the harmonic jungles of Schonberg and Stravinsky,"[35] while a search for the origins of jazz, begun years earlier by anthropologists and musicologists, had made a niche in bohemian culture for folk music. We have seen how jazz impresario John Hammond, for many years a champion of racial integration in the music, the discoverer of Billie Holiday, Count Basie, and Charlie Christian among others, had brought Alabama harmonica player Sonny Terry and Arkansas blues singer Big Bill Broonzy to New York in 1938 for his historic concert at Carnegie Hall; in 1962 this same man convinced skeptical Columbia executives to sign Bob Dylan, whose first album Hammond produced.

"Folkniks," Roger Abrahams recalls, looked with contempt on the narcissism and political lassitude of the beat movement, but at the same time shared with them a search for a "cultural center of gravity." The old Popular Front complaints about the Communist Party, that it was rigid and authoritarian, puritanical and self-important, without ideological tolerance and no understanding of plain human freedoms that the young were grasping by themselves, were now redirected toward Silber's *Sing Out!* and other stubborn hardliners such as Barbara Dane and Malvina Reynolds.[36] At the Cafe Figaro in Greenwich Village, where Edward Albee found his title *Who's Afraid of Virginia Woolf?* in a graffito on the wall, at the Cafe Rienzi or the Fig, folkniks and beatniks were making common cause, as existentialism yielded to D. T. Suzuki's metaphysical and Alan Watts's psychoanalytic Zen Buddhism, Jack Kerouac's new romance of the highway, and Allen Ginsberg's visionary poetry—galvanizing a younger generation's consciousness both of itself and of a forgotten America whose rediscovery was emerging as the field upon which to reenact the spiritual quests of jazzmen and disillusioned youth, with the power to open the eyes of the blinkered modern ego.

The bohemian way of life, amid empty wine bottles, mountains of dirty dishes, poetry leaflets and beat novels, unpaid rent, strangers coming and going at all hours, a typewriter clacking at the kitchen table, record player spinning interminably, a meager paycheck materializing from time to time on the mantelpiece either because one member of the household who knew how to dress for the real world actually held down a job, or out of some temporary employment to which from time to time the budding musical and literary lights in residence needed to submit themselves in order to buy a loaf of bread or a new ream of foolscap or a set of guitar strings—this existence, in every major city of the northeast and on the west coast, became the prevailing modus vivendi of the folk revivalists, most of whom imagined it their own invention.

Its historical models are of course many and various, in Moscow, Prague, Vienna, Berlin, London, and Paris; but while such manifestos as Paul Goodman's *Growing Up Absurd* or the novels of Kerouac and J. D. Salinger, alongside the City Lights editions of Ginsberg and Lawrence Ferlinghetti, may have lacked the disruptive energy of J. K. Huysmans, Lenin, or Tristan Tzara, they did shed a jaundiced light on the lapsed decade of the fifties, so saturated with the wartime precipitates of military bureaucracy and domestic propaganda, so deeply shadowed by the threat of nuclear annihilation, so glamorized with a resurgent corporate spectacle as to demand, among young people enjoying the first fruits of liberal-arts education and its inevitable skepticism, a revolutionary rejection.

But unlike the bohemian 1920s, the mode of the 1960s seemed more like a collective adolescent quest than a political or even a cultural revolution. Although the program of the New Left materialized only a few years later, the folk revival had no political agenda, beyond being vaguely against racism and war. By the middle of the decade, a kind of theme, "disillusionment," emerged as a code word or a self-explanation, depending on the audience; but this was already a reification, a dismissal: as soon as it found expression, always self-consciously, in response to the public construction put on "disillusioned" and "rebellious" youth by journalists and critics in the parent generation, indeed by parents themselves reading pop psychologists in supermarket magazines, it had lost its freshness and originality, had become a kind of ritual formula unconnected to the genuine wellsprings of the revivalist mood, which more resembled a massive "illusionment" than its negative.

The terms "straight" and "hip" entered sixties culture from gays and beats to describe the mysterious dichotomy between those young people who seemed to have bought into the institutional line and those who could not: those like seventeen-year-old Joan Baez, who in her first days at Boston University refused to wear the freshman beanie. Deeper than any philosophical or stylistic difference was the collective identity itself and the search for "connectedness." As Abrahams points out, the adoptive personal style that descended from Almanac House, as well as the shared repertory itself, operated within the subculture as a kind of "mason's handshake" negotiable throughout the urban folksong network; while singers sought new songs to distinguish themselves among their peers, it was their peers' embrace of the new material that authenticated it.

From the days of Edna St. Vincent Millay and John Reed, Greenwich Village was the seat of bohemian culture in New York. In 1935 Dominic Parisi imported an espresso machine into his Caffe Reggio, inaugurating the era of Village coffeehouses. Others opened—the Rienzi, the Cafe Wha, the Lion's Head, and the Fat Black Pussycat; folk clubs such as the Bitter End and Gerde's Folk City would spawn counterparts in bohemian enclaves throughout urban America. In Sausalito, San Francisco, and Los Angeles were the Unicorn, the Garret, the Ash Grove, the Hungry Eye, the Purple Onion, the Troubador; in Philadelphia, the Gilded Cage, the Second Fret, the Exodus, the Tarot; in Denver, the Spider; in Seattle, the White House and the Door; in Dallas, the House of Seven Sorrows; Chicago had the Gate of Horn, Mr. Kelly's, the Fickle Pickle (all nightclubs) and the Old Town School of Folk Music, under a local radio personality, the Burl Ives of the midwest, Wynn Strake.

Both the Village Vanguard and Cafe Society, of which the Communist Party was part owner, had occasionally featured folksingers in early postwar years. But the heart of folksinging in the Village, and a springboard for talent in the coffeehouses, was Washington Square. Who first strummed a guitar to accompany a folksong in the square is unknown—but legend identifies one George Margolin, a commercial printer, whose guitar playing in Washington Square one summer afternoon in 1945 attracted a small audience with whom he exchanged a few songs; all agreed to meet the following week. But Mayor LaGuardia had passed an ordinance against unlicensed street musicians; hence the first police permit, granted to Jean and Joe Silverstein, allowed only a "string instrument." Later Pete and Toshi Seeger took the permit out, renewing it yearly.

As the numbers of folksingers increased, the police attempted to control the crowd by dividing it into groups, many of whom formed around established figures whose recordings were supplying the repertories for the amateurs: the Weavers, the Tarriers, and the New Lost City Ramblers frequently joined the Sunday singing; Theo Bikel, Jack Elliot, and even Woody Guthrie himself, in the early stages of his deterioration, could be found there, imitated in his slouch, his old clothes, and his facial stubble by young would-be Okies who had to be told who he was.[37] Rinzler recalls Roger Sprung and a teenaged Eric Weissberg introducing the bluegrass banjo style to Washington Square, a singer named Jimmy Gavin, son of an Irish construction worker, singing labor songs, as well as the protegés of Norman Studer from Camp Woodland.

A fashion writer, Grace Jan Waldeman, offers us a glimpse at the lesser-knowns who lent the Sunday folk gatherings their real character. Her typology of the Washington Square scene included the Bore, "whose every song is an excuse for an explanation"; the Weeper, "who cries that true love is never true"; and the Peacemonger, "whose peculiar brand of pacifism advocates a good fight." On the square, she writes, "is an apple-cheeked, lute-voiced girl whose specialty is courtly but ribald Elizabethan songs . . . this is the law of naughty balladry; a madrigal-type singer can deliver the most lascivious songs in the best of taste just so long as her expression is every bit as unworldly as that of a choirboy or a countertenor in the New York Pro Musica."

"Numbered among the regulars," Waldeman notes, "are bearded boys and leotarded girls," including Sally, a magazine copywriter with a false ponytail, and Fred Gerlach, an iron craftsman who learned his music by listening to Leadbelly records. Gerlach's guitar "creates the effect of a staid, baroque harpsichord, yet, by contrast, he plays rolling blues songs learned from ex-convicts and chain-gang workers. One of his original songs is 'Goin' Down Slow,' about a once respectable citizen's disintegration on the Bowery. To compose it he rented a Bowery loft and spent several months listening to the stories and dialects of the men he met there." Then there was Ruth Jacobson, who specialized in lullabies she learned from streetsingers while her husband studied in a European medical school; and Ned Marcus, a third-year medical student, who spent his summers in Europe on a motorcycle, song catching in the Basque region and the Italian provinces.[38] "There's no other place in town where they will let you do this," said a thirteen-year-old from the Bronx, Ezra William Millstein. "You just come down here with your instrument and play on the edge of some group. If you are good they ask you to come in and join them."[39]

It was in Washington Square, nevertheless, that Peekskill met Montgomery, forging a new synthesis in American politics, what William Greider calls "the politics of moral drama," in which ordinary citizens turned to the civil-rights movement both as a model for effective political action and as a metaphor for their sense of powerlessness in postwar American society. After sixteen years of Sunday afternoon folksinging in Washington Square, in April 1961, six days after Pete Seeger's conviction as un-American by HUAC, Park Commissioner Newbold Morris, at the request of the Greenwich Village chamber of commerce, banned singing in the park. Inspired by King's demonstrations, a group of folksingers sat down in the dry fountain and sang "We Shall Not Be Moved" until the police drove them away with nightsticks.[40] What might have seemed at the time simply the appropriation by one disaffected group of the political tactics of another was actually the product of a common history probably unknown to many of the people who participated in the fountain sit-in.

Originally founded in 1932 as a labor college under Myles Horton, who had studied theology under Reinhold Niebuhr, the Highlander Folk School in Monteagle, Tennessee, initiated during the repressions of the fifties a conscientious campaign of voter registration among southern blacks. Both Martin Luther King and Pete Seeger had a long association with the school and with Horton. Highlander was and is a singing school, and its music director, Horton's wife Zilphia, was raised in an Ozark coal camp, educated in music at the College of the Ozarks, and collected hundreds of labor and folksongs from both black and white traditions. Among these was "We Shall Overcome," based on a gospel song written in 1901 by Charles Albert Tindley,[41] which she had learned from striking tobacco workers from North Carolina who came to Highlander. Pete Seeger learned the song from Zilphia in 1947 and conveyed it to California folksinger Frank Hamilton in 1955. Hamilton, cofounder in 1957 of Chicago's Old Town School of Folk Music, taught the song in turn to Guy Carawan, a young sociologist who went to work at Highlander in 1959—and Carawan carried it back to its starting place among blacks agitating not for better working conditions but for an end to segregation.

At Washington Square, then, even as the folk revival installed itself in an apolitical existentialist bohemia, the political alliances formed in the days of the Popular Front returned to touch it with an anonymous spirit of resistance. But police repression on the square could not stem the tide of the folk revival in New York. Young folksingers were gathering regularly at the American Youth Hostels headquarters on 8th Street, at Israel Young's

Folklore Center on MacDougal, where folksong itinerants enjoyed a mail service, a bulletin board, and small impromptu concerts; City, Brooklyn, Hunter, and Queens Colleges were all offering folklore courses, and the New School introduced "The Art of Singing Folk Songs and Ballads."

Indeed, many of the folksingers who were becoming prominent in the revival, such as Jean Ritchie, or who would find extraordinary commercial success in it, such as a teenaged Mary Travers, lived in Greenwich Village in the 1950s, and many found an audience there. Ritchie, a native of Viper, Kentucky, and a ballad singer in the traditional style, had come to New York in 1947 to teach children's songs and dances at the Henry Street Settlement House summer camp. The union official Lou Gordon had begun a folksinging series called Swapping Song Fair, originally connected to the Irish trio the Clancy Brothers and their show at the Cherry Lane Theater, *The Wise Have Not Spoken*. Begun in 1953, the series moved two years later to Circle in the Square, where Frank Warner, Jean Ritchie, Oscar Brand, Jack Elliott, Guy Carawan, Cynthia Gooding, Theo Bikel, Ed McCurdy, the Clancy Brothers, Tom Paley, Brownie McGhee, Sonny Terry, Reverend Gary Davis, the Trinidad Steel Band, Terisita La Tana, the Country Dance Society Dancers, Bob Gibson, the Tarriers, Hillel and Aviva, among others, all performed—that is, the entire community of singers and musicians negotiating the transition from the political folksong movement of the immediate postwar period to the countercultural folk revival of the sixties.[42]

Roger Abrahams recalls the Sunday evening sings in Paul Clayton's apartment at 190 Spring Street; Pete Seeger, Dave Van Ronk, Theo Bikel, Bob Gibson, and Odetta made regular visits there. Clayton had been collecting songs in the mountains above Charlottesville, bringing them to his Village companions with the bloom still on them; one of these, "Laid Around and Stayed Around," illicitly recorded on tape from Clayton's and Abrahams' singing at a concert, found its way to Nashville and into the repertory of Bill Monroe.

But the esoteric New York revival hadn't yet been sanctified by the cultural laying-on-of-hands accomplished in the thirties when, through Leadbelly and Woody Guthrie, the movement imagined itself in direct contact with the embodied spirit of the People. However painstakingly authentic, however technically accomplished, however rare and antiquated their aural sources, the folksingers of Washington Square were still mostly interpreters of folksong, not indigenous tradition bearers. Alan Lomax, driven to England by McCarthyism, had labored for nine years to create Columbia's collection of world folk music. The British skiffle movement was largely inspired, early in the decade, by the music of Leadbelly and Guthrie, whom Lomax introduced on British radio; one of the movement's most popular recordings, Lonnie Donegan's "Rock Island Line," an almost note-for-note imitation of Leadbelly's recording of the song, migrated to the top of the American charts as well in 1956, alongside Presley's "Hound Dog," carrying the flip-side "John Henry" along with it.

A country-music program was attempted at the 48th Street Theater in 1957, with Mother Maybelle Carter, the Coon Creek Girls, and Sunshine Sue. Shortly after his return to the United States in 1959, however, having introduced bluegrass music in *Esquire* magazine with the phrase "folk music in overdrive," Lomax was soon in the field again for both United Artists and Atlantic records, bringing to Carnegie Hall representatives of vernacular music in the urban and rural south and midwest, continuing the process begun by his father twenty-five years earlier.

Among these was Jimmie (Morris) Driftwood, a schoolteacher from Mountainview, Arkansas, who sang both traditional Ozark songs and compositions of his own such as "The Battle of New Orleans," country singer Johnny Horton's Top 40 hit of that year, and "Tennessee Stud," a hit for Eddie Arnold; Driftwood's method in effect was to work his classroom history lessons into lyrics fitted to traditional fiddle tunes. "A genuine bard," Lomax called him, one who marked the evening's cultural awkwardness by expressing his hope that "you-all can understand my southern brogue." A raw, take-no-prisoners bluegrass band, Earl Taylor and the Stony Mountain Boys, whom Mike Seeger had recorded in Baltimore—"from Balt-ee-more," Lomax sang, introducing a fiddle tune, "Fire on the Mountain," raising his voice to a shout—offered Flatt and Scruggs's "Roll in My Sweet Baby's Arms" and Jimmie Rodgers' "Muleskinner Blues," which Lomax wrongly attributed at the time to Woody Guthrie. Memphis Slim appeared, with what Lomax called "a blues you can relax on," alongside the great Muddy Waters. "The next song," Lomax cautioned theatrically, "is 'Hoochie Coochie Man,' a song about *voodoo* down in the Mississippi valley. Go ahead, Muddy."[43]

But Lomax caught on quickly; he jettisoned his old role as mountebank in the face of more sophisticated audiences less willing than the political idealists of the past to have their folk music constructed for them—or who insisted, at least, on constructing it in their own way. Lomax's Carnegie Hall concert reaffirmed that mood of secular optimism in which the beat generation had no share. One member of the audience, Ed Sherman, fully absorbed the old-fashioned prewar spirit in which Lomax had presented his performers: "the butcher's wife was there," he wrote, "the furniture salesman was there, the banker was there, a family from Fort Lee, New Jersey was there, the *people* were there."[44]

In fact, though, the spirit of the people had been summoned even in Lomax's absence. In March 1956 the Guthrie Children's Trust Fund trustees, Lou Gordon, Harold Leventhal, and Pete Seeger, settled on the idea of a benefit concert at Pythian Hall to help secure college educations for Woody's children by Marjorie Mazia (Arlo, Joady, and Nora); Guthrie's royalties on all of his work were at that point only about $1,000 a year. The concert was a kind of reunion, bringing the old left-wing community, the Almanac Singers and the People's Songs cohort, together with younger aficionados who had come under that generation's influence at school and camp.

Pete Seeger marked the evening, in retrospect, as the rebirth of the folk revival, and it was also the beginning of Woody Guthrie's canonization. Millard Lampell's script, which like *Ballad for Americans* alternated music and spoken text—both in this case of Woody's own composition—as well as a finale with the entire cast singing "This Land Is Your Land," restored to the bohemianized folk revival the populist glow of the thirties. "As the last verse ended," Klein writes,

> the spotlight swung suddenly to the balcony and settled on a spidery little man with salt-and-pepper hair who struggled to his feet and saluted the audience with a clenched fist—a perfect gesture, quite in keeping with the defiant spirit of the evening. Pete Seeger, tears streaming, began the last verse of "This Land" again, and now the entire audience was up and cheering the man in the balcony, and singing his song.[45]

*   *   *

"The folksong revival," Lee Haring gloomily predicted in 1963, "will inevitably become digested by mass culture and it will inevitably become mediocre and it will die the death . . . that is a fundamental pattern in the history of our culture."[46] Just as a jazz-centered bohemian culture had opened a place for the folk movement, so would the commercial establishment, led by jazz impresarios, embrace folk music, inevitably leading it toward the gargantuan pop music business that swept jazz out of the marketplace and the revivalists into it. A dramatic elevation in the social standing of jazz, as indicated by its enshrinement at Newport, would prove essential to its displacement by folk music, long the preserve of a cultural and intellectual elite.

Folk festivals had been mounted under a variety of banners and for a variety of ideological purposes in the period between the world wars, typically out of a convergence of certain cultural agendas with the interests of local-colorists and businessmen. Nativist and Anglo-Saxonist impulses, mixed with some high-minded cultural imperialism and a tincture of racism, had produced such affairs as the White Top Mountain Festival in

Virginia and Henry Ford's dealership fiddlers' conventions through the middle south. Though tourism, real estate, and boosterism had provided the occasion for Lunsford's folk festival at Asheville and Don Yoder's Kutztown festival in Pennsylvania, both reflected a genuine interest in the prescrvation of local folkways; court reporter Jean Thomas' "Traipsin' Woman" festival at Ashland, Kentucky, was more strictly touristic.

The history of Sarah Gertrude Knott's national folk festivals embodied, along with regional theater, settlement-house "folk festivals" and the emerging recreation movement, a variety of reformist aims, including the reinforcement of ethnic and regional identity, ethnic pride and tolerance, international understanding, and the cultural improvement of the industrial working class. "The festival scored a popular success," wrote Percival Chubb of Knott's first festival. "It was on the whole a good show—novel, quaint and at times sensational. But its more serious significance lay in its bearing on the pressing problem of developing leisure activities to fill the large increment of spare time now being forced upon the masses of laboring folk. How far does the solution lie in the recovery of these perishing forms of folk culture which specialists are hastening to record before it is too late?"[47]

Newport can be seen as the first and certainly the most influential festival of the urban folk revival. Tobacco magnates Elaine and Louis Lorillard first floated the notion of producing a music festival at Newport in 1954, after the failure of a New York Philharmonic concert; John Maxon, then the president of the Rhode Island School of Design, suggested a jazz festival—and Lorillard persuaded his colleagues on the Newport Casino's board of directors that its tennis court would make an ideal festival site.[48]

Newport was of course a famous watering spot for the super-rich. By the turn of the century, as the seventy-room cottages of the Vanderbilts and their social set went up along Bellevue Avenue and Ocean Drive, Newport became what a local guidebook called the "diadem of capitalism"; but global travel, the income tax, and rising maintenance costs broke up the Gilded Age summer community, leaving the splendid cottages to be sold for taxes, boarded up, destroyed by fire or vandalism, or converted into apartment houses. In 1954, the first year of the jazz festival, the Preservation Society of Newport County was organized to restore many of the remaining colonial houses and Gilded Age mansions and open them to the public, recognizing the importance of tourism to the town's economic survival.

Lorillard engaged the jazz impresario George Wein and secured the formal sponsorship of Cleveland Amory, jazz historian Marshall Stearns, Father Norman O'Connor, chaplain of the Newman Club at Harvard, Leonard Bernstein, and John Hammond. Jazz at Newport, the sponsors believed, would bring respectability to the music associated in popular culture with the beat generation and the Harlem underground.[49] But, as a kind of premonition of the cultural and generational faults shortly to appear in the larger society, the earnest hipsters and intellectuals who patronized the festival in its early years were replaced by masses of college-age partymakers who severely tried Newport's hospitality, roaming the streets until all hours, sleeping in their cars, in the public parks, and on the beaches, often with bottles of beer and occasional exhibitions of obnoxious behavior.

To Mrs. Louis Brugiere, "reigning Queen of Newport society," driving the festival out of Newport was worth ten million dollars. But where Mrs. Brugiere saw hooligans, the impresarios saw an audience. By the summer of 1959 folk music had ascended to such elite outdoor venues as Tanglewood, Stratford, and Ravinia—a fact not lost on the guardians of social legitimacy in the jazz community. "Folk artists," reported *Billboard* in June, "are being tied in, in one way or another, with various open air jazz scenes this summer, a fact which only seems to highlight the common heritage of both."[50]

Having experimented successfully with folksingers at his Storyville jazz clubs in Boston and Cape Cod, Wein planned

Newport's first afternoon of folksinging in 1959 for the weekend after the jazz festival, featuring the Kingston Trio, apparently conceiving the entertainment as a form of summer stock. Many of Newport's early performers had made their reputation in musical comedy, *Finian's Rainbow* and *Annie Get Your Gun* particularly, in nightclubs, or on television. Will Holt, for example, a graduate of Exeter Academy and the Dyer-Bennett School of Minstrelsy in Aspen, appeared on the *Today* and *Jack Parr* shows, where the growing popularity of folk music was a kind of news, and at the Village Vanguard, the Purple Onion, and the Gate of Horn. Holt "returns to Newport," the 1960 program notes announce to their small audience of summer people, from "roles in musical comedy, supplemented by a motorcycle tour of Europe during which Will absorbed a variety of musical idioms and styles."

Theodore Bikel came similarly recommended by his starring role opposite Mary Martin in *The Sound of Music,* as a southern sheriff in the film *The Defiant Ones,* and movie appearances in *The African Queen* and *Moulin Rouge.* Jimmie Driftwood, the high-school principal from Mountain View, was described in the program as a "rancher, writer, and sportsman," a sort of folksinging Zane Grey. Still more to the point—and to anyone familiar with the history of the folksong movement, even more incongruous—was the appearance of Bob Gibson, introduced in the program notes as follows: "A phenomenally successful New York businessman at the precocious age of 22 (his brilliant innovations in the management consulting field were acclaimed by the august *Harvard Business Review*), Bob first became interested in folk music while visiting Pete Seeger."

If the Newport Folk Festival was to succeed as radical chic, however, it would have to sail under different colors and answer the social elite's insistence on the authentic product—or at least on a convincing reproduction of it. The real audience at Newport, in any case, was not the summer elite but their sons and daughters, a new campus bohemia searching at once for a community, a politics, and forms of personal identity consonant with a developing mood of contempt for the commercial establishment of which hobbyists, actors, and other simulacra of folksong were perfect embodiments—and searching too for an authentic, noncommercial form of "folk music."

In 1959 the Ward Gospel Singers, the Abyssinian Choir, the Oranim Zabar Trio, a group of Nigerian dancer-drummers, and bluesman Robert Pete Williams, discovered in the Angola State Prison by folklorist Harry Oster, all performed at Newport, while Earl Scruggs, the bluegrass banjoist admired for his highly technical three-finger style, closed the program, assuring a place in the folk revival for what had been a commercial derivative of hillbilly music. But when Bob Gibson brought sweet-voiced Joan Baez to the stage, a professor's daughter who had made a small reputation singing to college students in Harvard Square, revivalists saw the possibility of a folk music that, though revived and interpreted, was nevertheless an original expression of the kind of alienation that the revivalists could scarcely acknowledge in themselves but recognize instantly in singers like Baez, a particularly gifted and beautiful representative of her generation.

Indeed, the Newport Folk Festival *was* its audience. "Each night the music continued long after the regular performances were over," Susan Montgomery reported in 1960, "when it became the property not of professionals but of small groups of students who carried their sleeping bags and instruments down to the beach."

> There, around fires built in holes scooped out of the sand to keep off the fog, boys from Yale's folk-singing clubs exchanged songs and instrumental solos with students from the University of Michigan's Folklore Society; and students from Cornell, the University of Vermont, Sweet Briar—along with others who didn't have their colleges emblazoned on their sweatshirts—sang and clapped to songs like "It Takes a Worried Man" . . . before the morning was over students would be playing and singing again—on the beaches, and on the narrow grass strip dividing the main boulevard. Inevitably students sat huddled in little groups as

if drawing warmth from one another. Their faces were solemn, almost expressionless, while they were singing, and they moved quickly from song to song without talking very much.[51]

Riots at the jazz festival in 1960 ended the festivities altogether until, under the auspices of the newly formed Newport Folk Foundation, the folk festival was revived in 1963. To stem the tide of commercialization, Toshi Seeger suggested paying a fifty-dollar union minimum to all the performers, while the governing board, which included Pete Seeger, Theo Bikel, and George Wein, outlined a program of which roughly half would consist of country stringbands, blues, gospel, and at least two examples of ethnic traditional music in America. Mike and Pete Seeger both called for scaled-down concerts, greater variety in programming, better balance among the various kinds, including representation for religious and political songs, as well as between men and women, young and old, the well-known and the lesser-known.

These formulas, and the enterprise of the Foundation itself, produced in 1963 and in the succeeding four years the greatest concentrations of traditional performers, both folksong professionals and rediscovered traditional musicians, ever assembled in one place. Early rural stringbands were represented by Tom Ashley, joined by his neighbors Clint Howard, Fred Price, and Doc Watson. Zeke and Wiley Morris, hillbilly duet of the thirties, were on the program, alongside Bill Monroe and the Bluegrass Boys, former Monroe lead singer Mac Wiseman, and Jim and Jesse and the Virginia Boys—bands that had never before appeared in the northeast. Other musicians rediscovered from early oldtime music discs and race records, such as Dock Boggs, Mississippi John Hurt, and Mother Maybelle Carter, appeared with the urban bluesman John Lee Hooker, introducing northeastern urban audiences to the mountain music and traditional blues styles formerly confined to particular regions and communities, decommercializing formerly commercial forms, reinventing cultural categories derived from race and region long

Mississippi John Hurt at a Newport workshop, 1964

axiomatic in folksong scholarship and presentation, and setting the revival's musical agenda for twenty years to come. "It was unreal," Cambridge Club 47 owner Jim Rooney and bluesman Eric Von Schmidt later said. "John Hurt was dead. *Had* to be. All those guys on that Harry Smith Anthology were dead."[52]

With its articles by Jean Ritchie on the history of the dulcimer, and by Lightnin' Hopkins and Von Schmidt on the blues, the 1963 program book rearticulated the festival's link to legitimate folksong scholarship, keeping at the same time the social resonances of Newport alive with a full-page photo of sailboats in drydock; an article by Robert Shelton on the "integration movement" sounded a political theme, while Wesleyan University ethnomusicologist David McAllister, who had brought in the Albuquerque Tribal Dancers, spoke to the moral and spiritual context:

One can still hear religious epics thousands of lines long sung by memory by chanters who have devoted a lifetime to their performance. It is as though we could still walk down the street and come upon Homer singing *The Iliad* or *The Odyssey* and sit down with him and ask him what it all means . . . It is a tradition in which man has a place of dignity and beauty: it has much to say to us in our present era of alienation and despair.[53]

The lion's share of the program, though, belonged to pioneer revivalists both from the folksong movement, such as Pete Seeger, Alan Lomax, and Bess Lomax Hawes, and from the postwar revival, an underground movement finally surfacing. The most commercially successful musicians, such as Peter, Paul, and Mary, the Canadians Ian and Sylvia, Judy Collins, and Tom Paxton headlined the evening concerts, seconded by nearly the entire community of professional revivalists dedicated to authentic forms, including Greenwich Village bluesman Dave Van Ronk, Jack Elliott, Jean Ritchie, the New Lost City Ramblers, the Maryland bluegrass bandleader Bill Clifton, bawdysinger Ed McCurdy, blues aficionado Sam Charters, country fiddler and mathematician Tex Logan, a Salem (Missouri) bluegrass band the Dillards, marine biologist and chanty singer Sam Hinton, among many others, veterans of Washington Square and the nightclub and college circuit.

Joan Baez and Bob Dylan, both aged twenty-two, appeared together to inspire the adulation of their peers and to secure their place in the pantheon of revival Olympians; and a nineteen-year-old John Hammond Jr., son of the impresario, inaugurated his lifelong career as an interpreter of the Delta blues, having "attended Antioch College but left to migrate South in search of the origins of rural blues."

Discovering its community in its own audience and its authentic music in the tradition bearers recalled from the country-music and blues circuits and from prewar discs, Newport, like Washington Square, found its politics in the civil-rights movement. The folk revival, as we have seen, was historically linked to civil rights both through the old left and through Highlander's voter-registration drives; *Sing Out!* had published an early civil-rights anthem, "Now, Right Now," in 1953, and after the 1956 Montgomery bus boycott began regularly featuring the songs of the civil-rights movement.[54]

In the previous year Pete Seeger had met, at the home of King's aide Andrew Young in Atlanta, a nineteen-year-old Bernice Johnson, a civil-rights worker with the Student Non-Violent Coordinating Committee and a powerful spiritual singer. Taking her cue from Seeger's recollections of the Almanac Singers and the labor movement, Johnson—known today as an outspoken African-American cultural leader, Smithsonian historian, and leader of the singing group Sweet Honey in the Rock—formed the SNCC quartet, the Freedom Singers, and undertook a national collegiate tour organized by Toshi Seeger along Pete's established folksong circuit, carrying the language, the ideas, the music, and the dress (cotton shifts and denim jackets, marking the movement's boycott of Jim Crow southern merchants) throughout the college population.

At the 1963 Newport Folk Festival, SNCC set up a photo exhibit on the grounds featuring pictures of Dylan, Bikel, and other folksingers at the voter-registration concert held in Greenwood, Mississippi, on July 6. On Saturday night, Baez and SNCC organizers led 600 people on a march through Newport, past the Vanderbilt mansions and into a rally in Truro Park, where SNCC executive secretary James Forman and the Freedom Singers urged supporters to join King's March in Washington on August 28.

The mood of protest, however, was far from unanimous. "These people told me before I came it wouldn't be like this," declared Reverend Buell Kazee, one of the Folkways Anthology immortals: "I don't want anything to do with tearing down America. I don't know why these folks don't do the honest thing and admit that this is ideology . . . If I'd known it was going to be like this I'd have stayed in Kentucky."[55]

Thus consolidated, Newport became, inevitably, a theater for the enactment of the generation gap well before the idea had emerged in the media. "The idea of staying and performing in the

shadows of mansions built by nineteenth century *nouveau riche,"*
Judy Collins recalls, "appealed to those who thought their role as
folksingers meant they should be advocates of 'the people,' dedicated to promoting social change by confronting power and
wealth." "Bob Dylan might very well have composed the words
to 'The Times They Are a-Changin,'" Ralph Rinzler speculated,
"while riding down Bellevue Avenue on the way to a concert that
was to feature Fannie Lou Hamer and the Freedom Singers."[56]

In 1964, some 70,000 people attended the festival to hear over
200 performers in various concerts, workshops, lectures, and
demonstrations. Remembering the disturbances of earlier years,
the city posted signs on the major arteries leading into Newport
warning people without tickets to keep out, and doubled its
police force with recruits from nearby towns. Its constant efforts
to disperse the crowds that gathered to play and sing, not only on
the beaches but on streetcorners, private lawns, and in restau-
rants and bars, were largely in vain. Night found thousands of
people sleeping in the city parks, on lawns, or in their cars, while
many rang doorbells asking for the use of porches and bathrooms.

A short time later the Newport town council introduced a
resolution to ban the festival from Peabody Park. In a letter to
the council Mrs. Vanderbilt Adams reported "that a man was
picked up for distributing subversive literature"; one Dr. John
Carr noted that "some of the lyrics advocate the overthrow of
all parental, church, and police authority . . . I don't think we
should give these people a pulpit to speak from."[57] "Under the
misguided conception that a couple of regiments of folk singers
were preferable to a handpicked two or three squads," Paul
Nelson complained of the Newport festival of 1964, "the Newport Committee enlisted what looked to be every folk singer, or
reasonable facsimile, on the North American continent . . .
scores of traditional artists remained virtually unnoticed in the
back pew."

"The festival badly needs a context," Nelson went on, "some
sort of intellectual setting into which both performer and audi-

ence can fit comfortably. It seems to exist now in a no-man's land of fantasy in which everyone is an alien."[58] Like Sarah Gertrude Knott's national folk festival and other festivals of the past, Newport had not solved the problem of context; efforts to address it, however, undertaken by the Newport Folk Foundation and especially by its fieldworker and talent director Ralph Rinzler, laid the foundation of the Cultural Conservation movement, so called after a federal document by that name, in which the folk revival found its institutional niche after its commercial phase had ended.

"Context" for Rinzler, following the lead of young folklore scholars such as Henry Glassie and Richard Bauman, as well as his own experience in the field, was to be found in the communities in which the authentic singers had absorbed their music—a broad cultural process that included the assimilation of adjunct or "cognate" folkways. "Often while listening to people sing," Rinzler noted with amusement, "I'd sit down on a folk chair or put my foot on a folk basket, or kick over a folk table."[59]

Rinzler first advised using the performers themselves, noting that Bessie Jones, of the Georgia Sea Island Singers, might offer a workshop on folktales, in which she was well versed, or that the Mississippi fife player Ed Young could teach the making of cane fifes; Cape Breton singers might knit a salmon net or assemble a lobster trap. His initial efforts in this direction occurred at an evening concert in 1965, in which the Cape Breton singers performed not in concert style but at the "waulking" table, singing while milling the tweed, accompanied by narratives from Rinzler and Alan Lomax linking the songs to the Hebrides and to ancient rowing songs performed at the funerals of Scottish kings.

Soon children's days and craft exhibits were added to the schedule, as Bruce Jackson put it, "to help people understand that folksong is really part of a broad cultural web rather than something that exists on LPs and in coffeehouses and folk festivals only."[60] Children's days, mounted for invited camp groups, state daycare programs, and federally funded programs for deprived children included concerts, workshops, and craft demonstrations, featuring workers who had learned their techniques directly in folk communities.

The festival program book, in an article by the folklorists Bruce Buckley and M. W. Thomas, elucidated the link between the festival's craft presentations and the "second nationalism" of the 1930s, citing the federal government's support of local history and folklore, the rearguard effort by Henry Ford and other industrialists to support the teaching of traditional crafts in economically depressed areas, the state guilds that stimulated local craftspeople to look more favorably on the traditional art forms of their districts, and college work programs, such as those at Berea, which attempted to ground local production in traditional crafts for a tourist and national market.[61]

But Rinzler's own program was more ambitious: he had begun to view the folk festival as an instrument of cultural promotion. In Newport's 1966 exhibits of textile production, Cape Breton weavers such as Malcolm Angus McLeod were joined with counterparts from America such as Taft Greer, from Johnson City, Tennessee, and with Scots weaver and balladeer Norman Kennedy, to exchange information in the shearing, washing, carding, spinning, and weaving of wool. Taking a page from the earlier craft movement, Rinzler had expanded his fieldwork into the realm of material culture, coordinating it with various community action programs, VISTA workers and other volunteers who had enlisted regional traditions in the interest of economic assistance and cultural empowerment.[62] Other craft items, including quilts, children's toys, chairs, baskets and jugs, lobster pots and fishing nets, as well as native American carving, patchwork, toys, and musical instruments were all on exhibit, many by the musicians themselves or by family members who had accompanied them to Newport. With the potter Nancy Sweezy, the documentary filmmaker Frederick Wiseman, Norman Kennedy, and John Kenneth Galbraith, Rinzler set up in 1966 a nonprofit craft foundation called Country Roads in Cambridge, as an outlet for the truckloads of objects he had obtained on his field trips.

By the late sixties, with the commercial folk revival drawing to a close and the new rock movement displacing it, Newport sought to revitalize itself through dance workshops, hootenannies, and an expanded Sunday morning religious program. Craft workshops were eventually scattered over nearly 20 of the 35-acre "festival field," anticipating what was to become Rinzler's Smithsonian Festival of American Folklife, beginning in 1967, which strove to narrow the gulf between performer and audience by recreating small community settings, scaled-down performance and exhibition venues, by limiting itself to authentically traditional participants, and by drawing on pertinent scholarship to frame and present the performances.[63] This style of exhibition, with its social and political subtexts, was to become the formula for the federal and state folklife programs that succeeded the revival.

Thronging the streets of Newport, by sheer numbers transforming the landscape into a kind of tactical field, the young had come each in his or her nascent individuality to find themselves involved in a mass movement, shockingly and exhilaratingly capable of arousing contempt, even hatred, in people of authority whom they had been taught all their lives to trust—and of returning that contempt with all the rage of a people betrayed. Like the antiwar movement that followed it, the folk revival gave vent to individual and collective demonstrations of protest which might otherwise have become entangled in the confusion and ambiguity of individual conscience; and, like the antiwar demonstrations, the festival was for many what Bruce Jackson called a narcotic, through which the "realization of the possibility of action substitutes for the action itself."[64]

Newport was not, for its audience, a rite of passage; but like any festival, it provided for the eruption into daylit social space the hidden underground life of an emergent youth culture, and for the symbolic elaboration of an inverted social order, in which many solitary ordeals of ritual anointment were taking place in a festive realm beyond the commercial marketplace. In place of the repudiated official elders were an elevated and revered folk; in place of the official ordeals of education and career were the revivalists' private struggles to incorporate an invented, imaginary music in which they could dimly discern the outline of a desired ideal world. More accurate, then, to see Newport as a kind of mass pilgrimage to a site made holy by the miracle of self-transformation: the resurrection of prewar blues and mountain musicians out of the tar pits of reissue records and into the living presence of their admirers. If the musically expert and charismatic young revivalists at Newport drew greater audiences and more enthusiastic ovations than the authentic musicians themselves, it is certainly because their performances sanctified the site by demonstrating the successful transmission of the folk character to the young—liberating them, in effect, from their own youth.

Like other new folk festivals at Monterey, Berkeley, Sun Valley, Mariposa, Chicago, and Philadelphia,[65] the Newport festival was a cultural dynamo, accelerating the circulation of information from arts and entertainment elites into a broader middle class of young people who had discovered in folk music an accessible instrument of dissent inflected at the same time with cultural prestige and legitimacy. The setting at Newport, symbolic seat of America's ruling class, is hardly incidental to this process. As Richard Flacks has observed, the young activist of the sixties was typically a child of the liberal intelligentsia—the growing postwar sector of researchers, teachers, and civil servants whose work, while in the vanguard of the welfare state, was in other ways calling the status quo into question; many revivalists came from politically liberal and affluent professional households in which concerns for art, ideas, values, and social justice prevailed over the practical issue of vocation.[66]

Postwar prosperity and its benefits, education in particular, had inculcated an unprecedented level of social and personal aspiration in the young, and provided plausible opportunities to attain it; at the same time, the anxieties of social mobility and middle-class status itself were aggravated by the intensified post-war competition for social and economic advantage that fell principally on the young. Deeply ambivalent about their unstable social situation, then, young collegians found in folk music what Pete Seeger had found in it—an arena for enacting social privilege in a capitalist, democratic, and egalitarian society where privilege is everywhere perceived and nowhere openly acknowledged as a factor in personal destiny. For though folk music was outwardly associated with the farmer, the mountaineer, the worker, and the black, the revival tradition was itself imbued with the quality of the exquisite—prized antique instruments, private schools and camps, concert halls and museums, exclusive vacation spots, rare recordings on esoteric labels. Like Rinzler's craft demonstrations, the lowly social status of the folk arts themselves was obviated by their traditional affiliation with ruling-class taste, philanthropy, social reform, and other forms of top-down cultural intervention.

Even more, as folk music and crafts symbolized the grassroots democracy of preindustrial America, they also embodied the values of rootedness and authenticity characteristic of patriarchal aristocracy. The very concept of the folk was a vertical one, of a traditional society pictured from above, where peasantry and nobility live in an interdependence literally grounded in land; to the industrial middle class, by contrast, society seemed to float on the social vagaries of the marketplace, money, and the power of transforming it into cultural capital. Newport posited, on the green lawns and behind the high hedges of the great estates, through the sanction of a socially and musically constructed imaginary world of traditional rank, place, and part, the temporary suspension of class in America and implicitly protested against the forces that perpetuate it, especially through alignment with social divisions grounded in race or ethnicity.

Shot through as it was with class motives, however, class itself was largely occluded, and hence all the more potent as an influence, by its general assimilation to the broader generational divide by which the yachts and palaces of Newport could be symbolically identified with an amorphous, remote, all-powerful "establishment." From this perspective, the generation gap emerges as a myth designed to explain to the young middle class the glass ceiling built above them by the traditional oligarchy, one through which the narrowing of opportunity in the face of rising expectations, and a burgeoning youth culture to bear them, could be seen in historical, even natural terms, rather than socially or politically.

The establishment after all—or at least *an* establishment, the commercial one—had created the Newport Folk Festival; and as the festival absorbed the ambient social energy, the barrier against commercial by elite culture could not but fall. The British invasion—that is, the return of America's socially and politically repressed rock-and-roll music, carried by young English aficionados—had already come to challenge the folk revival, itself implicated, with its higher class valuation, in that repression; the Beatles had encountered a mob scene such as only massive publicity can create when they arrived in New York for an appearance on the *Ed Sullivan Show* in February 1964. And on the airwaves that summer, with a dark, insinuating electric organ break and rumbling electric guitars, was a version of "Rising Sun Blues" by the British blues-rock group, the Animals, a song Alan Lomax had collected in Kentucky in 1937 and contributed to Leadbelly's repertory. The Animals had learned it from Bob Dylan, who had learned it from Dave Van Ronk and recorded it in 1962. Dylan was taken with the Animals' performance and began to experiment himself with rock accompanists and electric guitars.[67]

In the summer of 1965 Dylan's prolix and nagging "Like a Rolling Stone," backed by a full blues band including Al Kooper on electric organ, joined the Beatles and the Rolling Stones in saturating the atmosphere from jukeboxes and radio. When Dylan appeared at Newport with a satin motorcycle jacket and a four-piece electric band, an outraged Pete Seeger threatened to cut the power cables with an ax. He was restrained, but the response of the audience was confused. Some rose from their seats to dance; others hooted and booed—either because the amplification equipment muddied the sound, or because they took the gesture as Seeger had, as a betrayal of the folk revival. No one could hear, in any case; after two numbers Dylan quit the stage, returning with his acoustic guitar to sing "It's All Over Now, Baby Blue."[68]

"After some painful self-parody by Odetta, who seemed totally lost as an artist," Paul Nelson reported,

> the evening and festival drew to its absurd climax: what seemed like three hundred folksingers on stage, elbowing and shoving and posing for a future *Sing Out!* or *Broadside* cover, obviously running for President, and shrieking the most ghastly burlesque of "We Shall Overcome" as they fought tooth-and-nail for the cherished image areas next to the Freedom Singers. Bad to the point of negating everything positive and beautiful the song stands for, it was a brilliant and sickening microcosm of the vast and seedy macrocosm that is the current urban folk music scene.[69]

The efforts of the Newport Folk Foundation to assimilate the rock revolution failed. The San Francisco band Buffalo Springfield, precursor to Crosby, Stills, Nash, and Young, appeared in 1967, and Janis Joplin and the Holding Company came in 1968 to help recoup financial losses. After yet another jazz festival riot the following year, the city installed a chainlink fence around the arena, restricted seating to 18,000, and declared a midnight limit to evening concerts. State troopers, local police, and private security guards patrolled the streets and enforced a midnight-to-seven curfew on the beaches. But civil disturbance had become endemic to the jazz festival, and in 1971 both it and the folk festival were closed down—the Newport Folk Foundation, after two benefit concerts the next year to pay its debts, was dissolved.

Grafted onto beat culture in the Haight-Ashbury district of San Francisco, to which the older movement had shifted after a rise in rents in North Beach, a new millennialism, an apolitical and anti-intellectual mix of Zen mysticism, peyote-cult animism, and pueblo-inspired tribalism, became the wellspring from which a new youth culture flowed into what was being changed into a dazzling consumer spectacle, severing ties to the historical culture from which the folk revival drew its life and tying it instead to a psychedelic drug, LSD, sacrament of the hippie movement, a lineal descendant of the marijuana trips once associated with cool jazz on the one hand and Huxleyesque spiritual visions on the other.

With beat poets Gary Snyder, Lawrence Ferlinghetti, and Allen Ginsberg as spiritual teachers, and supported by a sumptuary economy overflowing with discretionary capital, the hippie movement gathered up a handful of Bay Area bluegrass, blues, and folk musicians and transformed them into megabands such as Jefferson Airplane and the Grateful Dead, whose lucrative recording contracts would help to saturate the youth movement with a contempt for money that only those amply supplied with it can feel.

With its last link to history broken, its moral and political center dispersed, all pretense to philosophical or ideological depth repudiated, all forms of discursive continuity abolished in the intensity of the hallucinatory splendor of an acid trip, all of it as congenial to the nature of the capitalist marketplace as soap, an enclaved, dissident, bohemian culture, like Fermi's uranium pile at Stagg Field, had become the site of postmodernity's first self-sustaining commercial chain reaction.

Bob Dylan and Joan Baez at Newport, 1963

9

Lady and the Tramp

For those who first heard it on the radio in 1958, "Tom Dooley" had its meaning not against the backdrop of folksong scholarship or left-wing politics but as an unexpected departure from, and at the same time an ingenious continuation of, what was then one of the most remarkable entrepreneurial successes in the youth market: rock-and-roll, remarkable because of its apparently obscure sociocultural origins and its violent overthrow of the class standards of popular music. Rock-and-roll grew out of the practice by white performers, begun sometime in the forties, of covering (emulating) black rhythm-and-blues recordings distributed primarily within the urban black community, often circulating to southern cities from Chicago and New York. Much of this music evolved directly from the traditional blues being played in the 1930s by small ensembles, such as those led by Washboard Sam, Big Bill Broonzy, and Muddy Waters, recently come from the Mississippi Delta to Chicago.[1]

When young white working-class southerners began in 1954 to cover black "jump" blues, rock-and-roll found a popular audience. This music, disseminated by the ever more portable radio and on 45-rpm discs, was unquestionably a kind of folk music, with roots extending deeply into the black and white folk culture of the south. The inexpensive and virtually indestructible 45-rpm rockabilly disc was in the weeks of its currency a kind of cryptogram that, much to the dismay of parents, could be deciphered only by constant repetition. If its message seemed an urgent one, established only by increments in the understanding of adolescent children, it was because at the moment of their sexual awakening an exotic sexual culture, the culture of the levee and the boondocks, where abandoned lovers take up lodgings at the end of Lonely Street, stand at their windows and moan, or sneak into one another's houses like dogs, was for the space of a few seconds borne in upon them on the rhythms of the juke joint and barrelhouse in trappings that disarmed their class- and race-derived resistance to it: the straining vocality, sinewy with sexual tension, of young white men. The arm languidly pointing, the sneer, the sideburns, the sidelong grin, the sexual footwork: Elvis Presley's image was the pattern for thousands of pubescent boys lip-synching before the bedroom mirror with their first cheap guitar. What did the fourteen-year-old know of the idiom and manners of the frankly erotic, unsentimental, and passionate black underworld of New Orleans, Little Rock, or Memphis? Nothing: but rockabilly music, like the thief that doffs his clothes to baffle the guard dog, made it a part of his life.

I have emphasized that one of the great contributory streams of American music and culture, what Alan Lomax calls the "Old Tar River," has for nearly two hundred years flowed from African-American life and culture into European and Anglo-American culture at every social level. Black performances, by singers such as Little Richard, Chuck Berry, and Fats Domino, and by the great rhythm-and-blues groups such as the Platters and the Orioles, continued to provide the touchstone of rock-and-roll throughout the period. From the viewpoint of the folk revival, however, our interest lies with the rockabilly singer, who could convincingly reproduce, in the African-American performance style, a jump blues or a rhythm-and-blues song—for this was a young man who *through* the music seemed to have thrown off, like blackface minstrels and white jazzmen before him, the weight of polite society and its constraints. Even at the Newport Folk Festival, where southern bluesmen such as Sleepy John Estes and Mississippi John Hurt, or mountain balladeers such as Sara Gunning or Almeda Riddle, were regarded with admiration, reverence, and even awe, it was still the young white revivalist, Baez or Dylan, who attracted the enormous crowds and inspired the most calculated musical and personal imitation.

The rockabilly sound swiftly declined in the face of massive commercialization, marketing and sex scandals, and, most of all, the strange disappearance of the founding performers: Elvis was drafted into the army, Carl Perkins seriously injured in an auto accident, Chuck Berry and Jerry Lee Lewis disgraced by liaisons with underage girls, Buddy Holly, Eddie Cochran, and Gene Vincent killed—so sweeping was the catastrophe that one could almost imagine some quasi-official conspiracy behind it, especially considering the hostility rock-and-roll had aroused in certain quarters.

Equally significant in its demise, however, were the social and cultural affinities of rockabilly. Though its popularity was hardly confined to the working class, rockabilly was a southern working-class music already identified, with a vigorous second from a terrorized Tin Pan Alley, with what was then officiously called "juvenile delinquency." Racists of course saw something still more sinister in it, and political paranoiacs regarded it as only another manifestation of the worldwide communist conspiracy.

The commercialization of this music alienated its young middle-class listeners, now entering college, from those who permitted themselves to be led by each new commercial imitation of it: Fabian and Frankie Avalon, men of European ethnic backgrounds, had been promoted with Frank Sinatra in mind. A vacuum in popular music had opened, and a broad sector of the middle-class young turned, with the blessing of a relieved commercial establishment, to a music that ingeniously subdued awakened musical proclivities on behalf of a new and more fastidious social self-awareness: and which, incidentally, promised to restore vitality to music publishing, since young listeners wanted not only to hear but to sing folksongs. The genie, it seemed, had been put back in the bottle.

A few songs from the nascent folk revival had migrated to the pop charts before "Tom Dooley." Among them was Johnny Horton's version of Jimmy Driftwood's "Battle of New Orleans," Ernie Ford's version of Merle Travis' "Sixteen Tons," and Jimmy Rodgers' version of the Weavers' "Kisses Sweeter Than Wine." The aforementioned "Rock Island Line," the Leadbelly song popularized by Scottish skiffle bandleader Lonnie Donegan in 1956, for a time rivaled Presley's hits; two recordings of "Freight Train," by Doug and Rusty Kershaw and by Rusty Draper—but composed by the Seeger family's housekeeper Libba Cotten in 1919, when she was twelve—reached the Top 40 in 1957.

But, like the rockabilly combos, the Kingston Trio and its many imitators—the Cumberland Three, the Chad Mitchell Trio, the Highwaymen—were small stringbands of three or four young white men singing in natural voices, accompanying themselves with open chords on at least one acoustic guitar. In fact, as Dave Guard recalls, the untrained vocal sound was the conscious product of professional coaching in phrasing, vowel sounds, and speech accent.[2] Thus, though it did not have the homegrown character of rockabilly, the Kingston Trio's music seemed essentially aural, amateur, and traditional—what would loosely be called "folk" music—and hence independently reproducible, theoretically, by any untrained person. The professional arrangements that marked its delivery, moreover, were ingeniously calculated to highlight the timbre of individual voices, the sounds of acoustic guitars and banjos, and the evocativeness of open harmonies.

This is the most important respect, perhaps, in which the new folk groups resembled the rockabilly bands. But the Kingston Trio's "Tom Dooley" had more strictly musical affinities with rockabilly as well. Like many other young men, Dave Guard had been a dedicated listener to urban black music: in his case, to the rhythm-and-blues radio stations broadcasting from San Francisco and Oakland. The Trio's "Tom Dooley" had a rhythmic shuffle and a vocal countermelody strongly reminiscent of rhythm-and-blues and a pronounced syncopation in the lyric; on this level the song might have been half-consciously received as a white imitation of the rhythm-and-blues style. Indeed this "Tom Dooley" could plausibly have been covered by the Coasters, with an irony even folk revivalists could appreciate.

Most important, though, "Tom Dooley" told a story, not frankly sexual but darkly so, of murder and execution, furnished like a folktale with vivid concretions—the knife, the white oak tree, a man called Grayson—putatively sung in a cloaked, melancholy voice by a hapless mountaineer with an Irish name, accompanied by a banjo that spoke obscurely of the frontier. It carried the listener's imagination away from highschool corridors and sock hops, where commercial songwriters had largely confined their material, into another world, a world that a century of popular literature and imagery, including that of the schoolroom, had stereotyped and legitimated.

At the same time, the Kingston Trio's music was delivered with an articulation and phrasing perceptibly polite and bookish, in musical settings wholesomely pianistic; with their colorful short-sleeved ivy-league shirts, close-cropped hair, their easy drollery and unambiguous enthusiasm, the group was collegiate, happily parodying the on-stage pedantry of the previous generation of balladeers and folksong collector-performers. One of Dave Guard's principal influences, Lou Gottlieb, leader of the Gateway Singers and later of the Limeliters, was himself a Ph.D. musicologist who played a comic "professor" part in his shows. Unlike their mentors, the Kingston Trio seemed to be on spring break somewhere, on the beach at Waikiki, perhaps, where one of their jacket photos pictured them. Yet, under the gleam of sporty arrangements and expensive harmonies, there was something solemnly beckoning, a horizon of possibilities; though unapologetically commercial and almost cunningly collegiate, they performed the principal office of music, what some of the great rock-and-roll tunes from Memphis such as "Heartbreak Hotel" or "Blue Suede Shoes" had done, which is to carry the imagination into regions where the human story tells itself unabridged and unencumbered.

As we have seen, there are elements in the folk revival with histories of their own: folklore and ballad scholarship, minstrelsy, left-wing politics, education, recreation, and leisure, popular music and culture; but their particular conjunction in the folk revival has its meaning in the psychosocial and economic setting of postwar America. As Elaine Tyler May points out in her perceptive study of the cold-war American family, *Homeward Bound,* the new social, domestic, and familial arrangements of the postwar period were anything but traditional. The economic pressures of the depression had both strengthened kinship ties and brought something close to gender equality; with the male role as breadwinner thus threatened, nostalgia developed for a strong paternal figure and a dependent housewife. But the new postwar suburbs were simply extensions of a corporate world that, having mostly swallowed the self-employed man and small entrepreneur, both eroded male autonomy and dispelled the "communities of obligation," ethnic and agrarian, in which traditional knowledge and value had been seated.

The "psychological fastness" of the nuclear family, then, took on an immense burden of social, personal, and sexual fulfillment that it would ultimately prove unable to bear—especially since its great expectations fell primarily on its children. Reared, many of them, in houses and tracts designed for young families, they would as adolescents chafe under constricted spaces, a lack of privacy, unrelieved programming and supervision, and especially the want of activity and variety once supplied by extended family and community in a town or city environment.[3]

If you were born between roughly 1941 and 1948 or 1950—born, that is, into the new postwar middle class but on the upward slope, not the crest, of the baby boom—you grew up in a reality perplexingly divided by the intermingling of an emerging mass society and a decaying industrial culture: a society in which the automobile, the television, the research laboratory, the transcontinental market, and the retail franchise, all of them in some sense precipitates of the war, would begin to displace the railroad, the radio, the factory, the regional market, and the local business, changes that in less than a generation would reshape patterns of settlement, the structure of the family, networks of communication, and the material environment itself. Obscurely taking shape around you, of a definite order and texture, was an environment of new neighborhoods, new schools, new businesses, new forms of recreation and entertainment, and technologies that would nearly abolish the world in which your parents had grown up.

At the same time, you had been born soon enough to take the lingering traces of an earlier way of life into your own imagination. You may have been reared, for example, in a slightly more rigorous style than that shortly to be advocated by Dr. Benjamin Spock. And you absorbed, as you grew to awareness, your parents' almost unlimited hopes for you—for to them, who had grown up in depression and war, the relatively prosperous and tranquil life of postwar America was the end of the rainbow, a new dispensation in which the inevitability of success seemed assured; probably you saw yourself growing up to be a doctor or lawyer, scientist or engineer, teacher, nurse, or mother—sexual discrimination was still marked—images held up to you at school and home as pictures of your special destiny. You probably attended, too, an overcrowded public school, typically a building built shortly before World War I to which a new wing had been added to accommodate the burgeoning school-age population, shared a desk with another student, and in addition to the normal fire and tornado drills had sometimes to climb under your desk in order to be sheltered from the explosion of an atomic bomb: "First there's a flash of light . . ."

That such a thing might come, and soon, was one of the axioms of daily life; you had seen the atomic explosion on the television, which had come into your livingroom around 1952 or 1953, and all around you, but particularly on television, in the Saturday movie matinees, and in the immediate memory of parents and teachers was evidence of a global catastrophe that had recently spent itself. There was, moreover, a dark colossus, the Soviet Union, and an insidious influence, the Communist Party, in some obscure way connected to one another, foreign in a colorless, unsavory way, and dedicated, you were taught, to conquering us from above, with a rain of bombs, or from within, through a picturesque technique called brainwashing. It is not inconceivable, in fact, that your neighbor was digging a fallout shelter in his backyard.

Your house in the suburbs, with its new television set, the two-car garage, the gleaming, garish cars parked inside, the new electric appliances, the college degree your parents persistently evoked as the key to happiness: these were trophies of the enthusiastic consumerism of the postwar period, the uninhibited reaching after a dream long deferred by wartime deprivations. Consequently in this vision of consumer Valhalla there was a lingering note of caution, even of dread. Being widely shared and widely promulgated, the vision brought with it a certain uniformity and consistency on the social landscape; and to grasp it probably required the principal wage-earner in your family, most likely your father, to give himself over to the tightly regimented, highly competitive bureaucracy of the postwar American business establishment that so resembled the army.

Bureaucratization, conformity, and consumerism did not perhaps touch you as immediately as they touched your parents; but they did touch you. You tended to identify yourself with children your own age, socially, economically, and culturally more or less like yourself, and to think of the homogeneous world of children in which your parents had moved to place you, as the aim of their escape from the small town or the urban ghetto, as a norm—you were not, in other words, much acquainted in your immediate experience with other classes or cultures and may have been inclined, or even taught, by means of ethnic or racial epithets, dimly allegorical science-fiction films, lingering wartime artifacts, attitudes, and expressions, to look on difference with suspicion or a kind of righteous hostility. The nuclear family to which you belonged, bivouacked in the suburbs with other families more or less like itself, had effectively reduced the generational spectrum to the bipolarity of parent and child, while the consolidated public school you attended was strictly stratified by grade and, in some schools even more scrupulously, by less visible standards like "aptitude." As you advanced in school, you were subject to ever more elaborate forms of quantitative evaluation to distinguish you from your fellows, so difficult to distinguish in other ways, a process of IQ tests, achievement tests, aptitude tests, and the like, whose crowning glory was the new Scholastic Aptitude Test with its inexorable power to define, delimit, and foreclose.

At the same time, though, intimations of a variegated and enigmatic world beyond the suburban street occasionally disturbed the tranquil surface of social reality. There were the desks in the old school building, for example, with their inkwells, and the elderly schoolmarms and schoolmasters, with their old-fashioned discipline. There were the old houses on Main Street, too, as well as Main Street itself, whose deterioration would not be complete until all the business had moved out to the shopping mall—a process requiring little more than a decade. Perhaps you had European-born grandparents, still in their stuffy East Side flat or out on the farm; or knew a "colored man," born in Mississippi, who came to mow the lawn and played the harmonica; or an Amish farmer who delivered eggs; or had a schoolmate with a southern accent, whose father had come from Kentucky to work at the foundry or the auto plant—and who, to your amazement, brought a giant flat-top guitar to the fifth-grade talent show, playing and singing in a piping voice "Your Cheatin' Heart."

Similarly disquieting, and certainly fascinating, was the gang of young toughs from the other side of town, slightly older perhaps—"hoods" or "greasers" you called them—who wore, with their long hair and sideburns, the uniform of the motorcyclist: black leather jackets with many zippers and pockets, a garrison belt, faded blue jeans, and black engineer boots with silver buckles. One of them, who sat behind you in mechanical drawing, may have failed out of school and been arrested for petty theft. Indeed, the fifth-grade country singer and the high-school dropout may have been, after the passage of a few years, the same person, an unwitting victim of cultural dislocation and the vicissitudes of postwar industrial restructuring.

If these figures in the remoter parts of the social landscape attracted your attention, it was perhaps because their certain strange resonance with realms of your cultural life more strictly imaginary made your own world seem insipid by comparison. Wild Bill Hickok, the Lone Ranger, the Cisco Kid, Wyatt Earp, and a hundred other western heroes galloped across television and movie screens on Saturday mornings and afternoons; frontiersmen Mike Fink and Davy Crockett conquered the wilderness in Disney's weekly after-dinner episodes; Ichabod Crane, Johnny Appleseed, Pecos Bill, and other folk legends came to life in Disney's cartoons. In music class you may have sung "Cindy" and "She'll Be Comin' Round the Mountain" and other folksongs, and very likely in reading class you learned of frontier childhoods in Laura Ingalls Wilder's "Little House" books, re-published in a new edition in 1953, or from Ralph Moody's *Man of the Family*. You may have sung folksongs at summer camp, where there was a college-age counselor with a banjo, or at scout camp, where you practiced the arts of wilderness survival and learned Indian lore; or you heard folksongs sung on the phonograph with discs from the Children's Record Guild or

Young People's Records, accompanied by pictures and narratives about John Henry and Barbara Allen.

In short, you were the beneficiary of traditions both learned and popular which had already enjoyed a long life in America. During the epoch of your childhood these were being hastily quarried out of literature and the arts to supply swelling school enrollments, a swiftly expanding youth market, and capacious new media such as television and the LP. In the various departments of domestic and public life in which it moved, the experience of your generation, what we may call for convenience (and only half in jest) the Pepsi generation, was chiefly of itself; but its awareness of itself *as* a generation was constituted in the marketplace by a series of entrepreneurial incursions that saturated the field of awareness with revelations of its own desire.

No one should be surprised that the imaginations of the "folkniks" had been shaped by their many cultural advantages.[4] Among these was of course education itself, the importance of which had been consistently emphasized at home, with the unforeseen consequence that certain young idealists, when introduced to the great philosophers, poets, and writers of Europe and America, tended to take them seriously—with disruptive effects, since middle-class postwar society showed little of the influence of, say, Nietzsche.

For once in college—and nearly half of the Pepsi generation would attend college—the folkniks encountered, in others like themselves, a new boldness, even a subtle nonconformity: a willingness, for example, to undertake academic majors in art, philosophy, or literature instead of more careerist professional programs. Allied to the interest in folk music, moreover, was an intriguing new style of uncertain origin: young women with long, natural hair, peasant skirts, handcrafted sandals and barrettes, young men whose hair had been clipped by their girlfriends, not by the barber, with sideburns or beards, workshirts, handmade leather belts with brass buckles—all brought to the campus by children of urban, middle-class background, perhaps from the galleries, street vendors, and import shops of Greenwich Village or from summer watering spots and artists' colonies such as Woodstock, Provincetown, Martha's Vineyard, or even a Colorado dude ranch.

Slowly a conception formed, more taste than ideology, more style than discourse, more interpersonal than historical, that the world had been gravely mismanaged by the parent generation. For set cruelly against the high expectations for the future which parents had inculcated, and against the richness and color of the promised world, was the nagging fear that the future might at any moment be withdrawn—precisely what happened in 1965 with Johnson's war—or that failure to measure up to some arbitrary standard would close off access to it; through the glory with which the world had been invested, then, ran a thick streak of the sinister. And in case anyone had forgotten about the Bomb, the Cuban missile crisis was there in 1962, on television, to refresh the national memory and to fill the atmosphere with a mood of apocalypse.

In such an atmosphere it seemed essential to take matters into your own hands. Young people, after all, seemed to fill the field of vision; commercially and institutionally consolidated, they had become a social and political power. This was an urgent and intoxicating idea—but it differed from the revolutionary ideas of the Vietnam-era counterculture, which would shortly bury the folk revival, in one important respect: it sought, and believed in, until deep political and social polarizations betrayed that belief, the blessing of the parent generation—for its high purposes were precisely the return on the moral, cultural, and indeed financial investment that generation had made in its children.

Recourse to magic, Roger Abrahams has said, will follow the collapse of authorized cultural forms; there is an analogy, he suggests, between the cholera-stricken tribe that western medicine has failed, turning to its traditional healers, and the revivalist turning to the imaginative resources of folk culture, or representations of it, in order to elaborate what Victor Turner calls a subjunctive world, not mere fantasy or make-believe but a symbolic system that grants us through purposeful manipulations the power to influence the actuality of which it is a scheme or map. This anthropological notion is no mere analogy. The ontological subjunctivity of which Turner speaks is in the folk revival amalgamated both with the adolescent psychosocial moratorium described by Erikson and the sequestered time and space of the college campus in which that moratorium was largely institutionalized, where the entire liberal enterprise is underwritten by an intellectual, social, and psychological subjunctivity that, however insulated from the real world, is at the same time variously threaded into and through it.

By the late 1950s, stirrings of activism, dormant since the thirties, now underwritten by a cautious and watchful confidence in its fundamental compatibility with the ideals and values that class and education had inculcated, began to appear on college campuses: politically in organizations such as the Student Peace Union, socially in liberalized attitudes—painfully modest by the anything-goes ethos that later evolved—toward sex, drugs, education, and career, and culturally in a new enthusiasm for folk music and everything associated with it. These developments were united in the goal of bringing about the world promised by the parent culture: politically by removing the most conspicuous impediment to it, the Bomb, socially by relaxing outmoded restraints, culturally by summoning up a visionary world in which a war- and weapon-liberated people might live, a culture rooted in prewar America, one that could not be suburbanized out of existence.

Thus the folk revival was neither reactionary nor revolutionary, though it borrowed the signs of other such movements to express its sense of difference from the parent culture; it was, instead, conservative or, more precisely, restorative, a kind of nonviolent cultural disobedience dedicated to picking up the threads of a forgotten legacy to reweave them into history—among which was precisely the tradition of the left itself, with its demand for the democratization of history, a history that can be "brought under the control of people in their daily lives."[5] In spite of appearances, this was the dream of children fundamentally obedient, good kids. "Despite his calculated artifice," wrote the music critic Paul Nelson of the young folksinger, "his well-made grubbiness, he was like a nervous debutante, afraid of not being asked to dance. Underneath that cultivated, ultimately clean-cut unkemptness there beat the heart not of a ramblin' gamblin' hobo (as he thought) but of a Boy Scout, one who is kind to his elders, helps old ladies across the street, walks the dog every night."[6]

For many, the amateur singing of folksongs was simply a dormitory pastime and after graduation went the way that tarot cards and love beads would a few years later. Like Pete Seeger, Jon Pankake complained in 1964, "but lacking his peculiar genius for presentation, the young revivalists have piled haphazardly into America's great traditions like so many grubby urchins grabbing at pennies":

> Flushed with Pete's encouragement, equipped with a week of perfunctory study in his banjo course, their heads till reverberating with the insane ring of the mass communications airwaves, young men and women have snatched up the lifeworks of centuries of dedicated country geniuses and degraded the integrity and dignity of these works by performing them as though they were so many Tin Pan Alley throwaways . . . The body of America's folk music has largely become like the proverbial Flemish description of life itself: "It is a haywain, and everybody snatches from it what he can."[7]

But, as Carl Sandburg suggested in 1927, the development of the musical skills required to perform a self-accompanied folksong can leave psychological traces more permanent than a parlor game or cosmetic jewelry. "A song is a role," he wrote. "The singer acts a part . . . all good artists study a song and live with it before performing it . . . There is something authentic about any person's way of giving a song which has been known, lived with and loved, for many years, by the singer."[8]

To study a song, concluded Israel Young, proprietor of Greenwich Village's Folklore Center, "makes a student feel allied to it. It enables a girl who grew up surrounded by the best of everything to sing with some conviction the kinds of blues and spirituals that, theoretically, could be sung honestly only by a prisoner on a Southern chain gang."[9] "There are certain qualities we demand from the music," John Cohen concurred: "a sense of immediacy, of personal involvement, a sense of tradition as well as appreciation for that which carries things to a point where they can go no further . . . a rejection of compromise . . . an obsession . . . with the song material and a sense of an event with every performance."[10]

"In order to acquire a folk singing style," Alan Lomax insisted, "you have to experience the feelings that lie behind it, and learn to express them as the folk singers do."[11] College students had begun to approach folk music in an ethnological spirit. Johns Hopkins and St. John's students were frequenting bluegrass bars and country-music parks around Baltimore, absorbing the music in its milieu. A Bennington junior took her guitar to a kibbutz to learn Israeli songs; a Duke graduate went "hill walking" through the Scottish highlands, learning stories and ballads from other students in youth hostels and pubs as well as from farmers and shepherds. "My great desire," testified Bonnie Robertson of Connecticut College, "is to go to the places where these songs began so I can know these people and their lives . . . and learn their music first hand. Only then can I feel content reproducing their songs with my voice, fingertips and emotions." Of this impulse Montgomery asks:

> Why American college students should want to express the ideas and emotions of the downtrodden and the heartbroken, of garage mechanics and millworkers and miners and backwoods farmers, is in itself an interesting question. But there is certainly good reason for students today to find the world brutal and threatening,

and one suspects that when they sing about the burdens and sorrows of the Negro, for example, they are singing out of their own state of mind as well.[12]

"Most of us," Cynthia Gooding recalled, "were initially drawn to folk singing by nebulous and partly indefinable reactions and yearnings. We love the traditional values and the honesty of the songs and of the rural performers. We wish to reassert the usefulness of ancient virtues, to find a link between past peasant cultures and ourselves that would demonstrate that in a bewildered time, there are roots we can touch and evoke in song. We had intended, I believe, to be responsible to the songs and to the art, each of us in his chosen way."[13]

In this setting, the revivalists' turn to dissent is more than superficially stylistic; it represents both a sense of affinity with the moral and emotional message of folksong as well as the personal influence of the dedicated practice of it. "Many of them," Montgomery observed of the early revivalists in Washington Square, "in some small detail of their appearance, looked ever so slightly beat."

> The badge of identity was sometimes a beard, worn as if in defiance of its owner's Shetland sweater or expensively tailored Madras shorts, or a workman's blue shirt tucked carelessly into faded jeans. Or a girl might go in for wrought-iron jewelry or long straight hair or a Mexican cotton skirt or handsome hand-crafted leather sandals . . . This generation of college students . . . is composed of young people who are desperately hungry for a small, safe taste of an unslick, underground world. Folk music, like a beard or sandals, has come to represent a slight loosening of the inhibitions, a tentative step in the direction of the open road, the knapsack, the hostel. To put it another way, some of the trappings and tastes of a Bohemian minority group have been gradually assimilated and adapted by the student middle class.[14]

By 1965, as Paul Nelson noted, the folksinger's persona had evolved into a loosely conventional form, that of the "casually road-weary" traveler in jeans and boots or peasant frocks, "clothes as rumpled as parents would allow," "erratic" hair, one who speaks a pidgin idiom neither south nor west but vaguely regional and proletarian, "that non-regional dialect of the Shangri-La West that Bob Dylan and Jack Elliott hailed from, that mythical nowhere where all men talk like Woody Guthrie and are recorded by Moses Asch."[15]

Pete Seeger, similarly transformed himself, understood the psychosocial project in which the revivalist was engaged. "When some people find that Jack Elliott was born in Brooklyn," he wrote—named Adnopoz, he might have added, the son of an ophthalmologist—"he with his cowboy hat and boots, rough lingo and expert guitar playing—their first reaction is 'Oh, he's a fake'."

> They're dead wrong. Jack reborned himself "in Oklahoma." He didn't just learn some new songs, but he changed his whole way of living . . . We are used to this happening in the opposite direction; a country youth goes off to college and then gets into business in the city . . . nobody calls him abnormal . . . My guess is that there will always be young people who for one reason or another will feel that they have to violently, radically reform themselves. A personal revolution. They abandon the old like a hated mask and rebuild on new foundations.[16]

John Cohen, himself a Yale graduate who became a leader in the revival of stringband music, noted the intensity arising "from the struggle with forces in the music itself—which become as real as any other problem of life."[17] Many students abandoned their studies, and their medical or legal careers with them, in response to those forces: to the demands of the bluegrass banjo style, the blues guitar, or the Appalachian fiddle. These, Montgomery concluded, were "bedeviled people . . . who should be counted among the casualties of contemporary American life."[18]

One such casualty was Cohen himself, a photographer by vocation; he joined with Tom Paley, a City College oldtime-music enthusiast, and Mike Seeger, Pete's younger half-brother, to form a stringband, the New Lost City Ramblers. Setting the pattern for the hundreds of amateur bands that followed them, the Ramblers offered concerts of oldtime music painstakingly reconstructed from rare discs recorded in the twenties by such bands as Charlie Poole and the North Carolina Ramblers, Gid Tanner and His Skillet Lickers, or J. E. Mainer's Mountaineers, many of which had been rerecorded from the Smith collection at the New York Public Library by Seeger and Ralph Rinzler.[19]

The New Lost City Ramblers raised the nap of the revival with newly esotericized discographic sources and a performance style that sounded as exotic as a Tibetan prayer. In addition to their expert musicianship, arcane scholarship, and a demeanor sober enough for the recital hall, they presented themselves like railroad stationmasters or telegraph operators of 1885, in vests, shirtsleeves, and neckties, and posed for an album photograph, its surface artificially mottled and cracked, with the blank faces and straight spines of a portrait studio of the last century. Yet they were not above self-parody: clowning with their many instrument changes on stage, which their own versatility and accuracy to their sources demanded, they typically identified themselves to nightclub audiences as an underground version of the Kingston Trio.[20]

We have detected traces of Left Bank and North Beach bohemianism, motorcycle errantry, old left-wing politics, and the rest in the folk revival; but it could not really be identified with any of these. Susan Montgomery, calling attention to the "open road, the knapsack, the hostel," was closer, I think, to the essential spirit of the developed folk revival, with its peculiar mix of youth, collegiality, holiday, rebellion, adventure, and idealism, and might have found it instructive to peruse the songbook from which the Kingston Trio learned the words to "Tom Dooley," Dick and Ruth Best's *New Song Fest*.

Originally issued in mimeograph, *New Song Fest* was a publication of the Intercollegiate Outing Club Association, founded in 1932 "to bring together students with a mutual interest in the out of doors"—students who took special delight in folk and international dancing and in singing folksongs around the campfire, to the strumming of a guitar or banjo. One of the largest of the club's chapters met at "Old Joe Clark" House in Cambridge, Massachusetts, hotbed of the folk revival, across the street from Radcliffe student Peggy Seeger's residence. The authors of *New Song Fest* appended to their signatures their class and college—"Cornell '44" and "Radcliffe '47"—and in a prefatory statement announced: "A reward of one dungaree patch, guaranteed not to rip, run, rust, tear, split, melt, break, etc. is hereby offered for the pelt of the first bohunk caught surreptitiously using this book at a songfest."[21]

Are we catching here an essence from an esoteric but vital phase of the sixties? Consider the IOCA song, which pictures young bohunks in "old dungarees, patched in the rear and on the knee," tramping high in the Adirondacks, "crashing through brush with heart so free," reveling in their disdain of hierarchy, manners, and rule:

> Our disorganization is perfect;
> Figureheads we have but a few,
> But no meetings among 'em, for we have hamstrung 'em
> 'Cause organization's taboo.

Collegiate as they are, they seem to prefer a vision of a simpler life to the fraternity mixer: "Give us an old-fashioned barn dance." The tone is cheerful and carefree; but the signal elements—rejection of authority, the dismantling of regimented structures, and pleasure in warm, informal association and casual fun, the idealization of folklife and the identification with the past—are all in place.

As Peter Yarrow (of Peter, Paul, and Mary), who graduated from Cornell in 1959, suggested, it was important for students to feel part of something, as they did at Seeger's communal sings. Yarrow outlined what had become a conventional pattern: having attended such an affair, and felt such elevated feelings as belong to hymn singing and revival meetings, the student begins by buying certain records, typically by Harry

Belafonte or the Kingston Trio, and slowly becomes acquainted, through friends, album notes, magazines, books, and other sources, with more "authentic" music such as that in the Library of Congress collection. Coffeehouse and concert performances intimate the possibility of her own transformation—and soon she has retired to her dorm room to compare her own efforts on the guitar to what she hears on the record albums.

"Students choose these records," Montgomery observes, "because, ironically, *they* think they are uncommercial."

> They like folk music because the whole country isn't singing it; it's something apart from the forty top tunes; it seems to them easy and comprehensible, not "hard" like progressive jazz . . . They are overjoyed by the discovery that after months, not years, of practice they can make pleasant sounds on a folk instrument like a guitar or a recorder.
>
> Since folkniks use folkmusic to set themselves apart . . . many of them will doubtless put their guitars aside before too long, when strumming and singing becomes the rage of Levittown and the matrons in Westchester.[22]

"In both their dress and their musical tastes," Irwin Silber comments, "these undergraduate folk music partisans seem to be protesting the innocuousness of the 'mass culture' which the soap-sellers are offering."

> In effect, they are rejecting the button-down collar and the button-down music. Since they realize that the realities of the world dictate their eventual dependence on the Establishment, they take advantage of their student years to express sentiments which will eventually be accommodated to the practicalities of life . . . No art can truly flourish outside its own time and place, and, in the long run, college students (along with the rest of us) will have to find a means of expression which is uniquely of our own age.[23]

In this testimony we can detect the sad contradiction inherent in a process that can throw off commercialism and other forms of hegemony only by means of them—a contradiction at the heart of Irwin's melancholy prediction not only that the revival would ultimately evaporate in its own commercial medium, but that the revivalists themselves had undertaken their project knowing of its transitory character. For as these contemporaneous reports indicate, it was neither the "innocuousness" of mass culture, that is, its formulaic, commercial aesthetic, nor its "exalted standards of performance," that is, its exclusionary appeal to class aspiration—mutually contradictory claims—that inspired dissent, but the concept of mass culture itself.

As Raymond Williams suggests, we can posit the existence of a mass culture only by positioning ourselves outside it; yet it is the very possibility of an outside perspective that calls the existence of a "mass" culture into question, even as we recognize everywhere the immense effort by institutions to circulate their own products, images, and associated ideologies, in effect to dominate the terrain at which culture and the marketplace converge. Hence it is not "mass culture" at issue, but cultural control:

> Theirs is a generation which has grown up in a world which seems beyond the realm of influence or change by the individual. It is a world of war and atomic diplomacy, of basic decisions made by remote men in remote places. Where an earlier generation marched for Spain or sang for the CIO, today's "protester" apparently believes that direct action is hopeless . . . Accordingly, a sizeable body of nonconformist opinion which might once have found itself on the intellectual barricades is today finding an outlet in a highly stylized, unlettered, individualistic folk music with an intense beauty and honesty which momentarily transcends the phony, grubby world of reality.[24]

What we can perhaps discern from our own postmodern perspective, and what the folk revivalist knew intuitively, is that what Silber calls "reality" is a matter of imaginative and material making, and as such can begin wherever the resources of culture become available for assent. While certainly acknowledging the power of corporate society to absorb not only her revival but herself, the folk revivalist would not, I think, have accepted the assumption implicit in Silber's remarks that her own world was somehow unreal and the other real, that in the end the fantasy would dissolve *because* it was a dream; on the contrary, in the making of culture, it is the fantasy, as a stronghold of value and the enactment of it, that has existential priority—which is what lends to the corporate hegemony, with its capacity to project desire, its pervasive presence. In the folk revival, as Joan Baez put it with reference to nonviolence, "the means would determine the ends," not the other way around.[25]

Precisely because they were college students, because they had enjoyed a lifetime of involvement in the structures, images, ideas, and narratives of postwar education, entertainment, and commerce, the revivalists of the sixties understood that they were enmeshed in the most colossal mythology industrial capitalist society had ever produced—that one history had ended and another begun with the explosion of the atomic bomb, and that the new history was nothing more or less than a total environment of institutional power.

The collectivizing, rationalizing, scientizing, and regimenting influences of that environment amounted to the appropriation by the commercial, educational and other establishments of what nature had given them most to enjoy, their own youth. To be young and middle-class in the postwar environment was not only to have your sexuality reduced to an elaborate set of prohibitions, exclusions, obsessions, and petty neuroses, but *at the same time* to have your sexual identity commodified, coarsened, and puerilized. To be young and female in the early sixties meant, in effect, to transform yourself into a rubber doll with plastic hair, purely a factory product; to be young and male demanded a practiced hypocrisy that sanctified women and at the same time demanded sexual conquests whose purpose was to provide materials for the minutely detailed narratives, graphic boasts, and outrageous claims familiar in men's dormitories.

Postwar culture, in short, even as it had given them everything, took away from the young all that they had. And as youth dissipated in the institutional structures of postwar society, so was the romantic energy characteristic of youth, redirected to the visible and immediate purpose of competition for individual rewards and personal distinction. To be young was, inevitably, to be a part of a true mass culture, in which the individual was no more than a punchcard, not to be bent, spindled, folded, or mutilated; it was to see the textured natural surfaces of the material world replaced by government-subsidized plastics, polymeric fibers, and cheap disposables; it was to be hygienically routed from middle school on through what amounted to a social assembly line akin to mass immunizations of scheduling routines, propagandistic history, "social studies," and other pedagogy riven with cold-war absolutes; tendentious educational films, the threadbare platitudes of scouting, sports, and gym, the mystical lottery of college admissions reminiscent of Calvinist election—all in preparation for membership in a suburban, corporate, consumerist, nucleated, economically stratified and segregated white-collar working class. "TV dinner by the pool," Frank Zappa crooned, "I'm so glad I finished school."

It became the immediate impulse of young adults enjoying the more liberal atmosphere of college life to emancipate themselves from bondage in their own youth—not to become old precisely but, like the "casually road-weary traveler," no longer to be young: to temper the callowness of youth with thoroughly typified "experiences" such as the cross-country road trip, immersion in abstruse philosophy or the fine frenzies of poetry or painting or song, and complicated sexual entanglements; more desperately, to harrow one's youth with alcohol binges and drug trips, impulsive acts of vandalism or theft. Some dropped school altogether either as a personal statement or in favor of some alternative occupation or traditional trade; some affected madness; some actually went crazy.

This contagious and dangerous rite of passage, at once hastening time and seeking to arrest it, arose in the dimensionlesss zone where self and the presentation of self flow into one another with mutually confirming and mutually actualizing potency; where conventional ordeals and constructed identities, and conventional outcomes, effects, and meanings, conferred personal identity through social assent and, conversely, won assent to personal identities fashioned within the broader patterns of recognition. The familiar sartorial and tonsorial practices of the young—the studiously careless personal grooming, the elegantly shabby utilitarian or secondhand clothes, the ethnic or exotic touch—these are all designed to historicize the body, to lengthen the temporal track on which the presented person has moved. What aspect of the person, indeed, is a more exacting timepiece, a sort of corporeal meridian, than a head of hair, which like growing grass visibly measures its own temporality? What more richly reveals the quality of that temporality, especially as it suggests the purposes to which one's individual life is turned? Molded with lotions and sprays, subdued with oils or sculpted with pastes, or like a soldier's shaved close with spartan or cruel intensity, hair affected a static form vainly attempting to stop time; left to itself in its luxuriousness, abundance, modesty, or plainness, it revealed the body's natural sexuality and its involvement with the cycles of natural time.

As Kathy Shirnberg testified, it was the "olderness" of the music that attracted her, for Helen Schneyer the "sense of yesteryear"; as Oscar Brand expressed it, the music "seemed to imply a passage of time." Folksongs sound historical; "they sound as if other people have sung them," used—like a pair of secondhand boots or an old guitar.[26] What distinguishes the folk revivalist in this broader rite of passage is that, in historicizing the body and temporalizing the self, she draws from the interrupted cultural narratives that folksong represents, attempting to reintegrate the body and the self with them, thereby revitalizing, like all proper rites, both the self and the culture. "My audiences," John Jacob Niles said at Newport in 1960, "thank all folk singers for comfort, for assurance, for the nostalgia that seems to connect them with times past."

As the revivalists knew, the meaning of their movement was thus most mysteriously and powerfully embodied in Joan Baez and Bob Dylan. In them youthful sexuality vivified the cultural forms to which certain ideals of American democracy had been aligned—innocence and freedom, independence, piety and duty, equality, conscience, and revolt; and at the same time those forms lent a kind of articulation, almost a poetry, to their considerable personal beauty, interest, and force. Like Pete Seeger, they were "absolutely coherent" and yet compounded of heterogeneous elements usually foreign and irreconcilable; they were arrestingly familiar, instantly recognizable, and yet somehow inscrutable; widely imitated, made themselves of imitation, mere types, long familiar in the revival and on the wider cultural landscape, and yet thoroughly inimitable and original. Between them they crystalized and defined, symbolically, the folk revival's gender roles, tapping the historical resources that touch sexuality with cultural meaning.

"Before Joan ever appeared on the folk scene," John Cohen writes, "there had been quite a parade of long-haired young ladies who sang the sad and lonesome ballads, mixing bel-canto singing with an idea of Elizabethan England and Victorian morality . . . In the 'forties and 'fifties these girls were as much a part of folksinging as was the idealism of the labor movement."[27] The folksong movement, it seems, used to have a distinctive if seldom acknowledged gender inflection—one that thrust the worksongs, chants, and blues of the levee, prison, and juke joint, or the complex techniques of bluegrass, into the masculine sphere, with the "remorseless authenticity" of such concern to patriarchy, while entrusting the tradition of British balladry and other forms such as the spiritual to the preserve of women. "I love the old ballads," wrote the columnist Harriet Van Horne, "and would run off tonight with any raggle-taggle gypsy-o who would teach me to play the zither and sing 'Rise Up, Lord Douglas,' 'The Nut-Brown Maid,' or any of the sixty-eight versions of Barbara Allen."[28]

Like many young women of her generation, Joan Baez vowed with her close highschool friends to preserve her virginity until she married—and, like many young women of her generation, forgot her vow almost as soon as the right young man presented himself. "We three maidens loved folk music," she reflected of herself and her college roommates who had grown their hair to their waists, recalling of her own hair that she "waited impatiently for it to grow out in tresses so that I could be like them, and like all the fair and tender maidens in all of the long and tragic ballads."[29] Singing duets with her sister Mimi in Cambridge coffeehouses, the young women "scanned the smokey room for our respective princes," shamelessly making eyes at them—"our boys," she called them, who "seemed satisfied to love us as they would two Mexican virgins who would eventually be given in marriage to the boy proven to be the truest and purest."

"To a handful of fans from Boston," the 1959 Newport festival program observed, "winsome, dark-haired 18-year-old Joan Baez was no 'discovery.'" As her collection of "utterly pure, nearly sacrosanct folk songs" grew, and came increasingly to be identified with her in the Cambridge revival, her "academic, rebellious coffee-drinking admirers listened single-mindedly to their madonna, and dared not touch her." By the time Bob Gibson introduced her at Newport, where she sang West Indian and American spirituals, "Virgin Mary" and "We Are Crossing Jordan's River," Baez's persona had been firmly fixed: "I looked like purity itself in long tresses, no makeup, and Bible sandals. No wonder the press labelled me 'the madonna' and 'the Virgin Mary' the next day."

In another sense, though, she *was* a discovery. Baez had unwittingly summoned the unconscious projections of a generation of young men and women for whom the sublimation of desire to ideality, passion to purity, was like a religious faith assuming the character of an emotional fiction, no longer grounded in social realities and yet still capable of summoning up the romantic quest in a context of persistent sexual guilt and doubt. The postwar reaction against the wartime expansion of women's economic role in the fifties had by the end of the decade produced the suburban housewife; but it also produced a generation of young women for whom liberal education and, in theory, increased economic opportunity had brought a new spirit of personal, professional, and, after the pill, sexual autonomy.

The sexual protocols that bourgeois society had adopted from late medieval French and Italian nobility to fuse its marriage and market systems under the principle of property, a four-hundred-year-old cultural artifact that by the Victorian period had become a middle-class commonplace, was by the 1950s near the end of its history, though still cherished by the respectable Anglo-American middle and upper classes. To call it up in its historical manifestations, then, in the transitional period that preceded our own sexual revolution, was to acknowledge its fictionality, to generate its tremendous erotic energy in a setting of increased sexual liberality and opportunity—precisely what Baez's highschool vow indicates.

Joan Baez began her musical career accompanying herself on the ukulele. Her repertory came from the bedside radio: "Earth Angel," "Pledging My Love," and "Your Cheatin' Heart"—rhythm-and-blues and country-western songs popular at a moment at which these forms had begun to go into solution with one another, needing only the catalyst of Elvis to produce the rock-and-roll explosion. The distinctive female stylists of rhythm-and-blues, Eartha Kitt and Della Reese, supplied vocal models until, after her rejection from the high-school glee club for lack of a vibrato, Baez began to develop her own style, and with it her "achingly pure soprano," ineffably light, unblemished, and fluid, with a kind of galvanic conductivity capable of carrying, through a medium as limpid and alive as the lens of the human eye, a powerful sexual current. Like that of traditional ballad singers, her vocal delivery was straightforward, even deadpan, without interpretation, sustaining her in the impersonally ideal realm; her exact but unpedantic articulation and unhurried phrasing preserved the "sanctity" of the ballad while bringing it completely from the textual into the aural and vocal, and manifestly female, domain.

It is important to recognize that the sanctity of the ballad in which Baez specialized resides not only in fair and tender maidens stabbing themselves, or being stabbed, through their snowy white breasts, but in the British and Anglo-American gentility with which the ballad and ballad scholarship had been associated in the late nineteenth century, and, further, with the property-based and virginity-centered sexual attitudes—"Victorian"—most associated with this class and most dramatically embodied in the ballad. To Anglo-American nativists and reformers, moreover, the ballad and other British folksongs surviving in Appalachian tradition had been taken as the Elizabethan residue of an authentic Anglo-American identity, even as the Elizabethan period itself symbolized a "merrie England" of festivity, pageantry, and sexual license. In this connection it is telling that Cecil Sharp's first trip to America had been to direct the music for Granville Barber's production of *A Midsummer Night's Dream* at Long Pond, the exclusive summer dance camp.

Baez embodied, symbolized, and enacted this powerful synthesis of sexual obsession, social prestige, erotic longing, and poetic representation; but what is most compelling about her is that in her personal life as well as her professional performances she consistently subverted it—as, indeed, many of the most distinguished women of the old Anglo-American ruling class, from Elizabeth Cady Stanton to Jane Addams, had done, women for whom virginity was less a commodity to be negotiated in the marriage market than the very key to emancipation from it.

From her parents and their experiences, Baez inherited her intriguing ethnic ambiguity, a durable memory of an idyllic prewar America, a social and moral commitment rooted in a religious tradition, the persistent nonconformity so congenial to the mood of the period, and a place at the wellspring of the folk revival around Harvard Square.

Her mother was Scots, daughter of an Episcopalian priest; to the eye, though, Joan Baez was no fair-haired, blue-eyed Protestant lady-in-waiting, but a dark Latin beauty imbued with Catholic exoticism and mystery. Throughout her school years in southern California she was consistently identified not with the Anglos but with Hispanic immigrants and illegal aliens—"girls with mountains of black hair, frizzed from sleeping all night on masses of pincurls, wearing gobs of violet lipstick, tight skirts and nylons," boys "who slicked back their gorgeous hair with Three Roses Vaseline Tonic and wore their pegged pants so low on the hip that walking without losing them had become an art"—but since she didn't speak Spanish, she was accepted by neither group.

Her father was Mexican, whose own father had left the Catholic church to work with the poor in Brooklyn as a Methodist minister. Imbued from his childhood with a sense of social responsibility, Albert Baez became a pacifist once his work as a research physicist had acquainted him with the destructive power of the atomic bomb. The family joined the Friends' church, drawing Joan out of the political as well as the ethnic mainstream and into one of the central traditions of dissent in America, toward what Jane Addams, daughter of a Hicksite Quaker, called "the old question eternally suggested by the inequalities of the human lot." Descended from abolitionist, social-settlement, and the antiwar movements, this was a tradition that elevated, in Addams' words, "mental integrity above all else."[30] At the height of the cold war, Baez was attending Quaker workcamps with her family, and in highschool, as a participant in an American Friends Service Committee conference in California, encountered the philosophy of nonviolence taught by Martin Luther King who, with her lifelong mentor, the committed pacifist Ira Sandperl, was at the meeting.

"We lived in a beautiful little house across from an open field of hay," Joan wrote of her earliest years in California.

> Mother grew sweet peas in our backyard on strings that stretched from the tops of the fence slats down to sticks placed firmly in the earth. I see the neighbor's mulberry tree whose branches hung down so low you could duck right under them and hide against the trunk, peeking out and staining your mouth and hands with mulberry juice. I see our rabbit in his cage over the lettuce rows in the vegetable garden, and the clothesline filled with sheets and tiny dresses, all stuck on the line with wooden clothespins. I see the trees lining the sidewalk in the front yard which bloomed in masses of deep pink in the spring.[31]

This vision is a sentimental one, but it recalls what for many revivalists was the elusive longing beneath their adolescent idealism: a childhood memory of the prewar domestic world that the depression had held in a kind of time warp, a world that suburbanization would eradicate and that many, like Baez herself, would leave behind.

Albert Baez's career took the family to Ithaca, New York, to a suburban house in Redlands, California, back to Palo Alto, and finally to MIT, when Joan enrolled at Boston University. Her school life had been a long series of refusals, beginning with her refusal in nursery school, among other kinds of bad behavior, to wear skirts, because the boys lifted them, in preference to overalls. In highschool she refused to participate in an air-raid drill, and at Boston refused to wear the customary beanie to the freshman class picnic—refusing, finally, to do any academic work at all, so that after one semester, she flunked out.

In a sense Baez's extraordinary vocal gift had already determined her career. Even before the emergence of the Kingston Trio she had been singing her popular repertory in the highschool cafeteria, at local proms, and at the parties and clubs of her parents and their friends; she was even offered an out-of-town gig by a highschool teacher, who paid her airfare to Paradise, California. By this time she had discovered Harry Belafonte and Odetta, and attended a Pete Seeger concert in San Francisco. On the trip to Massachusetts she heard "Tom Dooley" on the car radio—and when she arrived in Boston found a folk revival ready to embrace her. Eric Sackheim, a Harvard student and oldtime music aficionado, had brought from New York his collection of discs and tapes, while Arthur Gilette and Joan's college friend Debbie Green, graduates of the Putney School in Vermont, one of the more sequestered scenes of the folksong movement and of Pete Seeger's guerrilla warfare of the fifties, brought their guitar and banjo techniques to the new student folksingers around Harvard Square.[32]

Baez would begin to build her reputation, and her repertory, in the coffeehouses to which her father took her and her sisters, apparently out of an interest of his own. "Plaisir d'Amour," fresh and pure as a newborn baby, which appears on her first record album (produced by Fred Hellerman), she heard first at Tulla's Coffee Grinder from a young man accompanying himself on a classical guitar. Soon she met Eric Von Schmidt, who introduced her to his collection of Leadbelly, Woody Guthrie, and early blues recordings, and took a job two nights a week at a jazz club, the Club 47 on Mt. Auburn Street, whose owner wanted to convert it into a folk club—becoming the first folksinger to perform there. Other work followed, including an appearance at the Golden Vanity on a double bill with a screening of Marlon Brando's *The Wild One*, where she tranquilized an audience of Hell's Angels.

Though she ultimately signed with the classical label Vanguard, and enlisted the management of Boston Marxist and blues aficionado Manny Greenhill, her brief negotiation with promoter Albert Grossman, who would later manage Bob Dylan, Peter, Paul, and Mary, Janis Joplin, and Jimi Hendrix, took her to Grossman's Gate of Horn in Chicago, where she met, not a management consultant, but a hard-drinking hip iconoclast named Bob Gibson.

By 1961, a "rebellious, barefoot, antiestablishment young girl," Baez had twenty annual concerts on her calendar and in 1963 invited Bob Dylan, whom she'd seen first at Gerde's Folk City in 1961, to sing with her on the road. "I was getting audiences of up to ten thousand at that point," she recalled, "and dragging my little vagabond out onto the stage was a grand experiment and a gamble which I knew he and I would eventually win."[33]

It was the "little vagabond" whose audacious self-invention would consolidate the movement already abroad in youth culture. Dylan was another fascinating compound of contraries. He was born Robert Zimmerman in 1941 and grew up in working-class, predominantly Catholic, Hibbing, Minnesota, the son of a Jewish hardware merchant. As his biographer Anthony Scaduto points out, Zimmerman was subject to all the influences that marked the period for people his age: films such as *Blackboard Jungle* with its theme song "Rock Around the Clock," a rhythm-and-blues cover by Bill Haley and the Comets; James Dean's *Rebel Without a Cause* and *East of Eden;* and Little Richard, the first to bring the emotional energy of black gospel singing uncompromisingly into secular music. But having heard and imitated honkytonk singer Hank Williams on the radio, as well as blues singers such as Muddy Waters and Howlin' Wolf, Zimmerman probably had a deeper understanding of the roots of rock-and-roll than suburban youth who first encountered it in Elvis Presley.[34]

It is certain in any case that life on the Mesabi Iron Range, in a community of open-pit miners, differed from life in Great Neck, Long Island. In order to find acceptance among his schoolmates Zimmerman strove to efface his family background, which was not working-class Catholic, and by the time he was sixteen was riding with the local greasers and fronting at the piano a rock-and-roll band modeled on Little Richard's. When in September 1959 he pledged the Jewish fraternity at the University of Minnesota, Zimmerman abandoned his leather jacket and jeans for the button-down shirt, chinos, and white bucks of the day; but in a matter of months, after encountering the beatniks and folksingers in the Cedar Riverside quarter, Minneapolis' riverfront bohemia, and read Guthrie's autobiography *Bound for Glory,* he became "Bob Dylan": an orphan raised in Oklahoma or in Gallup or in Sioux Falls; a former pianist for Bobby Vee or a circus hand, carnie, railroad bum, or streetsinger—so he claimed to anyone who asked—but ultimately the youth in the fleece-lined jacket and corduroy cap who, sizing up his new audience from the cover of his first record album like a suitor who thinks he may be in love, had dared to offer himself, after a pilgrimage to Woody Guthrie's bedside, as the lad upon whom Guthrie's mantle would, and did, fall.

Whoever Bob Dylan was, Columbia's high-fidelity microgrooves brought his callow voice, wretchedly overwrought, his stagey panhandle dialect, his untutored guitar and harmonica—all of his gallant fraudulence—into dormitory rooms with shocking immediacy. And when, in the spoken preface to his shattering "Baby, Let Me Follow You Down," he waggishly reported he had learned the song from one Rick Von Schmidt, a blues guitar player from Cambridge, whom he had "met one day in the green pastures of . . . ah . . . Harvard University," the folk revival knew it had found one of its own.

To the parent generation, a folk revivalist like Dylan could scarcely be distinguished, on the one hand, from the motorcyclists and streetgangs of the fifties, whose crypto-fascist style was rooted in postwar social dislocations, or, on the other, from the beatniks. In fact, as we have seen, the folk revivalists *had* adapted, early on, these styles of youthful dissent, the one belonging to a disenfranchised class and the other largely to the affluent, educated, and well traveled—but not without subtle displacements. The aggressive black leathers and silver chains of the motorcycle highwayman were softened, and became a kind of dry-goods or surplus-store outfit of coarse textures and natural hues, strongly influenced by Clint Eastwood, James Arness, and other television cowboys—leather boots, chamois jackets, workshirts, wheat jeans—while the motorcycle itself remained: motorcycle accidents, in fact, seriously injured both John Hammond Jr. and Bob Dylan, and killed the singer-songwriter Richard Farina.

Bob Dylan's first album was not a commercial triumph, but it was a triumph for the folk revival. The role of desperado, tramp, poet, or peasant, earth mother or May queen, had been nurtured by the college campus and sanctioned by the broad complicity of one's peers; now it was ratified by the commercial establishment. Play had become an instrument for shaping reality and hence a means of laying claim to the social and historical initiative. This was the contribution of the folk revival to the sixties counterculture, which, with its social coherence and consistency, its relative freedom from social and economic constraints, and of course its youthfulness—that above all—acquired an enchanted, primitive, tribal quality that carnivalized the extant world with roles rooted in the imaginative life, which like all things imaginative urged, and for a time seemed to have achieved, their own actualization.

The folk revival, then, is really a moment of transformation in which an unprecedented convergence of postwar economic and demographic forces carried a culture of personal rebellion across normally impermeable social and cultural barriers under the influence and authority of folk music, at once democratic and esoteric, already obscurely imbued with a spirit of protest. This passage across social lines, again, transformed it, endowing it with new expressive forms, and with a legitimacy both wonderful and terrible—terrible because the massively politicizing issue of the Vietnam War, beginning in 1965, would swell it to a tidal wave of protest that swept destructively over the cultural landscape, leaving behind it deep racial, class, gender, and other moraines.

On the sources of that culture of rebellion one can only speculate. Angry, inarticulate, sullen, largely Anglo-American, it seems to have begun in the south, among the disenfranchised rural poor, though it trespassed regional boundaries swiftly and with impunity, following the wartime migrations of workers to southern cities such as Memphis and to the north and west, taking on a distinctly youthful cast in new highschool cultures of freedom and power centered on modified cars, motorcycles, and drive-ins. Was it rooted in the subversion of the economically fragile household by a war that drew young fathers into military service and young mothers into defense plants? Or was it something much older, a cultural relic of the Civil War and reconstruction, in which a feudal and agrarian order based in slavery fell to an industrial society with its subtler forms of servitude?

In any case, its first visible stirrings seem to be in the early fifties, when Hollywood idols such as Marlon Brando and James Dean made heroes of the teenagers hanging around the soda fountain and cruising the streets on motorcycles, the brooding sons and daughters who could neither understand nor be understood by their parents. In 1954, the year both films were released, Brando's roles wedded the identity of Elia Kazan's moody, inarticulate proletarian hero Terry Malloy of *On the Waterfront* to the implacable motorcycle outlaw of *The Wild One*.

But James Dean—restless but not warlike, diffident but not defiant, isolated but capable of love, with more than a trace of Steinbeck's Tom Joad in him—was the transitional figure: his *Rebel Without a Cause*, released in 1955 and shortly followed by *East of Eden*, presented a figure vulnerable both to parental indifference and to the insistent tribalism of the young—both of which were, by implication, emanations from the desperately acquisitive class-conscious society. Nicholas Ray, a folksong enthusiast closely associated as a radio producer in the forties with the left-wing folksong movement in New York, directed *Rebel Without a Cause;* it was Ray, perhaps, who detected in the film's theme of a young man's personal rebellion the messianic glow of New Deal populism[35]—and the film itself predicted the youth movement's substitution of peers for the nurture of parents distracted by the struggle for status.

Indeed in *Rebel Without a Cause* we can observe the myth of the generation gap almost at the instant of its formation, as from the old left perspective Ray maps the class struggles of the thirties onto the new postwar family: the socially uprooted, culturally destabilized middle-class parents seeking to define themselves by limning the outlook and deportment of Roosevelt's New York aristocracy, the neglected and isolated boy finding a virtual "family" in the working-class car culture ethnically nuanced by the actors Sal Mineo and Natalie Wood—and finding it, significantly, in the derelict rooms and gardens of an abandoned manor house.

This subtle drift of the moral center of gravity—from Brando to Dean, Zimmerman to Dylan, bandit to balladeer—reflects, I think, a deeper shift in the strata of our postwar cultural life. The Hell's Angel on his motorcycle declared war on authority by mounting a parody of its presiding symbol, the motorcycle cop. But he recalls the war-bereft rebel without a cause who like Tom Dula will not "conform to rules" and, still earlier, the Ringtail Roarer, the fiercely independent frontiersman of old Kentucky, who partakes of early America's persistent repudiation of privilege, an identity formed from negation.

But the sandy-haired, solitary son of the California grower we saw in *East of Eden,* abandoned by his mother, unable to please his father, descends from the egalitarian west, with its family-bound and community-building immigrant pioneers from central and northern Europe. James Dean, born in rural Indiana, lost his own mother as a boy and was after raised on a farm. The rebel is wild and will not be contained in representations—he becomes James Fenimore Cooper's noble savage, Mrs. Trollope's "remorseless spitting American," minstrelsy's buffoon, the magazine writer's caricature, Hollywood's outlaw or misfit; the farm boy abides with the possible in Willa Cather and John Steinbeck. One is parochial, born out of backcountry America, at once celebrated and despised, always the rebel, always the outsider; the other is provincial, the image of a youth in search of the human ties that tell him who he is. It is a westward migration of the spirit, betokening what such movement always has meant in America, a retreat from a society corrupted by entrenched power toward a vision of social harmony, cultural independence, and personal fulfillment.

Reflecting on the popularity of the Kingston Trio's "Tom Dooley," Dave Guard recalled that the title of the song coincidentally resonated with the name of a then-famous navy doctor, who had left the military to build hospitals in northern Laos. Dooley's fundraising efforts were buttressed by the popularity of the song, with which the Filipino people greeted him at the Manila airport on his homeward trip. This is fitting—Dooley's sense of mission prefigures the hundreds of young Peace Corps volunteers who followed the good doctor into the jungles of Southeast Asia a few years later, many of them with guitars and banjos on their backs, as well as the many who would not, finally, go as soldiers.

Dr. Tom Dooley, in fact, a gay sailor who was dying of cancer, exemplifies the fundamental shift in consciousness that lies at the heart of the folk revival. Like the utopian missionary movements, social and artistic programs, religious revivals and political crusades before it, as well as the liberation movements that followed it, the revival made the romantic claim of folk culture—oral, immediate, traditional, idiomatic, communal, a culture of characters, privileges, obligations, and beliefs—against a centrist, specialist, impersonal technocratic culture, a culture of types, functions, jobs, and goals.

Well after the commercial popularity of folksong had faded, many diehard revivalists, now parents and householders, endeavored, after the cataclysms of the sixties, to create a life that might somehow reverberate morally to folk music, even as the music itself, in the commercial marketplace at least, fell silent: a life radically less reliant on the accumulation of money; a life of participatory, not vicarious, recreation, with a recognition of the importance of small community to such enjoyment; a life, above all, that in the personal and domestic realms reflected an awareness of our involvement in the global ecological, economic, and political order. Chickens and goats, cottage crafts, organic gardening, home canning, wood heating, natural foods, natural fibers, natural childbirth—though inflation undercut most of these experiments, or sent them along commercial routes into exurbia to occupy the weekends of the rich—these came into American life from young adults for whom folk music had become, in Barbara Kirschenblatt-Gimblett's phrase, "the site of resistance to the centralization of power."[36] Some, like conservatory-trained Andy Cahan, who left Oberlin College for Low Gap, North Carolina, in order to apprentice himself to the great oldtime fiddler and banjo player Tommy Jarrell, adopted not only the music of their mentors but their way of life—a radical transformation akin to what William James, speaking of religious conversion, describes as "the throwing of our conscious selves upon the mercy of powers which, whatever they are, are more ideal than we are actually."[37] "The music was a first step back to the land," recalls the Chapel Hill banjoist Tom Carter, and "our world was dominated by powerful if dimly understood symbols like *the woodpile*."[38]

Through the folk revival, the broad typology of the American character, and with it the principle of cultural democracy, what Walt Whitman called the "democratic identity" and Kenneth Rexroth "the old free America," sought a new apotheosis on the social landscape. The old free America was of course an artifact too, of the poetic imagination—but without it we have only a winter of naked "society" to live in. It had emerged on the minstrel stage and in regionalist journalism and literature, in tent shows, vaudville, and Hollywood, out of the traffic in human encounter that crosses the intricate network of America's social boundaries, particularly those lying between urban and provincial societies.

The supreme moment in this national seance, in which the summons of folksong to the cultural dead populated the stage with a reunited family of heroes and heroines of the past, occurred at the closing concert of the Newport Folk Festival in 1963. Pete Seeger, Bob Dylan, Joan Baez, and Peter, Paul, and Mary linked arms with SNCC's Freedom Singers to sing the old Baptist hymn, "We Shall Overcome," and a parable of apocalypse, Bob Dylan's "Blowin' in the Wind"—litanies of the revival's dream of freedom, brotherhood, and peace. It was a moment in which, like a celestial syzygy, many independent forces of tradition, ideology, and culture, wandering at large in time, some of them in historical deep space and others only transient displays in the contemporary cultural atmosphere, briefly converge to reveal the truth of our collective life.

Peter, Paul, and Mary, for example, who looked like seminarians and bore New Testament names, might have flourished on the Christian Missionary Youth circuit. At a deeper level, the dust-bowl balladeer, Woody Guthrie, was present in spirit, as was the wandering Swedenborgian, Johnny Appleseed. But so were the Fisk Jubilee Singers of the 1870s and the Almanac Singers of the 1940s, after whom the Freedom Singers, at Seeger's suggestion, had modeled themselves; Tom Joad and James Dean were present in spirit, as was a dark Pocahontas with a Spanish name in the guise of a demure schoolgirl singing an Elizabethan ballad and dreaming of its hero, a dashing gypsy laddie. Perhaps Holden Caulfield, from Pencey Prep, was in attendance too: not out of Salinger's novel but in the unwritten sequel that Dylan, who once dreamed of playing Holden in a movie, was enacting in his own life.

Others, less palpable perhaps, lingered around the group—a Puritan man of the cloth, a plantation slave, a Jehovah's Witness, a blackface minstrel with a banjo, and a Yeshiva boy—all of them held together with the vast chorus of the audience whose 15,000 voices ascended into the summer night while "thousands of fans milled in the darkened streets outside, listening to the music drift over the stone walls of the arena."[39]

They were telling their own story; and for the space of a few years, ignorant of the last world war and united against the next, largely innocent of ideology, still protected from a consciousness of the realities of money, privilege, and power in which they were already swept up, they let it flow from their own voices, and their own hands, into the lives they had yet to live.

Finale at Newport, 1963, singing "Blowin' in the Wind." Left to right: Peter, Mary, Paul, Joan Baez, Bob Dylan, the Freedom Singers, Pete Seeger

10

Nobles, Patrons, Patriots, Reds

The folk revival, as described in this book, was a short-lived response—flowing out of various elite, progressive, radical, avant-garde, bohemian, and popular cultures and movements into the commercial marketplace, with little coherent ideology of its own but derived from many ideological traditions—to the conditions of life in America after World War II primarily as they affected young people at the threshold of adulthood.

That response took a variety of forms. For many it was simply a diversion, one that succeeded other kinds and would be succeeded by still others. Some retreated more deeply into the world of folk music, finding not only safety there but a "subjunctive" life, full of ideas and images, often dim and unrecoverable, of what seemed a historically verifiable alternative culture. Those ideas and images rebounded to shape the manner and bearing, the speech, dress, thoughts, and aspirations of many revivalists, turning what was for some shallow and transient into what for others was a coherent program for personal, domestic, social, and political life. For still others the response was straightforwardly a public protest, handmaiden to other struggles, civil rights, peace, the environment. Most important for its continuing life, the revival gave us a new generation of musicians with fresh and nearly inexhaustible musical resources.

As for the cultures and movements that shaped the revival, I have emphasized the contribution, on the one hand, of the left in New York, a largely European-American ethnic and political culture marked by revolutionary ideas of society and carried largely by immigrant groups, and, on the other hand, of a roughly contemporaneous Anglo-American tradition, emanating from the higher reaches of society, originating in abolitionist and settlement-house movements and later bound up with reactions to European immigration and to post-Civil War industrialization and urbanization. In a sense the folk revival represents a reconciliation of originally antagonistic sociopolitical developments, temporarily making common cause against what must have been understood, on some level, as the same adversary, mass or commercial culture. The various musics that prefigured or informed it—jazz, blues, calypso, rock-and-roll—were each of them touched with a spirit of protest.

In or behind the revival we have noted a coincidence of socialism and communism, nativism and Anglo-Saxonism, muscular Christianity, internationalism, feminism, the leisure-time and outdoor movements, tourism, pacifism, environmentalism, and a variety of other influences, none of which can quite explain the quality or the character of the revival—the desire of the postwar generation, quite simply the largest single generation in history, anywhere, through a magnetic performance form like folksong to draw out of the past the historical culture it had been raised to expect as a birthright, but which could not survive in a society that organized its peace as if it were still at war.

We in America are disinclined to explain ourselves with reference to hereditary caste, rank, grade, station, place, or even class, for, while our society is certainly stratified in complex ways—the forty zip-code marketing clusters and proliferating cable channels begin to suggest the inadequacy of our customary class analyses—and while all of us are daily buffeted by gusts of fashion, status, and celebrity, the fixed hierarchies of Europe and England have in general not been our lot; even when undeniable evidence of social inequality, gross maldistribution of wealth, oligarchy in government, the professions, business, or the media, lies plainly before us, so powerful is our dedication to the myth of social mobility that we pretend not to see it, or take it as a passing aberration that somehow in time will correct itself. Always there is appeal to the counterexample of someone's real social rise. After all, there *is,* for some people and families, social mobility in America, even if privilege does tend to perpetuate itself; historically, moreover, our class spectrum has been a comparatively narrow one—except, of course, where it has been egregiously wide.

A colonial squirarchy, a robber barony, a corporate oligarchy, or a Hollywood celebriate are in any case not true aristocracies. Our usual designations, "upper class," "upper-middle," "middle," "lower-middle," and so on, are hopelessly approximate; yet the terms we inherit from European tradition—bourgeoisie, working class, proletariat—carry in the American context a metaphorical resonance that, if enchantingly musical to some ears, lacks the hard precision of useful analytical categories.

All this being said, however, it is true that the traditions of ideas, values, norms, standards, and ideals that descend from the historical experience of hierarchy in Europe, because we are a diverse multicultural people, because culture is obdurate and does not easily depart even when material circumstances change radically, are still very powerful in America, often shaping the ways in which a person, a family, or a community will think about and present itself, upon what it will model itself, what it will try to achieve. As Michael Novak notes, "American experience melted the surfaces or appearances of the ethnics but not their 'inner feelings, aspirations, symbolic patterns,'" or their reactions "to pain, to authority, to dissent or rebellion, to fatherhood or family life, to mobility or home ownership."[1] All of these are of course bound up not only with inherited traditional attitudes but with the sense of one's own place, both perceived and invented, in the larger social system.

Much of our culture of hierarchy is simply bogus—mere signage meant to gain advantage in the status game; still it is the case that Old World peasantry, proletariat, bourgeoisie, gentility, and even nobility are given in the New World to maintain, through the operations of ethnic, regional, and class cultures, the social perspectives of their old situation—or, more significantly, to figure America's peculiar social promise in terms of the old class perspectives.

I know of no better way to illustrate this point than by recalling again my own mother, daughter of Russian-Jewish peasants. Her fascination with the ruling class of Chicago—more coldblooded than blueblooded, I'm afraid—its doctors, lawyers, judges, and financiers, and with the lavish aisles of Marshall Field's department store that society ladies used to frequent when she was a child, echoed the attitudes of her own mother, whose world had always been divided between peasants and *poritzim*, nobles. My mother was a brilliant assimilationist, and with the glamor, elegance, and self-possession of a queen—I can't help recollecting Harry Smith's remark that his mother thought of herself as the czarina of Russia—she cultivated a radiant personal presence that could have fooled, and often did fool, the starchiest Episcopalian.

Hers was emphatically not the view of the Anglo-American class of New England, who began their lives in this country within the narrow limits of East Anglia's yeoman, farmer, artisan, and merchant classes, but in two centuries grew accustomed to its position at the head of America's political and industrial oligarchy; nor, surely, the view of Virginia's ruling elite, actually descended from a landed aristocracy, its concepts of civil government and social order permanently installed in our founding documents. Nor, indeed, was her view that of the grandsons and granddaughters of the anarchists, syndicalists, Bolsheviks, Mensheviks, and Trotskyites—Russian, Polish, Ukrainian, Hungarian, and Lithuanian Jews brought here on the tide of the great immigrations—who after three generations still carried the spirit of revolution in their hearts but found ways of attaching it, in what is certainly a sublime cultural achievement, to the native strains of revolutionary idealism, from the New Deal to the New Frontier to the Great Society, the civil-rights movement, the peace movement, the environmental movement, the women's movement, and, need I add, the folk revival.

My point is that though the picture of social stratification in America is indistinct, our understanding of it spotty, and our experience of it particular and piecemeal, our ideas about it are venerable, compelling, and, as ideas go, powerful. Hence when we look at the alliance of upper-class Anglo-American and urban Jew, urban Jew and southern black, which can be observed at almost every point in the folk revival alongside equally strange and unlikely alliances, at the pungent but unstable solution of ruling-class ethnocentricism and a displaced cultural version of Marxist-Leninism, at lawyer's and doctor's sons and daughters playing bluegrass and blues and mixing on a "level of social equality" with mountain farmers, southern sharecroppers, and urban pariahs, we must recognize it not merely as a historical anomaly, but an instance of how received social ideas sometimes come together to create transient but definitive social and cultural transformation. These ideas, as we have seen, derive from many places and times, native and foreign—from late Puritan New England, the antebellum western frontier, the agrarian south and midwest, revolutionary Russia; but as ideas they are versatile, mobile, and protean.

There were great differences, as Raymond Williams writes, between Edmund Burke, "the first modern Conservative," and William Cobbett, "the first great tribune of the industrial proletariat," but both men "attacked the new England from their experience of the old England, and, from their work, traditions of criticism of the new democracy and the new industrialism were powerfully begun: traditions which in the middle of the twentieth century are still active and important."[2]

Burke, who died in 1797, was an opponent of democracy, which he believed would end in tyranny; the individual as such was inherently wicked, restrained in his vices and promoted in his virtues only by the forces of a "historical community" that extended throughout society and over generations, what Burke called a partnership: "a partnership in all science; a partnership in all arts; a partnership in every virtue, and in all perfection"—that is, in our terms, a high culture, trusted guardian of the true, the beautiful, and the good.

Burke's is the familiar voice of traditional authority, speaking before the onset of industrialism and modern "mass culture." Cobbett's voice, by contrast, is that of the countryman, as Williams calls him, who wished to preserve the economy and handicrafts of preindustrial England, the "England into which I was born," and of Cobbett the tribune, who championed, in a radically republican spirit, the claims of labor. In Cobbett these two strains so often at war, and just as often violently yoked together—a yearning for an ideal past and a fierce dedication to bringing about the collapse of the prevailing order on behalf of the better world to come—suggest the special idealism and anger, the naiveté and energy, the implacable dissatisfaction and restlessness of the political romantic, certainly out of sympathy with Burke the pragmatist, champion of incremental and evolutionary change.

At first the two voices would seem to be easily discriminated; but they are entangled in complex ways, have many traits in common, often occur in league with one another, and even adopt the other's livery quite convincingly; in the end they are joined not so much by the ends they desire as by their common recognition, and common antipathy, for the uncontrollable thing that has risen in their way. Folk revivalism is no doubt the least of the fields in which they meet and work, historically and politically; yet we find the two voices, in various configurations, in the ballad collections of the eighteenth century, in the sentiments and moods with which nineteenth-century poets and antiquarians take up the matter of peasants, rustics, and gypsies, and in every phase of the modern folk revival, from Cecil Sharp to Ralph Rinzler, New York to Newport, often bound up in the warring impulses of the same person.

For these are really two traditions of allegiance, which for the sake of discussion I will call the genteel and the revolutionary—and henceforth speak of them typologically rather than historically. The genteel, as we know, is the tradition of aristocracy, but it is a tradition bifurcated by the origins of power, whether of might or of money. A hereditary nobility and a capitalist aristocracy of graziers, planters, merchants, or manufacturers may look and act very much alike; in Regency England and Gilded Age America, at least, each attempted to look and act as much like the other as possible. But the differences between them are profound—deeper, probably, than the gulf between an ownership and a working class.

The old nobleman, whether rich as a king or impoverished as a monk, belongs together with peasant and artisan in a web of communal obligation and interdependency that inspires deference, without resentment, on the one hand, and true condescension, without contempt, on the other. It is the nobleman, maybe bereft of his fortune, whom we are likely to see in league with the peasant or worker against the capitalist or the king. The true bohemian is always of high degree. With his sense of traditionality and family, his attachment to old and well-made things living or dead, the noble has more in common, finally, with the common people than with his neighbor, the rich merchant or manufacturer—also in command of vast landholdings and numbers of dependents—and may yearn for a reunion with the common people whose love and allegiance over many generations he has won.

The noble is most at home, moreover, in the fiefdom, a type of folk community with its face-to-face relationships, than he is on the global stage, among trade routes, colonial outposts, and newfangled engines of progress. He knows that while his wealth lies in land, his power, originally acquired by force, lies ultimately in the loyalty of his dependents. His imagination ruminates on a conviction of vanished grandeur and the melancholy beauty of ruin, bound up with forces that transcend the moment such as family tradition and glory in war; he is a barbarian, who has come by his wealth and power by dint of the sword, and his poetic affinities are with the heroic or, in later ages, with romance and what Northrop Frye calls the "grave idealizing of heroism and purity." Passion and fury are likely to be the agents of his social and political power, so that acts of passion and fury will be admired and memorialized.

The noble has not wholly vanished: we may find some traces of him in Ford Madox Ford's Edward Ashburnham, who marries an Anglo-Catholic virgin, is a persistent adulterer, shows mercy to his hard-pressed tenants, and slits his throat for love. But his neighbor, the gentleman-capitalist, who has come by his land through enclosure, trade, or manufacture, is a very different sort of fellow. Though outwardly he has adopted the accoutrements of nobility, the cardinal point to remember is that he can only aspire to that rank and will use his wealth to generate the appearance of it. For he lives in a world of appearances, an existential one, of expedience rather than value, always in the process of becoming, because appearances may ultimately become material and ideological realities; inevitably in the moneyed family, a young man or woman in the third generation seems to capture the true spirit of nobility and scandalizes the family by professing values other than the value of money.

We must think of the moneyed patron on his estate as an isolated being, essentially alone in his wealth and power, remote from its sources in human labor and natural resources and deeply contemptuous of both. We might picture him at his drawing-room window, in a hall as splendid as a Florentine palace, gazing out on the park he has made of common fields, across the formal garden that lies at the foot of his grand verandah. Sheep graze; the fairway sweeps toward a vanishing point in the distance, through lanes of dowager elms and pastoral poplars, perhaps to a fountain at the terminus or, by the nineteenth century, to the towering stacks of the factory wherein his fortune lies.

It is a poignant and transcendent vision, for it turns on the solitude of the observer, projecting it into the infinitude of visual perspective and binding the experience of beauty to the sense of isolation, loss, bereavement. What has been lost perhaps is the old order of obligation, from which the patron is cut off—to create his park he has likely removed the peasant cottages and the peasants inside them, for he has no connection to them; they become paupers in the villages or workers in the new manufacturing cities or settlers in the colonies. The very notion of real property, and of Nature as the exfoliation of land, "methodized" by the artifices of its owner, originates with his class.

If the source of the noble's wealth is loyalty and hence, ultimately, Virtue, the source of the patron's is exploitation of natural and human resources and hence, ultimately, Science. In his isolation the patron has something the noble had not, leisure; and in his leisure he may become a man of literary and scientific learning. The noble has no truck with ideas; all he needs to know and believe, he knows and believes. For recreation, he hunts. But the patron places great faith in science, whose applications are connected directly to the sources of his wealth, while science itself, with its basis in number and quantity, has its origin in his medium of exchange. In time he may become an inventor or a collector or a philosopher; he is a great reader in hydraulics or mechanical engineering—but while his noble neighbor, insofar as he reads at all, favors the romance, the literary tastes of his class favor the mock-heroic, the picaresque, or the novel, in which romantic passions, constrained and sublimated, animate the rituals and personalities of bourgeois life.

The noble's bond to the folk is ancient and traditional; the patron's is sentimental. Like the Whig landowners who displaced Scots crofters, turning their farms to pastoral lands to furnish wool for the mills, only in another generation to adopt, under the influence of Sir Walter Scott, the tartan, shield, and piper's tunes of the ancient clans, the patron attempts to restore symbolically what he has eradicated in deed. Here we might think of Colonial Williamsburg or Greenfield Village. Where a gothic ruin, a classical temple, a Spenserian grotto, and even a village chapel may furnish the landscape, there is also, at the edge of a small lake, a peasant cottage in full scale, though not of course actually occupied: the appearance is preferred to the actuality, with its attendant responsibilities. The heart of the patron's existence is self, and he is a civilized being, capable of cultivating the nuances of sense and sensibility, of fashion and taste. For the patron, in short, the supplanted feudal system has supplied the pattern of a life built on different foundations, a life that has become literally recreational, a kind of elaborate picnic.

The genteel tradition, then, is complex, ambiguous, sometimes paradoxical, sometimes at odds with itself. It implies the everlasting involvement of class, rank, degree, power, and privilege with the love and idealization of common people. It is romantic in several senses: it projects on the folk, seen from afar, the deepest of the active principles of human desire, supposing the folk to represent a more direct and genuine expression of human nature, a tale or ballad heard from afar that is somehow more fundamentally satisfying of human yearnings than the life we really lead. But the genteel tradition is romantic in another sense too, in its drive toward acceptance *by* the folk. Looking on folklife from afar, and seeing in it something beautiful and worthy, both noble and patron feel excluded from it: and since it is their tradition or ambition to be denied nothing, they believe that access to the folk lies among traditional prerogatives or within range of economic power. The social impossibility of such access, and the means they may or may not have developed for shaping relations with groups below them in rank—a formal and respectful distance guarantees the dignity of both parties—may distinguish the true noble from his imitators. Social privilege, moreover, may bring about a deep sense of embarrassment; as Charles Seeger pointed out, the combative "I'm as good as you are" of the proletarian becomes the insistent "You're as good as I am" of bourgeois social superiors who do not really accept the legitimacy of their own situation.[3]

In the genteel tradition these forces combine to produce, at best, the person who will shoulder the prerogatives as well as the power of her class and, with a firm grip on her social role and a thoroughgoing acceptance of the realities of power, use her position to champion the cause of the underprivileged and the oppressed, fostering high culture and folk culture as the unitary thing they are, set not against one another but against the bourgeois culture that over centuries has driven a gulf between them. At worst, the tradition produces the gentleman who wants to preserve the folk only so that they will be available to please and delight him, and to provide handmade objects for the decoration of his home or even become instruments of financial gain; the folk are, for him, only extensions of his employees and servants—his millhand, his gardener, his carpenter, his housemaid, or perhaps his wilderness guide—and may receive a limited measure of his hospitality or, when circumstances permit it, on holiday or at college, the flattery of his imitation.

The romantic movement itself has roots in the genteel tradition, where the cult of sensibility emphasized impulses in human nature from which virtue springs; Rousseau's social contract was not Locke's cold accommodation between rational beings but a community joined by bonds of innate sympathy, the human warmth in which the seeds of family, community, and society finally lay. In landscape painting and gardening we can see the romantic vision of an inspiring natural world under-written by Newton's rational order.

But, again, the genteel tradition does not follow romanticism into the speculative realm, for aristocracies, as Matthew Arnold points out, have a "natural inaccessibility, as children of the established fact, to ideas." The noble may be a collector, a philologist, an explorer, and may perhaps write verse or prose; but strictly speaking he is not original, no poet or philosopher, unless it is a philosophy that simply celebrates the "established fact." For to think theoretically and deeply, to have doubts, to question, is not heroic; the hero acts out of immediate resolve, with a clear will and unalloyed intention; he does not grieve, he is not melancholy, he does not ruminate; his faith is strong, and it is the traditional faith.

Daring and exploratory thought, on the other hand, which sweeps away tradition and erects original conceptions in its place, is characteristic of science, and so long as science confines itself to the physical universe, the patron can embrace it; his view of nature, whether through windows, picture frames, or lenses, is essentially a scientific one, whether for beauty or for knowledge—both are a species of order, either of balance, tranquillity, and quiet, a "classical" order, or a sub-lime order contrived to challenge and expose the nature of the sensory-intellectual instrument. But when romanticism carried the spirit of scientific inquiry, if not the language and the method, into society, culture, and psyche, it proved more congenial to the revolutionary, who was in part its creation, than to the patron, even though democratic revolution had begun with moneyed gentlemen who wished to displace the old nobility. To achieve this the romantic had to work outside the bright luminosity of genteel rationalism and scientific posi-tivism, even outside the social order itself.

Just as there are at least two strains in the genteel tradition, aristocratic and capitalist, noble and patron, so there are at least two in the revolutionary tradition: preindustrial republicanism and postindustrial socialism—the patriot and the red. The eighteenth-century propertied gentleman, comparing himself to an elector of Rome, conceived of republican democracy in a way fundamentally different from the popular democracy that succeeded his system. For him democracy was simply an idea that legitimated the displacement of noblemen by capitalists, of inherited by acquired power; but, as the history of democratic revolutions amply illustrates, the idea escaped the grip of its promulgators and became a social as well as a political rallying cry for the independence of individuals and of the human spirit from all that bore the taint of traditional authority, including, in the spirit of Tom Paine, tradition itself.

This libertarian spirit, the spirit of the patriot, has often been characteristic of the folklorist in America, especially where mistrust of central authority, as in the post-Reconstruction south, has been particularly strong. Here one thinks of the Texas folklorist L. Frank Dobie, John Lomax, Jimmy Driftwood, the Ozark folklorist Vance Randolph—the person in love with her locality, the regionalist, often associated, after the invention of the rotary press, with a newspaper, the novelist who draws on the characters and stories of her place for her material, but with a sense that her audience lies in distant parts, who shares with her forebears a distrust of outsiders, especially if they represent urban sophistication, book learning, or central government. One thinks naturally of the chroniclers of the south, such as Augustus Longstreet or Fanny Kemble; Mark Twain belongs to it. But the tradition also embraces the great numbers of newspaper columnists, local historians, storytellers, collectors, and magazine writers, such as Joel Chandler Harris, Edward Everett Hale, and Thomas Wentworth Higginson, who in the decades after the Civil War documented regional American life to an expanding popular readership at a moment when that very expansion, the proliferation of printed information, the extension of the railroads into the mountains and plains, and the first significant rural-to-urban migration in our history, by commencing the long erosion of its foundations, had sharpened the popular consciousness of regionality as part of a shared national experience.

To the feeling for locality that emerged in the eighteen-seventies, faded in the nineties, and reemerged with new intensity after World War I, we owe not only our earliest folk festival, Bascom Lamar Lunsford's, but many of the folksong and tale collections that ground the study of American folklore: the work of Dobie, Phillips Barry, Howard Odum, Henry Belden, as well as Robert Winslow Gordon, Carl Sandburg, Louise Pound, the Lomaxes, and many others. The postwar period was also the golden age of the race and oldtime records and radio that, continuing the minstrel tradition, introduced folk music into popular culture.

The folklorist or revivalist in this democratic tradition is a populist; but unlike the socialist or communist, for whom the folk are at once ethereally abstract, "the People," and as intensely present as the workers in one's own shop, but in either case available for direct identification, the patriot's "folk," though local, immediate, and real, nevertheless represent a different, and subtly inferior, social stratum: brothers who live up on the mountain, telling tales, distilling whiskey, singing ballads, salvaging old washing-machine motors, and playing the fiddle; or the mayor, a florid and eloquent orator of quaint speech whose grandfather fought on the Union side in the Civil War; or the local craftspeople—smith, basketweaver, chairmaker, quilter, usually a handful of people who practice them all; old Annie, local historian, who has hundreds of times told the story of Barbara Foster's murder and sung the ballad she wrote about the event, seventy-eight years ago.

The patriot looks around her community and sees, not folklore in any romantic or scientific sense, and in fact may not see "folklore" at all until someone from the state university or the arts council suggests the idea, but sees instead interesting old tales, old songs, old crafts, and old people, colorful and memorable people whose scope of life, narrow and common as it may have been, suddenly appears fleeting and precious—for a new world, she understands, lies just over the horizon, connected to her own by telegraph or telephone and sending her own stories back to her community by rail, highway, or airwaves.

Conspirators, incendiaries, assassins, and terrorists there have always been; but the revolutionary will labor within the body of society, with the very material of it, to bring about more or less violent change under the spell of totalizing ideas that seem to have expanded his awareness beyond the seductions of the prevailing order and hence beyond the limits of the ordinary understanding he strives to alter and direct. In the republican period, in America and France, the revolutionary was an engineer of opinion, with his instrument the printing press, supposing that opinion, which like truth is a property of words and can be disseminated in print, was the basis of a civil society of discursive agents. Thus to promulgate ideas, the revolutionary works directly with people and communities, in writing and speech of course, in song, and, even more effectively, in those aspects of human relations where we normally don't expect some palpable design to be made upon us—but trust that gestures of friendship, appeals to vanity or pride, sexual overtures, or offers of economic advantage have no hidden object.

That is one stereotype, and it is insidious, of the revolutionary worker; another joins revolution to missionary or evangelistic impulses, in which the revolutionary is a kind of spiritual guide, living a spartan life, engaging with communities in various practical labors, from time to time sharing her political philosophy with her technical knowledge. Another conceives of it along the lines of military strategies and tactics. Still another sees the revolutionary simply as a terrorist with a bomb. Often the revolutionary is an idealist and often an ideologue, at best a saint, and as tiresome as a saint, incapable of a personal relation but inspiring as an example and vigilant to find in the moment its moral opportunity. At worst he is merely angry. She is often an intellectual too, a tireless reader of books, full of ideas and quick to dispute, conscientiously poor and negligent of the personal, so that his poverty has a kind of vanity in it, a kind of narcissism.

But his tradition is scholastic, not scientific; he thinks deductively, from received truths, and belongs to a community of oral discourse wherein those truths may be elaborated to meet new conditions and questions. Hence he has no detachment and is more concerned to maintain the integrity of his ideological system than to test it in the actual world. His explanatory system is powerful and persuasive, though it shows little tolerance for ambiguity; often his encounters with the real world are awkward, frustrating, or foolish. But his favored form of discourse, discussion, eloquence, persuasion, inclines him toward other communities of speech such as the union, cabaret, club, or salon. In this, of course, he resembles the noble.

And what of his class affinities? The revolutionary hates privilege. If he has been privileged himself, he will repudiate, or seem to repudiate, his advantages and, embracing the revolutionary life with the zealotry of the convert, try to prove to himself and others his genuine worth. Perhaps, having known privilege, he is in the best position to flout it—but in fact it is always with him, a part of his internal workings, and from it he derives his special sense of immunity.

In the end, however, the revolutionary animus arises neither from privilege nor from philosophy. It goes deeper than thought; it arises from a discovery, no doubt early in life to be as intractable as it is, of an injustice, one that he has felt keenly, that however great his effort, however fine his mind, however brave in battle, because of what he is he cannot flourish: because he is the son of a tailor or because he is a Jew or black or foreign or poor, or has an accent, or works on an assembly line, or because he is in some other way personally, socially, even physically crippled, as by a lack of love or an excess of wealth. It is not inevitable that a blacksmith's boy should find himself aspiring to gentility, or becoming a machine breaker, just because he is a blacksmith's boy. But if he is thrust into circumstances that frustrate him at this fundamental level, which can neither be changed nor transcended, his rage is equally fundamental, since it can only be directed against the entire order that has thus defined him. Unable to change himself, he has to change the world. It is a passion: one that can elaborate itself in a grand design or spend itself in a single explosive act.

Fearlessness, valor, independence, personal dignity, and faith are qualities of persons, not classes. The genteel and revolutionary traditions are not, strictly speaking, intellectual traditions, though each is involved with great intellectual movements, nor are they strictly traditions of class; rather they are social modalities, patterns formed where class and history, power and human attachments, intersect. One of the cardinal points of this intersection is the idea of the folk. Indeed, the science of folklore may be said to have been *formed*, historically, from a mixture of ideas at once aristocratic and radical; folk revivalism, by contrast, as in touristic folk festivals and popular entertainment, seems to have been mainly the work of patrons and patriots.

Other conceptions of the "folk"—those of the curate, the antiquarian, the colonialist, the scholar, the impresario—leave behind ineradicable traces of their thinking in the science of folklore as well as in folk revivalism. But for our purposes there are, to summarize, genteel and revolutionary conceptions and, within them, four types. First is the noble, whose folk are a dependent class, tenant families traditionally bound in mutual fealty and obligation to hereditary landlords. All are born to their relation; their essence is authenticity. In a different but comparable condition is the patron, whether grazier, planter, merchant, manufacturer, or capitalist, whose folk are, like hereditary tenants, laborers, and producers, compelled perhaps to play the roles of traditional dependents; but there are no bonds between them, either of obligation or fealty. They are in every sense both the commodity and the commodified, as indicated by the marketability of the folk product in the capitalist marketplace: like labor everywhere in capitalism, they *are* their product. The essence of the folk product is beauty—but, because it is a beauty that implies an eclipse, a disappearance, it is suffused with the melancholy that arises in the gap between hereditary and capitalist aristocracies, between noble and patron. If the noble condescends, the patron can only patronize.

Of revolutionaries there are, again, two types. There is first the literate patriot, whose folk are neighbors, farmers and townsfolk, familiar from youth, fondly recalled in adulthood, freed by a dimly remembered but duly commemorated war from subordination and deference, theoretically equal to all others, neither splendidly rich nor desperately poor, and, in this best of all possible worlds, vividly and emphatically human; their essence is character. And finally there is the red, whose folk are an abstraction, the proletariat, agents of a coming revolution. Their essence is mass; as such they are either glorious, like an army, Whitman's Americans en masse, or potentially so, like Trotsky's revolutionary peasants, or they are faceless: a mass market, a mass public, a mass culture. As such, however, they are amenable, paradoxically, to fleshly embodiment, either as the common or average man, the man on the street, or as a people's hero—as Clifton Fadiman said of Guthrie, "he *is* that People."

All of these perspectives figure in the making of the folk revival. One can without too lofty a suspension of disbelief distinguish some pure types: true nobles such as Jane Addams and Eleanor Roosevelt; rich patrons such as Henry Ford, with his workers' square dances and fiddle contests; dyed-in-the-wool patriots such as Bascom Lamar Lunsford or Sarah Gertrude Knott; and any number of ardent young reds in the schools, camps, and clubs of communist culture.

But the idea of the folk, to be fully achieved, must embrace these perspectives all at once, for it is a compound concept, evolved historically precisely from the interactions of these types, the site at which the voices of Cobbett and Burke converge. "Folklore" and "folksong" and "folklife" are never things in themselves, but a new cultural perception arising as mysterious modes of hegemony maneuver competing modes to the social margins, often to supersede them, though also to produce them as modes of opposition, but in any case to bring them into a kind of mutually defining relation—in the late eighteenth and early nineteenth centuries, for example, the relation between literate and preliterate consciousness; in the nineteenth, between industrial and preindustrial production; and in our own age of social deracination, between a nebulized postmodern life and imagined worlds of interdependency and community. In each of these phases the central interest of folklore—myth, narrative, and ritual in the first phase, modes of production in the second, social organization and the technics of communication in the third—arises, again, from the perception of relation, one in which the cultural dominant provides a frame of reference for the "folk" or residual form, around which, in turn, the emergent dominant form organizes itself conceptually as a kind of anthropological, historical, or moral touchstone.

The genteel tradition, then, looks on the life of some dependent group, peasants or workers, and sees in it a picture of human life in its perennial form, as well as a palpable source of life. It sees, in other words, something at once true and beautiful—and it finds the language, customs, tales, handcrafted objects, and music of that group true and beautiful too, perhaps even to the exclusion of the people who made the objects or sang the songs. In any case it is the genteel tradition that is sensitive to the aesthetic and moral dimensions of the folk group, and so it brings to the idea of the folk its *cultural* element. Generally speaking, the genteel tradition belongs to the other enterprises of high culture, as simply one dimension of its art, learning, and commerce.

The revolutionary tradition, by itself, is similarly truncated. The patriot represents and celebrates local life without recourse to any concept of the folk, which he may instinctively find alien or even offensive, for he understands its implicit denial of social equality; it is only when an east-coast editor wishes to republish his dialect columns or tale collections as "folklore" that he eases his way into the idea. The red, analogously, though embracing the idea of the folk as politically inspired, is ideologically blind to culture generally and hence to its role both in folklife and in the representation of it, including such cultural fountainheads of achieved feeling and moral value as art or religion, in which he sees only power oppressively reproducing itself.

But patriot and red, either by experience or by analysis, are mutually sensitive to what the genteel tradition often is not: the actual social and existential form, as well as the political meaning, of folklife. Hence the revolutionary tradition sees folklife as a part of its larger account of history; the genteel tradition sees it culturally, as a repository of imagination, invention, beauty, and truth.

By itself, folklore from the revolutionary perspective invariably dissolves into something else: an object of social science or social work, political advocacy or grassroots organizing, ethnic or regional humor, tourism. But these frameworks are for the folk revivalist never wholly satisfying: always, it seems, there are people who meet the terms of the sociological definition who don't create folklore or folksong, and people who don't who do. The genteel perspective, in turn, dissolves into the purely imaginary: the pastoral, the romantic, the quaint, antique, or picturesque—it belongs with all the pictorial and poetic imagery that gratifies the bourgeois longing for things ancient or rude, of whatever dramatizes or compensates the solitary condition of bourgeois consciousness. It may go so far as to associate folklore with a fancied *Volk* of German romantic nationalism—but these are inventions too, as surely a political fiction as the idea of equality, and just as surely an instrument of the state.

Merely this or merely that, the genteel and romantic traditions divide the idea of the folk between them and, in dividing the idea, render it fantastic. From either perspective alone, folklore is hallucinatory, either imaginary or theoretical. Join them together in some fashion, though, and the folk become real: an effect, at once social and material, conceptual and imaginative, of the dynamic relation among the ranks, classes, orders, and strata of society.

Consider the two traditions in their treatment of folksong. Genteel ballad collectors transcribed folk melodies and ballad narratives with, at first, little attention to the ballad style or its social context; instead these melodies, harmonies, and lyrics became a subcategory of the learned musical and poetic tradition, to be collected and published in books, to be performed by concert singers, perhaps to be incorporated into musical compositions—but in any case thoroughly assimiliated to the literary tradition, essentially fixed and closed.

Political singers, on the other hand, embraced folksong because they thought it could raise class consciousness in people not amenable to complex ideological argument. But their focus on ideological lyrics and conventionalized folk signifiers, largely at the expense of the real vernacular outlook—which they understood imperfectly and in any case had no background to reproduce in ways familiar to workers or farmers—was of course a feature of their own educations and socioeconomic backgrounds. Their song movement, with all its verbal wit and political sophistication, was powerless to bring about political or social change, while the commercial synthesis they would probably have found contemptible, rock-and-roll, would soon modify popular consciousness as surely as if it had been introduced into the national water supply.

All of this suggests, finally, that in the folk revivalist herself, by reason of upbringing, experience, training, and temperament, genteel and revolutionary attitudes divide imagination between them; it suggests that the social fault lines around which the idea of the folk coalesces also map the particular transit of possible ideas and experiences that shape the revivalist—suggests, finally, that the capacity to identify, to imitate, to invent, and finally to love the folk is a particular genius arising out of the revivalist's effort to unify a psyche divided by deeply opposed affinities, tendencies, and aspirations. It is a kind of sixth sense, capable of discovering where the arts of the poor, with what is often a curious precision, meet elite standards of taste, momentarily releasing in them what custom and convention have dulled, the emancipatory gleam.

Only consider some of the major figures of the folk revival: men and women whose class affinities were disrupted by experiences of another order, and who sublimated the opportunities afforded them by class to unify their psychic lives; or women and men born into folk communities who learned to exploit the prerogatives of the class into which they had risen to affirm the dignity of that community and others like it.

Consider Charles Seeger, shocked by others' poverty into radical politics, impelled by a Calvinist conscience to anneal his politics to his love of music; or Nancy Cunard, disinherited daughter of the steamship magnate, a lifelong radical who in the early thirties assembled a prodigious anthology on black culture, *Negro*. Or Diane Hamilton, of the Guggenheim family, who became a backer of the Clancy Brothers and Tradition Records, whose many influential albums included a collection of field recordings, *Instrumental Music of the Southern Appalachians* (1956).

Consider, too, John Hammond, who forged an idea of the folk out of his hatred of racial injustice; or the various captains of entertainment such as Albert Grossman and Harold Leventhal rediscovering in their folk-music projects their ethnicity, community, and politics. Consider musician, impresario, entrepreneur, manager, producer, and curator Ralph Rinzler, born into a genteel German- and Russian-Jewish family, son of a doctor with a largely Catholic and working-class practice, nephew of a Harvard-trained lawyer, socialist, and literary man, who found relief from his lifelong quarrel with authority in a fascination with nobility, whether of mountain potters and guitar pickers or of British peers. Or Bess Lomax Hawes, for many years the government's chief advocate of the folk at the National Endowment for the Arts: raised a patriot, educated to gentility, persuaded to radicalism, but in the fullness of time, and out of a life of personal obligation and difficulty, emerging as the grande dame of the public folklife establishment, unmistakably noble, her cultural work anchored in conviction, buoyed by hope, and driven by compassion.

Or Pete Seeger.

Or, indeed, John Lomax, by his own account from the "upper crust of the po' white trash," his family's first university graduate, his folklore interest endorsed by Harvard scholars, his restless middle life disrupted by loss and failure, essentially a patriot aspiring to gentility; or his son Alan, virtually baptized in the Old Tar River, a graduate of Choate and Harvard, as a young man immersed in Nietzsche, Veblen, Marx, Lenin, and Freud, a lifelong champion of the cultural equity that neither he nor his father, as descendants of East Texas dirt farmers, had ever been granted. "Now if you speak out and sing eloquently," he told a congressional committee, "and all that ever comes back to you through the communication channel—TV, radio, records—is the voice of somebody else singing, advocating; if you dance and move well and the only image you see is another kind of behavior, representing another culture, you feel inferior; you feel forced into silence."[4]

Arguably the most important figure in this entire story, Alan Lomax brought a leftist program of active intervention, often under the patronage of major publishing houses and recording companies, to bear on an epic vision of American folklife shaped by the messianism of the Popular Front. Though the means were red, the ends were egalitarian, those of a global patriot for whom the origins of democracy were anthropological, not philosophical, exemplified by the egalitarian Mbuti Pygmy society where, he writes, "we find social solidarity in its earliest and purest form," coming "unbidden to everyone present in the form of tuned-in, interlocked synchrony of voice, of hands outstretched with food, and with naked, dancing, frolicsome, bodily synchrony."[5]

In Africa, Lomax thought, "the electric current of sexuality touches everyone." Though he grounds his cultural argument in Marx and Freud, its genuine elements are romantic, racial, and erotic, like all noble stories driven by imperatives of blood flowing from the wound of humankind's original innocence. Again and again Lomax retells Colin Turnbull's story of the crippled Pygmy girl too ashamed to use a crutch—until all the villagers fashioned one for themselves and "playfully hobbled about the camp."

Most intriguing in this respect is the complex Jewish cultural tradition in America: a people of the book, who place a high premium on literacy and learning but who are also heir to a rich oral tradition; who have historically strived for assimilation into prevailing economic and political orders but who have consistently been driven back into communal enclaves where both the learned and the oral traditions, even as they become more strange and incomprehensible, take on an added trenchancy; a people whose assimilationist tradition has given them a special vision, often wildly idealistic, of the hegemonic culture, and who become poignant and precise interpreters of it when they wear the masks created out of their ideas of America, masks that have a curious way, over a generation, of installing themselves as social realities; a people who are, finally, themselves socially stratified—a bourgeois German-Jewish class, whose early arrival brought them economic leadership in business and industry, and a peasant class, Russian and eastern European, of a medieval village culture, who when they came to America fell by virtue of their common heritage into a relationship with their German-Jewish predecessors not unlike the Old World division between noble and peasant.

Jews are well represented in the academy and in entertainment—but if they seem to have a special role as folk revivalists, it may be because their historical experience has volatilized out of the embodied forms of race, nation, language, and even religion the ethnomimetic atmosphere of pure culture. At one level, the mask of the "casually road-weary traveler" speaking a "pidgin idiom vaguely regional and proletarian," replaces, like blackface, a foreign identity with a native one; at another level, representations of American folk culture offer a model for reconciling a dispersed people's culture to the historical experience of a particular place, a particular language, a particular religion and race, embodying itself in these particularities but, by putting its own accent on them, never disappearing altogether.

My own life is illustrative. My father was a country doctor, son of a Methodist preacher, born in the last year of the nineteenth century and raised in the rural midwest. By a process too unlikely to try to explain, he married, late in life, a young second-generation Russian Jew whose father, a fishmonger, had built an empire in Chicago real estate only to lose it in the crash of 1929, when my mother was seventeen. I grew up in a working-class community in the Calumet region of northern Illinois, half industrial and half agricultural, the two sectors divided by a narrow precinct of tranquil tree-lined streets, in a house that was, by the standards of the community, baronial; but my friends and schoolmates were the sons and daughters of southern migrants, African-American and Appalachian, who had come to work in the mills and foundries of the Calumet. At fifteen I was suddenly transplanted, after my father's death, into an aging Old World Jewish enclave on the north side of Chicago, long since abandoned for the suburbs by those who could afford it, in which no palpable evidence of my former life survived.

My father was a hayseed, my mother a peasant. Both aspired to, and outwardly achieved, a kind of gentility. His tireless dedication to ordinary people, black and white, most of his patients poor, was my reality, day and night; she filled me with dreams of some indistinct higher existence not to be encountered in this world. My old friends and schoolmates were the sons and daughters of working-class southern migrants, and they brought out the Elvis in me; but the bright, ambitious kids

in Chicago, with few advantages but their own youthful optimism, looked for, and found, the Jew.

In this strange new world, my first friend was Marvin Green-
baum. He played the banjo.

*   *   *

> Wordsworth saw that when we become uncertain in a world of
> apparent strangers who yet, decisively, have a common effect on
> us, and when the forces that will alter our lives are moving all
> around us in apparently external and unrecognizable forms, we
> can retreat, for security, into a deep subjectivity, or we can look
> around us for social pictures, social signs, social messages, to
> which, characteristically, we try to relate as individuals but so as
> to discover, in some form, community.

So writes Raymond Williams. He was no folk revivalist, as far
as I know, but he has much to say concerning our revival.
"Much of the content of modern communications," he writes,
"is this kind of substitute for directly discoverable and transitive
relations to the world . . . a form of shared consciousness rather
than merely a set of techniques." Williams is writing about what
we have come to call the postmodern spectacle—"a form of
unevenly shared consciousness of persistently external events,"
that which "appears to happen, in these powerfully transmitted
and mediated ways, in a world with which we have no other
perceptible connections but which we feel is at once central and
marginal to our lives."

Against this form of shared consciousness belonging to modernity, Williams sets the long, persistent poetic tradition of lost
lives in which we may identify, I think, sentiments strongly
reminiscent of the folk revival:

> The old urban working-class community; the delights of corner
> shops, gas lamps, horsecabs, trams, piestalls: all gone, it seems, in
> successive generations. These urban ways and objects seem to
> have, in the literature, the same real emotional substance as the
> brooks, commons, hedges, cottages, festivals of the rural scene.
> And the point of saying this is not to disprove or devalue either

kind of feeling. It is to see the real change that is being written about, as we discern its common process.

For what is at issue, in all these cases, is a growth and alteration of consciousness . . . What was once close, absorbing, accepted, familiar, internally experienced becomes separate, distinguishable, critical, changing, externally observed. In common or back-street, village or city quarter, this process happens. We can say, of course, that it is an inevitable process; that this growth of adult consciousness is profoundly necessary . . . Great confusion is caused if the real childhood memory is projected, unqualified, as history. Yet what we have finally to say is that we live in a world in which the dominant mode of production and social relation-ships teaches, impresses, offers to make normal and even rigid, modes of detached, separated, external perception and action: modes of using and consuming rather than accepting and enjoy-ing people and things.[6]

"It is not so much the old village or backstreet that is significant," Williams concludes—and so we might add, in a retrospect of thirty years, not so much the banjo or the guitar or the folksong, though we still from time to time pick them up to play and sing our tribute. Rather it is the beliefs with which they are indelibly associated, "the perception and affirmation of a world in which one is not necessarily a stranger and an agent, but can be a member, a discoverer, in a shared source of life."

That is close to what, when we were good, we somehow understood; it is what our youth movement, our revival, was about.

Notes

Prologue: Tom Dooley

1. Anne Warner, *Traditional American Folksongs from the Anne and Frank Warner Collection* (Syracuse: Syracuse University Press, 1984), 1.
2. Ibid., 261.
3. Alan Lomax, *Folk Song U.S.A.* (New York: Duell, Sloan, Pearce, 1947), 285.
4. Joe Hickerson, interview with the author, 31 March 1988.
5. Richard and Ruth Best, *New Song Fest* (New York: International Outing Club, 1955), i.
6. The Kingston Trio's sung version goes: "Down in some lonesome valley, / Hangin' from a white oak tree."
7. Dave Guard, interviews, 15 June and 1 September 1989.
8. Oscar Brand, *The Ballad Mongers* (New York: Funk and Wagnalls, 1962), 144.
9. Roger Abrahams, interview, 4 February 1986.
10. Charles K. Wolfe, *Tennessee Strings: The Story of Country Music in Tennessee* (Knoxville: University of Tennessee Press, 1977), 46–47. The great success of the Kingston Trio's "Tom Dooley" eventually provoked a lawsuit involving Ludlow Music, which held Lomax's and Warner's rights to the song, and Capitol Records; the outcome was an equal division of royalties after 1962, well after its popularity had peaked. See O. Wayne Coon, "Some Problems with Musical Public-Domain Materials under United States Copyright Law as Illustrated Mainly by the Recent Folk-Song Revival," in *Copyright Law Symposium*, no. 19 (New York, 1971), 189–194. Coon observes that John Lomax, while director of the folksong archive at the Library of Congress, coincidentally collected a version of "Tom Dula" in North Carolina in 1936, and that the

music division's *Check-List of Recorded Songs* includes three additional versions collected by others as early as 1935. My thanks to Neil Rosenberg for this reference.

11. Brand, *Ballad Mongers*, 66.
12. Ralph Rinzler, interview, 19 January 1986.
13. A version by Watson can be heard on his album, *Doc Watson* (New York: Vanguard Records 9152, 1963).
14. Warner, *Traditional American Folksongs*, 290.

1. We Are the Folk

1. John Cohen, "In Defense of City Folksingers," *Sing Out!* 9 (Summer 1959), 33.
2. David Hackett Fischer, *Albion's Seed* (New York: Oxford University Press, 1989), 388–389.
3. Roger D. Abrahams, *Singing the Master: The Emergence of Afro-American Culture in the Plantation South* (New York: Pantheon, 1992), 133.
4. Dena J. Epstein, *Sinful Tunes and Spirituals* (Urbana: University of Illinois Press, 1977), 318.
5. See David Whisnant, *All That Is Native and Fine: The Politics of Culture in an American Region* (Chapel Hill: University of North Carolina Press, 1983).
6. Jane Addams, *Twenty Years at Hull House* (1910; New York: New American Library, 1981), 175.
7. T. J. Jackson Lears, *No Place of Grace: Antimodernism and the Transformation of American Culture, 1880–1920* (New York: Pantheon, 1981).
8. Addams, *Twenty Years*, 65.
9. Deborah Kodish, *Good Friends and Bad Enemies: Robert Winslow Gordon and the Study of American Folksong* (Urbana: University of Illinois Press, 1986), 134.
10. Annabel Morris Buchanan, "The Function of a Folk Festival," *Southern Folklore Quarterly* 1 (March 1937), 30. See also Whisnant's discussion in *All That Is Native*, 180–252.
11. Buchanan, "Folk Festival," 34.
12. Loyal Jones, *Minstrel of the Appalachians: The Story of Bascom Lamar Lunsford* (Boone, N.C.: Appalachian Consortium Press, 1984).
13. Archie Green, "The National Folk Festival Association," *John Edwards Memorial Foundation Newsletter* 11 (Spring 1975), 23–32.

14. Sarah Gertrude Knott, "The National Folk Festival after Twelve Years," *California Folklore Quarterly* 5 (January 1946), 93.

15. David Allen Evans, "Folk Revival Music," record review, *Journal of American Folklore* 92 (1979), 110–111.

16. Roger Abrahams, personal communication, 10 August 1994.

17. Evans, "Folk Revival Music," 111.

18. Mike Seeger, personal communication, 16 March 1995.

19. *Mike Seeger, Solo,* compact disc (Cambridge: Rounder Records CD 0278, 1991).

2. The New Minstrelsy

1. Elaine Tyler May, *Homeward Bound: American Families in the Cold War Era* (New York: Basic Books, 1988), 25.

2. Alan Lomax at the hearings on S.1591 (American Folklife Foundation Act), Subcommittee on Education, U.S. Senate, 91st Congress, *Hearings*, vol. 351 (18 May 1970), 26.

3. Phil Cohen, "Subcultural Conflict and Working-Class Community," in Stuart Hall et al., eds., *Culture, Media, Language: Working Papers in Cultural Studies, 1972–79* (London: Hutchison and the Centre for Contemporary Cultural Studies, University of Birmingham, 1980), 82.

4. Jack Whalen and Richard Flacks, *Beyond the Barricades: The Sixties Generation Grows Up* (Philadelphia: Temple University Press, 1989), 272.

5. Christopher Lasch, *The New Radicalism in America: The Intellectual as a Social Type* (New York: Knopf, 1966), 36.

6. David K. Dunaway, *How Can I Keep from Singing: Pete Seeger* (New York: McGraw-Hill, 1981), 93.

7. John Cohen, "Roscoe Holcomb at Zebriskie Point," *Sing Out!* 20 (September–October 1970), 20–21.

8. Robert Toll, *Blacking Up: The Minstrel Show in Nineteenth-Century America* (New York: Oxford University Press, 1974), 45.

9. Eric Lott, *Love and Theft: Blackface Minstrelsy and the American Working Class* (New York: Oxford University Press, 1993), 96.

10. David R. Roediger, *The Wages of Whiteness: Race and the Making of the American Working Class* (London: Verso, 1991), 13–14.

11. Roger Abrahams, personal communication, 10 August 1994.

12. Nathan Irvin Huggins, *The Harlem Renaissance* (New York: Oxford University Press, 1971).

13. Lott, *Love and Theft*, 97.

14. Toll, *Blacking Up*, 13–14.

15. Jacob A. Riis, How the Other Half Lives (1890; New York: Dover, 1971), 19.

16. William R. Taylor, "The Launching of a Commercial Culture: New York City, 1860–1930," in *Power, Culture, and Place: Essays on New York City*, ed. John Hull Mollenkopf (New York: Russell Sage Foundation, 1988), 107–133.

17. Irving Howe, *World of Our Fathers: The Journey of the East European Jews to America and the Life They Found and Made* (New York: Simon and Schuster, 1976), 563.

18. Michael Rogin, "Blackface, White Noise: The Jewish Jazz Singer Finds His Voice," *Critical Inquiry* 18 (1992), 440.

19. Lott, *Love and Theft*, 21.

20. Ibid., 43.

21. Robert Callahan, "Irish Mornings and African Days on the Old Minstrel Stage: An Interview with Leni Sloan," *Callahan's Irish Quarterly* 2 (Spring 1982), 49–56.

22. Robert Cantwell, *Bluegrass Breakdown: The Making of the Old Southern Sound* (Urbana: University of Illinois Press, 1984), 224.

23. Charles Hamm, *Music in the New World* (New York: Norton, 1983), 449–450.

24. "John Hammond, Discoverer of Musical Talent, Dies," *New York Times*, 11 July 1987, 1, 17.

25. John Hammond and Charles Edward Smith, album notes by Sterling Brown, *A Gateway in Time—The Spirituals to Swing Concerts* (New York: Vanguard VRS 8523/4, n.d.).

26. John A. and Alan Lomax, *American Ballads and Folk Songs* (New York, Macmillan, 1934), xxx.

27. Roger Abrahams, interview, 4 February 1986.

28. John A. and Alan Lomax, *Cowboy Songs and Other Frontier Ballads*, rev. ed. (New York: Collier/Macmillan, 1910, 1916, 1938), xvii.

29. John S. Patterson, "The Folksong Revival and Some Sources of the Popular Image of the Folksinger, 1920–1963" (M.A. thesis, Indiana University, 1963), 33.

30. John A. Lomax, "Some Types of American Folk-Song," *Journal of American Folklore* 27 (January–March 1915), 1–17.

31. Henry B. Fuller, *The Cliff Dwellers* (1893; New York: Irvington, 1981), 224.

32. Sam Hinton, "Reply to Eric Molin," *Journal of American Folklore* 71 (1958), 77; Joe Klein, *Woody Guthrie: A Life* (New York: Ballantine, 1980), 143.

33. John A. and Alan Lomax, *Our Singing Country: A Second Volume of American Ballads and Folksongs,* Ruth Crawford Seeger, music ed. (New York: Macmillan, 1949).

34. Klein, *Woody Guthrie,* 144; Gene Bluestein, "Moses Asch, Documentor," *American Music* 5 (Fall 1987), 299; Patterson, *Folksong Revival,* 24–25.

35. Lomax, *American Ballads,* xxii–xxiii.

36. Patterson, "Folksong Revival," 24–25.

37. Frederic Ramsey Jr., "Leadbelly: A Great Long Time," *Newport Folk Festival Program* (1969), 36–45.

38. Statement by C. J. Rogers in *New York Clipper,* 20 June 1874, quoted in Hans Nathan, *Dan Emmett and the Rise of Early Negro Minstrelsy* (Norman: University of Oklahoma Press, 1963), 110. Its source is impresario Al G. Fields, *Watch Yourself Go By* (Columbus, Ohio, 1912).

39. Richard A. Reuss, "American Folklore and Left-Wing Politics, 1927–1957" (diss., Indiana University, 1971), 163.

40. Alan Lomax, *Folk Songs of North America* (New York: Doubleday, 1960), 551.

41. Constance Rourke, *American Humor: A Study of the National Character* (1931), in W. T. Lhamon Jr., ed. (Tallahassee: Florida State University Press, 1986), 92.

42. Sterling Brown, album notes, *A Gateway in Time.*

3. Ballad for Americans

1. Gene Bluestein, "Moses Asch, Documentor," *American Music* 5 (Fall 1987), 299.

2. "Folk Music Today: A Symposium," *Sing Out!* 2 (February–March 1961), 27.

3. Bluestein, "Moses Asch," 294.

4. "Folk Music Today," 27.

5. Bluestein, "Moses Asch," 295, 299, 300.

6. Norm Cohen, *Folk Song America: A 20th Century Revival,* booklet (Washington, D.C.: Smithsonian Collection of Recordings, 1990), 61–62.

7. David P. Peeler, *Hope among Us Yet: Social Criticism and Social Solace in Depression America* (Athens: University of Georgia Press, 1987), 14–22.

8. Jonathan Frankel, *Prophesy and Politics: Socialism, Nationalism, and the Russian Jews, 1862–1917* (Cambridge: Harvard University Press, 1981), 4.

9. Ibid., 455.

10. Joe Klein, *Woody Guthrie* (New York: Ballantine, 1980), 224.

11. Jane Addams, *Twenty Years at Hull House* (1910; New York: New American Library, 1981), 193.

12. Richard A. Reuss, "American Folklore and Left-Wing Politics, 1927–1957" (diss., Indiana University, 1971), 28. My account of the evolving Soviet position on folksong is based primarily on Reuss's excellent summary.

13. John A. and Alan Lomax, *American Ballads and Folk Songs* (New York, Macmillan, 1934), xxxiv.

14. Reuss, "American Folklore," 72–73. Both Gorky and the Lomaxes were familiar with the pioneering work of Milman Parry on the formulaic composition of oral epic. Parry's work on the process in Homer had begun to reach print in 1930; by 1933 he was studying oral singers in Yugoslavia. See Albert B. Lord, *The Singer of Tales* (Cambridge: Harvard University Press, 1960).

15. Reuss, "American Folklore," 159.

16. See Archie Green, *Songs about Work: Essays in Occupational Culture* (Bloomington: Indiana University Press, 1994), and his *Wobblies, Pile Butts, and Other Heroes: Laborlore Explorations* (Urbana: University of Illinois Press, 1993).

17. Reuss, "American Folklore," 35.

18. Green, *Wobblies,* 83.

19. Reuss, "American Folklore," 34.

20. On the portraiture of the 1930s and 1940s, see Green, *Wobblies,* 77–96.

21. Quoted in Peeler, *Hope among Us Yet,* 106–108.

22. William Leach, *Land of Desire: Merchants, Power, and the Rise of a New American Culture* (New York: Random House, 1993), 41–42.

23. David K. Dunaway, "Unsung Songs of Protest: The Composers' Collective of New York," *New York Folklore* 5 (Summer 1979), 1–2.

24. Ibid., 5.

25. Klein, *Woody Guthrie,* 145.

26. Reuss, "American Folklore," 63, 89.

27. Ibid., 83.

28. David K. Dunaway, "Charles Seeger and Charles Sands: The Composers' Collective Years," *Ethnomusicology* 24 (May 1980), 168.

29. Charles Seeger, "Folk Music in the Schools of a Highly Industrialized Society," *Journal of the International Folk Music Council* 5 (1953); reprinted in *Studies in Musicology, 1935–1977,* 40–44. See also his "Music and Class Structure in the United States," *American Quarterly* 9 (Fall 1957), 281–294.

30. Dunaway, "Unsung Songs," 6.

31. Reuss, "American Folklore," 263; Dunaway, "Unsung Songs," 12. See also Serge Denisoff, *Great Day Coming: Folk Music and the American Left* (Urbana: University of Illinois Press, 1971), 38–39.

32. Oakley C. Johnson, "A Memory of Times Past," *Broadside* 23 (March 1963), 19.

33. Carl Sandburg, *American Songbag* (New York: Harcourt, Brace, Jovanovich, 1927), viii.

34. Kenneth Rexroth, review of *Letters of Carl Sandburg,* in *New York Times,* 28 September 1969.

35. Sandburg, *American Songbag,* 459, 246.

36. Ibid., 51, 404, 464, 428.

37. "Folk Music Today," 19.

38. Dunaway, "Unsung Songs," 12.

39. Ibid., 167.

40. Charles Seeger, "Confidential Report to Adrian Dornbush, Resettlement Administration, August 1936" (typescript), Archive of Folk Culture, Library of Congress.

41. Wilson quoted in William Leach, *Land of Desire: Merchants, Power, and the Rise of a New American Culture* (New York: Random House, 1993), 379.

42. William E. Leuchtenberg, *The Perils of Prosperity, 1914–1932* (Chicago: University of Chicago Press, 1958), 2.

43. Benjamin A. Botkin, comp., "The Folksong Revival: A Symposium." *New York Folklore Quarterly* 19 (1963), 121.

44. Stephen J. Whitfield, *The Culture of the Cold War* (Baltimore: Johns Hopkins University Press, 1991), 2.

45. Tony Scherman, "This Man Captured the True Sounds of a Whole World," *Smithsonian* 18 (August 1987), 111–123.

46. William R. Taylor, "The Launching of a Commercial Culture: New York City, 1860–1930," in *Power, Culture, and Place: Essays on New York City,* ed. John Hull Mollenkopf (New York: Russell Sage Foundation, 1988), 128.

47. Barbara Melosh, *Engendering Culture: Manhood and Womanhood in New Deal Public Art and Theater* (Washington, D.C.: Smithsonian Institution Press, 1991), 112.

48. Peeler, *Hope among Us Yet,* 64, 82.

49. Alan Lomax, *Folk Song U.S.A.* (New York: Duell, Sloan, Pearce, 1947), viii.

50. Oscar Brand, *The Ballad Mongers* (New York: Funk and Wagnalls, 1962), 73, 77–78.

51. Lomax, *Folk Song U.S.A.,* xi.

52. Klein, *Woody Guthrie,* 147.

53. Denisoff, *Great Day,* 71–72.

54. Earl Robinson and John Latouche, *Ballad for Americans,* record album (New York: Vanguard VRS-9193, 1940, 1976).

55. Michael Rogin, "Blackface, White Noise: The Jewish Jazz Singer Finds His Voice." *Critical Inquiry* 18 (1992), 438.

56. Reuss, "American Folklore," 221.

57. Millard Lampell and Earl Robinson, record album, *The Lonesome Train* (New York: Decca DL 9065, 1945).

58. Green, *Wobblies,* 288–298, 300–309.

59. Klein, *Woody Guthrie,* 142–143.

60. Reuss, "American Folklore," 92.

61. Bluestein, "Moses Asch," 302.

62. Klein, *Woody Guthrie,* 259.

63. Ibid., 160.

64. Lomax, "Woody Guthrie," Archive of American Folk Song, Library of Congress, 1940.

4. Ramblin' Round Your City

1. Joe Klein, *Woody Guthrie: A Life* (New York: Ballantine, 1980), 187.

2. Richard A. Reuss, "American Folklore and Left-Wing Politics, 1927–1957" (diss., Indiana University, 1971), 204.

3. Jack Whalen and Richard Flacks, *Beyond the Barricades: The Sixties Generation Grows Up* (Philadelphia: Temple University Press, 1989), 2.

4. David K. Dunaway, *How Can I Keep from Singing: Pete Seeger* (New York: McGraw-Hill, 1981), 82.

5. Reuss, *American Folklore*, 219.

6. Klein, *Woody Guthrie*, 217.

7. Ibid., 129.

8. Robert Warshow, *The Immediate Experience: Movies, Comics, Theatre and Other Aspects of Popular Culture* (Garden City: Doubleday, 1962), 60–62.

9. Robbie Lieberman, *"My Song Is My Weapon": People's Songs, American Communism, and the Politics of Culture, 1930–1950* (Urbana: University of Illinois Press, 1989), 6.

10. Dunaway, *How Can I*, 85.

11. "Besides," Kenneally writes, "the Jews of Cracow were accustomed—in a way that could best be described as congenital—to the idea of a ghetto. And now that it had been decided, the very word had a soothing, ancestral ring. Their grandfathers had not been permitted to emerge from the ghetto of Kazimierz until 1867 . . . Although their liberty had come so late, there was among the older Cracow Jews a nostalgia for the old ghetto of Kazimierz. A ghetto implied certain squalors, a crowding in tenements, a sharing of bathroom facilities, disputes over drying space on clotheslines. Yet it also consecrated the Jews to their own special-ness, to a richness of shared scholarship, to songs and Zionist talk, elbow to elbow, in coffeehouses rich in ideas if not in cream." *Schindler's List* (New York: Simon and Schuster, 1993), 85–86.

12. Reuss, "American Folklore," 207.

13. Dunaway, *How Can I*, 98–102.

14. Reuss, "American Folklore," 358.

15. Jane Addams, *Twenty Years at Hull House* (New York: New American Library, 1981), 197–198.

16. Bert Spector, "The Weavers: A Case History in Show Business Black-listing," *Journal of American Culture* (1982), 114.

17. Klein, *Woody Guthrie*, 213.

18. Robert Shelton, "A Man To Remember: Woody Guthrie," *Newport Folk Festival Program* (1960).

19. This recording can be heard on *Folk Song America: A 20th Century Revival* (Smithsonian Collection of Recordings, 1990).

20. David P. Peeler, *Hope among Us Yet: Social Criticism and Social Solace in Depression America* (Athens: University of Georgia Press, 1987), 6.
21. Michael Rogin, "Blackface, White Noise: The Jewish Jazz Singer Finds His Voice," *Critical Inquiry* 18 (1992), 439.
22. Dunaway, *How Can I*, 87.
23. Moses Asch and Alan Lomax, *The Leadbelly Songbook* (New York: Oak Publications, 1962), 7.
24. Peeler, *Hope among Us*, 233.

5. Wasn't That a Time

1. Herman G. James, "Oratory: Demagogue Is Still a Demagogue, Even If Unseen," *Newsweek* 5 (18 May 1935), 2.
2. Herbert I. Schiller, *Culture, Inc.: The Corporate Takeover of Public Expression* (New York: Oxford University Press, 1989), 13.
3. Frederick F. Siegel, *Troubled Journey: From Pearl Harbor to Ronald Reagan* (New York: Hill and Wang, 1984), 73. Except where noted, my historical account draws largely from this book.
4. Ibid., 56.
5. Ibid., 57, 59.
6. Robbie Lieberman, *"My Song Is My Weapon": People's Songs, American Communism, and the Politics of Culture, 1930–1950* (Urbana: University of Illinois Press, 1989), 9–10; Schiller, *Culture, Inc.*, 15.
7. Quoted in Lieberman, *My Song*, 11.
8. This is the heart of Richard Freeland's argument in *The Truman Doctrine and the Origins of McCarthyism* (1985).
9. Siegel, *Troubled Journey*, 44.
10. Frank Kofsky, *Harry S. Truman and the War Scare of 1948: A Successful Campaign to Deceive the Nation* (New York: St. Martin's, 1993). See also Kofsky's letter to the editor, *Harper's* (October 1993), 7–8.
11. Lieberman, *My Song*, 11.
12. Joe Klein, *Woody Guthrie* (New York: Ballantine, 1980), 347. To get the full lunacy of America's anticommunist hysteria, see Stephen J. Whitfield's grippingly thorough and wickedly funny *The Culture of the Cold War* (Baltimore: Johns Hopkins University Press, 1991).
13. Siegel, *Troubled Journey*, 75–77.
14. Elaine Tyler May, *Homeward Bound* (New York: Basic Books, 1988), 10.

15. Ibid., 90–93.

16. Schiller, *Culture, Inc.*, 16.

17. "Folk Music Today: A Symposium," *Sing Out!* 2 (February–March 1961), 27.

18. Quoted in May, *Homeward Bound*, 162.

19. Lieberman, *My Song*, 130.

20. John S. Patterson, "The Folksong Revival and Some Sources of the Popular Image of the Folksinger, 1920–1963" (M.A. thesis, Indiana University, 1963), 39.

21. Oscar Brand, *The Ballad Mongers* (New York: Funk and Wagnalls, 1962), 84–85.

22. Lieberman, *My Song*, 140; David K. Dunaway, *How Can I Keep from Singing: Pete Seeger* (New York: McGraw-Hill, 1981), 16–23; Siegel, *Troubled Journey*, 143.

23. Quoted in Michael W. Munley, "Stories of Work for the American Century." *American Quarterly* 46 (September 1994), 468.

24. James Gilbert, *Perfect Cities* (Chicago: University of Chicago Press, 1991), 37–43.

25. Siegel, *Troubled Journey*, 101–102. See also Stephen J. Whitfield, *The Culture of the Cold War* (Baltimore: Johns Hopkins University Press, 1991), 74–75, 90.

26. Siegel, *Troubled Journey*, 102.

27. These are the principal arguments of William Greider's *Who Will Tell the People: The Betrayal of American Democracy* (New York: Simon and Schuster, 1992). See also Frum's *Dead Right*.

28. Forthcoming work by Avery Gordon and Christopher Newfield in this area promises to shed considerable new light on corporate culturalism. See their (as editors) *Mapping Multiculturalism* (Minneapolis: University of Minnesota Press, 1995).

29. Richard A. Reuss, "American Folklore and Left-Wing Politics, 1927–1957" (diss., Indiana University, 1971), 254.

30. "Folk Music on the Radio," *Journal of American Folklore* 57 (1944), 215; 59 (1946), 73.

31. Brand, *Ballad Mongers*, 84. Among the recordings of folksongs for children from this period were Pete Seeger's *American Folk Songs for Children* (Folkways FC 7601) of 1954, based on Ruth Seeger's collection, which included "She'll Be Comin' Around the Mountain," "Jim

Crack Corn," and "Frog Went A-Courting"; Burl Ives's *Burl Ives Sings Songs for All Ages* (Columbia CL 980) in 1957; Woody Guthrie's *Songs to Grow On* (Folkways FC 7675) in 1958; and Pete Seeger's and Erik Darling's *Camp Songs* (Folkways FC 7028) in 1959. Leadbelly also recorded children's records for both Folkways and Stinson.

32. Theatre Guild, *Sing Out, Sweet Land* (New York: Decca Records A-404, 1946).
33. Lieberman, *My Song,* 21, 62, 69; Klein, *Woody Guthrie,* 354–355; Dunway, *How Can I,* 138.
34. *The Weavers at Carnegie Hall,* album notes (New York: Vanguard Records VRS 9010-A, 1956).
35. Bert Spector, "The Weavers: A Case History in Show Business Blacklisting," *Journal of American Culture* (1982), 114.
36. Reuss, "American Folklore," 337.
37. Hyman quoted in Patterson, *Folksong Revival,* 44.
38. Dunaway, *How Can I,* 156.
39. This account of Schneyer's career is summarized from Robert J. Clayton, "Folk Voices: Three Urban Folk Performers Speak of Their Lives" (unpaginated paper, George Washington University, April 1976), Archive of Folk Song, Library of Congress.
40. May, *Homeward Bound,* 40, 137.
41. Siegel, *Troubled Journey,* 93.
42. Lynn Spigel, *Make Room for TV: Television and the Family Ideal in Postwar America* (Chicago: University of Chicago Press, 1992), 5.

6. Smith's Memory Theater

1. Arlene Liebenau et al., eds., "Folkways Records: The Legacy of Moses Asch Comes to the Smithsonian," *Festival of American Folklife Program Book* (Washington: Smithsonian Institution, 1987), 7–8.
2. Archie Green, "Hillbilly Music: Source and Symbol," *Journal of American Folklore* 78 (July–September 1965), 204–228; Nolan Porterfield, *Jimmie Rodgers: The Life and Times of America's Blue Yodeler* (Urbana: University of Illinois Press, 1979), 88–101.
3. Harry Smith, album notes, *American Folk Music* (New York: Folkways Records, FA 2951-53, 1952).
4. Daniel J. Czitrom, *Media and the American Mind: From Morse to McLuhan* (Chapel Hill: University of North Carolina Press, 1982), 164.

5. My biographical account, including quotations, is based on John Cohen, "A Rare Interview with Harry Smith," *Sing Out!* 9 (April–May 1969), 2–11, 41.

6. See Frances A. Yates, *The Rosicrucian Enlightenment* (Boulder: Shambala Press, 1978), 70.

7. Frances A. Yates, *The Art of Memory* (Chicago: University of Chicago Press, 1966), 342–367.

8. Archie Green pointed this out to me.

9. Yates, *Rosicrucian Enlightenment*, 79.

10. Paul Oliver, *Songsters and Saints: Vocal Traditions on Race Records* (Cambridge, Eng.: Cambridge University Press, 1984), 247.

11. Oliver writes: "Sousa's marches, the two-steps, cakewalks and quadrilles combined with the popular 'coon' songs of the 1890s to stimulate a period of unprecedented excitement over new dances. Some of these were still reflected in some degree in the songs of folk musicians thirty years later. Jim Jackson, for instance, whose markedly syncopated jig rhythm must have been close to the folk dances he mentioned on *Bye, Bye Policeman*:

> Now first thing honey is the Bombashay,
> Oh turn right round, go the other way.
> To the Worldly Fair, the Turkey Trot,
> Oh, don't that girl think she's very hot?
> She puts her hand on her head
> And lets her mind rove on—
> Stands way back, lookin' to stop—
> Oh! She dance so nicely, and politely
> She do the Pas-a-Ma-La.

"A guitar player born in Hernando, Mississippi, Jim Jackson spent most of his life there, on the road, or in Memphis. In performance his song was rural Southern in character but the words were directly from the original *Pas Ma La* by Ernest Hogan, published in 1895.

> Fus yo' say, my niggah, Bombashay
> Then turn 'round and go the other way
> To the World's Fair and do the Turkey Trot,
> Do not dat coon tink he look very hot?
> Hand upon 'yo head, let your mind roll far,

> Back, back, back and look at the stars,
> Stand up rightly, dance it brightly
> That's the Pas Ma La.

"Possibly French Creole in origin, and known as La Pas Ma Le, the dance had been parodied by a black composer, Irving Jones, as the *Possumala Dance* a year earlier. In the mid-1890s it was widely popular" (33–34). Note how the ugly racism of the original coon song, whose World's Fair allusion associates it with the Columbian Exposition of 1893, becomes in Jim Jackson's version a fond and subtle expression of sexuality.

12. Oliver, *Songsters,* 34, 267; Sam Charters, *The Country Blues* (New York: Da Capo Press, 1975), 132.

13. Loyal Jones, *Minstrel of the Appalachians: The Story of Bascom Lamar Lunsford* (Boone, N.C.: Appalachian Consortium Press, 1984), 9.

14. Charlie Seeman, "The American Cowboy: Image and Reality," album notes, *Back in the Saddle Again* (New York: New World Records 314/315, 1983), 3.

15. Oliver, *Songsters,* 131.

16. *Henry Thomas Sings the Texas Blues!* (Origin Jazz Library, 1962).

17. Tony Russell, *Blacks, Whites, and Blues* (London: Studio Vista, 1970), 47.

7. He Shall Overcome

1. Gene Bluestein, "Moses Asch, Documentor," *American Music* 5 (Fall 1987), 291–304.

2. Alan Wald, "Remembering the Answers," *Nation* 233 (26 December 1981), 710.

3. Roger Abrahams, interview, 4 February 1986.

4. Ibid.; Ralph Rinzler, interview, 19 January 1986.

5. John Cohen, "In Defense of City Folksingers," *Sing Out!* 9 (Summer 1959), 32–33.

6. Karen Linn, *That Half-Barbaric Twang: The Banjo in American Popular Culture* (Urbana: University of Illinois Press, 1991), 48.

7. My biographical account, including quotations, is based on David K. Dunaway, *How Can I Keep from Singing: Pete Seeger* (New York: McGraw-Hill, 1981).

8. Pete Seeger, "The American Folk Song Revival," in the *Newport Folk Festival Program* (1960), n.p.

9. Archie Green, *Wobblies, Pile Butts, and Other Heroes: Laborlore Explorations* (Urbana: University of Illinois Press, 1993), 302.

10. John Pankake, "Pete's Children: The American Folk Song Revival, Pro and Con," *Little Sandy Review* 29 (March–April 1964), 26.

11. Bert Spector, "The Weavers: A Case History in Show Business Blacklisting," *Journal of American Culture* (1982), 114.

12. Cheryl Anne Brauner, "A Study of the Newport Folk Festival and the Newport Folk Foundation" (M.A. thesis, Department of Folklore, Memorial University of Newfoundland, 1983), 162.

13. Pete Seeger, "Statement to the Court," *Sing Out!* 11 (Summer 1961), 10.

8. Happy Campers

1. "Folk Music Today: A Symposium," *Sing Out!* 2 (February–March 1961), 31.

2. John S. Patterson, "The Folksong Revival and Some Sources of the Popular Image of the Folksinger, 1920–1963" (M.A. thesis, Indiana University, 1963), 54; Irwin Silber, "15 Years of *Sing Out!* Notes from an Editor's Diary," *Sing Out!* 16 (February–March 1966), 43.

3. Elaine Tyler May, *Homeward Bound: American Families in the Cold War Era* (New York: Basic Books, 1988), 78, 169.

4. Pete Seeger, "The Theory of Cultural Guerrilla Tactics," in "Johnny Appleseed Jr.," *Sing Out!* 2 (October–November 1961), 60.

5. Seeger, *Sing Out!* 4 (February 1954), 30.

6. John Cohen, "Folk Festivals: Rural, Urban, and Commercial," *Newport Folk Festival Program* (1964), 22.

7. Mike Seeger, "Mountain Music Bluegrass Style," enclosure in album (New York: Folkways Records FA 2318, 1959, 1962), 2. Ralph Rinzler, interview, 19 January 1986.

8. Irwin Silber, "Traditional Folk Artists Capture the Campus," *Sing Out!* 14 (April–May 1964), 8–14; Grace Jan Waldeman, "Life among the Guitars," *Mademoiselle* (May 1959), 32.

9. Susan Montgomery, "The Folk Furor," *Mademoiselle* (December 1960), 117.

10. Rinzler interview; Joe Hickerson, interview, 31 March 1988.

11. "Folksmiths," *Sing Out!* 8 (Spring 1958), 17.

12. Norm Cohen, *Folk Song America: A 20th Century Revival* (Washington, D.C.: Smithsonian Collection of Recordings, 1990), 88.

13. Reuss, "American Folklore," 185.

14. Pete Seeger, "Johnny Appleseed Jr.," *Sing Out!* 6 (Summer 1956), 34.

15. Beatrice Freedman, review, "People's Festival in a People's War. Third Annual Folk Festival of the Catskills, 1942," *California Folklore Quarterly* 5 (January 1946), 222.

16. Hickerson interview, 1988.

17. Jane Farwell, "Folk Camp," *Recreation,* 40 (January 1947), 540.

18. Archie Green, "Commercial Music Graphics: Twenty-Two (the Victor in Rural Schools)," *JEMF Quarterly* 8 (Autumn 1972), 141–147.

19. John A. and Alan Lomax, *Our Singing Country: A Second Volume of American Ballads and Folksongs,* Ruth Crawford Seeger, music ed. (New York: Macmillan, 1949), viii.

20. "Folk Music on the Radio," *Journal of American Folklore* 57 (1944), 215.

21. Ruth Crawford Seeger, *American Folk Songs for Children,* illus. Barbara Cooney (New York: Doubleday, 1948), 13.

22. Ibid., 25.

23. Based on Robert J. Clayton, "Folk Voices: Three Urban Folk Performers Speak of Their Lives" (paper, George Washington University, April 1976).

24. Joseph Janeti, "Folk Music's Affair with Popular Culture," in *New Dimensions in Popular Culture,* ed. Russell Nye (Bowling Green: Bowling Green University Popular Press), 231.

25. Patterson, *Folk Song Revival,* 57–58.

26. Margot Mayo, "Five Years of Folk Song Favorites," *Sing Out!* 12 (April–May 1962), 37–39. See also "Folk Music Goes to School," *Sing Out!* 12 (February–March 1962), 5–6.

27. Sam Hinton, "Reply to Eric Molin," *Journal of American Folklore* 71 (1958), 77. According to Archie Green, this songbook was published by the Cooperative Recreation Association at Delaware, Ohio, edited by Gus Danzig.

28. Simeon Loring, "A Folksinging Camp," *Sing Out!* 12 (Summer 1962), 12–13.

29. Richard A. Reuss, "Summer Is Icumen In! (And Louder Sing the Guitar-Pickers and Banjo-Players at Summer Camps Throughout the Country)," *Sing Out!* 2 (Summer 1961), 25–27.

30. Benjamin A. Botkin, comp., "The Folksong Revival: A Symposium," *New York Folklore Quarterly* 19 (1963), 118.

31. *Newport Folk Festival Program* (1959), n.p.

32. Ed Sherman, "Alan Lomax Presents: Folk Song Festival at Carnegie Hall," album notes (New York: United Artists Records UAL 3050, 1959).

33. Mike Collins, "Personal Observations on the Folk Craze," *Catholic Times,* Columbus, Ohio, 28 February 1964.

34. Harriet Van Horne, "Square Toes Blues," *New York World-Telegram and Sun,* 17 June 1960.

35. Alan Lomax, "Bluegrass Background: Folk Music with Overdrive," *Esquire* 52 (October 1959), 108.

36. Abrahams interview; see also David P. Peeler, *Hope among Us Yet* (Athens: University of Georgia Press, 1987).

37. Oscar Brand, *The Ballad Mongers* (New York: Funk and Wagnalls, 1962), 158–162; Joe Klein, *Woody Guthrie* (New York: Ballantine, 1980), 421.

38. Waldeman, "Life among the Guitars," 89, 91.

39. Michael James, "Balladeers Lure Crowd to Washington Square," "Free Songfest Is a Tourist Magnet—Beatniks Frown," *New York Times,* 25 May 1959.

40. Dunaway, *How Can I,* 206; Ben Botkin, "The Folk Song Revival: Cult or Culture?" *Sing Out!* 15 (March 1965), 30.

41. Cohen, *Folk Song America,* 77.

42. Israel Young, "Israel Young's Notebook," *Sing Out!* 18 (February–March 1968), 47–49. Klein, *Woody Guthrie,* 410–411.

43. "Alan Lomax Presents: Folk Song Festival at Carnegie Hall" (United Artists UAL 3050, 1959).

44. Ed Sherman, ibid., album notes.

45. Klein, *Woody Guthrie,* 411.

46. Botkin, *Symposium,* 118.

47. Percival Chubb, "Folk Culture and Leisure," *Recreation* 28 (September 1934), 278.

48. Cheryl Anne Brauner, "A Study of the Newport Folk Festival and the Newport Folk Foundation" (M.A. thesis, Department of Folklore, Memorial University of Newfoundland, 1983), 278.

49. George Freyer, "Blue Notes and Blue Stockings," *Esquire* 48 (August 1955), 38.

50. Ren Grevatt, "Folkniks on the March; Hill Sound Upsurge," *Billboard* (8 June 1959), 1.

51. Montgomery, "Folk Furor," 99.

52. Eric Von Schmidt and Jim Rooney, *Baby, Let Me Follow You Down: The Illustrated Story of the Cambridge Folk Years* (New York: Anchor Books, 1979), 189.

53. David McAllister, "On Listening to Indian Music," *Newport Folk Festival Program Book* (1963), 15.

54. Silber, "15 Years of Sing Out!," 45.

55. Brauner, "Study of Newport," 91–93.

56. Ibid., 90.

57. Quoted in Bruce Jackson, editorial, *Sing Out!* 14 (January 1964), 2.

58. Paul Nelson, "Newport: Down There on a Visit," *Little Sandy Review* 30 (1965), 60.

59. Brauner, "Study of Newport," 127.

60. Bruce Jackson, "Newport '66: Good Music, Diabolical Programming," *Sing Out!* 16 (November 1966), 17.

61. Bruce Buckley and M. W. Thomas, "Traditional Crafts in America," *Newport Folk Festival Program* (1966), 70.

62. Ralph Rinzler, "Field Report," *Newport Folk Festival Program* (1967), 7.

63. David Whisnant, "Folk Festival Issues: Report from a Seminar," *John Edwards Memorial Foundation Quarterly* special series 12 (2–3 March 1978), 8.

64. Jackson, editorial (1964), 2.

65. "Folk Festivals Are 'In,'" *Sing Out!* 13 (October–November 1963), 24–27.

66. Jack Whalen and Richard Flacks, *Beyond the Barricades: The Sixties Generation Grows Up* (Philadelphia: Temple University Press, 1989), 8.

67. Klein, *Woody Guthrie*, 432.

68. Brauner, "Study of Newport," 116–118.

69. Nelson, "Newport," 66.

9. Lady and the Tramp

1. See Robert Palmer, *Deep Blues* (New York: Viking, 1981).

2. Dave Guard, interviews 15 June and 1 September 1989.

3. Elaine Tyler May, *Homeward Bound* (New York: Basic Books, 1988), 38–48, 136–161, 174.

4. Susan Montgomery, "The Folk Furor," *Mademoiselle* (December 1960), 118. Israel Young, of the Folklore Center, seems to have the strongest

claim to coining the term—an echo of San Francisco columnist Herb Caen's Yiddish-inspired "beatnik."

5. Jack Whalen and Richard Flacks, *Beyond the Barricades* (Philadelphia: Temple Unversity Press, 1989), 9.

6. Paul Nelson, "Newport: Down There on a Visit," *Little Sandy Review* 30 (1965), 53.

7. John Pankake, "Pete's Children: The American Folk Song Revival, Pro and Con," *Little Sandy Review* 29 (March–April 1964), 28.

8. Carl Sandburg, *American Songbag* (New York: Harcourt, Brace, Jovanovich, 1927), ix.

9. Quoted in Montgomery, "Folk Furor," 118.

10. "Folk Music Today: A Symposium," *Sing Out!* 2 (February–March 1961), 23.

11. Alan Lomax, "The 'Folkniks'—and the Songs They Sing," *Sing Out!* 9 (Summer 1959), 31.

12. Montgomery, "Folk Furor," 118.

13. "Folk Music Today," 24.

14. Montgomery, "Folk Furor," 99.

15. Nelson, "Newport," 51.

16. Pete Seeger, "Johnny Appleseed Jr.," *Sing Out!* 14 (February–March 1964), 71–73.

17. John Cohen, "In Defense of City Folksingers," *Sing Out!* 9 (Summer 1959), 33–34.

18. Montgomery, "Folk Furor," 118.

19. Ralph Rinzler, interview, 19 January 1986.

20. Neil Rosenberg, personal communication, 23 May 1989.

21. Richard and Ruth Best, *New Song Fest* (New York: International Outing Club, 1955), i.

22. Montgomery, "Folk Furor," 118.

23. Irwin Silber, "Traditional Folk Artists Capture the Campus," *Sing Out!* 14 (April–May 1964), 14.

24. Ibid., 9.

25. Joan Baez, *And a Voice to Sing With: A Memoir* (New York: Summit Books, 1987), 41.

26. Benjamin A. Botkin, comp., "The Folksong Revival: A Symposium." *New York Folklore Quarterly* 19 (1963), 92.

27. John Cohen, "Joan Baez," *Sing Out!* 13 (Summer 1963), 6.

28. Harriet Van Horne, "Square Toes Blues," *New York World-Telegram and Sun* (17 June 1960), 17.

29. Baez, *And a Voice*, 66. Except where noted, my biographical account, including quotations, is based on this book.

30. Jane Addams, *Twenty Years at Hull House* (New York: New American Library, 1981), 27–28.

31. Baez, *And a Voice*, 19.

32. Eric Von Schmidt and Jim Rooney, *Baby, Let Me Follow You Down* (New York: Anchor Books, 1979), 26–28.

33. Baez, *And a Voice*, 91.

34. Anthony Scaduto, *Bob Dylan: An Intimate Biography* (New York: Grosset and Dunlap, 1971).

35. Joe Klein, *Woody Guthrie* (New York: Ballantine Books, 1980), 206.

36. Barbara Kirschenblatt-Gimblett, "Mistaken Dichotomies," *Journal of American Folklore* 101 (April–June 1988), 151.

37. William James, *The Varieties of Religious Experience* (1902; New York: New American Library, 1958), 172.

38. Thomas Carter, "Looking for Henry Reed," in Daniel W. Patterson, ed., *Sounds of the South* (Chapel Hill: Southern Folklife Collection, 1991), 81.

39. Cheryl Anne Brauner, "A Study of the Newport Folk Festival and the Newport Folk Foundation" (M.A. thesis, Department of Folklore, Memorial University of Newfoundland, 1983), 86–87.

10. Nobles . . . Reds

1. Michael Novak, "What the Melting Pot Didn't Melt," *Christian Century* 89 (19 April 1972), 437.

2. Raymond Williams, *Culture and Society, 1780–1950* (New York: Columbia University Press, 1983), 3–4.

3. Charles Seeger, "Music and Class Structure in the United States," *American Quarterly* 9 (Fall 1957), 281–294.

4. Alan Lomax at the hearings on S.1591 (American Folklife Foundation Act), Subcommittee on Education, U.S. Senate, 91st Congress, *Hearings*, vol. 351 (18 May 1970).

5. Alan Lomax, *Folk Song Style and Culture* (Washington, D.C.: American Association for the Advancement of Science, 1968), 203.

6. Raymond Williams, *The Country and the City* (New York: Oxford University Press, 1973), 295, 297–298.

Acknowledgments

This book grew out of research conducted at the Library of Congress Archive of Folk Song in connection with another project, on the Smithsonian's Festival of American Folklife, since published as *Ethnomimesis: Folklife and the Representation of Culture* (University of North Carolina Press, 1993). I want to thank Joe Hickerson, then director of the Archive of Folk Song, for his patient guidance through the masses of ephemeral material housed in the library, as well as for his own important personal testimony. I must again express my gratitude to the Office of Folklife Programs and Cultural Studies at the Smithsonian Institution.

From that time to this, Roger Abrahams has been wonderfully generous with his insights and ideas; I hope he will not be too dismayed to find them shamelessly deployed here without attribution, simply because I have so long relied on them that I mistake them for my own. Archie Green will find himself reflected here as well: not only in numerous small suggestions and corrections but, to the extent I am capable of it, in the intellectual and political forthrightness he consistently demands.

Often I have turned to the wise counsel of Bess Lomax Hawes. Few understand better than she the actual human ground on which we must conduct the relations between ourselves and those people we deem "the folk," or the collaborative character of folk-cultural work, which without conscientious human sympathy and mutual respect can never ultimately succeed. Bess's leadership in folk arts at the National Endowment for the Arts has extended the central contribution of the Lomax family in the folk revival of this century to the generation that will no doubt refashion it for the next. I count her friendship, with Archie's and Roger's, an honor and a privilege.

I should like to pay tribute to David Guard, who in what turned out to be the last months of his life shared with me his memories of the early days of the Kingston Trio, as well as his own fascination with the folk revival as a phenomenon of American culture. In his music he never stopped growing and experimenting. Dave gave me some useful information, but the model of grace, generosity, and courage with which he left me is permanently installed in my memory.

For me this project can have had no better outcome than to have initiated a highly gratifying association with my gifted contemporary Greil Marcus, whose writing I have always admired and whose friendship has fortified me through the final stages of this work. My colleague John Kasson generously intervened in the project at a time when it seemed overwhelming and, with the knowledge and skill of a professional historian, helped me to bring conceptual problems and bibliographical solutions into alignment. I am grateful to my editors at Harvard University Press: Joyce Backman who, with precise surgical strokes and bold interrogations, clarified my often turgid prose and made me confront my own evasions; and Lindsay Waters, who appreciated my work on its own terms and inspired me with his enthusiasm and his learning. And for valuable assistance with photographs, I would like to thank Diane Hamilton, David Gahr, Jackie Alper, Matt Walters, Jeff Place, Judith Gray, and Archie Green.

Portions of my book appeared in different form in the *New England Review,* in Robert Baron's and Nick Spitzer's *Public Folklore* (Smithsonian Institution Press, 1992), and in Neil Rosenberg's *Transforming Tradition: Folk Music Revivals Examined* (University of Illinois Press, 1993). To Neil I am further indebted for his many helpful suggestions and to Terry Hummer, former editor-in-chief of the *New England Review*, for his interest in my work.

Among my sources have been several important books: David Dunaway's *How Can I Keep from Singing*, a detailed and entertaining biography of Pete Seeger; Robbie Lieberman's *My Song Is My Weapon*, an informed and sympathetic discussion of left-wing culture, the Popular Front, and the Wallace campaign; Richard Reuss's important dissertation "American Folklore and Left-Wing Politics, 1927–1957"; Cheryl Ann Brauner's master's thesis on the Newport Folk Festival; and Joe Klein's rich and imaginative *Woody Guthrie*, by far the best work in print on the folksong movement. I recommend to anyone who wishes better to understand the revival Norm Cohen's anthology album *Folk Song America*, issued by the Smithsonian Collection of Recordings, with Cohen's succinct but comprehensive accompanying booklet, an excellent short history of the revival. I can recommend too Rosenberg's *Transforming Tradition*, with its retrospective essays by revivalists now in scholarly or public-sector folklore professions. Judith Tick's biography of Ruth Crawford Seeger, Nolan Porterfield's of John Lomax, Roger Abrahams' *Folkways-Smithsonian Book of American Folksongs*, Millie Rahn's history of the Club 47, as well as histories of the revival by Ronald Cohen and Benjamin Filene, are as of this writing still in progress.

I could not have conceived this project at all, and certainly never finished it, were it not for Lydia Wegman's support, companionship, and love. What strengths are in the book reflect her considerable intellectual vigor and clarity; its weaknesses reflect what even all the opportunities of the written word cannot compensate, the writer's own failings of mind and heart.

Index

Bob Dylan alone